264 wood and ivory carvings none of them larger than a matchbox: potter Edmund de Waal was entranced when he first encountered the collection in the Tokyo apartment of his great uncle Iggie. Later, when Edmund inherited the 'netsuke', they unlocked a story far larger than he could ever have imagined . . .

The Ephrussis came from Odessa, and at one time were the largest grain exporters in the world; in the 1870s, Charles Ephrussi was part of a wealthy new generation settling in Paris. Marcel Proust was briefly his secretary and used Charles as the model for the aesthete Swann in *Remembrance of Things Past*. Charles's passion was collecting, and the netsuke, bought when Japanese *objets* were all the rage in the salons, were sent as a wedding present to his banker cousin in Vienna.

Later, three children – including a young Ignace – played with the collection as history reverberated around them. The Anschluss and Second World War swept the Ephrussis to the brink of oblivion. Almost all that remained of their vast empire was the netsuke collection, smuggled out of the huge Viennese palace (then occupied by Hitler's theorist on the 'Jewish Question'), one piece at a time, in the pocket of a loyal maid – and hidden in a straw mattress.

In this stunningly original memoir, Edmund de Waal travels the world to stand in the great buildings his forebears once inhabited. He traces the network of a remarkable family against the backdrop of a tumultuous century. And, in prose as elegant and precise as the netsuke themselves, he tells the story of a unique collection which passed from hand to hand – and which, in a twist of fate, found its way home to Japan.

# The Hare with Amber Eyes

## A HIDDEN INHERITANCE

### Edmund de Waal

Chatto & Windus
LONDON

Published by Chatto & Windus 2010

6 8 10 9 7 5

Copyright © Edmund de Waal 2010

All quotations from *À la Recherche du Temps Perdu* by Marcel Proust
are from the translation by C.K. Scott Moncrieff, revised by Terence
Kilmartin, 1981

We are grateful to the following for permission to use these images: *Le Pont
de l'Europe*, Gustave Caillebotte © Musée du Petit Palais, Geneva; *Une botte
d'asperges*, Edouard Manet © Rheinisches Bildarchiv, Cologne; Schottentor,
Vienna, 1885 © Österreichische Nationalbibliothek; Palais Ephrussi frontal
view, plan from the *Allgemeine Bauzeitung* © Österreichische Nationalbibliothek; Vienna Anschluss, 1938 © Österreichische Nationalbibliothek.

First published in Great Britain in 2010 by
Chatto & Windus
Random House, 20 Vauxhall Bridge Road,
London SW1V 2SA

www.rbooks.co.uk

Addresses for companies within The Random House Group Limited
can be found at: www.randomhouse.co.uk/offices.htm

The Random House Group Limited Reg. No. 954009

A CIP catalogue record for this book
is available from the British Library

ISBN 9780701184179

The Random House Group Limited supports The Forest Stewardship
Council (FSC), the leading international forest certification organisation.
All our titles that are printed on Greenpeace approved FSC certified paper
carry the FSC logo. Our paper procurement policy can be found at
www.rbooks.co.uk/environment

**Mixed Sources**
Product group from well-managed
forests and other controlled sources
www.fsc.org  Cert no. TT-COC-2139
© 1996 Forest Stewardship Council
FSC

Typeset by Palimpsest Book Production Limited,
Falkirk, Stirlingshire

Printed and bound in Great Britain by
Clays Ltd, St Ives plc

for Ben, Matthew and Anna
and for my father

'Even when one is no longer attached to things, it's still something to have been attached to them; because it was always for reasons which other people didn't grasp . . . Well, now that I'm a little too weary to live with other people, these old feelings, so personal and individual, that I had in the past, seem to me – it's the mania of all collectors – very precious. I open my heart to myself like a sort of vitrine, and examine one by one all those love affairs of which the world can know nothing. And of this collection to which I'm now much more attached than to my others, I say to myself, rather as Mazarin said of his books, but in fact without the least distress, that it will be very tiresome to have to leave it all.'

*Charles Swann*

Marcel Proust, *Cities of the Plain*

# CONTENTS

**Charles Joachim Ephrussi** *m1* **Belle Levensohn**    *m2* **Henriette Halperson** *

b 1793 Berdichev  d 1864 Vienna    d 1841    b 1822 Lemberg  d 1888 Vienna

**Leon Ephrussi** *m* Mina Lindau

b 1826 Berdichev d 1871 Paris    b 1824 Brody  d 1888 Paris

**Jules** *m* Fanny Pfeiffer    **Ignace**    **Charles**    **Betty** *m* Max Hirsch Kann

b 1846 Odessa  d 1915 Paris    b 1848 Odessa  d 1908 Paris    b 1849 Odessa  d 1905 Paris    b 1851 Odessa d 1871 Paris

**Fanny Kann** *m* Theodore Reinach

b 1870 Anvers  d 1917 Paris

*four sons*

**\* *m2* Henriette Halperson**

b 1822 Lemberg d 1888 Vienna

**Michel** *m* Liliane Beer    **Therese 'Bacha'** *m* Leon Fould

b 1845 Odessa   d 1914 Paris    b 1851 Odessa d 1911 Paris

*three daughters*    *one son one daughter*

**Maurice** *m* Charlotte Beatrice de Rothschild    **Marie 'Mascha'** *m* Guy de Percin

b 1849 Odessa d 1916 Paris    b 1853 Odessa d 1924 Paris

*one daughter*

# EPHRUSSI FAMILY TREE

**Ignace von Ephrussi** *m* Emilie Porges

b 1829 Berdichev d 1899 Vienna — b 1836 Vienna d 1900 Vichy

**Stefan** *m* Estiha

b 1856 Odessa d 1911

**Anna** *m* Herz von Hertenried

b 1859 Odessa d 1938 Vienna

*one son one daughter*

**Viktor** *m* Emmy Schey von Koromla

b 1860 Odessa d 1945 Tunbridge Wells

**Elisabeth** *m* Hendrik de Waal

b 1899 Vienna d 1991 Monmouth

**Gisela** *m* Alfredo Bauer

b 1904 Vienna d 1985 Mexico

*three sons*

**Ignace**

b 1906 Vienna
d 1994 Tokyo

**Rudolf** *m* Mary Raley

b 1918 Vienna d 1971 New York

*two sons three daughters*

**Victor** *m* Esther Moir

b 1929 Amsterdam

**Constant Hendrik** *m* Julia Jessel

b 1931 Vienna

*two sons*

**Jiro Sugiyama**

b 1926 Shizuoka

**John**

b 1962 Cambridge

*one son one daughter*

**Alexander**

b 1963 Cambridge

*two sons one daughter*

**Edmund** *m* Susan Chandler

b 1964 Nottingham

**Thomas**

b 1966 Nottingham

*one daughter*

**Benjamin**

b 1998 London

**Matthew**

b 1999 London

**Anna**

b 2002 London

# PREFACE

In 1991 I was given a two-year scholarship by a Japanese foundation. The idea was to give seven young English people with diverse professional interests – engineering, journalism, industry, ceramics – a grounding in the Japanese language at an English university, followed by a year in Tokyo. Our fluency would help build a new era of contacts with Japan. We were the first intake on the programme and expectations were high.

Mornings during our second year were spent at a language school in Shibuya, up the hill from the welter of fast-food outlets and discount electrical stores. Tokyo was recovering from the crash after the bubble economy of the 1980s. Commuters stood at the pedestrian crossing, the busiest in the world, to catch sight of the screens showing the Nikkei Stock Index climbing higher and higher. To avoid the worst of the rush hour on the underground, I'd leave an hour early and meet another, older scholar – an archaeologist – and we'd have cinnamon buns and coffee on the way in to classes. I had homework, proper homework, for the first time since I was a schoolboy: 150 kanji, Japanese characters, to learn each week; a column of a tabloid newspaper to parse; dozens of conversational phrases to repeat every day. I'd never dreaded anything so much. The other, younger scholars would joke in Japanese with the teachers about television they had seen or political scandals. The school was behind green metal gates, and I remember kicking them one morning and thinking what it was to be twenty-eight and kicking a school gate.

Afternoons were my own. Two afternoons a week I was in a ceramics studio, shared with everyone from retired businessmen making tea-bowls to students making avant-garde statements in rough red clay and mesh. You paid your subs and grabbed a bench or wheel and were left to get on with it. It wasn't noisy, but there was a cheerful hum of chat. I started making work in porcelain for the first time, gently pushing the sides of my jars and teapots after I'd taken them off the wheel.

I had been making pots since I was a child and had badgered my father to take me to an evening class. My first pot was a thrown bowl that I glazed in opalescent white with a splash of cobalt blue. Most of my schoolboy afternoons were spent in a pottery work-shop, and I left school early at seventeen to become apprenticed to an austere man, a devotee of the English potter Bernard Leach. He taught me about respect for the material and about fitness for pur-pose: I threw hundreds of soup-bowls and honey-pots in grey stoneware clay and swept the floor. I would help make the glazes, careful recalibrations of oriental colours. He had never been to Japan, but had shelves of books on Japanese pots: we would discuss the merits of particular tea-bowls over our mugs of milky mid-morning coffee. Be careful, he would say, of the unwarranted gesture: less is more. We would work in silence or to classical music.

I spent a long summer in the middle of my teenage apprentice-ship in Japan visiting equally severe masters in pottery villages across the country: Mashiko, Bizen, Tamba. Each sound of a paper screen closing or of water across stones in the garden of a tea-house was an epiphany, just as each neon Dunkin' Donuts store gave me a moue of disquiet. I have documentary evidence of the depth of my devotion in an article I wrote for a magazine when I returned: 'Japan and the Potter's Ethic: Cultivating a reverence for your materials and the marks of age'.

After finishing my apprenticeship, and then studying English literature at university, I spent seven years working by myself in silent, ordered studios on the borders of Wales and then in a grim inner city. I was very focused, and so were my pots. And now here I was in Japan again, in a messy studio next to a man chatting away about baseball, making a porcelain jar with pushed-in, gestural sides. I was enjoying myself: something was going right.

Two afternoons a week I was in the archive room of the Nihon Mingei-kan, the Japanese Folk Crafts Museum, working on a book about Leach. The museum is a reconstructed farmhouse in a suburb, which houses the collection of Japanese and Korean folk crafts of Yanagi Soetsu. Yanagi, a philosopher, art historian and poet, had evolved a theory of why some objects – pots, baskets, cloth made by unknown craftsmen – were so beautiful. In his view, they expressed unconscious beauty because they had been made in such numbers that the craftsman had been liberated from his ego. He and Leach had been inseparable friends as young men in the early part of the twentieth century in Tokyo, writing animated letters to each other about their passionate reading of Blake and Whitman and Ruskin. They had even started an artists' colony in a hamlet a convenient distance outside Tokyo, where Leach made his pots with the help of local boys and Yanagi discoursed on Rodin and beauty to his bohemian friends.

Through a door the stone floors would give way to office linoleum, and down off a back corridor was Yanagi's archive: a small room, twelve feet by eight, with shelves to the ceiling full of his books and stacked with Manila boxes containing his notebooks and correspondence. There was a desk and a single bulb. I like archives. This one was very, very quiet and it was extremely gloomy. Here I read and noted and planned a revisionist history of Leach. It was to be a covert book on *Japonisme*, the way in which the West has passionately and creatively misunderstood Japan for more than a hundred years. I wanted to know what it was about Japan that produced such intensity and zeal in artists, and such crossness in academics as they pointed out one misinterpretation after another. I hoped that writing this book would help me out of my own deep, congested infatuation with the country.

And one afternoon a week I spent with my great-uncle Iggie.

I'd walk up the hill from the subway station, past the glowing beer-dispensing machines, past Senkaku-ji temple where the forty-seven samurai are buried, past the strange baroque meeting hall for a Shinto sect, past the sushi bar run by the bluff Mr X, turning right at the high wall of Prince Takamatsu's garden with the pines. I'd let myself in and take the lift up to the sixth floor. Iggie would be reading in his armchair by the window. Mostly Elmore Leonard or John Le Carré. Or memoirs in French. It is odd, he said, how some languages are warmer than others. I would bend down and he'd give me a kiss.

His desk held an empty blotter, a sheaf of his headed paper, and pens ready, though he no longer wrote. The view from the window behind him was of cranes. Tokyo Bay was disappearing behind forty-storey condominiums.

We'd have lunch together, prepared by his housekeeper Mrs Nakano or left by his friend Jiro, who lived in the interconnecting apartment. An omelette and salad, and toasted bread from one of the excellent French bakeries in the department stores in the Ginza. A glass of cold white wine, Sancerre or Pouilly Fumé. A peach. Some cheese and then very good coffee. Black coffee.

Iggie was eighty-four and slightly stooped. He was always impeccably dressed; handsome in his herringbone jackets with a handkerchief in the pocket, his pale shirts and a cravat. He had a small white moustache.

After our lunch he'd open the sliding doors of the long vitrine that took up most of one wall of the sitting-room and would get out the netsuke one by one. The hare with amber eyes. The young boy with the samurai sword and helmet. A tiger, all shoulder and feet, turning round to snarl. He would pass me one and we'd look at it together, and then I'd put it carefully back amongst the dozens of animals and figures on the glass shelves.

*Iggie with the netsuke collection in Tokyo, 1960*

I'd fill the little cups of water kept in the case to make sure the ivories didn't split in the dry air.

Did I tell you, he would say, how much we loved these as children? How they were given to my mother and father by a cousin in Paris? And did I tell you the story of Anna's pocket?

Conversations could take strange turns. One moment he would be describing how their cook in Vienna would make their father *Kaiserschmarrm* for his birthday breakfast, layers of pancakes and icing sugar bathed in a syrupy liqueur; how it would be brought in with a great flourish by the butler Josef into the dining-room and cut with a long knife, and how Papa would always say that the Emperor couldn't hope for a better start to his own birthday. And the next moment he would be talking about Lilli's second marriage. Who was Lilli?

Thank God, I'd think, that even if I didn't know about Lilli I knew enough to know where some of the stories were set: Bad Ischl, Kövesces, Vienna. I'd think, as the construction lights on the cranes came on at dusk, stretching deeper and deeper into Tokyo Bay, that I was becoming a sort of amanuensis and that I should probably record what he said about Vienna before the First World War, sit at his elbow with a notebook. I never did. It seemed formal and inappropriate. It also seemed greedy: that's a good rich story, I'll have that. Anyway, I liked the way that repetition wears things smooth, and there was something of the river stone to Iggie's stories.

Over the year of afternoons I'd hear about their father's pride in the cleverness of his older sister Elisabeth, and of Mama's dislike of her elaborate language. Do talk sensibly! He often mentioned, with some anxiety, a game with his sister Gisela, where they had to take something small from the drawing-room, get it down the stairs and across the courtyard, dodge the grooms, go down the cellar steps and hide it in the arched vaults under the house. And dare each other to get it back, and how he lost something in the dark. It seemed an unfinished, fraying memory.

Lots of stories about Kövesces, their country house in Czechoslavakia. His mother Emmy waking him before dawn to go out with a gamekeeper with a gun for the first time by himself to shoot hares in the stubble, and how he couldn't pull the trigger when he saw their ears tremble slightly in the cool air.

Gisela and Iggie coming across gypsies with a dancing bear on a chain, camping on the edge of the estate by the river, and running all the way back terrified. How the *Orient-Express* stopped at the halt and how their grandmother, in her white dress, was helped down by the stationmaster, and how they ran to greet her and take the parcel of cakes wrapped in green paper that she'd bought for them at Demel's in Vienna.

And Emmy pulling him to the window at breakfast to show him an autumnal tree outside the dining-room window covered in goldfinches. And how when he knocked on the window and they flew, the tree was still blazing golden.

I washed up after lunch while Iggie had his nap, and I would try to do my kanji homework, filling one chequered paper after another with my jerky efforts. I'd stay until Jiro came back from work with the Japanese and English evening newspapers and the croissants for tomorrow's breakfast. Jiro would put on Schubert or jazz and we would have a drink and then I'd leave them be.

I was renting a very pleasant single room in Mejiro, looking out over a small garden filled with azaleas. I had an electric ring and a kettle and was doing my best, but my life in the evenings was very noodle-focused and rather lonely. Twice a month Jiro and Iggie would take me out to dinner or a concert. They would give me drinks at the Imperial and then wonderful sushi or steak tartare or, in homage to banking antecedents, *boeuf à la financière*. I refused the foie gras that was Iggie's staple.

That summer there was a reception for the scholars in the British Embassy. I had to make a speech in Japanese about what I had learnt during my year and how culture was the bridge between our two island nations. I had rehearsed it until I could bear it no longer. Iggie and Jiro came and I could see them encouraging me across their glasses of champagne. Afterwards Jiro squeezed my shoulder and I got a kiss from Iggie and, smiling, complicit, they told me that my Japanese was *jozu desu ne* – expert, skilled, unparalleled.

They had sorted it well, these two. There was a Japanese room in Jiro's apartment with tatami mats and the little shrine bearing photographs of his mother and Iggie's mother, Emmy, where prayers were said and the bell rung. And through the door in Iggie's apartment on his desk there was a photograph of them together in a boat on the Inland Sea, a mountain of pines behind them, dappled sunshine on the water. It is January 1960. Jiro, so good-looking with his hair slicked back, has an arm over Iggie's shoulder. And another picture, from the 1980s, on a cruise ship somewhere off Hawaii, in evening dress, arm in arm.

Living the longest is hard, says Iggie, under his breath.

Growing old in Japan is wonderful, he says more loudly. I have lived here for more than half my life.

Do you miss anything about Vienna? (Why not come straight out and ask him: So what do you miss, when you are old and not living in the country you were born in?)

No. I didn't go back until 1973. It was stifling. Smothering. Everyone knew your name. You'd buy a novel in the Kärntner Strasse and they'd ask you if your mother's cold was better yet. You couldn't move. All that gilding and marble in the house. It was so dark. Have you seen our old house on the Ringstrasse?

Do you know, he says suddenly, that Japanese plum dumplings are better than Viennese plum dumplings?

Actually, he resumes, after a pause, Papa always said that he'd put me up for his club when I was old enough. It met on Thursdays somewhere near the Opera, with all his friends, his Jewish friends. He came back so cheerful on Thursdays. The Wiener Club. I always wanted to go there with him, but he never took me. I left for Paris and then New York, you see, and then there was the war.

I miss that. I missed that.

Iggie died in 1994 soon after I returned to England. Jiro rang me: there had been only three days in hospital. It was a relief. I came back to Tokyo for his funeral. There were two dozen of us, their old friends, Jiro's family, Mrs Nakano and her daughter, clouded in tears.

There is the cremation, and we gather together and the ashes are brought out, and in turns a pair of us pick up long black chopsticks and put the fragments of unburnt bone into an urn.

We go to the temple where Iggie and Jiro have their interment plot. They had planned this tomb twenty years before. The cemetery is on a hill behind the temple, each plot marked with small stone walls. There is the grey gravestone with both their names already inscribed on it, and a place for flowers. Buckets of water and brushes and long wooden signs with painted inscriptions on them. You clap three times and greet your family and apologise for the delay since you were last there, and clean up, remove old chrysan-themums and put new ones in water.

At the temple the urn is placed on a small dais and a photograph of Iggie – the photograph of him on the cruise ship in his dinner jacket – is placed in front of it. The abbot chants a sutra and we offer incense, and Iggie is given his new Buddhist name, his *kaimyo*, to help him in his next life.

Then we speak of him. I try to say, in Japanese, how much my great-uncle means to me and cannot because I am in tears and because, despite my expensive two-year scholarship, my Japanese isn't good enough when I need it. So instead, in this room in this Buddhist temple, in this Tokyo suburb, I say the Kaddish for Ignace von Ephrussi who is so far from Vienna, for his father and his mother, and for his brother and sisters in their diaspora.

After the funeral Jiro asks me to help sort out Iggie's clothes. I open the cupboards in his dressing-room and see the shirts ordered by colour. As I pack the ties away, I notice that they map his holi-days with Jiro in London and Paris, Honolulu and New York.

When this job is done, over a glass of wine, Jiro takes out his brush and ink and writes a document and seals it. It says, he tells me, that once he has gone I should look after the netsuke.

So I'm next.

There are 264 netsuke in this collection. It is a very big collection of very small objects.

I pick one up and turn it round in my fingers, weigh it in the palm of my hand. If it is wood, chestnut or elm, it is even lighter than the ivory. You see the patina more easily on these wooden ones: there is a faint shine on the spine of the brindled wolf and on the tumbling acrobats locked in their embrace. The ivory ones come in shades of cream, every colour, in fact, but white. A few have inlaid eyes of amber or horn. Some of the older ones are slightly worn away: the haunch of the faun resting on leaves has lost its markings. There is a slight split, an almost imperceptible fault line on the cicada. Who dropped it? Where and when?

Most of them are signed – that moment of ownership when it was finished and let go. There is a wooden netsuke of a seated man holding a gourd between his feet. He's bending over it, both hands on a knife that is half into the gourd. It is hard work, his arms and shoulder and neck show the effort: every muscle concentrates on the blade. There is another of a cooper working on a half-finished barrel with an adze. He sits leaning into it, framed by it, brows puckered with concentration. It is an ivory carving about what it is like to carve into wood. Both are about finishing something on the subject of the half-finished. Look, they say, I got there first and he's hardly started.

When you tumble them in your hands there is a pleasure in finding where these signatures have been placed – on the sole of a sandal, the end of a branch, the thorax of a hornet – as well as the play between the strokes. I think of the moves when you sign your name in Japan with ink, the sweep of the brush into the ink, the first plosive moment of contact, the return to the ink stone, and wonder at how you could develop such a distinctive signature using the fine metal tools of the netsuke-maker.

Some of these netsuke carry no name. Some have bits of paper glued to them, bearing tiny numbers carefully written in red pen.

There are a great number of rats. Perhaps because they give the maker the chance to wrap those sinuous tails round each other, over the pails of water, the dead fish, the beggars' robes, and then fold those paws underneath the carvings. There are also quite a lot of rat-catchers, I realise.

Some of the netsuke are studies in running movement, so that your fingers move along a surface of uncoiling rope, or spilt water. Others have small congested movements that knot your touch: a girl in a wooden bath, a vortex of clam shells. Some do both, surprising you: an intricately ruffled dragon leans against a simple rock. You work your fingers round the smoothness and stoniness of the ivory to meet this sudden density of dragon.

They are always asymmetric, I think with pleasure. Like my favourite Japanese tea-bowls, you cannot understand the whole from a part.

When I am back in London I put one of these netsuke in my pocket for a day and carry it round. Carry is not quite the right word for having a netsuke in a pocket. It sounds too purposeful. A net-suke is so light and so small that it migrates and almost disappears amongst your keys and change. You simply forget that it is there. This was a netsuke of a very ripe medlar fruit, made out of chestnut wood in the late eighteenth century in Edo, the old Tokyo. In autumn in Japan you sometimes see medlars; a branch hanging over a wall of a temple or from a private garden into a street of vending machines is impossibly pleasing. My medlar is just about to go from ripeness to deliquescence. The three leaves at the top feel as if they would fall if you rubbed them between your fingers. The fruit is slightly unbalanced: it is riper on one side than the other. Under-neath, you can feel the two holes – one larger than the other – where the silk cord would run, so that the netsuke could act as a toggle on a small bag. I try and imagine who owned the medlar. It was made long before the opening up of Japan to foreign trade in the 1850s, and thus created for the Japanese taste: it might have been carved for a merchant or a scholar. It is a quiet one, undemonstrative, but it makes me smile. Making something to hold out of a very hard material that feels so soft is a slow and rather good tactile pun.

I keep my medlar in my jacket pocket and go to a meeting at a museum about a piece of research I am supposed to be doing, and then to my studio and then to the London Library. I intermittently roll this thing through my fingers.

I realise how much I care about how this hard and soft, losable object has survived. I need to find a way of unravelling its story. Owning this netsuke – inheriting them all – means I have been handed a responsibility to them and to the people who have owned them. I am unclear and discomfited about where the parameters of this responsibility might lie.

I know the bones of this journey from Iggie. I know that these netsuke were bought in Paris in the 1870s by a cousin of my great-grandfather called Charles Ephrussi. I know that he gave them as a wedding-present to my great-grandfather Viktor von Ephrussi in Vienna at the turn of the century. I know the story of Anna, my great-grandmother's maid, very well. And I know that they came with Iggie to Tokyo, of course, and were part of his life with Jiro.

Paris, Vienna, Tokyo, London.

The medlar's story starts where it is made. Edo, the old Tokyo before the Black Ships of the American Commodore Perry opened Japan up to trade with the rest of the world in 1859. But its first resting-place was in Charles's study in Paris. It was in a room looking over the rue de Monceau in the Hôtel Ephrussi.

I start well. I'm pleased because I have one direct, spoken link to

Charles. As a child of five, my grandmother Elisabeth met Charles at the Chalet Ephrussi in Meggen, on the edge of Lake Lucerne. The 'chalet' was six storeys of rusticated stone surmounted by small baronial turrets, a house of stupendous ugliness. It had been built in the early 1880s by Charles's oldest brother Jules and wife Fanny, as a place to escape the 'horrid oppression of Paris'. It was huge, grand enough to house all the 'clan Ephrussi' from Paris and Vienna, and assorted cousins from Berlin.

The chalet had endless small paths that crunched underfoot, with neat box edging in the English manner, small flowerbeds filled with bedding plants, and a fierce gardener to tell the children off for playing; gravel did not stray in this severe Swiss garden. The garden went down to the lake, where there was a small jetty and boathouse, and more opportunities for reprimand. Jules, Charles and their middle brother Ignace were Russian citizens and the Russian imperial flag flew from the boathouse roof. There were endless slow summers at the chalet. My grandmother was the expected heir of the fabulously wealthy and childless Jules and Fanny. She remembered a large painting in the dining-room of willows by a stream. She also remembered that there were only manservants in the house, and that even the cook was a man, which was wildly more exciting than her own family's household in Vienna with only old Josef the butler, the porter who would wink at her as he opened the gates to the Ring and the grooms amidst all the maids and cooks. Apparently manservants were less likely to break the porcelain. And, she remembered, there was porcelain on every surface in this childless chalet.

Charles was middle-aged, but seemed old by comparison with his infinitely more glamorous brothers. Elisabeth remembered only his beautiful beard and that he had an extremely delicate watch that he produced from a waistcoat pocket. And that, in the manner of elderly relatives, he had given her a golden coin.

But she also remembered with great clarity, and more animation, that Charles had bent down and ruffled her sister's hair. Her sister Gisela – younger and far, far prettier – always got this kind of attention. Charles had called her his little gypsy, his *bohémienne*.

And that is my oral link to Charles. It is history and yet, when I write it down, it doesn't feel like much.

And what there is to go on – the number of manservants and the slightly stock story of the gift of a coin – seems held in a sort of melancholic penumbra, though I quite like the detail of the Russian flag. I know that my family were Jewish, of course, and I know they were staggeringly rich, but I really don't want to get into the sepia saga business, writing up some elegiac Mitteleuropa narrative of loss. And I certainly don't want to turn Iggie into an old great-uncle in his study, a figure like Bruce Chatwin's Utz, handing over the family story, telling me: Go, be careful.

It could write itself, I think, this kind of story. A few stitched-together wistful anecdotes, more about the *Orient-Express*, of course, a bit of wandering round Prague or somewhere equally photogenic, some clippings from Google on ballrooms in the Belle Epoque. It would come out as nostalgic. And *thin*.

And I'm not entitled to nostalgia about all that lost wealth and glamour from a century ago. And I am not interested in *thin*. I want to know what the relationship has been between this wooden object that I am rolling between my fingers – hard and tricky and Japanese – and where it has been. I want to be able to reach to the handle of the door and turn it and feel it open. I want to walk into each room where this object has lived, to feel the volume of the space, to know what pictures were on the walls, how the light fell from the windows. And I want to know whose hands it has been in, and what they felt about it and thought about it – if they thought about it. I want to know what it has witnessed.

Melancholy, I think, is a sort of default vagueness, a get-out clause, a smothering lack of focus. And this netsuke is a small, tough explosion of exactitude. It deserves this kind of exactitude in return.

All this matters because my job is to make things. How objects get handled, used and handed on is not just a mildly interesting question for me. It is *my* question. I have made many, many thousands of pots. I am very bad at names, I mumble and fudge, but I am good on pots. I can remember the weight and the balance of a pot, and how its surface works with its volume. I can read how an edge creates tension or loses it. I can feel if it has been made at speed or with diligence. If it has warmth.

I can see how it works with the objects that sit nearby. How it displaces a small part of the world around it.

I can also remember if something invited touch with the whole hand or just the fingers, or was an object that asked you to stay away. It is not that handling something is *better* than not handling it. Some things in the world are meant to be looked at from a distance and not fumbled around with. And, as a potter, I find it a bit strange when people who have my pots talk of them as if they are alive: I am not sure if I can cope with the afterlife of what I have made. But some objects do seem to retain the pulse of their making.

This pulse intrigues me. There is a breath of hesitancy before touching or not touching, a strange moment. If I choose to pick up this small white cup with its single chip near the handle, will it figure in my life? A simple object, this cup that is more ivory than white, too small for morning coffee, not quite balanced, could become part of my life of handled things. It could fall away into the territory of personal story-telling; the sensuous, sinuous intertwining of things with memories. A favoured, favourite thing. Or I could put it away. Or I could pass it on.

How objects are handed on is all about story-telling. I am giving you this because I love you. Or because it was given to me. Because I bought it somewhere special. Because you will care for it. Because it will complicate your life. Because it will make someone else envious. There is no easy story in legacy. What is remembered and what is forgotten? There can be a chain of forgetting, the rubbing away of previous ownership as much as the slow accretion of stories. What is being passed on to me with all these small Japanese objects?

I realise that I've been living with this netsuke business for too long. I can either anecdotalise it for the rest of my life – my odd inheritance from a beloved elderly relative – or go and find out what it means. One evening I find myself at a dinner telling some academics what I know of the story, and feel slightly sickened by how poised it sounds. I hear myself entertaining them, and the story echoes back in their reactions. It isn't just getting smoother, it is getting thinner. I must sort it out now or it will disappear.

Being busy is no excuse. I have just finished an exhibition of my porcelain in a museum and can postpone a commission for a collector, if I play my cards right. I have negotiated with my wife and cleared my diary. Three or four months should see me right. That gives me enough time to go back to see Jiro in Tokyo and to visit Paris and Vienna.

As my grandmother and my great-uncle Iggie have died, I must also ask for my father's help to get started. He is eighty and kindness itself and will look out family things for me, he says, for background information. He seems delighted that one of his four sons is interested. There isn't much, he warns me. He comes down to my studio with a small cache of photographs, forty-odd. He also brings two thin blue files of letters to which he has added yellow Post-it notes, mostly legible, a family tree annotated by my grandmother sometime in the 1970s, the membership book for the Wiener Club in 1935 and, in a supermarket carrier bag, a pile of Thomas Mann novels with inscriptions. We lay them out on the long table in my office up the stairs, above the room where I fire my pots in the kilns. You are now the keeper of the family archive, he tells me, and I look at the piles and am not sure how funny I should find this.

I ask, somewhat desperately, if there is any more material. He looks again that evening in his small flat in the courtyard of retired clergymen where he lives. He telephones me to say that he has found another volume of Thomas Mann. This journey is going to be more complicated than I had thought.

Still, I can't start with a complaint. I know very little of substance about Charles, the first collector of the netsuke, but I have found where he lived in Paris. I put a netsuke in my pocket and set out.

*Part One*

PARIS 1871–1899

# I. LE WEST END

One sunny April day I set out to find Charles. Rue de Monceau is a long Parisian street bisected by the grand boulevard Malesherbes that charges off towards the boulevard Pereire. It is a hill of golden-stone houses, a series of hotels playing discreetly on neoclassical themes, each a minor Florentine palace with heavily rusticated ground floors and an array of heads, caryatids and cartouches. Number 81 rue de Monceau, the Hôtel Ephrussi, where my net-suke start their journey, is near the top of the hill. I pass the headquarters of Christian Lacroix and then, next door, there it is. It is now, rather crushingly, an office for medical insurance.

It is utterly beautiful. As a boy I used to draw buildings like this, spending afternoons carefully inking in shadows so that you could see the rise and fall of the depth of the windows and pillars. There is something musical in this kind of elevation. You take classical elements and try to bring them into rhythmic life: four Corinthian pilasters rising up to pace the façade, four massive stone urns on the parapet, five storeys high, eight windows wide. The street level is made up of great blocks of stone worked to look as if they have been weathered. I walk past a couple of times and, on the third, notice that there is the double back-to-back E of the Ephrussi family incorporated into the metal grilles over the street windows, the tendrils of the letter reaching into the spaces of the oval. It is barely there. I try to work out this rectitude and what it says about their confidence.

I duck through the passageway to a courtyard, then through another arch to a stable block of red brick with servants' quarters above; a pleasing diminuendo of materials and textures.

A delivery man carries boxes of Speedy-Go Pizza into the medical insurers. The door into the entrance hall is open. I walk into the hall, its staircase curling up like a coil of smoke through the whole house, black cast iron and gold filigree stretching up to a lantern at the top. There is a marble urn in a deep niche, chequerboard marble tiles. Executives are coming down the stairs, heels hard on marble, and I retreat in embarrassment. How can I start to explain this idiotic quest? I stand in the street and watch the house and take some photographs, apologetic Parisians ducking past me. House-watching is an art. You have to develop a way of seeing how a building sits in its landscape or streetscape. You have to discover how much room it takes up in the world, how much of the world it displaces. Number 81, for instance, is a house that cannily disappears into its neighbours: there are other houses that are grander, some are plainer, but few are more discreet.

I look up at the second-floor windows where Charles had his suite of rooms, some of which looked across the street to the more robustly classical house opposite, some across the courtyard into a busy roofscape of urns and gables and chimneypots. He had an antechamber, two salons – one of which he turned into his study – a dining-room, two bedrooms and a '*petite*'. I try to work it out; he and his older brother Ignace must have had neighbouring apartments on this floor, their elder brother Jules and their widowed mother Mina below, with the higher ceilings and grander windows and the balconies on which, on this April morning, there are now some rather leggy red geraniums in plastic pots. The courtyard of the house was glazed, according to the city records, though all that glass is long gone. And there were five horses and three carriages in these stables which are now a perfect bijou house. I wonder if that number of horses was appropriate for a large and social family wanting to make the right kind of impression.

It is a huge house, but the three brothers must have met every day on those black-and-gold winding stairs, or heard each other as the noise of the carriage being readied in the courtyard echoed from the glazed canopy. Or encountered friends going past their door on the way up to an apartment above. They must have developed a way of not seeing each other, and not hearing each other, too: to live so close to your family takes some doing, I think, reflecting on my own brothers. They must have got on well. Perhaps they had no choice in the matter. Paris was work, after all.

The Hôtel Ephrussi was a family house, but it was also the Parisian headquarters of a family in its ascendancy. It had its counterpart in Vienna, the vast Palais Ephrussi on the Ringstrasse. Both the Parisian and Viennese buildings share a sense of drama, of a public face to the world. They were both built in 1871 in new and fashionable areas: the rue de Monceau and the Ringstrasse were so of-the-minute that they were unfinished, untidy, loud and dusty building sites. They were still spaces that were inventing themselves, competitive with the older parts of town with their narrower streets, and spikily arriviste.

If this particular house in this particular streetscape seems a little stagey, it is because it is a staging of intent. These houses in Paris and Vienna were part of a family plan: the Ephrussi family was 'doing a Rothschild'. Just as the Rothschilds had sent their sons and daughters out from Frankfurt at the start of the nineteenth century to colonise European capital cities, so the Abraham of my family,

Charles Joachim Ephrussi, had masterminded this expansion from Odessa in the 1850s. A true patriarch, he had two sons from his first marriage, Ignace and Leon. And then when he remarried at fifty he had continued producing children: two more sons, Michel and Maurice, and two daughters, Therese and Marie. All of these six children were to be deployed as financiers or married into suitable Jewish dynasties.

Odessa was a city within the Pale of Settlement, the area on the western borders of imperial Russia in which Jews were allowed to live. It was famous for its rabbinical schools and synagogues, rich in literature and music, a magnet for the impoverished Jewish shtetls of Galicia. It was also a city that doubled its population of Jews and Greeks and Russians every decade, a polyglot city full of speculation and traders, the docks full of intrigues and spies, a city on the make. Charles Joachim Ephrussi had transformed a small grain-trading business into a huge enterprise by cornering the market in buying wheat. He bought the grain from the middlemen who transported it on carts along the heavily rutted roads from the rich black soil of the Ukrainian wheat fields, the greatest wheat fields in the world, into the port of Odessa. Here the grain was stored in his warehouses before being exported across the Black Sea, up the Danube, across the Mediterranean.

By 1860 the family had become the greatest grain-exporters in the world. In Paris, James de Rothschild was known as the *le Roi des Juifs*, the King of the Jews. The Ephrussi were *les Rois de Blé*, the Kings of Grain. They were Jews with their own coat of arms: an ear of corn and a heraldic boat with three masts and full sails. Their motto, *Quod Honestum*, unfurled below the ship: *We are above reproach. You can trust us.*

The masterplan was to build on this network of contacts and finance huge capital projects: bridges across the Danube, railways across Russia and across France, docks and canals. Ephrussi et Cie would change from being a very successful commodity trading house into an international finance house. It would become a bank. And each helpful deal struck with a government, each venture with an impoverished archduke, each client drawn into serious obligation with the family would be a step towards even greater respectability, a step further from those wagons of wheat creaking in from the Ukraine.

In 1857 the two elder sons and their families were sent out from Odessa to Vienna, the capital city of the sprawling Hapsburg Empire. They bought a huge house in the city centre, and for ten years this was home to a shifting population of grandparents, children and grandchildren as the family moved backwards and forwards between the two cities. One of the sons, my great-great-grandfather Ignace, was tasked with handling Ephrussi business in the Austro-Hungarian Empire from this Vienna base. Paris came next: Leon, the older son, was tasked with establishing the family and business here.

I'm standing outside Leon's outpost on a honey-coloured hill in the 8th arrondissement. Actually I am leaning against the house opposite and thinking of that fiercely hot summer of 1871 when they arrived from Vienna to this newly built, golden mansion. It was a city still in trauma. The siege by the Prussian army had only ended a few months before with the defeat of France and the declaration of the German Empire in the Hall of Mirrors in Versailles. The new Third Republic was shaky, assailed by communards on the street and by factionalism in government.

*The Hôtel Ephrussi in the rue de Monceau*

Their house may have been finished, but all the neighbouring buildings were still under construction. The plasterers had only just left, the gilders were lying uncomfortably on the shallow stairs burnishing the finials on the handrail. Furniture, pictures, crates of crockery are shifted slowly up to their apartments. There is noise inside and noise outside, and all the windows are open onto the street. Leon is unwell with a heart complaint. And the family have a terrible start to their life in this beautiful street. Betty, the youngest of Leon and Mina's four children, married to a young Jewish banker of unimpeachable suitability, dies within weeks of giving birth to a daughter, Fanny. They have to build a family tomb in the Jewish section of the cemetery in Montmartre in their newly adopted city.

It is Gothic, large enough for the whole clan, a way of making it clear that they are staying here, whatever is going to happen. I finally find it. The gates are gone and it has caught drifts of autumn's chestnut leaves.

This hill was the perfect setting for the Ephrussi family. Just as the Ringstrasse in Vienna, where the other half of the family lives, was acerbically known as Zionstrasse, so Jewish money was a key denominator of life here in the rue de Monceau. The area was developed in the 1860s by Isaac and Emile Péreire, two Sephardic brothers who had made their fortunes as financiers, railroad-builders and property magnates, creating colossal developments of hotels and department stores. They acquired the plaine de Monceau, a large nondescript area that was originally beyond the city limits, and set to work developing houses for the burgeoning financial and commercial elite, an appropriate landscape for the newly arrived Jewish families from Russia and the Levant. These streets became a virtual colony, a complex of inter-marriage, obligation and religious sympathy.

The Péreires relandscaped the existing eighteenth-century park in order to improve the views of the new houses around it. New cast-iron gates with gilded emblems of the Péreires' activities now led into it. There was an attempt to call the area around the parc Monceau *le West End*. If you are asked where the boulevard Malesherbes leads, a contemporary journalist wrote, 'answer boldly: to *Le West End* . . . One could give it a French name, but that would be vulgar; an English name was far more fashionable.' This was the park in which, according to a waspish journalist, you could watch 'the great dames of the noble Faubourg . . . the female "illustrations" of "La Haute Finance" and "La Haute Colonie Israelite" promenade'. The park had sinuous paths and flowerbeds in the new English style with displays of colourful annuals that had to be constantly renewed, far removed from the grey, clipped formalities of the Tuileries.

As I walk down the hill from the Hôtel Ephrussi at what I consider to be a good flaneurial pace, slower than usual, weaving from one side of the road to the other to check on details of the mouldings of windows, I'm conscious that many of the houses I pass have these stories of reinvention embedded in them. Almost everyone who built them started somewhere else.

Ten houses down from the Ephrussi household, at number 61, is the house of Abraham Camondo, with his brother Nissim at 63 and their sister Rebecca over the street at number 60. The Camondos, Jewish financiers like the Ephrussi, had come to Paris from Constantinople by way of Venice. The banker Henri Cernuschi, a plutocratic supporter of the Paris Commune, had come to Paris from Italy and lived in chilly magnificence with his Japanese treasures on the edge of the park. At number 55 is the Hôtel Cattaui, home to a family of Jewish bankers from Egypt. At number 43 is the palace of Adolphe de Rothschild, acquired from Eugène Péreire and rebuilt with a glass-roofed exhibition room for his Renaissance art collection.

But nothing compares to the mansion built by the chocolate magnate Émile-Justin Mernier. It was a building so splendidly excessive, so eclectic in its garnished decorations, glimpsed above its high walls, that Zola's description of it as 'an opulent bastard of every style' still seems about right. In his dark novel of 1872, *La Curée*, Saccard – a rapacious Jewish property magnate – lives here on the rue de Monceau. You feel this street as the family move in: it is a street of Jews, a street full of people on display in their lavish golden houses. *Monceau* is slang in Paris for nouveau riche, newly arrived.

This is the world in which my netsuke first settled. On this street down the hill I feel this play between discretion and opulence, a sort of breathing-in and breathing-out of invisibility and visibility.

Charles Ephrussi was twenty-one when he came to live here. Paris was being planted with trees, and wide pavements were taking the place of the cramped interstices of the old city. There had been fifteen years of constant demolition and rebuilding under the direction of Baron Haussmann, the civic planner. He had razed medieval streets and created new parks and new boulevards. Vistas were opened up with extraordinary velocity.

If you want to taste this moment, taste the dust sweeping along the newly paved avenues and across the bridges, look at two paintings of Gustave Caillebotte. Caillebotte, a few months older than Charles, lived around the corner from the Ephrussi family in another grand hotel. You see in his *Le Pont de l'Europe* a young man, well dressed in his grey overcoat and black top hat, maybe the artist,

*Gustave Caillebotte,* Le Pont de l'Europe, *1876*

walking over the bridge along the generous pavement. He is two steps ahead of a young woman in a dress of sedate frills carrying a parasol. The sun is out. There is the glare of newly dressed stone. A dog passes by. A workman leans over the bridge. It is like the start of the world: a litany of perfect movements and shadows. Everyone, including the dog, knows what they are doing.

The streets of Paris have a calmness to them: clean stone façades, rhythmic detailing of balconies, newly planted lime trees appear in his painting *Jeune homme à sa fenêtre*, shown in the second Impressionist exhibition in 1876. Here Caillebotte's brother stands at the open window of their family apartment looking out onto the intersection of the rue de Monceau's neighbouring streets. He stands with his hands in his pockets, well dressed and self-assured, with his life before him and a plush armchair behind him.

Everything is possible.

This could be the young Charles. He was born in Odessa and had spent the first ten years of his life in a yellow-stuccoed *palais* on the edge of a dusty square fringed with chestnut trees. If he climbs to the attics of the house he can see all the way across the masts of the ships in the port to the sea. His grandfather occupies a whole floor and all the space. The bank is next door. He cannot move along the promenade without someone stopping his grandfather or father or uncles to ask them for information, a favour, a kopek, something. He learns, without knowing it, that to move in public means a series of encounters and avoidances; how to give money to beggars and pedlars, how to greet acquaintances without stopping.

Then Charles moves to Vienna, living there for the next decade with his parents, his siblings, his uncle Ignace and glacial aunt Emilie, and his three cousins – Stefan (haughty), Anna (acerbic) and the little boy Viktor. A tutor comes each morning. They learn their languages: Latin, Greek, German and English. They are always to speak French at home, and are allowed to use Russian amongst themselves, but must not be caught speaking the Yiddish that they picked up in the courtyards in Odessa. All these cousins can start a sentence in one language and finish it in another. They need these languages, as the family travels to Odessa, to St Petersburg, to Berlin and Frankfurt and Paris. They also need these languages as they are denominators of class. With languages, you can move from one social situation to another. With languages, you are *at home anywhere*.

They visit Breughel's *Hunters in the Snow* with its patchwork of dogs busy on the ridge. They open the cabinets of drawings in the Albertina, the watercolours by Dürer of the trembling hare, the outstretched wing of a lapidary bird. They learn to ride in the Prater. The boys are taught to fence and all the cousins take dance lessons. All the cousins dance well. Charles, at eighteen, has a family nickname, *Le Polonais*, the Pole, the waltzing boy.

It is in Vienna that the oldest boys, Jules, Ignace and Stefan, are taken to the offices off the Ringstrasse on the Schottenbastei. It is a forbidding building. This is where the Ephrussi conduct business. The boys are told to sit quietly as shipments of grain are discussed and percentages on stock are queried. There are new possibilities in oil in Baku and gold near Lake Baikal. Clerks scurry. This is where they are blooded in the sheer scale of what will be theirs, taught the catechism of profit from the endless columns in the ledgers.

This is when Charles sits with his youngest cousin Viktor and draws Laocoön and the snakes, the statue he loved in Odessa, making the coils extra specially tight around muscly shoulders to impress the boy. It takes a long time to draw each of those snakes well. He sketches what he has seen in the Albertina. He sketches the servants. And he talks to his parents' friends about their pictures. It is always pleasing to have your paintings discussed by such a knowledgeable young man.

And then at last there is the long-planned move to Paris. Charles is good-looking, slightly built with a neatly trimmed dark beard, which has a haze of red in particular lights. He has an Ephrussi nose, large and beaked, and the high forehead of all the cousins. His eyes are dark grey and alive, and he is charming. You see how well dressed he is, with his cravat beautifully folded, and then you hear him talk: he is as good a talker as a dancer.

Charles is free to do what he wants.

I want to think this is because he was the youngest son and the third son and, as in all good children's stories, it is always the third son who gets to leave home and go adventuring – pure projection, as I am a third son. But I suspect that the family know this boy is not cut out for the life of the Bourse. His uncles Michel and Maurice have moved to Paris: perhaps there were enough sons for the offices of Ephrussi et Cie at 45 rue de l'Arcade not to miss this pleasant bookish one, with his habit of withdrawing when money comes up and that aptitude for losing himself in conversation.

Charles has his new apartment in the family house, gilded and clean, and empty. He has somewhere to come back to, a new house on a newly paved Parisian hill. He has languages, he has money and he has time. So now he sets off wandering. Like a well-brought-up young man, Charles goes south. He goes to Italy.

In the prehistory of my netsuke collection this is the first age of Charles's collections. Perhaps as a boy he had picked up conkers from the trees in the promenade in Odessa, or collected coins in Vienna, but this is where I know he starts. What he starts with and brings back to his apartment at 81 rue de Monceau shows avidity. Avidity or greed or liberated excitement: he certainly buys a lot.

He has a year away from his family, a gap year, a conventional *Wan derjahr*, a Grand Tour through the canon of Renaissance art. This journey turns Charles into a collector. Or perhaps, I think, it allows him to collect, to turn looking into having and having into knowing.

Charles buys drawings and medallions, Renaissance enamels and sixteenth-century tapestries made after Raphael cartoons. He buys a marble child in the manner of Donatello. He buys a beautiful faience sculpture of a young faun by Luca della Robbia, an ambiguous, vulnerable creature turning round to look back at us, glazed in deep Madonna blue and yolky yellows. Back in his second-floor apartment Charles frames it in a niche in his bedroom hung with sixteenth-century Italian broderies, thickly embroidered textiles. It becomes a sort of satyric altarpiece, with the faun taking the place of a martyred saint.

There is an illustration of this altarpiece in a vast maroon three-volume elephant folio in the library at the Victoria and Albert Museum. I order it up, and there is much jocularity when it is brought into the Reading Room on a hospital trolley. This *Musée Graphique* contains engravings of all the major collections of Renaissance art in Europe, principally those of Sir Richard Wallace (of the Wallace Collection in London), assorted Rothschilds – and the twenty-three-year-old Charles. These folios are vanity publishing on a colossal scale, produced by collectors to impress other collectors. Three pages after his sumptuous niche for the faun – a deep burgundy with raised golden threads, panels of saints, coats of arms – another part of his collection is revealed.

It makes me laugh out loud: a huge Renaissance bed, a *lit de parade* also hung with broderies. A high canopy with putti embowered in intricate patterns, grotesque heads, heraldic emblems, flowers and fruit. Two rich curtains are held back with heavily tasselled ropes, each with an E on a golden background. On the bedhead itself is another E. It is a sort of ducal bed – almost a princeling's bed. It belongs to fantasy. It is a bed from which to rule a city state, give audiences, to write sonnets in, certainly to make love in. What kind of young man would buy a bed like this?

I write down this long list of his new possessions and try to imagine being twenty-three, with these crates of treasures heaved up the winding stairs to the second floor and opened with all the shavings and splinters flying; arranging them in my own suite of rooms, trying out their disposition in relation to the morning sun that floods in from the street. As visitors come into the salon, should they see a wall of drawings or a tapestry? Should they glimpse my *lit de parade*? I imagine showing the enamels to my parents and my brothers, showing off to my family. And I have a sudden, embarrassed return to being sixteen and hauling my bed into the corridor in order to sleep on the floor, and tacking up a carpet over my mattress to make a canopy. And weekends spent rehanging my pictures and rearranging my books, trying out how it felt to change my own space. It feels eminently possible.

It is, of course, a stage-set. All these things that Charles collected are objects that need a connoisseur's eye, all are things that speak of knowledge, history, lineage, of collecting itself. Unpick this list of treasures – tapestries *woven after* Raphael cartoons, sculpture *after* Donatello – and you can feel that Charles has begun to internalise how art unfolds through history. Back in Paris he donates a rare fifteenth-century medallion of Hippolytus torn apart by wild horses to the Louvre. I think I can begin to hear the young art historian talking to visitors. You sense the notebook, not just the money.

But I also begin to feel his pleasure in stuff here: the surprising weight of damask, the chill of the surface of enamels, the patina of bronzes, the heft of the raised thread on the embroideries.

This first collection is totally conventional. Many of his parents' friends would have had similar objects within their houses, and would have brought them together to make set-pieces of decorative sumptuousness, just as the young Charles created his own burgundy-and-gold *mise en scène* in his Parisian bedroom. It is just a smaller version of what was happening elsewhere in other Jewish house-holds. He is showing, rather emphatically for a young man, how grown-up he is. And he is preparing himself for a life in public.

If you wanted to see set-pieces at scale you could go to any of the Rothschild houses in Paris or, indeed, to James de Rothschild's new palace at Ferrières, just outside the city. Here the works of the Renaissance Italy of merchants and bankers were celebrated: remember that great patronage comes through the astute use of money and is not hereditary. Rather than having a Great Hall, chivalric and Christian,

Ferrières had a central indoor piazza with four great doorways leading to different parts of the house. Under a Tiepolo ceiling there was a gallery of tapestries of the Triumphs, sculptured figures in black-and-white marble, and pictures by Velázquez, Rubens, Guido Reni and Rembrandt. Above all, there was a lot of gold: gold on the furniture, on the picture frames, on the mouldings, in the tapestries, and embedded – everywhere – were gilded symbols of the Rothschilds. *Le gout Rothschild* had become a shorthand for gilding. Jews and their gold.

Charles's sensibility stops short of Ferrières. As does his space, of course: he only has his two salons and his bedroom. But Charles not only has a place in which he could arrange his new possessions and his books, but also has a sense of himself as a young scholar-collector. He is in the extraordinary position of being both ridiculously affluent and very self-directed.

And neither of these things warms me to him at all. In fact the bed makes me feel a little queasy: I am not sure how much time I can face with this young man and his good eye for art and interior decoration, netsuke or no. *Connoisseur*, goes the alarm. And *thinks he knows too much, too young.*

And, of course, *much, much too rich for his own good.*

I realise that I must understand how Charles looked at things, and for this I must read his writings. I am in safe academic territory here: I will make a complete bibliography, and I will work my way through it in chronological order. I start by reading old volumes of the *Gazette des Beaux-Arts* from the time when Charles comes to live in Paris, noting down his first, rather dry published comments on Mannerist painters, bronzes and Holbein. I feel focused, if dutiful. He has a favourite Venetian painter, Jacopo de Barbari, who was keen on St Sebastian, the combat of Tritons and writhing bound nudes. I'm not sure how significant this taste for eroticised subjects will prove. I remember Laocoön and feel a little anxious.

He starts poorly. There are notes on exhibitions, books, essays, and notes on publications: the expected art-historical detritus on the margins of other people's scholarship ('notes towards an authentication of', 'responses to the catalogue raisonné of'). These texts are a little like his Italian collections and I feel I am making scant headway. But, as the weeks go by, I find myself starting to relax into Charles's company: this first collector of the netsuke begins to write more fluidly. There are unexpected registers of feeling. Three weeks of my precious spring go by, and then another fortnight, a mad expense of days unspooling in the dimness in Periodicals.

Charles learns to spend time with a picture. He has been and looked, you feel, and then gone back and looked again. There are essays on exhibitions where you feel this touch on the shoulder, that turn to look again, move closer, move further away. You feel his growing confidence and his passion, and then at last the beginning of a steeliness in his writings, a dislike of set opinions. Charles holds his feelings in balance with his judgements, but writes so that you are aware of both. This is rare in writing on art, I think, as the weeks fall away from me in the library and my stack of *Gazettes* builds around me, a tower of new questions, each volume a matrix of bookmarks and yellow Post-it notes and reserve slips.

My eyes hurt. The type is eight-point, less for the notes. At least my French is returning. I begin to think that I can work with this man. He is not showing off about how much he knows, most of the time. He wants to make us see more clearly what is in front of him. That seems honourable enough.

## 3. 'A MAHOUT TO GUIDE HER'

It is not yet time for the netsuke to enter the story. Charles in his twenties is always elsewhere, in transit to somewhere, sending regards and his apologies for missing family gatherings, from London, Venice, Munich. He is starting to write a book on Dürer, the artist he fell for in the collections of Vienna, and he needs to find every drawing, every scribble in every archive, in order to do him justice.

His two older brothers are safely ensconced in their own worlds. Jules is at the helm of Ephrussi et Cie in the rue de l'Arcade with his uncles. His early training in Vienna has paid off and he turns out to be very good with money. And he has got married in the synagogue in Vienna to Fanny, the clever, wry young widow of a Viennese financier. She is very rich, and it is all appropriately dynastic. The gossip in the papers in Paris and Vienna is that he danced with her every night until she wearied, gave in and married him.

Ignace has cut loose. He is prone to falling spectacularly, serially, in love. As an *amateur de la femme*, his particular skill is an ability to climb buildings and into high windows for assignations – something I later find recalled in memoirs of elderly society ladies. He is a *mondain*, a Parisian man of the world, living between love-affairs, evenings at the Jockey Club – the epicentre of bachelor society – and duelling. This is illegal, but occupies the time of wealthy young men and army officers, who resort to rapiers over issues of minute transgressions of honour. Ignace turns up in the duelling manuals of the day, one newspaper recording an accident where his eye is almost taken out in a bout with his tutor. Ignace is 'relatively tall but a little under the average height . . . Gifted with energy which is also luckily backed up by steel muscles . . . Mr Ephrussi is one amongst the keenest . . . he is also one of the most friendly and frankest fencers I know.'

Here he is, posed nonchalantly with a rapier, like a Hilliard miniature of an Elizabethan courtier: 'an untiring sportsman, you will find him in the forest early in the morning, riding a superb dapple-grey; he has already taken his fencing lesson . . .' I think of Ignace checking the lengths of the stirrups in the stables in the rue de Monceau. When he rides, his horse is arrayed 'in the Russian manner'. I'm not quite sure what this entails, but it sounds splendid.

It is in the salons that Charles first comes into view. He is noticed by the acidic novelist, diarist and collector Edmond de Goncourt in his journal. That people such as Charles were invited to salons at all disgusted the novelist: the salons had become 'infested with Jews and Jewesses'. He comments on these new young men that he encounters: these Ephrussi were '*mal élevés*', badly brought up, and '*insupportables*', insufferable. Charles, he intimates, is ubiquitous, the trait of someone who does not know his place; he is hungry for contact, does not know when to shade eagerness and become invisible.

De Goncourt is jealous of this charming boy with the slightest of accents to his French. Charles has walked, seemingly without effort, into the formidable, fashionable salons of the day, each of which was a minefield of fiercely contested geographies of political, artistic, religious and aristocratic taste. There were many, but the three principal salons were those of Madame Straus (the widow of Bizet), of the Countess Greffuhle, and of a rarefied painter of water-colours of flowers, Madame Madeleine Lemaire. A salon consisted of a drawing-room full of regularly invited guests, meeting at a set time in the afternoon or evening. Poets, playwrights, painters, 'club-men', *mondains* would meet under the patronage of a hostess to engage in conversation around issues of note, or purposeful gossip, or to listen to music or see a new society portrait unveiled. Each salon had its own distinct atmosphere and its own acolytes: those who offended Mme Lemaire were 'bores' or 'deserters'.

Mme Lemaire's Thursday salon is mentioned in an early essay of the young Marcel Proust. He evokes the scent of lilacs filling her studio and drifting into the rue de Monceau, crowded with the carriages of the beau monde. You could never get through the rue de Monceau on a Thursday. Proust notices Charles. There is a hubbub and he moves closer through the throng of writers and socialites. Charles is there in a corner talking to a portrait painter, their heads bowed and conversing so softly and intensely that, though he hovers nearby, Proust cannot overhear even a scintilla of their conversation.

De Goncourt, splenetic, is particularly furious that young Charles has become a confidant of *his* Princess Mathilde, the niece of Bona-parte. She lives nearby in a vast mansion in the rue de Courcelles. He records gossip that she has been seen at Charles's house in the rue de Monceau along with the '*gratin*', the upper crust, of the aris-tocracy, that the Princess had found in Charles 'a mahout to guide her through her life'. It is an unforgettable image of the formidable, aged Princess in her black, an elephantine presence rather like Queen Victoria, and this young man in his twenties, able to guide her with the merest of suggestions, of touch.

Charles is starting to find a life for himself in this complex and snobbish city. He is beginning to discover the places where his conversation is welcomed, where his Jewishness is either acceptable or where it is overlooked. As a young writer on art, he goes to the offices of the *Gazette des Beaux-Arts* in the rue Favart each day – taking in six or seven salons en route, adds the omniscient de Goncourt. From family house to these editorial offices is exactly twenty-five minutes' brisk walk, or on my April morning forty-five minutes of flaneurial stroll. I suppose Charles might go in a carriage, I worry, but I can't time that.

The *Gazette*, the '*Courrier Européen de l'art et de la curiosité*', has a canary-yellow cover and on its title page an aesthetic display of Renaissance artefacts on top of a classical tomb surmounted by a furious-looking Leonardo. For your seven francs you get reviews of the different exhibitions jockeying for position in Paris, the *Exposition des Artistes Indépendants*, the official Salons hung floor to ceiling with paintings, the surveys at the Trocadéro and the Louvre. It is cuttingly described as 'an expensive art-magazine which every great lady kept open but unread on her table' and it certainly holds a reputation as an essential part of society life, a *World of Interiors* as well as an *Apollo*. In the beautiful oval library of the Camondo mansion down the hill from the Hôtel Ephrussi are shelves and shelves of its bound volumes.

Here at the offices are other writers and artists, and the best art library in Paris, full of periodicals from all over Europe and catalogues of exhibitions. It is an exclusive arts club, a place to share news and gossip about which painter is working on which commission, who is out of favour with the collectors or with the jurists for the Salon. It is also busy. The *Gazette* is published monthly and so it is a real place of work. There are all the decisions to be taken on who will be writing on what, the ordering of engravings and illustrations. You can learn a lot by being here day by day, watching the arguments.

When Charles, just back from his plundering of Italian art dealers, starts to write for the *Gazette*, it includes lavish engravings of the pictures of the day, artefacts mentioned in the scholarly reviews and key pictures from the Salon represented in careful reproduction. I pick out an issue at random from 1878. It includes, amongst other things, articles on Spanish tapestry, Greek archaic sculpture, the architecture of the Champ de Mars, and Gustave Courbet – all, of course, with illustrations interleaved with tissue mounts. It is the perfect journal for a young man to write for, a calling-card into those places where society and art intersect.

I find the traces of these intersections by hacking my way assiduously through the social columns of Parisian newspapers of the 1870s. I start this as a necessary clearing of the undergrowth, but it becomes strangely compelling and a relief from my dogged attempt to chart every single one of Charles's exhibition reviews. There are the same labyrinthine lists of encounters and guests, the minutiae of who wore what, who is to be seen, each run of names a calibration of snubs and fine judgements.

I get particularly hooked by the listings of wedding-presents at society marriages, telling myself that this is all good research on cultures of gift-giving, and waste an embarrassing amount of time trying to work out who is being over-generous, who a cheapskate and who is just dull. My great-great-grandmother gives a set of golden serving dishes shaped as cockle shells at a society wedding in 1874. Vulgar, I think, with nothing to back this up.

And amongst all these Parisian balls and musical soirées, the salons and receptions, I start to find mentions of the three brothers. They stick together: the MM Ephrussi are seen in the box at a premiere at the Opéra, at funerals, at the receptions of Prince X, Countess Y. The Tsar has made a visit to the city and they are there to greet him as prominent Russian citizens. They give parties jointly, are noted for the 'grand series of dinners they are hosting together', have been spotted, along with other *sportsmen*, on the latest thing, the bicycle. One column of *Le Gaulois* is devoted to *déplacements* – who is off to Deauville and who to Chamonix – so I know when they leave Paris for their holidays in Meggen at Jules and Fanny's baronial Chalet Ephrussi. From their golden house on the hill they seem to have become an accepted part of Parisian society within a few years of their arrival. *Monceau*, I remember, quick-going.

The elegant Charles has new interests apart from rearranging his rooms and perfecting his sinuous art-historical sentences. He has a mistress. And he has started to collect Japanese art. These two things, sex and Japan, are intertwined.

He owns no netsuke yet, but he is getting much closer. I am willing him on as he starts his collection, buying lacquer from a dealer in Japanese art called Philippe Sichel. De Goncourt writes in his journal that he has been to Sichel's, 'the place where Jewish money comes'; he goes into a back room in search of the latest *objet*, the newest album of erotic prints, a scroll maybe. Here he comes across 'La Cahen d'Anvers, crouched over a Japanese lacquer box with her lover, the young Ephrussi'.

She is indicating to him 'the time and place that he can make love with her'.

## 4. 'SO LIGHT, SO SOFT TO THE TOUCH'

Charles's lover is Louise Cahen d'Anvers. She is a couple of years older than Charles and very pretty, with red-gold hair. 'La Cahen d'Anvers' is married to a Jewish banker and they have four small children, a boy and three girls. The fifth child arrives and Louise calls him Charles.

I only know about Parisian marriages from the novels of Nancy Mitford, but this strikes me as extraordinarily sanguine. And rather impressive – I want to be bourgeois and ask how you find time for five children, a husband *and* a lover? The two clans are very close. In fact, as I stand in the place d'Iéna outside Jules and Fanny's marital home, his initials floridly entwined with hers above the grander doors, I find that I am looking straight across the road to Louise's equally baroque new palace at the corner of the rue Bassano. At this point I wonder if the clever, indefatigable Fanny arranged this affair for her best friend.

There was certainly something very intimate about the whole arrangement. They met constantly at the round of receptions and balls and the two families often holidayed together at the Chalet Ephrussi in Switzerland or at the Cahen d'Anvers's chateau at Champs-sur-Marne just outside Paris. What was the etiquette of meeting your friend on the way up the stairs to your brother-in-law's apartment? These lovers might have needed the back rooms of dealers just to get away from all this smothering, knowing amiability. And the children.

Charles, this increasingly adept and helpful young man of the salons, arranged for his society friend Léon Bonnat to do a pastel portrait of Louise. She is pictured in a pale dress, looking down demurely, her hair half-hiding her face.

In fact, Louise was far from demure. De Goncourt records her with his novelist's eye, on Saturday 28th February 1876, in her salon:

The Jews retain, from their oriental origin, a peculiar nonchalance. Today, I was charmed as I observed Mme Louise Cahen fishing in the bottom of her vitrine of porcelain and lacquer ware, wanting to hand me some; she moved like a lazy cat. And when they are blond – these Jews – there is, at the heart of their blondness, something golden, like the painting of the MISTRESS OF TITIAN. Her search completed, the Jewess dropped onto a chaise longue, her head flung back to one side and revealing at the head, a coil of hair that resembled a nest of snakes. Pulling various amused, questioning expressions, and, wrinkling her nose, she complained of the unreasonableness of men and of novelists expecting women not to be human creatures and not to have, in love, the same disgust as men.

It is an unforgettable image of eroticised langour: the mistress of Titian is indeed very golden and very naked, one hand loosely covering herself. You sense Louise's power over the famous writer, her control of the situation. She is, after all, '*La muse alpha*' for Paul Bourget, another popular novelist of the day. In the portrait she commissioned of herself for her own salon from Carolus-Duran, *the* society painter of the moment, she is barely contained in her swirling gown, her lips slightly parted. There is a lot of drama in this muse. It makes me wonder why she wanted this aesthetic young man as a lover.

It may have been his lack of histrionics, the deliberative pace of an art historian. Or it may have been due to her having two huge households, a husband and a run of children, whilst Charles was unencumbered, perfectly free to entertain her when she needed distraction. It is certain that the lovers shared a real interest in music, art and poetry – and in musicians, artists and poets. Louise's brother-in-law, Albert, was a composer, and Charles and Louise went with him to the Opéra in Paris, and to the more radical premieres in Brussels to hear Massenet. They were both passionate about Wagner, a kind of passion that is hard to dissemble, but good to share. Wagner's operas, I imagine, also give the couple plenty of time to themselves in one of those deep, plush boxes at the Opéra. They were present at a small and select dinner party (*sans* the husband) followed by a recital of poetry by Anatole France, hosted by Proust.

And they buy Japanese black-and-gold lacquer boxes together for their parallel collections: they start their love-affair with Japan.

It is with Louise, weary after an argument with her husband or with Charles, indolently fishing in her vitrine of Japanese lacquer bibelots, then falling back on to her chaise longue, that I know that I am getting closer to the netsuke. They are coming into focus, part of a complex, fractious Paris life that really existed.

I want to find how these nonchalant Parisians, Charles and his lover, handled Japanese things. What was it like to have something so alien in your hands for the first time, to pick up a box or a cup – or a netsuke – in a material that you had never encountered before and shift it around, finding its weight and balance, running a fingertip along the raised decoration of a stork in flight through clouds? There must be a literature on touch somewhere, I think; someone must have recorded in a diary or a letter the fugitive moment of what they felt when they picked one up. There must be a trace of their hands somewhere.

De Goncourt's aside is a good place to start. Charles and Louise bought their first pieces of Japanese lacquer from the house of the Sichel brothers. It was not a gallery where each collector was reverently shown *objets* and prints in separate booths, as at the up-market gallery of Siegfried Bing, the Oriental Art Boutique, but an over-flowing morass of everything Japanese. The quantities were overwhelming. Philippe Sichel sent forty-five crates with 5,000 objects back from Yokohama after one buying trip in 1874 alone. This created a febrile atmosphere. What was here, and where was it? Would other collectors find the treasure before you?

This mass of Japanese art inspired reverie. De Goncourt recorded a day spent at the Sichels soon after a delivery had arrived from Japan, surrounded by '*tout cet art capiteux et hallucinatoire*' – all this intoxicating, mesmerising art. Since 1859 prints and ceramics had begun to seep into France; by the early 1870s this had become a flood of *things*. A writer looking back on the very earliest days of this infatuation with Japanese art wrote in the *Gazette* in 1878:

One kept oneself informed about new cargoes. Old ivories, enamels, faience and porcelain, bronzes, lacquer, wooden sculptures . . . embroidered satins, playthings, simply arrived at a merchant's shop and immediately left for artists' studios or writers' studies . . . They entered the hands of . . . Carolus Duran, Manet, James Tissot, Fantin-Latour, Degas, Monet, the writers Edmond and Jules de Goncourt, Philippe Burty, Zola . . . the travellers Cernuschi, Duret, Emile Guimet . . . The movement was established, the amateurs followed.

Even more extraordinary was the occasional sight of:

young men in our great faubourgs, on our boulevards, in the theatre, whose appearance surprises us . . . They wear top hats or small rounded felt ones resting on fine and lustrous black hair, long and straight back, the cloth frock coat is correctly buttoned, clear grey trousers, fine shoes and with a cravat of some dark colour floating on the elegant linen. If the jewel that fixes this cravat was not too visible, the trousers not splayed by the instep, the top boots not too glossy, the cane not too light, – these nuances betray the man who submits to the taste of his tailor instead of imposing his taste on them, – we would take them to be Parisians. You cross them on the pavement, you look at them: their skin is lightly bronzed, the beard rare; some of them have adopted the moustache . . . the mouth is large, conformed to open squarely, in the fashion of masks in Greek comedy; the cheek-bones become round and the forehead protuberant on the oval of the face; the external angles of the small bridled eyes, but black and alive, with a piercing gaze, lift towards the temples. They are the Japanese.

It is a breath-catching description of being a stranger in a new culture, almost imperceptible except for your meticulous dress. The passer-by takes a second look, and it is only the completeness of your disguise that gives you away.

It also reveals the strangeness of this encounter with Japan. Though Japanese were extremely rare in Paris in the 1870s – there were delegations and diplomats and the odd prince – their art was ubiquitous. Everyone had to get their hands on these *Japonaiseries*: all the painters Charles was starting to meet in the salons, all the writers Charles knew from the *Gazette*, his family, his family friends, his lover, all were living through this convulsion. Fanny Ephrussi records in her letters shopping trips to Mitsui, a fashionable shop in the rue Martel that sold Far Eastern objects, to buy Japanese wallpaper for the new smoking-room and guest bedrooms in the house that she and Jules had just finished building in the place d'Iéna. How could Charles, the critic, the well-dressed *amateur d'art* and collector, *not* buy Japanese art?

In the Parisian artistic hothouse it mattered when you started your collection. Earlier collectors, *Japonistes,* had the edge as they were men of superior appreciation and creators of taste. De Goncourt, naturally, managed to suggest that he and his brother had actually seen Japanese prints *before* the opening up of Japan. These early adopters of Japanese art, though fiercely competitive with each other, shared their discernment. But, as George Augustus Sala wrote in *Paris Herself Again* in 1878, the collegiate atmosphere of earlier collecting soon disappeared. '*Japonisme* has become to some very artistic amateurs, the Ephrussi, the Camondos, like a sort of religion.'

Charles and Louise were 'neo-*Japonistes*', young and rich artistic latecomers. For with Japanese art there was an exhilarating lack of connoisseurship, none of the enmeshed knowledge of art historians to confound your immediate responses, your intuitions. Here was a new Renaissance unfolding and the chance to have the ancient and serious art of the East in your hands. You could have it in quantity and you could have it now. Or you could buy it now and make love later.

When you held a Japanese *objet*, it revealed itself. Touch tells you what you need to know: it tells you about yourself. Edmond de Goncourt offered his view: 'here, in respect to politeness, gentleness, unctuousness so to speak, of perfect things in one's hands: an aphorism. Touch – it is the mark by which the amateur recognises himself. The man who handles an object with indifferent fingers, with *clumsy* fingers, with fingers that do not envelop lovingly is a man who is not passionate about art.'

For these early collectors and travellers to Japan, it was enough to pick up a Japanese object to know whether it was 'right' or not. Indeed, the American artist John La Farge on his trip in 1884 made a pact with his friends 'that we should bring no books, read no books, but come as innocently as we could'. Having a *feel* for beauty was enough: touch was a kind of sensory innocence.

Japanese art was a brave new world: it introduced new textures, new ways of feeling things. Though there were all those albums of wood block prints to buy, this was not art simply to hang on walls. This was an epiphany of new materials: bronzes of a depth of patina that seemed far greater than those of the Renaissance; lacquers of an unequalled depth and darkness; folding screens of gold leaf to bisect a room, throw light. Monet painted *Mme Monet in a Japanese Dress* (*La Japonaise*); Camille Monet's robe had 'certain gold embroideries several centimetres thick'. And there were objects that were unlike anything seen in Western art, objects that could only be described as 'playthings', small carvings of animals and beggars called 'netsuke' that you could roll in your hands. Charles's friend and editor of the *Gazette*, the collector Louis Gonse, described a particular boxwood netsuke beautifully as '*plus gras, plus simple, plus caresse*' – very rich, very simple, very tactile. It is difficult to beat this cadence of response.

This was all stuff to have in your hands, stuff to add texture to your salon or your boudoir. As I look at the images of Japanese things, I see that the Parisians are layering one material on another:

an ivory is wrapped in a silk, a silk is hanging behind a lacquer table, a lacquer table is spread with porcelain, fans fall across a floor.

Passionate touch, discovery in the hands, things enveloped lovingly, *plus caresse*. *Japonisme* and touch were a seductive combination for Charles and Louise, amongst many others.

Before the netsuke comes a collection of thirty-three black-and-gold lacquer boxes. It was a collection to place with Charles's other collections in his apartment at the Hôtel Ephrussi, something to sit near his burgundy Renaissance hangings and his pale Donatello sculpture in marble. Charles and Louise put this collection together from Sichel's chaotic house of treasures. It was a stellar group of seventeenth-century lacquers, as good as any in Europe: to choose them they must have been regular visitors to Sichel's. And very pleasingly for me as a potter, alongside these lacquers, Charles also had a sixteenth-century stoneware covered jar from Bizen, the Japanese pottery village in which I studied when I was seventeen, excited to finally get my passionate hands on those simple, tactile tea-bowls.

In *Les Lacques Japonais au Trocadero*, a long essay published in the *Gazette* in 1878, Charles describes the five or six vitrines full of lacquer on exhibition at the Trocadéro in Paris. This is his fullest writing about Japanese art. As elsewhere, he is in turn academic (he is exercised about dating), descriptive and ultimately lyrical about what he sees in front of him.

He mentions the term *Japonisme* 'coined by my friend Philippe Burty'. For three whole weeks, before I find an even earlier mention, I think this is the first ever use of the term in print, and am filled with excitement that my netsuke and *Japonisme* are linked so beautifully, a told-you-so moment of visceral happiness in the Publications section of the library.

*Japanese box of golden lacquer from the
collection of Louise Cahen D'Anvers*

Charles gets very, very excited in this essay. He has discovered that Marie Antoinette had a collection of Japanese lacquer, and uses this knowledge to negotiate a lovely correspondence between the civilised world of the eighteenth-century rococo and that of Japan. In his essay, women, intimacy and lacquer seem to be woven together. Japanese lacquer, Charles explains, was rarely seen in Europe: 'One simultaneously needed wealth and the fortune of being a favourite or a queen to reach for the envied possession of these almost unobtainable objects.' But this is a moment – Paris in the Third Republic – when two remote and alienated worlds have collided. These lacquers, of a legendary rarity and so technically complex that they are almost unmakeable, the possessions of Japanese princes or Western queens, are now *here* in a Parisian shop, available to buy. For Charles, this lacquer has a quality of embedded poetry: not just rich and strange, but latent with stories of desire. His passion for Louise is palpable. The unobtainability of this lacquer creates the aura that surrounds it. You feel him reaching towards the golden Louise as he writes.

And then Charles picks a box up: 'Take one of these lacquer boxes in your hand – so light, so soft to the touch, on which the artist has represented apple trees in blossom, sacred cranes flying across the water, and topping a mountain range, undulating under a cloud-filled sky, some people in flowing robes, in poses that seem bizarre to us but always gracious and elegant, under their large parasols . . .'

Holding this box, he talks about its exoticism. Its accomplishment requires a suppleness of the hand that is 'entirely feminine, a persevering dexterity, a sacrifice of time' that we in the West could not achieve. When you see and hold these lacquers – or netsuke or bronzes – you are immediately conscious of this work: they embody all the travail, and yet they are miraculously free.

The images in the lacquer interlace with his growing love of the paintings of the Impressionists: the images of flowering apple trees, cloud-filled skies and women in flowing robes are straight out of Pissarro and Monet. Japanese things – lacquers, netsuke, prints – conjure a picture of a place where sensations are always new, where art pours out of daily life, where everything exists in a dream of end-less beautiful flow.

And embedded in Charles's essay on lacquer are engravings of pieces from Louise's collection and his own. His prose becomes a little much here, a little breathless, as he describes the interior of Louise's cabinet of golden lacquer, over which morning glories trail. Their collections are formed by 'the caprice of an opulent amateur who can satisfy all his covetousness'. In talking of their collections of these strangely rich objects he quietly brings himself and Louise together. They are both covetous and capricious, led by sudden desire. What they collect are objects to discover in your hands, 'so light, so soft to the touch'.

It is a discreetly sensual act of disclosure, showing their pieces together in public. And assembling these lacquers also records their assignations: the collection records their love-affair, their own secret history of touch.

There is a review in *Le Gaulois* of an exhibition in 1884 of Charles's lacquers. 'One could spend days in front of these vitrines,' writes the reviewer. I agree. I cannot trace which museums Charles and Louise's lacquers have disappeared into, but I go back to Paris for a day to the Musée Guimet in the avenue d'Iéna, which now holds Marie Antoinette's collection, and stand in front of their vitrines full of the mazy reflections of these softly gleaming things.

He brings these dense black-and-gold *objets* to his salon in the rue de Monceau, where he has recently laid down a golden Savonnerie carpet. It is finely woven from silk, made originally for a gallery in the Louvre in the seventeenth century. Its imagery is an allegory of Air: the four winds blowing their trumpets with fat cheeks, and everything is interlaced with butterflies and undulating ribbons. The carpet has been cut down in size so that it fits. I imagine walking across this floor. The whole room is golden.

## 5. A BOX OF CHILDREN'S SWEETS

To buy a little of Japan the best thing to do was to visit the place. This was the ultimate bit of one-upmanship of Charles's neighbour Henri Cernuschi, or the industrialist Emile Guimet, the organiser of the Trocadéro exhibition.

If you could not match that, then you had to visit Parisian galleries for Japanese bibelots. These shops were known as places for encounters, popular sites for rendezvous for beau-monde lovers – *rendez-vous des couples adultères*, like Charles and Louise. In the old days, you would find these couples in the Jonque Chinoise, the shop in the rue de Rivoli, or its companion shop the Porte Chinoise in the rue Vivienne, where the galleriste Madame Desoye – who had sold Japanese art to the first wave of collectors – sat 'enthroned in her jewels . . . almost a historic figure in our time like a fat Japanese idol'. Now Sichel's had taken over.

Sichel was a great salesman, but not a curious or observant anthropologist. In a pamphlet published in 1883, *Notes d'un bibeloteur au Japon*, he wrote, 'The country was entirely new to me: if I speak frankly I wasn't interested in day-to-day life at all: all I wanted was to get the lacquers from the bazaar.'

And this is all he did. Soon after his arrival in 1874 in Japan, Sichel discovered a group of lacquer writing-boxes hidden under layers of dust in a Nagasaki bazaar. He 'paid one dollar for each, and today many of these objects are valued at over 1,000 francs'. These were the writing-boxes that he sold – he fails to say – to his Parisian clients like Charles or Louise or Gonse for a great deal more than 1,000 francs.

Sichel continues:

In those days Japan was a treasure trove of art objects to be had at bargain prices. The streets of its cities were lined with shops of curios, textiles and pawn goods. Throngs of tradespeople would gather at one's door at dawn: vendors of *fukusa* [scrolls] or bronze merchants carrying their goods in carts. There were even passers-by who would quite willingly sell the *netsuke* from their *obi* [belts].The barrage of offers was so incessant that one was almost overwhelmed by a weariness and a distaste for buying. Nevertheless, these merchants in exotic objects were amiable tradesmen. They acted as your guide, bargained on your behalf in return for just a box of children's sweets, and concluded business deals by throwing grand banquets in your honour which ended with enticing performances by female dancers and singers.

Japan was that box of sweets. Collecting in Japan encouraged a striking greed. Sichel writes of the urge *'d'évaliser le Japon'* – to plunder or rape the country. The stories of destitute daimyos selling their heirlooms, samurai their swords, dancers their bodies – and passers-by their netsuke – became a story of endless possibility. Anyone would sell you anything. Japan existed as a sort of parallel country of licensed gratification, artistic, commercial and sexual.

Japanese things carried an air of eroticised possibility, not simply the shared encounter of lovers over a lacquer box or ivory bibelots. Japanese fans, bibelots and robes would only come alive in private encounters. They were props for dressing up, role-playing, the sensuous reimagining of the self. Of course they appealed to Charles with his ducal bed, canopied with swags of brocade, and his endless reconfiguring of his rooms in the rue de Monceau.

In James Tissot's *La Japonaise au bain* a girl is naked but for a heavy brocade kimono, loose on her shoulders, standing on the threshold of a Japanese room. In Monet's provocative portrait of his wife Camille, she is shown in a golden wig, clothed in a swirling robe of embroidered red on which a samurai unsheathes his sword. Behind her is a scattering of fans across the wall and the floor, like a burst of Whistler's fireworks. It is very much a performance for the artist, one akin to that in Proust's *Du côté de chez Swann* of the *demi-mondaine* Odette receiving Swann, dressed in her kimono in her drawing-room of Japanese silk cushions and screens and lanterns, filled with its heavy scent of chrysanthemums, an olfactory *Japonisme*.

Ownership seemed transposed. These objects seemed to induce insatiability, to own you, make demands on you. Collectors themselves speak of the intoxication of hunting and buying, a process that could send you towards mania: 'Of all the passions, of all without exception, the passion for the bibelot is perhaps the most terrible and invincible. The man smitten by an antique is a lost man. The bibelot is not only a passion, it is a mania,' claimed the young writer Guy de Maupassant.

A haunting self-description of this comes in a strange book written by Charles's scourge, Edmond de Goncourt. In *La Maison d'un artiste* de Goncourt describes each room of his own house in Paris in painstaking detail – the *boiseries*, the pictures, the books, the objects – in an attempt to evoke each object and picture and their placement as an act of homage to his dead brother, with whom he had lived. In two volumes, each of more than 300 pages, de

Goncourt constructs an autobiography and a travelogue, as much as an exhaustive inventory of a house through objects. Japanese art saturates the house. There are Japanese brocades and *kakemonos*, scrolls, in the hall. Even the garden is a carefully curated assortment of Chinese and Japanese trees and shrubs.

In a moment worthy of Borges, *his* collection even incorporates a grouping of Chinese art put together by a seventeenth-century Japanese '*bibeloteur exotique*'. There is endless play in de Goncourt's display between pictures, screens, scrolls on open display and those objects held in vitrines.

I imagine de Goncourt, dark-eyed, an unruly white silk scarf knotted under his chin, pausing for effect at the door of his pear-wood vitrine. He is holding one of his netsuke, and he starts to tell a story of the obsessive search for perfection that lies behind each object:

a whole class of exceptionally fine artists – usually specialists – are responsible for . . . fabrication and dedicate themselves exclusively to the reproduction of an object or a creature. Thus, we hear of an artist whose family has for three generations sculpted rats in Japan, nothing but rats. Alongside these professional artists, amid this manually gifted populace, there would be amateur netsuke sculptors, who amuse themselves by sculpting a little masterpiece for themselves. One day, Mr Philippe Sichel approached a Japanese man sitting on his threshold, notching a netsuke that was in its last stages of completion. Mr Sichel asked him if he would like to sell it . . . when it was completed. The Japanese man started laughing, and ended up telling him that that would take approximately a further eighteen months; then he showed him another netsuke that was attached to his belt, and informed him that it had taken him several years of work to make it. And as the conversation progressed between the two men, the amateur artist confessed to Mr Sichel that he did 'not work like that in such a long-drawn out manner . . . that he needed to be in the process . . . that it was only on certain days . . . on days when he had smoked a pipe or two, after he felt gay and refreshed', essentially letting him know that for this work, he needed hours of inspiration.

These bibelots of ivory or lacquer or mother-of-pearl all seemed to express the fact that Japanese workers had the imagination of '*bijoux-joujoux lilliputien*', charming Lilliputian trinket-makers. That the Japanese are small, and make small things, was a commonplace in Paris. This idea of the miniature was often held as the reason that Japanese art seemed to lack ambition. They were brilliant at the laborious fashioning of rapid feeling, but fell down when it came to the grander feelings of tragedy or awe. That is why they lacked a Parthenon, a Rembrandt.

What they could do was everyday life. And emotion. It was these emotions that entranced Kipling when he first saw netsuke in Japan on his travels in 1889. He writes in one of his letters from Japan of:

a shop full of the wrecks of old Japan . . . The Professor raves about the cabinets in old gold and ivory studded with jade, lazuli, agate, mother-o'-pearl and cornelian, but to me more desirable than any wonder of five-stoned design are the buttons and netsuke that lie on cotton wool, and can be taken out and played with. Unfortunately the merest scratch of Japanese character is the only clue to the artist's name, so I am unable to say who conceived, and in creamy ivory executed, the old man horribly embarrassed by a cuttle-fish; the priest who made the soldier pick up a deer for him and laughed to think that the brisket would be his and the burden his companion's; or the dry, lean snake coiled in derision on a jawless skull mottled with the memories of corruption; or the Rabelaisian badger who stood on his head and made you blush though he was not half an inch long; or the little fat boy pounding his smaller brother; or the rabbit that had just made a joke; or – but there were scores of these notes, born of every mood of mirth, scorn and experience that sways the heart of man; and by this hand that has held half a dozen of them in its palm I winked at the shade of the dead carver! He had gone to his rest, but he had worked out in ivory three or four impressions that I had been hunting after in cold print.

And the Japanese could do erotica. This was hunted with a particular passion: de Goncourt talked of his 'debauches' buying it at Sichel's. *Shunga* – prints of acrobatic sexual positions or bizarre encounters between courtesans and fantastical creatures – were hunted out by Degas and Manet. Octopuses were especially favoured as their sinuosity offered great inventive possibilities. De Goncourt records that he has just bought 'an album of Japanese obscenities . . . They amuse me, enchant my eyes . . . The violence of the lines, unexpected conjunctions, the arrangement of the accessories, the caprice in their positioning and the clothes, the . . . picturesque quality of the genitals.' Erotic netsuke were also highly popular with Parisian collectors. Stock themes included countless octopuses embracing naked girls, monkeys carrying very large and phallic mushrooms, and burst persimmons.

These erotic *objets* complemented other Western objects for male pleasure: the bronzes, small classical nudes perfect for the hand, that connoisseurs would keep in the study for learned discussion of the quality of the modelling, or of patination. Or the collections of small enamelled snuff-boxes that, when opened, showed priapic fauns or startled nymphs, little stagings of concealment and revelation. These small things to handle and to be moved around – slightly, playfully, discerningly – were kept in vitrines.

The chance to pass round a small and shocking object was too good to miss in the Paris of the 1870s. Vitrines had become essential to the witty and flirtatious intermittencies of salon life.

## 6. A FOX WITH INLAID EYES, IN WOOD

And so Charles buys the netsuke. He buys 264.

A fox with inlaid eyes, in wood
A curled snake on a lotus leaf, in ivory
A boxwood hare and the moon
A standing warrior
A sleeping servant
Children playing with masks, in ivory
Children playing with puppies
Children playing with a samurai helmet
Dozens of ivory rats
Monkeys and tigers and deer and eels and a galloping horse
Priests and actors and samurai and craftsmen and a bathing woman in
  her wooden tub
A bundle of kindling tied with a rope
A medlar
A hornet on a hornet's nest, the nest attached to a broken branch
Three toads on a leaf
A monkey and its young
A couple making love
A reclining stag scratching his ear with a hind leg
A Noh dancer in a heavy embroidered robe holding a mask in front of
  his face

An octopus

A naked woman and an octopus

A naked woman

Three sweet chestnuts

A priest on a horse

A persimmon.

And over 200 more, a huge collection of very small things.

Charles bought them, not piece by piece like his lacquers, but as a complete and spectacular collection from Sichel.

Had they just come in, each one folded in its square of silk, then placed in wood-shavings, then crated from Yokohama on one of those four-month shipments by way of the Cape? Had Sichel recently put them out in a cabinet to tempt his rich collectors, or did Charles unwrap them one by one, finding my favourite tiger turning in surprise on a branch of bamboo, carved in ivory at the end of the eighteenth century in Osaka; or the rats looking up as they are caught on the husk of a dried-out fish?

Did he fall in love with the startlingly pale hare with amber eyes, and buy the rest for company?

Did he order them from Sichel? Were they put together over a year or two from the newly impoverished, by some canny dealer in Kyoto, and sold on? I look carefully. There are a very few that have been made for the Western market, knocked up in a hurry ten years before. The plump boy, simpering with his mask, is definitely one of these. It is crudely done, vulgar. The vast majority are netsuke that were carved before the coming of Commodore Perry, some from a hundred years before. There are figures and animals and erotica and creatures from myth: they cover most of the subjects that you could expect in a comprehensive collection. Some are signed by famous carvers. Someone with knowledge has put this group together.

Did he just happen to be there at Sichel's with Louise, amongst the landslide of silks, the folders of prints, the screens and the porcelain, before the other collectors could spot the trove? Did she turn to him or did he turn to her?

Or was Louise elsewhere? And was it intended as a surprise for her when she next came up to his rooms?

How much did they cost this young man, this capricious, charming collector? His father Leon had just died of heart failure, aged only forty-five, and had been buried next to Betty in the family grave in Montmartre. But Ephrussi et Cie was doing very well indeed. Jules had recently bought the land on the Lake Lucerne for his holiday chalet. His uncles were buying chateaux and running racehorses at Longchamps in the Ephrussi colours of blue-and-yellow polka dots. The netsuke must have been very expensive indeed, but Charles could choose to afford this extravagance as his fortune went on growing year by year with that of his family.

There are things I cannot know. But I do know that Charles bought a black vitrine to put them in, wood polished like lacquer. It was taller than him, just over six foot high. You could see in through the glass door at the front and through the glass at the sides. A mirror at the back let the netsuke slide away into infinities of collecting. And they were all placed on green velvet. There are many different subtle variations of colours in netsuke, all the colours of the ivory, the horn and the boxwood: cream, wax, nut-brown, gold in this field of dense dark green.

They are in front of me now, Charles's collection within a collection.

Charles places the netsuke on the green velvet in their dark vitrine with the mirrored back, in this, their first resting-place in the story. They are near the lacquer boxes, near the great hangings he brought back from Italy, close to the golden carpet.

I wonder if he could resist going out onto the landing and turning left to tell his brother Ignace about his new acquisition.

Netsuke cannot knock around your salon or your study unprotected. They get lost or dropped, dusty, chipped. They need a place to rest, preferably in company with other bibelots. This is why vitrines come to matter. And in this journey towards the netsuke, I became more and more intrigued by vitrines, glass display cases.

I kept coming across them in Louise's salon. I had seen them preserved in Belle Epoque mansions, read about them in Charles's exhibition reviews in the *Gazette* and in descriptions in Rothschild inventories. And now that Charles has one of his own, I realise they are part of the performance of salon life, not just part of the furnishings. A collector friend of Charles is described in the act of placing Japanese objects in a vitrine, 'like a painter applying a stroke to his canvas. The harmony is complete and the refinement exquisite . . .'

The vitrines exist so that you can see objects, but not touch them: they frame things, suspend them, tantalise through distance.

This is what I realise now I failed to understand about vitrines. I spent the first twenty years of my life as a potter earnestly trying to get objects out of the glass cases in which my pots were often placed in galleries and museums. They die, I'd say, behind glass, held in that airlock. Vitrines were a sort of coffin: things need to be out and to take their chances away from the protection of formal display, to be liberated. 'Out of the drawing-room and into the kitchen!' I wrote in a sort of manifesto. There was too much in the way. There was *trop de verre*, too much glass, as a great architect commented on seeing a rival Modernist's house of glass.

But the vitrine – as opposed to the museum's case – is for opening. And that opening glass door and the moment of looking, then choosing, and then reaching in and then picking up is a moment of seduction, an encounter between a hand and an object that is electric.

Charles's friend Cernuschi had a great collection of Japanese art just down the road next to the gates to the parc Monceau, displayed on radical white walls. It made the Japanese objects 'look unhappy', as if they were in the Louvre, a critic remarked. Displaying Japanese art as Art made it problematic, over-serious. But Charles's salon up the hill, a place for a strange encounter between old Italian things and new Japanese things, is not a museum.

Charles's vitrine is a threshold.

And these netsuke are perfect for the life of Charles's salon. The golden Louise opening up her vitrine of Japanese things, fishing, handing things out to be looked at and handled, to be caressed, shows that Japanese things are made for digressive conversation, made for distraction. These netsuke add something very particular to Charles's way of living, I think. They are the first things that have any connection to everyday life, even an exotic everyday life. They are wonderful and highly sensual, of course, but they are not princely like his Medici bed or his Marie Antoinette lacquers. They are for touching.

Above all, they make you laugh in many different ways. They are witty and ribald and slyly comic. And now that I have finally got the netsuke up the winding stairs and settled in Charles's salon in the honey-coloured hotel, I find I am relieved that this man whom everyone liked so much had enough of a sense of humour to enjoy them. I don't have just to admire him. I can like him too.

## 7. THE YELLOW ARMCHAIR

The netsuke – my tiger, my hare, my persimmon – have settled in Charles's study where he was finally finishing his book on Dürer. It is a room lit up in a breathless letter to Charles from the young poet Jules Laforgue:

Every line of your beautiful book recalled so many memories. Especially the hours spent working alone in your room where the note of a yellow arm-chair bursts out! And the Impressionists! Two fans by Pissarro, solidly constructed of painstaking small strokes. The Sisleys, the Seine and the tele-graph wires and the sky in springtime. The barge near Paris, with that loafer in the lanes. And Monet's flowering apple trees scaling a hill. And Renoir's dishevelled little savage and Berthe Morisot's deep and fresh undergrowth, a seated woman, her child, a black dog, a butterfly net. And another Morisot, a maid with her charge – blue, green, pink, white, dappled with the sun. And the other Renoirs, the Parisienne with red lips in a blue jersey. And that carefree woman with a muff and the lacquer rose in her button-hole . . . And the bare-shouldered dancer by Mary Cassatt in yellow, green, blond, rust on the red fauteuil. And the nervous dancers by Degas, Duranty by Degas – and of course Manet's *Polichinelle* with Banville's poem! . . . Ah! The tender hours spent there, losing myself in the catalogue of *Albert Dürer*, dreaming . . . in your bright room where bursts the note of the yellow arm-chair, yellow, so yellow!

*Albert Dürer et ses dessins* was Charles's first proper book, a book that had taken him 'vagabonding' across Europe. Laforgue, twenty-one years old and new to Paris, had been recommended as a secretary to sift the lists, emendations, notes of ten years of study into appendices, tables and indices for publication. For Laforgue, Charles in his Chinese dressing-gown was an intoxicating patron in an intoxicating setting.

I'm pretty excited too, because I had no idea that Laforgue had worked for him, before coming across a footnote in a book on Manet. Laforgue is a wonderful poet of cities, park benches dripping wet, telegraph wires on roads that no one passes.

Charles is no longer the rushing young man. He has become the 'benedictine-dandy of the rue Monceau', a black-coated scholar, but flaneurial, whose top hat is tilted at an angle; someone who carries his cane under his arm with a sense of correctness and *amour propre*. Someone who has a valet to make sure that his hat is brushed. Someone, I am sure, who never carried things in his jacket pockets and spoilt the fall of the cloth. We see him here at thirty, with his mistress and his new role as the recently appointed editor of the *Gazette*, and find that he has grown into himself. He is a *mondain* art historian with a secretary. And a collector now not only of netsuke, but of pictures.

And he is so alive in this room. These colours – the black of his coat, and the black of his top hat, and the slightly reddish tinge to his beard – against the stream of fantastic paintings, set alight by this fierce clarity of the note of the yellow armchair. A study, you think, of a man who not only needs colour, but constructs his life around it. A man who wears the perfect uniform of rabbinical black in the rue de Monceau, and who has this other life behind this study door.

What kind of study could possibly go on in a room like this?

Jules Laforgue started work for Charles on 14th July 1881. He worked all summer in this study, staying up half the night. He was, I note with some severity, very badly paid by this Jewish Maecenas. It is through his eyes that we see Charles completing his book: 'stone by stone you slowly and solidly build the pyramid which supports your beautifully bearded monument'. In a throwaway bit of marginalia Laforgue scribbles a picture of the two of them together. Laforgue, tiny with bouffant hair, walks in front, arms and legs akimbo blowing clouds of smoke, while the debonair, upright, tall, monumental, Assyrian-profiled Charles walks behind him. He has filled out splendidly.

Laforgue adores him, teases him. He is anxious to prove himself in this his first job. 'And now, oh dandy-scholar of the Rue Monceau, what are you up to? I always see the summaries of the *Gazette* and *Art*. What are you plotting between Monet's *Grenouillère*, Manet's

*The 'Benedictine-dandy of the rue de Monceau':*
*a self-portrait with Charles, by Jules Laforgue, 1881*

*Constantin Guys*, and the . . . strange archaeologies of Moreau – tell me.'

Laforgue wishes to be remembered to 'our' room, signs off with 'good wishes to the Monet – you know which'. His summer with Charles was an encounter with Impressionism, an encounter that would challenge him to find a new kind of poetic language. He tries out a kind of prose-poem, calls it 'Guitare', and dedicates it to Charles. But surely these descriptions of Charles's study are prose-poems themselves: there are the mixtures of the exact markings of colour – '*la tache colorée*' – the yellow armchair, the red lips and blue jersey of Renoir's girl. The letters, pell-mell with sensation, high on ideas, are close to Laforgue's description of Impressionist style as one in which spectator and spectacle are knitted together: '*irrémédiablement mouvants, insaisissables et insaissants*'.

Charles was very attached to Laforgue. After the long summer in Paris he arranged for the young poet to get a job in Berlin as reader of French to the Empress – Charles had a casually impressive social reach – and wrote to him, sent him money, advised him, critiqued his reviews and then helped Laforgue to get published. Charles kept more than thirty letters from Laforgue from this time, publishing them in the journal *La Revue blanche* after the poet's early death from tuberculosis.

In these letters you *feel* the room. I wanted to be here with the netsuke, and have worried that I would never get beyond a connoisseurial inventory of the grand furnishings of Charles's apartment. I've worried how I could construct a life entirely through objects. The room overflows, like Laforgue's writings, with unexpected conjunctions and disjunctions. I can hear their digressive night-time conversations and am here at last.

Everything in this salon is heightened emotion. It is difficult not to feel alive in a place saturated with images of freedom and lassitude, days out in the countryside, young women, a gypsy girl, bathers in the Seine, a loafer in a lane with nowhere to go, a gorgeous faun framed amongst the broderies and all those curious, funny, tactile netsuke.

## 8. MONSIEUR ELSTIR'S ASPARAGUS

I am in the library again, hesitating. Dürer's self-portrait – Christ-like, long-haired and bearded – stares back at me as I open Charles's *Albert Dürer et ses dessins*. There is a challenge in this stare. I have spent ages thinking about how this careful, delicate skein of thinking, and all these properly edited tables and lists, could have been written in a study with Monet's breezy summer day *there* on the wall.

When I read of Charles's animation as he describes his search for Dürer's lost drawings, I can hear the catch of his voice: 'We traced the drawings of our master wherever we suspected they might be hidden: museums of capital cities and secondary towns abroad, of Paris and the provinces, famous collections and little-known private ones, the *cabinets* of amateurs and of forbidding people, we rummaged and raked up, we examined everything.' Charles might be a flâneur, might take his time in the salons, be seen at the races and the Opéra, but his 'vagabonding' is done with real intensity.

Vagabonding was his phrase. It sounds recreational rather than diligent or professional. As an extremely rich Jewish *mondain*, it would have been contrary to social practice to be seen to work. He was an '*amateur de l'art*', an art lover, and his phrase is carefully self-deprecating. But it does get the pleasure of the searching right, the way you lose your sense of time when you are researching, are pulled on by whims as much as by intent. It makes me think of the rummaging that I am doing through *his* life as I track the netsuke, the noting of other people's annotations in the margins. I vagabond in libraries, trace where he went and why. I follow the leads of whom he knew, whom he wrote about, whose pictures he bought. In Paris I go and stand outside his old offices in the rue Favart in the summer rain like some sad art-historical gumshoe and wait to see who comes out.

I find that as the months pass I have a strangely increased sensitivity to the quality of paper.

And I find that I have fallen for Charles. He is a passionate scholar. He is well dressed *and* good at art history *and* dogged in research. What a great and unlikely trinity of attributes to have, I think, aspirationally.

Charles had a very particular reason to do his research work. He believed that 'all of Dürer's drawings, even the lightest of sketches, merited a special mention, that nothing that was attributed to the hand of our master should be omitted . . .' Charles knows that it is intimacy that matters. Picking up a drawing enables us to 'catch the thought of the artist in all its freshness, at the very moment of manifestation, with perhaps even more truth and sincerity than in the works that require arduous hours of labour, with the defiant patience of the genius'.

This is a wonderful manifesto for drawing. It celebrates the moment of apprehension and the fugitive moment of response a few traces of ink or a few strokes of the pencil. It is also a beautifully coded claim for a conversation between a particular kind of the old and the very new in art. Charles intended this book to 'make better known in France the greatest German artist', the first artist he fell in love with during his childhood in Vienna. But it also gave Charles an emotional as well as an intellectual platform from which to argue that different ages informed each other, that a sketch by Dürer could talk to a sketch by Degas. He knew that it could work.

Charles was becoming an advocate in print for the living artists he was getting to know. He was a critic both in his own name and under pseudonyms, arguing the merits of particular paintings, fighting for the cause of Degas's *Little Dancer*, 'standing in her working clothes, tired and worn out . . .' Now, as editor of the *Gazette*, he started to commission reviews of the exhibitions of painters he admired. And, passionate and partisan, he had also started buying pictures for the room with the yellow armchair.

Charles's first pictures were by Berthe Morisot. He loved her work: 'She grinds flower petals onto her palette, in order to spread them later on her canvas with airy, witty touches, thrown down a little haphazardly. These harmonise, blend, and finish by producing something vital, fine and charming that you do not so much see as intuit . . . one step further and it will be impossible to distinguish or understand anything at all!'

In three years he put together a collection of forty Impressionist works – and bought twenty more for his Bernstein cousins in Berlin. He bought paintings and pastels by Morisot, Cassatt, Degas, Manet, Monet, Sisley, Pissarro and Renoir: Charles created one of the great early collections of the Impressionists. All the walls of his rooms must have been filled with these pictures, they must have been hung above each other three deep. Forget the Degas pastel glowing solitary on a gallery wall at the Metropolitan, five feet from another picture on either side, nothing above or below. In this room this pastel (*Two Women at the Haberdashers*, 1880) must have shaded the Donatello, knocked against a score of other glowing pictures, rubbed up against the vitrine of netsuke.

Charles was in the vanguard. He needed audacity. The Impressionists had their passionate supporters, but were still assailed in the press and by the Academy as charlatans. His advocacy was significant; he had the gravitas of a prominent critic and editor. He also had straightforward utility as a patron for painters who were struggling: it was 'in the mansion of an American or of a young Israelite banker' that you would find these paintings, wrote Philippe Burty. And Charles acted as a mahout to other wealthy friends, persuading Madame Straus, giver of the fiercely aesthetic salon, to purchase one of Monet's *Nympheas*.

But he was much more than this. He was a real interlocutor, a visitor to their studios to see work in progress, to buy a picture from the easel, 'an older brother to young artists', as one critic wrote. He and Renoir talked at length about which paintings might be best to send to the Salon, Whistler asked him to check one of his pictures for damage. 'It was due to him,' wrote Proust in a later character sketch of Charles as '*un amateur de peinture*', 'that many paintings, which had been left at a half-way stage, were actually completed.'

And he was a friend of the artists. 'It is now Thursday,' writes Manet to Charles, 'and I still haven't heard from you. You are evidently enthralled by your host's wit . . . Come on, take up your very best pen and get on with it.'

Charles bought a picture of some asparagus from Manet, one of his extraordinary small still lifes, where a lemon or rose is lambent in the dark. It was a bundle of twenty stalks bound in straw. Manet wanted 800 francs for it, a substantial sum, and Charles, thrilled, sent 1,000. A week later Charles received a small canvas signed with a simple M in return. It was a single asparagus stalk laid across a table with an accompanying note: 'This seems to have slipped from the bundle.'

Proust, who knew Charles's paintings well from visits to his apartment, retells the story to his credit. In his novels there is an

*Edouard Manet,* Une botte d'asperges, *1880*

Impressionist painter, Elstir, modelled partly on Whistler and partly on Renoir. The Duke de Guermantes fumes that 'There was nothing else in the picture. A bundle of asparagus exactly like what you're eating now. But I must say I declined to swallow Monsieur Elstir's asparagus. He asked three hundred francs for a bundle of asparagus. A Louis, that's as much as they're worth, even if they are out of season. I thought it a bit stiff.'

Many of the pictures on the walls of Charles's working study were of his friends. There was a pastel by Degas of Edmond Duranty, captured in a description by the young writer J. K. Huysmans: 'Here is Monsieur Duranty, among his prints and his books, sitting at a desk. And his neighbouring tapering fingers, his sharp mocking eyes, his acute searching expression, his wry smile of an English humorist . . .'

There was a canvas by Constantin Guys, the 'painter of modern life', as well as a portrait of him by Manet, looking very unkempt and bushy and slightly wild-eyed. From Degas, Charles bought the double portrait of General Mellinet and the Chief Rabbi Astruc, in which the heads of these two redoubtable men – friends from their shared experiences of the war of 1870 – are seen in half-profile together.

Then there were Charles's pictures of his Paris life: a scene by Degas of the start of the races at Longchamp, where he would go to see his uncle Maurice Ephrussi's famous racehorses. 'Courses – Ephrussi – 1000 [francs],' writes Degas in his notebook. And images of the demi-monde, of dancers and a scene at the milliner's with the backs of the heads of two young women on a sofa (2,000 francs), and one of a solitary woman in a café nursing a glass of absinthe.

Most of Charles's pictures were of the country, of the fast-moving clouds and wind in the trees that spoke to his feeling for the disappearing moment. There were five landscapes by Sisley and three by Pissarro. From Monet he purchased, for 400 francs, a view of Vétheuil with scudding white clouds across a field with willows, and a picture of apple trees, *Pommiers,* painted in the same village. He also bought a scene of a wintry early morning on the Seine, *Les Glaçons,* with the break-up of the ice, a painting beautifully described by Proust in his early novel *Jean Santeuil* as 'a day of thaw . . . the sun, the blue of the sky, the broken ice, the mud, and the moving water turning the river to a dazzling mirror'.

Even the portrait of the 'dishevelled little savage' to whom Laforgue asked to be remembered captures this feeling of impermanence, of imminent change. *La Bohémienne,* the red-headed gypsy girl with her unkempt hair, is in country clothes standing amongst grasses and trees in fierce sunlight. She is clearly part of her landscape, about to run off and keep running.

These were all paintings, Charles wrote, that could 'present the living being, in gesture and attitude, moving in the fugitive, ever-changing atmosphere and light; to seize in passing the perpetual mobility of the colour of the air, deliberately ignoring individual shades in order to achieve a luminous unity whose separate elements melt together into an indivisible whole and to arrive at a general harmony even by way of discords'.

He also bought a spectacular painting by Monet of bathers, *Les Bains de la Grenouillère*.

Back in London, on my way to the library, I go into the National Gallery to see this picture and reimagine it near the yellow *fauteuil* and the netsuke. It shows a popular place on the Seine in midsummer. Figures in bathing costumes walk along a narrow wooden gangway out into the sun-dappled water, while the non-bathers in their dresses walk towards the shore, a single patch of vermilion on the hem of a dress. Rowing boats – Laforgue's 'gloriously imagined boats' – jumble up into the foreground, a canopy of trees hangs over the scene. The water ripples away, becoming enmeshed with the bobbing heads of the bathers, the 'perpetual mobility of the colour of the air'. It is only just warm enough to go in the water, you think, almost too cold to come out. You feel alive looking at it.

This conjunction of Japanese objects and the shimmering new style of painting seems right: though *Japonisme* might be a 'sort of religion' to the Ephrussi, it was in Charles's circle of artist friends that this new art had the most profound effect. Manet, Renoir and Degas were, like him, avid collectors of Japanese prints. The structure of Japanese pictures seemed to rehearse the meaning of the world differently. Inconsequential gobbets of reality – a pedlar scratching his head, a woman with a crying child, a dog wandering off to the left – each had as much significance as a great mountain on the horizon. As in the netsuke, everyday life went on without rehearsal. This almost violent conjunction of story-telling with graphic, calligraphic clarity was catalytic.

The Impressionists learnt how to cut life up into glances and inter-jections. Rather than formal views, you have a trapeze-wire dissecting a picture, the backs of the heads at the milliner's, the pillars of the Bourse. Edmond Duranty, whose portrait in pastels by Degas hung in Charles's study, saw this happening. 'The person . . . is never in the centre of the canvas, in the centre of the setting. He is not always seen as a whole: sometimes he appears cut-off at mid-leg, half-length, or longitudinally.' When you see the strange portrait by Degas of *Viscount Lepic and His Daughters: Place de la Concorde*, now in the Hermitage in St Petersburg – three figures and a dog moving across a strange emptiness stretching through the canvas – the influence of the flat perspective of Japanese prints seems palpable.

Like the repeated themes in the netsuke, Japanese prints also give the possibility of the series – forty-seven views of a famous mountain suggested a way of returning in differing ways and reinterpreting formal pictorial elements. Haystacks, the bend of the river, poplars, the cliff face of Rouen Cathedral – all share this poetic return. Whistler, the master of 'variations' and 'caprices', explained that 'On any given canvas the colours must, so to speak, be embroi-dered on; that is, the same colour must reappear at intervals, like a single thread in an embroidery.' Zola, an early advocate, wrote of Manet's paintings that 'This art of simplification is to be likened to that of Japanese prints; they resemble it in their strange elegance and magnificent patches of colour.' Simplification seemed to lie at the heart of this new aesthetic, but only if it was combined with 'patchiness', with an abstraction of colour or with its repetition.

Sometimes all it took was to paint Parisian life in the rain. A flotilla of patchy grey umbrellas taking the place of parasols turns Paris into a kind of Edo.

When Charles writes – beautifully and with precision – about his friends, he understands how radical they are, both in technique and subject matter. It reminds one of the best critiques of Impressionism. Their aim was:

to make the figures indivisible from their background, as though they were the product of it, so that to appreciate the picture the eye must take it in as a whole, looking at it from the correct distance – such are the ideals of the new school. It has not learnt its optical catechism, it disdains pictorial rules and regulations, it renders what it sees as it sees it, spontaneously, well or badly, uncompromisingly, without comment, without verbiage. In its horror of platitude it seeks for fresh themes, it haunts the corridors of theatres, cafés, cabarets, even low music-halls; the glare of cheap dance-halls does not alarm its members; and they go boating on the Seine in the Paris suburbs.

This was to be the setting of Renoir's bravura *Le Déjeuner des canotiers*, the *Luncheon of the Boating Party*. It shows a pleasingly louche afternoon at the Maison Fournaise, a restaurant by the Seine at one of the newly popular places that Parisian day-trippers could reach by train. Pleasure boats and a skiff can be seen through the silvery-grey willows. A red-and-white striped awning protects the party from the glare of the sun. It is after lunch in Renoir's new world of painters, patrons and actresses, and everyone is a friend. Models smoke, drink and talk amongst the detritus of the empty bottles and the meal left on the tables. There are no rules or regulations here.

The actress Ellen Andrée, in a hat with a flower pinned to it, raises her glass to her lips. Baron Raoul Barbier, a former mayor of colonial Saigon, his brown bowler hat pushed back, talks to the young daughter of the proprietor. Her brother, straw-hatted like a professional oarsman, stands in the foreground surveying the lunch. Caillebotte, relaxed and fit in a white singlet and boater, sits astride his chair looking at the young seamstress Aline Charigot, Renoir's lover and future wife. The artist Paul Lhote sits with a proprietorial arm around the actress Jeanne Samary. It is a matrix of smiling conversation and flirtation.

And Charles is there. He is the man at the very back, in the top hat and black suit, turning slightly away, seen glancingly. You can just see his red-brown beard. He is talking with a pleasantly open-faced, poorly shaved Laforgue, dressed as a proper poet in a working man's cap and what could even be a corduroy jacket.

I doubt that Charles really wore his benedictine clothes, heavy and dark, to a boating party in the summer sunshine, a top hat instead of a boater. This is an in-joke about his Mécène uniform between friends, Renoir suggesting that patrons and critics are needed, somewhere in the background, on the edge, even on the sunniest and most liberated of days.

Proust writes of this picture, noting a 'gentleman . . . wearing a top hat at a boating party where he was clearly out of place, which proved that for Elstir he was not only a regular sitter, but a friend, perhaps a patron'.

Charles is clearly out of place, but he is a sitter, friend and patron and he is there. Charles Ephrussi – or at least the back of Charles's head – enters art history.

It is July and I'm in my studio in south London. It is down a track between a betting shop and a Caribbean takeaway, sandwiched in amongst car repairers. It's a noisy area, but it is a beautiful space, with my wheels and kilns in a long and airy workshop and a room up some steep white stairs for my books. It is here that I display some of my finished work, groups of porcelain cylinders placed in lead-lined boxes at this moment; and it is here that I stack my piles of notes on early Impressionism and continue to write about the first collector of my netsuke.

It is a calm space, books and pots being good companions. And this is where I bring clients who want to commission something from me. It is very strange for me to be reading so much about Charles as a patron and his friendship with Renoir and Degas. It is not just the vertiginous descent from doing the commissioning to being commissioned. Or, indeed, from having paintings to writing about them. It is that I have been working long enough as a potter to know that being commissioned is an extremely delicate business. You are grateful, of course, but gratitude is different from feeling indebted. It is an interesting question for any artist: how long must you go on feeling grateful once someone has bought your work? It must have been especially complex given the youth of this patron – thirty-one in 1881 – and the age of some of the artists: Manet was forty-eight when he painted that bundle of asparagus. And, I think when I look at an image of a Pissarro that Charles owned, of poplar trees in a breeze, it must be especially delicate if your artistic credo is of freedom of expression, and spontaneity and lack of compromise.

Renoir was in need of money, and so Charles persuaded an aunt to sit for him; then he began work on Louise. It took a long summer of delicate negotiation between the lovers and the painter; Fanny, writing from the Chalet Ephrussi where Charles was staying, details the lengths to which he went to make sure it all came off successfully. It was quite a labour to bring about these two paintings. The first is of Louise's elder daughter Irene, with reddish-golden hair, like her mother's, falling around her shoulders. The second, impossibly saccharine portrait is of the younger girls, Alice and Elisabeth. The two girls also have their mother's hair. They stand in front of a dark burgundy curtain, held open to reveal the salon beyond, holding hands, as if for reassurance – a confection of pink-and-blue ruffles and ribbons. Both pictures were exhibited at the Salon of 1881. I'm not sure how much Louise liked them. After all this work she was shockingly late in paying the modest charge of 1,500 francs. I find myself similarly embarrassed when I discover a cross note from Degas reminding Charles about a bill.

All this commissioned work for Renoir made some of Charles's other painter friends mistrustful. Degas was especially severe: 'Monsieur Renoir, you have no integrity. It is unacceptable that you paint to order. I gather that you now work for financiers, that you do the rounds with Monsieur Charles Ephrussi, next you'll be exhibiting at the Mirlitons with Monsieur Bouguereau!' This anxiety was compounded when Charles started buying pictures by other artists; this patron seemed to be moving on, looking for new sensations. And it was at this point that Charles's Jewishness made him suspect.

Charles had bought two paintings by Gustave Moreau. De Goncourt described his work as the 'watercolours of a poet goldsmith, which seem to have been washed with the gleams and patina of the treasures in the *Thousand and One Nights*'. They were rich, highly symbolic, Parnassian paintings of Salome, Hercules, Sappho, Prometheus. Moreau's subjects are barely clothed, except for a fall of gauze. The landscapes are classical, full of ruined temples, the details exactingly coded. It was all a very, very long way from a meadow in the wind, the currents of a river amongst ice, or a seamstress bent over her work.

Huysmans would write his scandalous novel *À rebours* (*Against the Grain*) about what it felt like to live with a Moreau painting. Or, to be more exact, in the atmosphere created by a Moreau painting. His hero, Des Esseintes, was based closely on the decadent Comte Robert de Montesquiou, a man dedicated to achieving a totally aestheticised existence, finessing the details of his house so that every sensory experience would immerse him totally. The apogee was a tortoise whose shell was encrusted with gemstones so that its slow passage across a room would enliven the pattern of a Persian carpet. This impressed Oscar Wilde, who noted in French in his Paris journal that 'a friend of Ephrussi has an emerald-encrusted tortoise. I also need emeralds, living bibelots . . .' This was substantially better than opening the door of a vitrine.

In Des Esseintes's attenuated existence there was one artist 'who most ravished him with unceasing transports of pleasure – Gustave Moreau. He had purchased his two masterpieces, and night after night he would stand dreaming in front of one of these, a picture of Salome': he is so involved in these intensely charged paintings that he becomes one with them.

And this is close to how Charles felt about his two great pictures. He wrote to Moreau that his work had 'the tonalities of an ideal dream' – an ideal dream being one where you are held in a state of weightless reverie and lose the boundaries of your self.

And Renoir was absolutely furious. 'Ah that Gustave Moreau, to think he is taken seriously, a painter who has never even learnt how to paint a foot . . . he knew a thing or two. It was clever of him to take in the Jews, to have thought of painting with gold colours . . . Even Ephrussi fell for it, who I really thought had some sense! I go and call on him one day, and I come face to face with a Gustave Moreau!'

I imagine Renoir entering the marble hall and coming up those winding stairs past Ignace's apartment to Charles's rooms on the second floor, and being let in and finding Moreau's *Jason* in front of him: standing naked on the slaughtered dragon, holding up his broken spear and the golden fleece. Medea carries the small flask that contains the magic potion and rests her hand adoringly on his shoulder – 'a dream, a flash of enchantment', Laforgue's 'strange archaeologies of Moreau'.

Or perhaps he came face to face with *Galatée*, dedicated '*à mon ami Charles Ephrussi*', a picture described by Huysmans as 'a cavern illuminated by precious stones like a tabernacle, and containing that inimitable and radiant jewel, the white body, its breast and lips tinted with pink, Galatée, asleep . . .' There is certainly a lot of gold here alongside the yellow armchair: Galatée is immured in a faux-Renaissance frame worthy of a Titian.

It is 'Jew Art', Renoir writes, galled to find his patron, the editor of the *Gazette,* with this *gout Rothschild* stuff on the walls, jewelled and mythic, contaminatingly close to his own paintings. Charles's salon in the rue de Monceau has become 'a cavern . . . like a taber-nacle'. It has become a room that could anger Renoir, inspire Huysmans and even impress the sanguine Oscar Wilde: '*Pour écrire il me faut de satin jaune,*' he writes in his Paris journal – 'To write I need yellow satin.'

I realise that I am trying to police Charles's taste. I am worried by gold and by Moreau. And even more so by the work of Paul Baudry, the decorator of the ceilings of the Paris Opéra, adept at working in the baroque cartouches of the new Belle Epoque build-ings of Paris. Baudry's work was reviled by the Impressionists as meretricious pap – an academic painter like the hated William-Adolphe Bouguereau. He was particularly successful with his nudes. He still is. There is a hugely popular poster of a Baudry with a wave about to break over a stretched-out girl, called *Pearl and the Sea*, that you can find in the racks of museum shops and on fridge magnets. And Baudry was Charles's closest painter friend, their letters laced with endearments. Charles was his biographer and was named as his executor.

Perhaps I should continue to hunt down every picture that was in Charles's room with the netsuke. I start to list all the museums in which his pictures now hang and to trace how they got there. I con-sider how long it would take to go from the Art Institute of Chicago to the Musée de la Ville de Gerardmer to put Manet's *Races at Longchamp* alongside Degas's double portrait of the General and the Rabbi. I wonder if I should take my white netsuke of the hare with amber eyes in my pocket to reunite object and image. For the span of a cup of coffee I mull this over as a real possibility, a way of keep-ing moving.

My timetable has disappeared. My other life as a potter is on hold. A museum needs a response. I am away, my assistants say when people ring, and cannot be reached. Yes, a big project. He will return your call.

Instead I make the familiar trip to Paris and stand beneath Baudry's ceilings in the Opéra and then rush over to the Musée d'Orsay to look at Charles's single asparagus stem by Manet and the pair of Moreau pictures they now own, to see if it all coheres, if it all sings, if I can see what his eye saw. And, of course, I cannot, for the simple reason that Charles buys what he likes. He is not buying art for the sake of coherence, or to fill gaps in his collection. He is buying pictures from his friends, with all the complexities that brings with it.

Charles has many friendships beyond the studios of painters. Saturday evenings would be spent at the Louvre with colleagues, each collector or writer bringing a sketch or an object, or a problem of attribution for discussion: 'anything could be brought to the table, save for pedantry! What we would learn there, and never need to doubt! What tireless voyages we made in those beautiful chairs in the Louvre, across all the museums of Europe!' remembered the art historian Clément de Ris. Charles had stimulating colleagues working at the *Gazette*. He had friends for neighbours, the Camondo brothers and Cernuschi, men to whom you could happily show an acquisition.

Charles was becoming a public figure. In 1885 he had become the proprietor of the *Gazette*. He helped raise money for the purchase of a Botticelli for the Louvre. He had his writing. There was his curatorial work: he helped to organise exhibitions of Old Master drawings in 1879, and two of portraits in 1882 and 1885. It was one thing to be a covetous, vagabonding young man and quite another to have these responsibilities and this scrutiny. He had just received the *Légion d'honneur* for his contribution to the arts.

Most parts of this busy life were lived in the public view of colleagues, neighbours, friends, his young secretaries, his lover and his family.

Proust, a neophyte if not yet quite a friend, had become a regular visitor to the apartment, drinking in Charles's empyrean conversation, the way he arranged his new treasures, his span across society. Charles knows the socially ravenous Proust well enough to tell him that it is time to leave a dinner after midnight, as the hosts are desperate for bed. For some long-buried slight, Ignace in the apartment next door pins him down as the 'Proustaillon' – a rather adept description of Proust's butterfly flitting from one social occasion to another.

Proust has also become a presence in the offices of the *Gazette* in the rue Favart. He is diligent here: sixty-four works of art that will appear later in the twelve novels that make up *À la recherche du temps perdu* were illustrated in the *Gazette*, a huge proportion of the works' visual texture. Like Laforgue before him, he has sent Charles his early writings on art and has received a tough critique and then a first commission. For Proust it is to be a study of Ruskin. The preface to Proust's translation of Ruskin's *Bible of Amiens* has as its dedicatee 'M. Charles Ephrussi, always so good to me'.

Charles and Louise are still lovers, though I am not sure if Louise has another lover, or several other lovers. Charles, who has a quality of discretion, leaves no traces here, and I feel frustrated that I cannot find more. I note that Laforgue was the first of a number of much younger men who would work for him more as acolytes than as secretaries, and I wonder at this series of intense relationships in his heady cavern-like rooms lit by up by yellow satin and those Moreaus. The gossip in Paris was that Charles was *entre deux lits*, bisexual.

That spring of 1889 Ephrussi et Cie prospers, but family matters are exceedingly complicated. The robustly heterosexual Ignace, along with other wistful bachelors, was devoted to the Countess Potocka. This intriguing Countess, with looks that Proust described as 'at once delicate, majestic and malicious', her black hair pulled apart in a centre parting, held sway over a coterie of young men who would wear sapphire badges inscribed with the motto '*À la Vie, à la Mort*'. She holds 'Maccabee' dinners at which they would pledge to perform outrageous acts in her honour. As the Maccabees were Judaean martyrs, this must make her Judith, I realise belatedly, the heroine who cut off the head of Holofernes when he was drunk. After one dinner a letter to de Maupassant records that 'Ignace is a little more far-gone than the others . . . and has the bright idea of walking completely naked through the Paris streets . . .' and has been packed off to the country to recover.

Charles, at forty, was poised between all these different worlds. His private taste had become public property. Everything about him was aesthetic. He was known in Paris as an aesthete whose commissions and pronouncements and cut of jacket were scrutinised. He was a devotee of the Opéra.

Even his dog was called Carmen.

I find a letter to her, c/o Monsieur C. Ephrussi, 81 rue de Monceau, in the archives of the Louvre, from Puvis de Chavannes, the Symbolist painter of pallid figures and washed-out landscapes.

It wasn't just Renoir who disliked the Jews. A string of financial scandals throughout the 1880s were laid at the door of the new Jewish financiers, and the Ephrussi family was a particular target: 'Jewish machinations' were supposed to be behind the collapse in 1882 of the *Union Générale*, a Catholic bank that had strong ties to the Church, with many small Catholic depositors. The popular demagogue Edouard Drumont wrote in *La France Juive*:

The audacity with which these men treat these enormous operations, which for them are just simple game parties, is incredible. In one session, Michel Ephrussi buys or sells oil or wheat worth ten or fifteen million. No trouble; seated for two hours near a column at the Stock Exchange and phlegmatically holding his beard in his left hand, he distributes orders to thirty courtiers who crowd around him with their pencils extended.

Courtiers come and whisper in Michel's ear the day's news. Money is seen to be a bagatelle to these Jewish money-men, implies Drumont, a plaything. It has no connection to the savings carefully taken into the bank on market day, or hidden in the coffee pot on the mantelpiece.

It is a vivid image of covert power, of plotting. It has the intensity of Degas's painting *At the Bourse* of a whispered conversation between hook-nosed, red-bearded financiers amongst the pillars.

The Bourse and its players segue into the Temple and the money-changers.

'Who shall stop these men from living then, who shall soon make France look like a wasteland then? . . . it is the speculator in foreign wheat, it is the Jew, the friend of the Count of Paris . . . the favourite of all the salons of the aristocratic quarter; it is Ephrussi, the chief of the Jewish band who speculate on wheat.' Speculation, the making of money out of money, is seen as a particular Jewish sin. Even Theodor Herzl, the apologist of Zionism, always eager to raise money for the cause from wealthy Jewry, is rude in a letter about 'the Ephrussi, *spekulant*'.

Ephrussi et Cie did wield extraordinary power. The absence of the brothers from the Bourse was noted with panic during one crisis. Their threat to flood the markets with grain in response to Russian pogroms was taken seriously in an excited report in a newspaper during another crisis. '[The Jews] . . . have learned the potency of this weapon when they made Russia hold her hand in the last Jewish persecution . . . by reducing Russian securities twenty-four points in thirteen days. "Touch another of our people and not another ruble you shall have, to save your empire," said Michel Ephrussi, head of the great house at Odessa, the largest grain dealers in the world.' The Ephrussi were, in short, very rich, very visible and very partisan.

Drumont, the editor of a daily anti-Semitic newspaper, acted as the marshaller of opinion into print. He told the French how to spot a Jew – one hand is larger than another – and how to counter the threat that this race posed to France. His *La France Juive* sold 100,000 copies in its first year of publication in 1886. By 1914 it had gone into 200 editions. Drumont argued that Jews, because they were inherently nomadic, felt they owed nothing to the State. Charles and his brothers, Russian citizens from Odessa and Vienna and God knows where, looked after themselves – whilst leaching the life-blood of France by speculating with real French money.

The Ephrussi family certainly thought they belonged in Paris. Drumont certainly thought not: 'Jews, vomited from all the ghettos of Europe, are now installed as the masters in historic houses that evoke the most glorious memories of ancient France . . . the Rothschilds everywhere: at Ferrières and at Les Vaux-de-Cernay . . . Ephrussi, at Fontainebleau, in the palace of Francis I . . .' Drumont's ridicule of the speed in which this family has moved from being 'penniless adventurers' to this ascent into society, their attempts at hunting, their recently commissioned coats of arms, became vicious anger when he thought of his patrimony soiled by the Ephrussi and their friends.

I force myself to read this stuff: Drumont's books, newspaper, the endless pamphlets in numerous editions, the English versions. Someone has annotated a book on the Jews of Paris in my London library. Written very carefully and approvingly next to Ephrussi is the word *venal* pencilled in capitals.

There are quantities and quantities of this stuff, swinging wildly between hectoring generalities and splenetic detail. The Ephrussi family come up again and again. It is as if a vitrine is opened and each of them is taken out and held up for abuse. I knew in a very general way about French anti-Semitism, but it is this particularity that makes me feel nauseated. It is a daily anatomising of their lives.

Charles is pilloried as someone 'who *operates* . . . in the world of literature and the arts'. He is abused as someone who has power in French art, but treats art as commerce. Everything Charles does comes back to gold, say the writers in *La France Juive*. Meltable, transportable, mutable gold to be carried, bought and sold by Jews who do not understand land or country. Even his book on Dürer is scrutinised for Semitic tendencies. How can Charles understand this great German artist, writes one angry art historian, for he is only a '*Landesman aus dem Osten*', an oriental.

His brothers and uncles are excoriated and his aunts, now married into the French aristocracy, are savagely parodied. All the Jewish finance houses of France are anathematised by rote: '*Les Rothschilds, Erlanger, Hirsch, Ephrussi, Bamberger, Camondo, Stern, Cahen d'Anvers ... Membres de la finance internationale*'. The complex intermarriage between the clans is repeated endlessly to build up a picture of one terrible spider's web of intrigue, a web even more tightly bound when Maurice Ephrussi marries Beatrice, the daughter of the head of the French Rothschilds, Alphonse de Rothschild. These two families now count as one.

The anti-Semites need to pull these Jews back to where they came from, to strip them of their sophisticated Parisian life. One anti-Semitic pamphlet, *Ce Bons Juifs*, describes an imagined conversation between Maurice Ephrussi and a friend:

– Is it true that you soon have to leave for Russia?

– Within 2 or 3 days, said M. de K . . .

Well! Maurice Ephrussi replied, if you are going to Odessa, go to the stock exchange to tell my father some news of me.

M. de K promises, and after having finished his business work in Odessa, goes to the stock exchange and asks for Ephrussi the father.

– You know, he is told, if you want it to be done, it is the Jews you need. Ephrussi the father arrives, an awful-looking Hebrew with long and dirty hair, wearing a pelisse which is completely covered with grease stains.

M. de K . . . delivers the message to the old man and wants to leave, when he suddenly feels pulled by his clothing, and hears the Ephrussi father who tells him:

– You forgot my small profits.

– What do you mean by your small profits? exclaimed M. de K . . .

You understood perfectly well, dear Sir, replies the father of Rothschild's son in law, while bowing to the ground, I am one of the curiosities of the Odessa stock exchange; when strangers come to see me without doing any business they always give me a small present. My sons thus send me over 1000 visitors a year and this helps me to make ends meet.

And with a large smile, the noble patriarch adds: they know well that they will one day be rewarded . . . my sons!

The Ephrussi, *les Rois de Blé*, are simultaneously loathed as upstarts and fêted as patrons. One minute they are to be reminded of the Odessan grain merchant, a patriarch with his grease-stained coat and his outstretched hand. The next, Beatrice is at a society ball wearing her tiara of hundreds of slender ears of trembling golden corn. Maurice, the owner of a vast chateau at Fontainebleau, put himself down on his marriage certificate to Beatrice de Rothschild as 'landowner', rather than banker. This was no slip. For Jews, owning land was still a comparatively new experience: it was only since the Revolution that Jews had full citizenship, a mistake – according to some commentators – as Jews were not capable adults. Just look at how the Ephrussi lived, suggested one screed, *The Original Mr Jacobs,* 'the love of bric-a-brac, of all odds and ends, or rather the Jews' passion for possession, is often carried to childishness'.

I wonder how these brothers lived their lives in these conditions.

Did they shrug their shoulders, or did it get to them, this incessant hum of vilification, mutterings about venality, the sort of constant, bubbling animosity that the narrator in Proust's novels remembers of his grandfather: 'Whenever I brought a new friend home my grandfather seldom failed to start humming "O, God of our fathers" from *La Juive*, or else "Israel, break thy chains" . . . The old man would call out "On guard! On guard!" upon hearing the name of any new friend and if the victim had admitted his origins, 'then my grandfather . . . would look at us, humming under his breath the air of "What! Do you hither guide the feet of this timid Israelite?"'

There were duels. Though outlawed, duels were nonetheless popular amongst young aristocrats, members of the Jockey Club and army officers. Many of the quarrels were inconsequential, issues of territoriality amongst young men. A disparaging reference to an Ephrussi-owned horse in an article in *Le Sport* started a quarrel with the journalist, 'which led to an altercation and then a hostile meeting' with Michel Ephrussi.

But some of the disputes reveal the growing, alarming fissures within Parisian society. Ignace was an accomplished dueller, but choosing not to fight was regarded as a particularly Jewish failing. A gloating report tells of one example of this when a business deal between Michel and the Count Gaston de Breteuil had ended with substantial losses on the part of the Count. Michel, a man of business, did not see it as a matter for a duel and failed to give satisfaction by fighting. When the Count returned to Paris after the refused invitation, 'according to the story current in club circles . . . he encountered Ephrussi . . . and twisted the latter's nose with the bank notes representing the balance, the pin with which they were fastened together severely scratching the proboscis of the great wheat operator. He resigned from the Rue Royale Club and gave a million francs to be distributed amongst the poor of Paris . . .' This is recounted as a comedy – rich Jews, gross and without honour, and their noses.

They are not above reproach: Jews just don't know how to behave.

Michel did fight a bitter run of duels with the Comte de Lubersac on behalf of a Rothschild cousin whose honour had been impugned, and who was too young to stand up for himself. One took place on the island of the Grand Jatte, in the River Seine. 'At the fourth onslaught, Ephrussi was wounded in the breast, the count's sword striking a rib . . . The count attacked vigorously from the outset, and the combatants parted at the finish without the customary handshake. The count left the scene in a landau, and was greeted with cries of "*À bas les Juifs*" and "*Vive l'Armée*".'

Protecting your name and your family's honour was increasingly difficult as a Jew in Paris.

In October 1891 Charles took the netsuke to a new home on the avenue d'Iéna. Number 11 is larger than the Hôtel Ephrussi on the rue de Monceau and more austere on the outside – no swags, no urns. It is so large that it is practically invisible. I stand and look. The spaces between the floors are greater: these are rooms with volume. Charles moved here with his brother Ignace three years after their widowed mother died. I chance my luck and ring a bell and explain my mission to a woman with a perfect and unwavering smile, who explains, quite slowly to me, that I am completely wrong about who lived here, that it is private and that she has never heard of this family. She watches me until I am back in the street.

I'm furious. A week later I find that the brothers' house was torn down and rebuilt in the 1920s.

This new area is even grander than the rue de Monceau. It is only twenty years since the Ephrussi arrived in Paris, but this was a family that now felt secure. The bachelor brothers' house was 300 yards down the hill from the grandeur of Jules and Fanny's mansion, with its emblems of ears of corn above the windows and their entwined initials over the huge gateway into the courtyard. Louise's palace was directly across the road in the rue Bassano. The area is on the hill to the north of the Champ de Mars, where the Eiffel Tower had just been erected. It was the place to be: it was talked of as the 'hill of arts'.

Charles's taste was still changing. His passion for the Japanese was being slowly overtaken. The cult had become so widespread that everyone in the 1880s had houses full of *Japonaiseries*: they were now regarded as bric-a-brac, settling like dust on every available surface. 'Everything,' said Alexandre Dumas in 1887, 'is Japanese now': Zola's house outside Paris, awash with Japanese *objets*, was considered slightly risible. It had become much more difficult to make a claim for their special attributes when they had become mainstream, when the posters for bicycles or absinthe flapping off the hoardings now resembled Japanese woodblock prints. There were still serious collectors of Japanese art – including Guimet, who lived next door – and much more art-historical knowledge than in the melee of ten years before. De Goncourt had published his studies of Hokusai and Utamaro, Siegfried Bing had his journal *Le Japon artistique*, but it was no longer followed with religious intensity in Charles's fashionable circle.

Proust records this moment of transition in the drawing-room of Swann's lover, the *demi-mondaine* Odette: 'the Far East was retreating more and more before the invading forces of the eighteenth century . . . nowadays it was rarely in Japanese kimonos that Odette received her intimates, but rather in the bright and billowing silk of a Watteau housecoat'.

It was a change of exoticisms that was noticed in Charles, critic, collector and curator. A journalist wrote that Charles had begun 'little by little to detach himself from . . . [Japan] . . . and to turn more and more towards the French XVIIIth century, the productions of Meissen and of the Empire, of which he has collected an ensemble of creations of the highest quality'. In his new house Charles hung on the walls of his study a suite of tapestries depicting children's games, woven from silver thread. And he created a series of enfilade rooms, which he decorated with formal suites of pale Empire furniture with its bronze mounts, on which he placed garnitures of Sèvres and Meissen porcelain: there were careful rhythms here. And then he hung the Moreaus, Manets and Renoirs.

Proust has the Duchesse de Guermantes rhapsodising over this kind of neoclassical furniture, seen in the house of the Duc d'Iéna: 'all those things invading our houses, the Sphinxes crouching at the feet of the armchairs, the snakes coiled round candelabra . . . all the Pompeian lamps, the little boat-shaped beds which look as if they have been floating on the Nile'. A bed has a siren stretched out in relief, she says, that looks just like a Moreau.

It is in this new house that Charles replaces his *lit de parade* with an Empire bed. It is a *lit à la polonaise* hung with silks.

In a second-hand bookshop in Paris I find the sale catalogues of parts of Michel and Maurice's art collections that were dispersed after they had died. A dealer had been bidding for the clocks, unsuccessfully, annotating every lot with the price as it had come up: 10,780 francs for a Louis XV astronomical clock inlaid with bronze signs of the zodiac. All this porcelain, the Savonnerie carpets, the paintings by Boucher, the *boiseries* and the tapestries speak of the need of the Ephrussi family to settle seamlessly into society. And I began to realise that Charles's new taste for Empire paintings and furniture as he approached his mid-forties was more than just a way of creating an ensemble in which to live. It was also a claim on an essential Frenchness, on belonging somewhere properly. And perhaps a way of putting more space between those first, jostlingly heterodox rooms and his authoritative life as an arbiter of taste. Empire is not *le gout Rothschild*, not Jewish. It is patrician, French.

I wonder how the netsuke looked here: it is in these formal rooms that Charles begins to grow away from them. His rooms in the rue de Monceau had not 'learnt their optical catechism'; they were cut through by the note of the yellow armchair. They were congeries of different things to pick up and handle. But I feel that Charles is becoming grander. He is now called 'the opulent Charles' by a Parisian wit. There is less to touch here: you would not dare to pick up those Meissen vases in their bronze mounts and hand them round for inspection. The furnishings of these rooms are described by a critic after Charles's death as the very best of their kind: they are *'pompeux, ingénieux et un peu froids'*, grandiose, clever and a little cold. Cold is right, I think, as I surreptitiously reach a hand over a velvet rope to stroke the arm of an Empire *fauteuil* in the Musée Nissim de Camondo in the rue de Monceau, for research.

I find it harder to imagine the vitrine opening and a hand havering over the netsuke in indecision between a scramble of ivory puppies and a girl soaping herself in a wooden tub. I'm not sure they fit in at all.

In their new house the brothers gave larger dinner parties and soirées. On 2nd February 1893 *Le Gaulois* records one in its column *'Mondanités'*. There was a 'Very brilliant *five o'clock* last evening, at Messrs Charles and Ignace Ephrussi, in honour of the princess Mathilde,' it records:

Her Imperial Highness, accompanied by the Baronesse de Galbois, arrived at the splendid salons of the avenue d'Iéna, where more than 200 people, the upper echelons of the Parisian and foreign world, gathered together.

Let us mention at random:

Comtesse d'Haussonville, in black satin; Comtesse von Moltke-Hvitfeldt, also in black; Princesse de Léon, in dark blue velvet; the Duchesse de Morny in black velvet; Comtesse de Louis de Talleyrand-Périgord, in black satin; Comtesse Jean de Ganay, in red and black; Baronesse Gustave de Rothschild, in black velvet . . . Comtesse Louise Cahen d'Anvers, in mauve velvet; Mme Edgard Stern, in green grey; Mme Manuel de Yturbe, née Diaz, in lilac velvet; Baronesse James de Rothschild, in black; Comtesse de Camondo, née Cahen, in grey satin; Baronesse Benoist-Méchin, in black velvet and fur, etc.

Among the men, notable men included:

The minister of Sweden, Prince Orloff, Prince de Sagan, Prince Jean Borghèse, Marquis de Modène, Messrs Forain, Bonnat, Roll, Blanche, Charles Yriarte Schlumberger, etc.

Mme Léon Fould and Mme Jules Ephrussi did the honours in greeting the guests, one in a gown of deep grey and the other in clear grey.

The elegant apartments were much appreciated, notably the grand salon Louis XVI, where one admired the head of king Midas, a marvel by Luca della Robbia, and Charles Ephrussi's rooms, of the most pure Empire.

The reception was very lively, and there was a very beautiful musical programme performed by the tziganes.

The Princesse Mathilde didn't leave the avenue d'Iéna until 7 o'clock

It was a good turn-out for the brothers. According to the paper it was a cold and bright evening with a fullish moon. The avenue d'Iéna is wide, with plane trees sweeping down the centre, and I imagine the carriages for the brothers' party blocking the road, and the gypsy music coming from their apartments. I imagine Louise, red-gold and Titian-like in mauve velvet, walking the few hundred yards up the hill to her vast faux-Renaissance mansion and her husband.

A 'very brilliant five o'clock' would have been difficult to give the following year. In 1894, as the painter J. E. Blanche put it, 'the Jockey club deserted the table of the Princes of Israel'.

It was the start of the Dreyfus Affair, twelve years that convulsed France and polarised Paris. Alfred Dreyfus, a Jewish officer on the French General Staff, was accused of being a spy for Germany on the forged evidence of a slip of paper found in a waste-paper basket. He was court-martialled and found guilty, though it was quite clear to the Army General Staff that the evidence was fabricated. Dreyfus was cashiered in front of a howling crowd demanding his execution. Toy gallows were sold on the streets. He was sent to Devil's Island to serve life-imprisonment in solitary confinement.

The campaign to have him retried began almost immediately, provoking an intense and violent anti-Semitic backlash; the Jews were seen to be overthrowing natural justice. Their patriotism was impugned: by supporting Dreyfus they were proving that they were Jewish first and foremost, and French only second. Charles and his brothers, still Russian citizens, were typical Jews.

Two years later evidence emerged that another French officer, Major Esterhazy, was behind the forgery, but Esterhazy was exonerated on only the second day of his military trial, and Dreyfus was reconfirmed in his conviction. Additional forgeries were produced to back up the sham. Despite Zola's impassioned plea to the President, *J'accuse . . . !*, published in the newspaper *L'Aurore* in January 1898, Dreyfus was brought back in 1899 and reconvicted for a third time. Zola was convicted of criminal libel and fled to England. It was not until 1906 that Dreyfus would finally be cleared.

There were seismic splits into bitter Dreyfusard and anti-Dreyfusard camps. Friendships were curtailed, families separated and salons where Jews and veiled anti-Semites used to meet became actively hostile. Amongst Charles's artist friends, Degas became the most savage anti-Dreyfusard, and stopped speaking to Charles and to the Jewish Pissarro. Cézanne, too, was convinced of Dreyfus's guilt, and Renoir became actively hostile to Charles and his 'Jew art'.

The Ephrussi family were Dreyfusard by faith and by inclination – and simply by living in the public eye. In a letter written to André Gide in the febrile spring of 1898, a friend recounts hearing a man catechising his children outside the Ephrussi house in the avenue d'Iéna. Who lives here? '*Le sale juif!*' The dirty Jew! Ignace was followed back home from the Gare du Nord after a late dinner in the country, by inspectors of the police who had mistaken him for the exiled Zola. 'Five agents,' reported the anti-Dreyfusard *Le Gaulois* on 19th October 1898, 'spent the night in surveillance. Inspector Frecourt arrived in the afternoon to convey the summons to court to M. Zola, whom he believed was taking refuge chez Ephrussi . . . When he dares to return M. Zola will not escape the vigilant eye of the police.'

And it was a family battle: Charles and Ignace's niece Fanny, the adored daughter of their late sister Betty, had married Theodore Reinach, an archaeologist and Hellenist from a prominent Jewish family of French intellectuals. And Theodore's politician brother Joseph was the principal mover in Dreyfus's defence – and the later author of the magisterial *Histoire de l'affaire Dreyfus*. Reinach became a lightning conductor for anti-Semitism: much of Drumont's ire was directed against this 'personification of the counterfeit Frenchman'. The 'Jew Reinach' was stripped of his own military rank at a court martial, beaten up while leaving Zola's trial and became the subject of a national campaign of vilification of great viciousness.

Paris changed for Charles. He was a *mondain* with doors shut in his face, a patron ostracised by some of his artists. I think of what it must have been like, and recall Proust writing of the Duc de Guermantes's anger:

as far as Swann is concerned . . . they tell me now that he is openly Dreyfusard. I should never have believed it of him, an epicure, a man of practical judgement, a collector, a connoisseur of old books, a member of the Jockey, a man who enjoys the respect of all, who knows all the good addresses and used to send us the best port you could wish to drink, a dilettante, a family man. Ah! I feel badly let down.

In Paris I haunt the archives and pace my routes between old houses and offices, vagabonding in museums, aimless one moment and over-purposeful the next. I am charting a journey into memory. I have a netsuke of a brindled wolf in my pocket. It is almost too strange to find how interwoven Charles is with Proust's figure of Swann.

I keep coming on the places where Charles Ephrussi and Charles Swann intersect. Before I started my journey I knew in the broadest terms that my Charles was one of the two principal models for Proust's protagonist – the lesser, it was said, of the two. I remember reading a dismissive remark on him ('a Polish Jew . . . stout, bearded and ugly, his manner was ponderous and uncouth') in the biography of Proust published by George Painter in the 1950s and taking it at face value. The other model acknowledged by Proust was a charming dandy and clubman called Charles Haas. He was an older man, neither a writer nor a collector.

If there has to be a first owner of my wolf, I want him to be Swann – driven, loved, graceful – but I don't want Charles to disappear into source material, into literary footnotes. Charles has become so real to me that I fear losing him into Proust studies. And I care too much about Proust to turn his fiction into some Belle Epoque acrostic. 'My novel has no key,' Proust said, repeatedly.

I try to map the straightforward correspondences that my Charles and the fictional Charles share, the lineaments of their lives. I say 'straightforward', but when I start to write them out they become quite a list.

They are both Jewish. They are both *mondain.* They have a social reach from royalty (Charles conducted Queen Victoria round Paris, Swann is a friend of the Prince of Wales) via the salons to the studios of artists. They are art-lovers deeply in love with the works of the Italian Renaissance, Giotto and Botticelli in particular. They are both experts in the arcane subject of Venetian fifteenth-century medallions. They are collectors, patrons of the Impressionists, incongruous in the sunshine at a boating-party of a painter-friend.

Both of them write monographs on art: Swann on Vermeer, my Charles on Dürer. They use their 'erudition in matters of art . . . to advise society ladies what pictures to buy and how to decorate their houses'. Both Ephrussi and Swann are dandies and they are both Chevaliers of the *Légion d'honneur.* Their lives traverse *Japonisme* and reach into the new taste for Empire. And they are both Dreyfusards who find that their carefully constructed lives are deeply riven by their Jewishness.

Proust played with the interpenetration of the real and the invented. His novels have a panoply of historical figures who appear as themselves – Mme Straus and the Princess Mathilde, for instance – mingling with characters reimagined from recognisable people. Elstir, the great painter who leaves behind his infatuation with *Japonisme* to become an

Impressionist, has elements of Whistler and Renoir in him, but has another dynamic force. Similarly Proust's characters stand in front of actual pictures. The visual texture of the novels is suffused not just with references to Giotto and Botticelli, Dürer and Vermeer, alongside Moreau, Monet and Renoir, but, by the act of looking at paintings, by the act of collecting them and remembering what it was to see something, with a memory of the moment of apprehension.

Swann catches resemblances in passing: Odette to a Botticelli, the profile of a footman at a reception to a Mantegna. And so did Charles. I cannot help wondering if my grandmother, so undishevelled, so very kempt in her white laundered frock on those gravel paths in the garden of the Swiss chalet, ever knew what made Charles bend down and ruffle her pretty sister's hair and compare her to his Renoir of the gypsy girl?

And when I encounter Swann, he is funny and charming, but he has a quality of reserve 'like a locked cabinet'. He moves through the world leaving people more alive to the things he loves. I think of how the young narrator, in love with Swann's daughter, visits the household and is met with such courtesy, introduced to the sublimities of his collection.

That is my Charles, taking endless pains to show books or pictures to young friends, to Proust, writing about objects and sculpture with acuity and honesty, animating the world of things. I know. It is how I have come to see Berthe Morisot for the first time, how I learn to stand back and then move forward. It is how I have come to listen to Massenet, look at Savonnerie carpets, see that Japanese lacquer is worth spending time with. I pick up one after another of Charles's netsuke and think of him choosing them. And I think of his reserve.

He belongs in this glittering Parisian world, but he never stops being a Russian citizen. He always has this secret hinterland.

Charles had a poor heart like his father. He was fifty when Dreyfus was brought back from Devil's Island to undergo his second farcical trial and be reconvicted in 1899. In the delicate engraving of him done in that year by Jean Patricot he is looking downwards, inwards, his beard still neatly trimmed, his cravat held by a pearl. He is more involved in music and is now a patron of the Comtesse Greffuhle's Société des Grandes Auditions Musicales, 'where his advice is greatly appreciated, and where he has put himself to work with ardour'. He had almost stopped buying pictures, except for a Monet of the rocks at low tide at Pourville on the Normandy coast. It is a beautiful painting, scumbled rocks in the foreground and strange calligraphies of the fishermen's wooden poles emerging from the sea. It is, I think, rather Japanese.

*Engraving of Charles Ephrussi by Patricot published with his obituary in the* Gazette des Beaux Arts, *1905*

Charles had slowed his writing too, though he was punctilious in his duties at the *Gazette*, clear about what should get published, 'never ever late, ever diligent down to the very minutiae of every article, ever seeking perfection', happy to bring on new writers.

Louise had a new lover. Charles was superseded by Crown Prince Alphonse of Spain, thirty years her junior and rather weak-chinned, but nonetheless a future king.

On the cusp of the new century, Charles's first cousin in Vienna was to be married. Charles had known Viktor von Ephrussi since boyhood, when the whole family had lived together, all the generations under one roof, the evenings spent in planning their move to Paris. Viktor was the bored little boy, his youngest cousin, for whom Charles drew caricatures of the servants. The clan was close and they had seen each other at parties in Paris and Vienna, on holiday in Vichy and St Moritz, at Fanny's summer gatherings at the Chalet Ephrussi. And they shared Odessa – the city they were both born in, the starting place that is not mentioned.

The three brothers in Paris all send a wedding-present to Viktor and his young bride, the Baroness Emmy Schey von Koromla. The couple will start their new life in the enormous Palais Ephrussi on the Ringstrasse.

Jules and Fanny send them a beautiful Louis XVI desk of marquetry with tapering legs ending in small gilt hooves.

Ignace sends them an Old Master painting, Dutch, of two ships in a gale. Perhaps a coded joke about marriage from a serial avoider of commitment.

Charles sends them something special, a spectacular something from Paris: a black vitrine with green velvet shelves, and a mirrored back that reflects 264 netsuke.

*Part Two*

## VIENNA 1899–1938

## 12. DIE POTEMKINISCHE STADT

In March 1899, Charles's generous wedding gift for Viktor and Emmy is carefully crated up and taken from the avenue d'Iéna, leaving the golden carpet, the Empire *fauteuils* and the Moreaus. It travels across Europe and is delivered to the Palais Ephrussi in Vienna, on the corner of the Ringstrasse and the Schottengasse.

It is time to stop walking with Charles and reading about Parisian interiors, and start reading *Die Neue Freie Presse* and concentrating on Viennese street life at the turn of the century. It is October and I find I have spent almost a year with Charles – far longer than I thought possible, unwarranted skeins of time reading about the Dreyfus Affair. I do not have to move floors in the library: French literature and German literature are next to each other.

I am anxious about where my boxwood wolf and my ivory tiger are moving to. I book a ticket to Vienna and set out for the Palais Ephrussi.

This new home for the netsuke is absurdly big. It looks like a primer on classical architecture; it even makes the Paris houses of the Ephrussi look demure. The Palais has Corinthian pilasters and Doric columns, urns and architraves, four small towers at the corners, rows of caryatids holding up the roof. The first two storeys are powerfully rusticated, surmounted by two storeys of pale pink-washed brick, and stone behind the fifth-storey caryatids. There are so many of these massive, endlessly patient Greek girls in their half-slipped robes

– thirteen down the long side of the Palais on the Schottengasse, six on the main Ringstrasse front – that they look a little as if they are lined up along a wall at a very poor dance. I cannot escape gold: there is lots of gilding to the capitals and balconies. There is even a name glittering across the façade, but this is comparatively new: the Palais is now the headquarters of Casinos Austria.

I do my house-watching here, too. Or, rather, I attempted to do my house-watching, but the Palais is now opposite a tram stop above an underground station pushing people out in a constant stream. There is nowhere that I can lean against a wall and pause and look. I try to place the roofline against the winter sky and almost walk into the path of a tram, and a bearded man in three coats and a balaclava harangues me for my carelessness, and I give him too much money to make him go away. The Palais is opposite the main building of the University of Vienna, where three campaigns of protest – American policies in the Middle East, carbon emissions, something to do with fees – compete for noise and signatures. It is an impossible place to stand.

The house is just too big to absorb, taking up too much space in this part of the city, too much sky. It is more of a fortress or a watchtower than a house. I try to accommodate its size. It is certainly not a house for a wandering Jew. And then I drop my glasses and one of the arms fractures near the joint, so that I have to pinch them together to see anything at all.

I am in Vienna, 400 yards across a small park from the front door to Freud's apartment, outside my paternal family house, and I cannot *see clearly*. Bring on the symbolism, I mutter, as I hold my glasses up to try and see this pink monolith; prove to me that this bit of my journey is going to be difficult. I am wrong-footed already.

*The Palais Ephrussi looking along the Schottengasse
towards the Votivkirche, Vienna, 1881*

So I go for a walk. I push my way through the students and I'm
on the Ringstrasse, and I can move and can breathe.

Except that it is a windingly ambitious street, breath-catchingly
imperial in scale. It is so big that a critic argued, when it was built,
that it had created an entirely new neurosis, that of agoraphobia.
How clever of the Viennese to invent a phobia for their new city.

The Emperor Franz Josef had ordered a modern metropolis to
be created around Vienna. The old medieval city walls were to be
demolished, the old moats filled in and a great arc of new buildings,
a city hall, a Parliament, an opera house, a theatre, museums and a
university constructed. This Ring would have its back to the old city
and would look out into the future. It would be a ring around

Vienna of civic and cultural magnificence, an Athens, an ideal efflorescence of *Prachtbauten* – buildings of splendour.

These buildings would be of different architectural styles, but the ensemble would pull together all this heterogeneity into a whole, the grandest public space in Europe, a ring of parks and open spaces; the Heldenplatz, the Burggarten and the Volksgarten would be ornamented with statues celebrating the triumphs of music and poetry and drama.

To produce this spectacle meant colossal engineering works. For twenty years it was dust, dust, dust. Vienna, said the writer Karl Kraus, was being 'demolished into a great city'.

All the Emperor's citizens from one end of the Empire to the other – Magyars, Croats, Poles, Czechs, Jews from Galicia and Trieste, all the twelve nationalities, the six official languages, the five religions – would encounter this *Kaiserlich-königlich*, imperial and royal civilisation.

It works: I find that it is curiously difficult to stop on the Ring, with its endless deferred promise of a moment when you can see it all, together. This new street is not dominated by any one building; there is no crescendo towards a palace or a cathedral; but there is this constant triumphant pull along from one great aspect of civilised life to another. I keep thinking there will be one defining view through these bare winter trees, one framed moment glimpsed through my broken glasses. The wind sweeps me on.

I walk away from the university, built in its new Renaissance style, steps sweeping up to a great portico flanked by rows of arched windows, busts of scholars in every niche, classical sentinels on the rooftops, golden scrolls labelling anatomists, poets, philosophers.

I walk on past the Town Hall, fantasy Gothic, towards the bulk of the Opera, then past the museums and the Reichsrat, the Parliament, built by Theophilus Hansen, the architect of the moment. Hansen was a Dane who had made his name by studying classical archaeology in Athens and designing the Academy of Athens. Here, on the Ring, he built the Ringstrasse Palais for the Archduke Wilhelm, then the Musikverein, then the Academy of Fine Arts, then the Vienna Stock Exchange. And the Palais Ephrussi. He had won so many commissions by the 1880s that other architects suspected a conspiracy by Hansen and 'his vassals . . . the Jews'.

It was no conspiracy. He was just very good at giving his clients what they wanted; his Reichsrat is one Greek detail after another. Birth of democracy, says the great portico. Protector of the city, says the statue of Athena. There is a little something everywhere you look to flatter the Viennese. There are chariots on the roof, I notice.

In fact, as I look up, I see figures everywhere against the sky.

On and on. It becomes a musical series of buildings, spaced with parks, punctuated by statues. It has a rhythm that suits its purpose. Ever since it was officially opened on 1st May 1865 with a procession by the Emperor and Empress, this had been a space for progresses, for display. The Hapsburg court lived according to Spanish court ceremonial, a severe code of ritual, and there were innumerable opportunities for complex court processions. And there was the daily marching of the City Regiment, and marches on major feast days of the Hungarian Guards, celebrations of the Imperial Birthday, jubilees, honour guards for the arrival of a Crown Princess, and funerals. All the guards had different uniforms: confections of sashes, fur trimmings and plumed hats and epaulettes. To be on the Vienna Ringstrasse was to be within earshot of a marching band, the drumming of feet. The Hapsburg regiments were the 'best-dressed army in the world', with a stage to match.

I realise that I am going too fast, walking as if I had a destination, rather than a point of departure. I remember that this was the street that was made for the slower movement of the daily 'Corso', the ritualised stroll for society along the Kärntner Ring to meet and flirt and gossip and be seen. In the illustrated scandal sheets that proliferated in Vienna around the time that Viktor and Emmy got married, there were often sketches showing '*Ein Corso Abenteuer*', an adventure on the Corso, advances from bewhiskered men with canes or glances from *demi-mondaines*. There was a 'regular jam', wrote Felix Salten, 'of knights of fashion, monocled nobles, members of the pressed-trouser brigade'.

This was a place to get dressed up for. In fact, it was the site of the most spectacular bit of dressing up in Vienna. In 1879, twenty years before Viktor and Emmy marry and Charles's netsuke arrive, Hans Makart, a wildly popular painter of vast canvases of historical fantasy, orchestrated a *Festzug* or procession of artisans for the twenty-fifth anniversary of the Emperor's wedding. The artisans of Vienna were deployed in forty-three guilds, each of which had its own float decorated in allegorical fashion. Musicians and heralds and pikemen and men with banners milled around each float. Everyone wore Renaissance costume, and Makart led the whole swaggering cavalcade on a white charger, wearing a wide-brimmed hat. It occurs to me that this slippage – a bit of Renaissance, a bit of Rubens, some cod-classicism – fits the Ringstrasse perfectly.

It is all so self-consciously grand, and yet a bit Cecil B. de Mille. I am the wrong audience for it. A young painter and architecture student, Adolf Hitler, had a proper visceral response to the Ringstrasse:

'From morning until late at night I ran from one object of interest to another, but it was always the buildings that held my primary interest. For hours I could stand in front of the Opera, for hours I could gaze at the Parliament; the whole Ringstrasse seemed to me like an enchantment out of "The Thousand-and-One-Nights".'

Hitler would paint all the great buildings on the Ring, the Burgtheater, Hansen's Parliament, the two great buildings opposite the Palais Ephrussi, the university and the Votivkirche. Hitler appreciated how the space could be used for dramatic display. He understood all this ornament in a different way: it expressed 'eternal values'.

All of this enchantment was paid for by selling building lots to the rapidly growing class of financiers and industrialists. Many of them were sold to create the Ringstrasse Palais, a type of building where a series of apartments lay behind one formidable façade. You could have the imposing Palais address, with a great front door and balconies and windows onto the Ringstrasse, a marble entrance hall, a salon with a painted ceiling- and yet live on just one floor. This floor, the *Nobelstock*, would have all the main reception rooms centred on a large ballroom. The *Nobelstock* is easy to spot as it has the most swags around its windows.

And because many of the inhabitants of these new Palais were the families who had recently made good, this meant that the Ringstrasse was substantially Jewish. Walking away from the Palais Ephrussi, I pass the Palais of the Liebens, the Todescos, the Königswaters, the Wertheims, the Gutmanns, the Epsteins, the Schey von Koromlas. These bravura buildings are a roll-call of intermarried Jewish families, an architectural parade of self-confident wealth where Jewishness and ornament were interlocked.

As I walk with the wind at my back, I think of my 'vagabonding' around the rue de Monceau and I remember Zola's rapacious Saccard in his vulgarly opulent mansion, intrusive on the street. Here in Vienna there are subtly different arguments about the Jews of Zionstrasse behind the great façades of their Palais. Here, the common talk goes, the Jews had become so assimilated, had mimicked their Gentile neighbours so well, that they had tricked the Viennese and simply disappeared into the fabric of the Ring.

Robert Musil in his novel *The Man Without Qualities* has the old Count Leinsdorf muse on this disappearing act. These Jews have muddled social life in Vienna by not staying true to their decorative roots:

The whole so-called Jewish Question would disappear without a trace if the Jews would only make up their minds to speak Hebrew, go back to their old names, and wear Eastern dress . . . Frankly, a Galician Jew who has just recently made his fortune in Vienna doesn't look right on the Esplanade at Ischl, wearing a Tyrolean costume with a chamois tuft on his hat. But put him in a long, flowing robe . . . Imagine them strolling along on our Ringstrasse, the only place in the world where you can see, in the midst of Western European elegance at its finest, a Mohammedan with his red fez, a Slovak in sheepskins, or a bare-legged Tyrolean.

Go into the slums of Vienna, Leopoldstadt, and you can see Jews living as Jews should live, twelve in a room, no water, loud on the streets, wearing the right robes, speaking the right argot. In 1863 when Viktor arrived in Vienna from Odessa as a three-year-old child, there were fewer than 8,000 Jews in Vienna. In 1867 the Emperor gave civic equality to Jews, removing the last barriers to their rights to teach and their ownership of property. By the time Viktor was thirty in 1890 there were 118,000 Jews in Vienna, many of the newcomers the *Ostjuden* driven out of Galicia by the horrors of the pogroms that had erupted throughout the previous decade. Jews also came from small villages in Bohemia, Moravia and Hungary, shtetls where their living conditions were abject. They spoke Yiddish and sometimes wore caftans : they were immersed in their Talmudic heritage. According to the popular Viennese press, these incomers were possibly involved in ritual murder, and certainly were involved in prostitution, hawking second-hand clothes, peddling goods all over the city with their strange baskets on their backs.

By the time of Viktor and Emmy's marriage in 1899 there were 145,000 Jews in Vienna. By 1910 only Warsaw and Budapest had a larger Jewish population in Europe; only New York had a larger Jewish population in the world. And it was a population like no other. Many of the second generation of the new migrants had achieved remarkable things. Vienna was a city, said Jakob Wassermann at the turn of the century, where 'all public life was dominated by the Jews. The banks. The press, the theatre, literature, social organisations, all lay in the hands of the Jews . . . I was amazed at the hosts of Jewish physicians, attorneys, clubmen, snobs, dandies, proletarians, actors, newspapermen and poets.' In fact, 71 per cent of financiers were Jewish, 65 per cent of lawyers were Jewish, 59 per cent of doctors were Jewish and half of Vienna's journalists were Jewish. *Die Neue Freie Presse* was 'owned, edited and written by Jews', said Wickham Steed in his casually anti-Semitic book on the Hapsburg Empire.

And these Jews had perfect façades – they vanished. It was a

Potemkin city and they were Potemkin inhabitants. Just as this Russian general had put a wood-and-plaster town together to impress the visiting Catherine the Great, so the Ringstrasse, wrote the young firebrand architect Adolf Loos, was nothing but a huge pretence. It was *potemkinische*. The façades bore no relation to the buildings. The stone was only stucco, it was all a confection for parvenus. The Viennese must stop living in this stage-set 'hoping that no one will notice they are fake'. The satirist Karl Kraus concurred. It was the 'debasement of practical life by ornament'. What was more, through this debasement, language had become infected by this 'catastrophic confusion. Phraseology is the ornament of the mind.' These ornamental buildings, their ornamental disposition, the ornamental life that went on around them: Vienna had become orotund.

This is a very complex place to send the netsuke to, I think, as I circle back to the Palais Ephrussi towards dusk, feeling calmer. It is complex because I'm not sure what all this ornament means. My netsuke are one material or another, boxwood or ivory. They are hard all the way through. They are not *potemkinische*, not made of stucco and paste. And they are funny little things, and I can't see how they will survive in this self-consciously grandiloquent city.

But then again, no one could accuse them of being practical, either. They can certainly be thought of as ornamental, even as a sort of enchantment. I wonder at the appropriateness of Charles's wedding-present once it reaches Vienna.

When the netsuke arrived at the Palais, the house was almost thirty years old, built around the same time as the Hôtel Ephrussi in the rue de Monceau. The building is a piece of theatre, a show-stopping performance by the man who commissioned it, Viktor's father, my great-great-grandfather Ignace.

There are, I am afraid, three Ignace Ephrussi in this story, stretching across three generations. The youngest is my great-uncle Iggie in his Tokyo flat. Then there is Charles's brother, the duelling Parisian

*Baron Ignace von Ephrussi, 1871*

with his string of love-affairs. And here in Vienna we meet the Baron Ignace von Ephrussi, holder of the Iron Cross Third Class, ennobled for his services to the Emperor, Imperial Counsellor, Chevalier of the Order of St Olaf, Honorary Consul to the King of Sweden and Norway, Holder of the Bessarabian Order of the Fleece, Holder of the Russian Order of the Laurel.

Ignace was the second-richest banker in Vienna, owning another huge building on the Ringstrasse and a block of buildings for the bank. And that was just in Vienna. I find an audit which notes that in 1899 he had assets in the city of 3,308,319 florins, roughly the current equivalent of $200 million; 70 per cent of this wealth was in stocks, 23 per cent in property, 5 per cent in works of art and jewellery and 2 per cent in gold. That is a lot of gold, I think, as well as a splendidly Ruritarian list of titles. You would need a façade with extra caryatids and gilding, if you had to live up to that list.

Ignace was a *Gründer*, a founding father, of the *Gründerzeit*, the founding age of Austrian modernity. He had come to Vienna with his parents and older brother Leon from Odessa. When the Danube flooded Vienna catastrophically in 1862, water lapping the altar steps of St Stephen's Cathedral, it was the Ephrussi family who loaned money to the government for the construction of embankments and new bridges.

I own a drawing of Ignace. He must be about fifty, and he is wearing a rather beautiful jacket with wide lapels and a fatly knotted tie with a pearl stuck through it. Bearded, with his dark hair swept back from his brow, Ignace is looking straight back at me appraisingly and his mouth is set for judgement.

I have a portrait of his wife Emilie too, grey-eyed with a rope of pearls spun round and round her neck and sweeping down over a black shot-silk dress. She is also pretty judgemental, and every time I've hung this painting at home I've had to take it down, as she looks down on our domestic life in disbelief. Emilie was known in the family as 'the crocodile', with a most engaging smile – whenever she smiled. As Ignace had affairs with both of her sisters, as well as keeping a series of mistresses, I feel lucky that she is smiling at all.

Somehow I imagine that it was Ignace who chose Hansen as architect; he understood how to make symbols work. What this rich Jewish banker wanted was a building to dramatise the ascendancy of his family, a house to sit alongside all these great institutions on the Ringstrasse.

The contract between the two men was signed on 12th May 1869, with building permission granted by the city at the end of August. By the time he came to work on the Palais Ephrussi, Theophilus Hansen had been raised to the nobility; he was now Theophil Freiherr von Hansen, and his client – now knighted – was Ignace Ritter von Ephrussi. Ignace and Hansen started by disagreeing about the scale of the elevation: the plans record endless revisions as these two strong-willed men worked out how to use the spectacular site. Ignace demanded stables for four horses as well as a coach-house 'for two to three carriages'. His chief requirement was for a staircase just for himself, one that couldn't be used by anyone else living in the house. It is all spelt out in an article from 1871 in the architectural journal *Allgemeine Bauzeitung*, illustrated with splendid plans and elevations. The Palais would be a grandstand onto Vienna: its balconies would overlook the city, and the city would pass by its huge oak doors.

I stand outside. This is the last moment when I can choose to turn away, cross the road, take the tram and leave this dynastic house and story alone. I breathe in. I push the left door, cut into the huge oak double gates, and am in a long, high, dark corridor, a gold coffered ceiling above me. I go on and I am in a glazed courtyard five storeys high, with internal balconies punctuating the huge space. There is a life-size statue of a rather muscle-bound Apollo half-heartedly strumming his lyre in front of me, held on his pedestal.

There are some small trees in planters and a reception desk, and I explain, poorly, who I am and that this is my family house, and that I would love to look around if it is not too much of a problem. It is certainly not a problem. A charming man emerges and asks me what I would like to see.

All I can see is marble: there is lots of marble. This doesn't say enough. Everything is marble. Floor, stairs, walls of staircase, columns on staircase, ceiling over staircase, mouldings on ceiling of staircase. Turn left and I go up the family stairs, shallow marble steps. Turn right and I go into another entrance hall. I look down and the patriarch's initials are set in the marble floor: JE (for Joachim Ephrussi) with a coronet above them. By the grand stairs are two torchères, taller than me. The steps go on and on, trippingly shallow. Black marble frames to the huge double doors – black and gold – I push, and I enter the world of Ignace Ephrussi.

For rooms covered in gold, it is very, very dark. The walls are divided into panels, each delineated by ribbons of gilding. The fireplaces are massive events of marble. The floors are intricate parquet. All the ceilings are divided into networks of lozenges and ovals and triangular panels by heavy gilded mouldings, raised and coffered into intricate scrolls of neoclassical froth. Wreaths and acanthus top the heady mixture. All the panels are painted by Christian Griepenkerl, the acclaimed decorator of the ceilings of the auditorium of the Opera. Each room takes a classical theme: in the billiard-room we have a series of Zeus's conquests – Leda, Antiope, Danae and Europa – each undraped girl held up by putti and velvet draping. The music-room has allegories of the muses; in the salon, miscellaneous goddesses sprinkle flowers; the smaller salon has random putti. The dining-room, achingly obvious, has nymphs pouring wine, draped with grapes or slung with game. There are more putti, for no good reason, sitting on doorway lintels.

Everything in this place, I realise, is very shiny. There is nothing to grip onto with these marbled surfaces. Its lack of tactility makes me panic: I run my hands along the walls and they feel slightly clammy. I thought I'd worked through my feelings about Belle-Epoque architecture in Paris, craning my neck to see the Baudrys on the ceilings of the Opéra. But here it is all so much closer, so much more personal. This is aggressively golden, aggressively lacking in purchase. What was Ignace trying to do? Smother his critics?

In the ballroom, with its three great windows looking across the square to the Votivkirche, Ignace suddenly lets something slip. Here, on the ceiling – where in other Ringstrasse Palais you might find something Elysian – there is a series of paintings of stories from the biblical Book of Esther: Esther crowned as Queen of Israel, kneeling in front of the Chief Priest in his rabbinical robes, being blessed, with her servants kneeling behind her. And then there is the destruction of the sons of Hamam, the enemy of the Jews, by Jewish soldiers.

It is beautifully done. It is a long-lasting, covert way of staking a claim for who you are. The ballroom is the only place in a Jewish household – however grand, and however rich you might be – that your Gentile neighbours would ever see socially. This is the only Jewish painting on the whole of the Ringstrasse. Here on Zionstrasse is a little bit of Zion.

This implacably marble Palais is where Ignace's three children were brought up. In the cache of family photographs that my father gave me is a salon picture of these children, caught stiffly between velvet drapes and a potted palm. Stefan is the eldest son, handsome and rather anxious. He is spending his days at the office with his father, learning grain. Anna is long-faced and huge-eyed, with massed curls, and looks utterly bored, her picture album almost falling out of her hands. She is fifteen and, apart from dancing lessons, spends her days in a carriage going between at-homes with her glacial mother. And my great-grandfather is the young Viktor. He is called by his Russian family patronymic, Tascha, and is in a velvet suit, clutching a velvet hat and a cane. He has black, glossy, waved hair and looks as if he has been promised a reward for spending this long afternoon away from his schoolroom, under all these heavy drapes.

Viktor's schoolroom has a window looking out towards the building site where they were finishing the university, with its rational series of columns telling the Viennese that knowledge is secular and new. For years every window in this new family house on the Ringstrasse looked out onto dust and demolition. And while Charles talks to Mme Lemaire about Bizet in the salons of Paris, Viktor sits in this schoolroom in the Palais Ephrussi with his German tutor, the Prussian Herr Wessel. Herr Wessel made Viktor translate passages of Edward Gibbon's *Decline and Fall of the Roman Empire* from

English into German, taught him how history worked from the great German historian Leopold von Ranke, '*wie es eigentlich gewesen*' – history as it actually happened. History was happening now, Viktor was told; history is rolling like wind through fields of wheat onwards from Herodotus, Cicero, Pliny and Tacitus through one empire to another, to Austria-Hungary and on towards Bismarck and the new Germany.

To understand history, taught Herr Wessel, you must also know Ovid and you must know Virgil. You must know how heroes encounter exile and defeat and return. So after history lessons, Viktor must learn parts of the *Aeneid* by heart. And after this, as recreation I suppose, Herr Wessel teaches Viktor about Goethe, Schiller and von Humboldt. Viktor learns that to love Germany is to love the Enlightenment. And German means emancipation from backwardness, it means *Bildung*, culture, knowledge, the journey towards experience. *Bildung*, it is implied, is in the journey from speaking Russian to speaking German, from Odessa to the Ringstrasse, from grain-trading to Schiller-reading. Viktor starts to buy his own books.

Viktor, it is understood in the family, is the bright one and must get this kind of education. Viktor, like Charles, is the spare son and will not have to be the banker. Stefan is being groomed for this, just like Leon's eldest son Jules. In a photograph of Viktor a few years later, he is just twenty-two and looks like a good Jewish scholar with his neatly trimmed beard, already slightly plumper than he should be, a high white collar and a black jacket. He has the Ephrussi nose, of course, but what is most noticeable are his pince-nez, the mark of a young man who wants to become a historian. Indeed, in 'his' café, Viktor is able to discourse at length, as his tutor has taught him, on this moment in time and how the forces of reaction must be seen in the context of progress. And so on.

Every young man has his own café, and each is subtly different. Viktor's was the Griensteidl, at the Palais Heberstein close to the Hofburg. This was a meeting place for young writers, the Jung Wien of the poet Hugo von Hofmannsthal, and the playwright Arthur Schnitzler. The poet Peter Altenberg had his post delivered to his table. There were mountains of newspapers and a complete run of *Meyers Konversations-Lexicon*, Germany's answer to the *Encyclopaedia Britannica*, to provoke or answer arguments or fuel journalistic copy. You could spend your whole day here, nursing a single cup of coffee under the high vaulted ceilings, writing, not-writing, reading the morning newspaper – *Die Neue Freie Presse* – while waiting for the afternoon edition. Theodor Herzl, the paper's Paris correspondent with his apartment in the rue de Monceau, used to write here and argue his absurd idea of a Jewish state. Even the waiters were rumoured to join in the conversations around the huge circular tables. It was, in a memorable phrase of the satirist Karl Kraus, 'an experimental station for the end of the world'.

In a café you could adopt an attitude of melancholic separation. This was an attitude shared by many of Viktor's friends, the sons of other wealthy Jewish bankers and industrialists, other members of the generation that had grown up in the marble Palais of the Ringstrasse. Their fathers had financed cities and railways, made fortunes, moved their families across continents. It was so difficult to live up to the *Gründer* that the most one could be expected to do was talk.

These sons had a common anxiety about their futures, lives set out in front of them on dynastic tram-lines, family expectations driving them forward. It meant a life lived under the gilded ceilings of their parents' homes, marriage to a financier's daughter, endless dances, years in business unspooling in front of them. It meant *Ringstrassenstil* – Ringstrasse-style – pomposity, over-confidence, the parvenu. It meant billiards in the billiard-room with your father's friends after dinner, a life immured in marble, watched over by putti.

These young men were seen as either Jewish or Viennese. It doesn't matter that they may have been born in the city: Jews had an unfair advantage over the *natural-born Viennese,* who had gifted liberty to these Semitic newcomers. As the English writer Henry Wickham Steed said, this was:

Liberty for the clever, quick-witted, indefatigable Jew to prey upon a public and a political world totally unfit for defence against or competition with him. Fresh from Talmud and synagogue, and consequently trained to conjure with the law and skilled in intrigue, the invading Semite arrived from Galicia or Hungary and carried everything before him. Unknown and therefore unchecked by public opinion, without any 'stake in the country' and therefore reckless, he sought only to gratify his insatiable appetite for wealth and power . . .

The Jews' insatiability was a common theme. They simply did not know their limits. Anti-Semitism was part of common day-to-day life. The flavour of Viennese anti-Semitism was different from Parisian anti-Semitism. In both places it happened both overtly and covertly. But in Vienna you could expect to have your hat knocked off your head on the Ringstrasse for looking Jewish (Schnitzler's Ehrenberg in *The Way into the Open*, Freud's father in *The Interpretation of Dreams*), be abused as a dirty Jew for opening a window in a train carriage (Freud), be snubbed at a meeting of a charity committee (Emilie Ephrussi), have your lectures at the university disrupted by cries of '*Juden hinaus*' – 'Jews out' – until every Jewish student had picked up his books and left.

Abuse also came in more generalised ways. You could read the latest pronouncements by Vienna's own version of Edouard Drumont in Paris, Georg von Schönerer, or hear his thuggish demonstrations churning their way along the Ring under your window. Schönerer came to prominence as the founder of the Austrian Reform Meeting, declaiming against 'the Jew, the sucking vampire . . . that knocks . . . at the narrow-windowed house of the German farmer and craftsman'. He promised in the Reichsrat that if his movement did not succeed now, 'the avengers will arise from our bones' and 'to the terror of the Semitic oppressors and their hangers-on' make good the principle '"An eye for an eye, a tooth for a tooth"'. Retribution against the injustices of the Jews – successful and affluent – was especially popular with artisans and students.

Vienna University was a particular hotbed of nationalism and anti-Semitism, with the *Burschenschaften* or student fraternities leading the way with their avowal of kicking the Jews out of the university. This is one of the reasons why many Jewish students considered it necessary to become exceptionally expert and dangerous fencers. In alarm, these fraternities instituted the Waidhofen principle, which meant there could be no duelling with Jews, that Jews had no honour and should not be expected to live as if they did: 'It is impossible to insult a Jew; a Jew cannot therefore demand satisfaction for any suffered insult.' You could still beat them up, of course.

It was Dr Karl Lueger, the founder of the Christian Social Party, with his amiability and Viennese patois, his followers with their white carnations in their buttonholes, who seemed even more dangerous.

His anti-Semitism seemed more carefully considered, less overtly rabble-rousing. Lueger made his play as an anti-Semite by necessity rather than conviction: 'wolves, panthers, and tigers are human compared to these beasts of prey in human form . . . We object to the old Christian Austrian Empire being replaced by a new Jewish Empire. It is not hatred for the individual, not hatred for the poor, the small Jew. No gentlemen, we do not hate anything but the oppressive big capital which is in the hands of the Jews.' It was *Bankjuden* – the Rothschilds and Ephrussi – who had to be put in their place.

Lueger gained huge popularity and was finally appointed Mayor in 1897, noting with some satisfaction that 'Jew-baiting is an excellent means of propaganda and getting ahead in politics'. Lueger then reached an accommodation with those Jews he had assailed in his rise to power, remarking smugly that 'Who is a Jew is something I determine.' There was still considerable Jewish anxiety: 'Can it be considered appropriate for the good name and interests that Vienna be the only great city in the world administered by an anti-semitic agitator?' Though there was no anti-Semitic legislation, the penalty of Lueger's twenty years of rhetoric was a legitimisation of bias.

In 1899, the year that the netsuke arrived in Vienna, it was possible for a Deputy in the Reichsrat to make speeches calling for *Schussgeld* – bounties – for shooting Jews. In Vienna the most outrageous statements were met with a feeling from the assimilated Jews that it was probably best not to make too much fuss.

It looks as if I am going to spend another winter reading about anti-Semitism.

It was the Emperor who held out against this agitation. 'I will tolerate no *Judenhetze* in my Empire,' he said. 'I am fully persuaded of the fidelity and loyalty of the Israelites and they can always count on my protection.' Adolf Jellinek, the most famous Jewish preacher of the time, pronounced that 'The Jews are thoroughly dynastical, loyalist, Austrian. The Double Eagle is for them a symbol of redemption and the Austrian colours adorn the banners of their freedom.'

Young Jewish men in their cafés had a slightly different view. They were living in Austria, part of a dynastic empire, part of a stifling bureaucracy where every decision was endlessly deferred, where everything aspired to be '*Kaiserlich-königlich*', *k & k*, imperial and royal. You could not move in Vienna without seeing the double-headed Hapsburg eagle or the portraits of the Emperor Franz Josef, with his moustaches and sideburns and his chest of medals, and his grandpaternal eyes following you from the window of the shop where you bought your cigars, over the little desk of the maître d' in the restaurant. You could not move in Vienna if you were young, wealthy and Jewish, without being observed by a member of your extended dynastic family. Anything you did might end up in a satirical magazine. Vienna was full of gossips, caricaturists – and cousins.

The nature of the age was much discussed around these marble café tables and between these earnest young men. Hofmannsthal, the son of a Jewish financier, argued that the nature of the age 'is multiplicity and indeterminacy'. It can rest only, he said, on '*das Gleitende*', moving, slipping, sliding: 'what other generations believed to be firm is in fact *das Gleitende*'. The nature of the age was change itself, something to be reflected in the partial and fragmentary, the melancholy and lyric, not in the grand, firm, operatic chords of the *Gründerzeit* and the Ringstrasse. 'Security,' said Schnitzler, the well-off son of a Jewish professor of laryngology, 'exists nowhere.'

Melancholy fits with the perpetual dying fall of Schubert's *Abschied*, Farewell. *Liebestod*, the love of death, was one response. Suicide was terribly common among Viktor's acquaintances. Schnitzler's daughter, Hofmannsthal's son, three of Ludwig Wittgenstein's brothers and Gustav Mahler's brother would all kill themselves. Death was a way of separating oneself from the mundane, from the snobbery and the intrigues and the gossip, drifting into *das Gleitende*. Schnitzler's list of reasons for shooting yourself in *The Way into the Open* encompasses 'Grace, or debts, from boredom with life, or purely out of affectation'. When, on 30th January 1889 the Crown Prince, Archduke Rudolf, committed suicide after murdering his young mistress Marie Vestera, suicide gained its imperial imprimatur.

It was understood that none of the sensible Ephrussi children would go as far as that. Melancholy had its place. A café. It shouldn't be brought home.

But other things were brought home.

On 25th June 1889 Viktor's sister, the long-faced, *belle laide* Anna, converted to Catholicism in order to marry Herz von Hertenreid. She has a long list of possible husbands, and now she has found a banker and a baron who comes from the right kind of family, even if he is Christian. The von Hertenreids are a family that – approving tones from my grandmother – *always spoke French*. Conversion was relatively common. I spend a day looking up the records of the Viennese Rabbinate in the archives of the Jewish community next to the synagogue in Judengasse, the names of every Jew born, married or buried in Vienna. I'm searching for her when an archivist turns. 'I remember her marriage,' she says, '1889. She has the firmest signature, confident. It almost goes through the paper.'

I can believe this. Anna seems to have been able to create trouble wherever she went. On the family tree my grandmother made for my father in the 1970s, there are pencil annotations. Anna has two children, she writes, a beautiful daughter who marries and then flees with her lover to the East, and a son who is 'not married, did nothing'. 'Anna', she continues, 'witch'.

Eleven days after Anna's wedding to her banker, Stefan, the heir-apparent – groomed for the life of the bank, with his fantastic waxed moustaches – elopes with his father's Russian Jewish mistress Estiha. Estiha only spoke Russian – this is written on the annotated family tree – *and broken German.*

Stefan was immediately disinherited. He was to receive no allowance, live in no family property, communicate with no member of the family. It was a proper Old Testament banishment, admittedly with the particularly Viennese slant of marrying your father's lover. One sin piled on another: apostasy on filial disgrace. And linguistic incompetence in a mistress. I'm not sure how to read this. Does it reflect badly on father or son, or both?

Cut off, this couple went first to Odessa, where there were still friends and a name to use. Then on to Nice. Then a succession of progressively less smart resorts along the Côte d'Azur as their money ran out. In 1893 an Odessa newspaper notes that the Baron Stefan von Ephrussi has been received into the Lutheran Evangelical faith. By 1897 he is working as a cashier in a Russian bank for foreign trade. A letter comes from a shabby Paris hotel in the 10th arrondissement in 1898. They have no children, no heirs to complicate Ignace's plans. I wonder, in passing, if Stefan kept his fine moustaches as he travelled downwards with Estiha through these circles of shabbier hotels, waiting for a telegram from Vienna.

And Viktor's world stopped still as a slammed book.

Café mornings or not, Viktor was suddenly going to be in charge of a very large and complex international business. He was to be blooded in stocks and shipments, sent to Petersburg, Odessa, Paris, Frankfurt. Precious time had been lost on the other boy. Viktor had to learn quickly what was expected of him. And this was just the start. Viktor also had to marry, and he had to have children: specifically he had to have a son. All those dreams of writing a magisterial history of Byzantium were lost. He was now the heir.

I think it might have been at around this point that Viktor developed his nervous tic of taking off his pince-nez and wiping his hand across his face from brow to chin, a reflex movement. He was clearing his mind, or arranging his public face. Or perhaps he was erasing his private face, catching it in his hand.

Viktor waited until she was seventeen and then proposed to the

*The young scholar: Viktor aged 22, 1882*

Baroness Emmy Schey von Koromla, a girl he had known since her childhood. Her parents, the Baron Paul Schey von Koromla and the English-born Evelina Landauer, were family friends, business associates of his father's, neighbours on the Ringstrasse. Viktor and Evelina were close friends, as well as contemporaries in age. They shared a love of poetry, would dance together at balls and go on shooting parties to Kövesces, the Scheys' Czechoslovakian estate.

Viktor and Emmy were married on 7th March 1899 in the synagogue in Vienna. He was thirty-nine and in love, and she was eighteen and in love. Viktor was in love with Emmy. She was in love with an artist and playboy who had no intention of marrying anyone, let alone this young decorative creature. She was not in love with Viktor.

Alongside appropriate wedding-presents from all over Europe, laid out after the wedding breakfast in the library, was a famous rope of pearls from a grandmother, the Louis XVI desk from cousin Jules and Fanny, the two ships in a gale from cousin Ignace, an Italian Madonna and Child *nach* Bellini in a huge gilt frame from uncle Maurice and aunt Beatrice, and a large diamond from someone whose name is lost. And, from cousin Charles, there was the vitrine containing the netsuke lined up on the green velvet shelves.

And then, on 3rd June, ten weeks after the wedding, Ignace died. It was sudden: there was no malingering. According to my grandmother, he died in the Palais Ephrussi with Emilie holding one hand and his mistress the other. This must have been another mistress, I realise, a mistress who was neither his son's wife nor one of his sisters-in-law.

I have a photograph of Ignace on his deathbed, his mouth still firm and decisive. He was buried in the Ephrussi family mausoleum. It is a small Doric temple that he had built with characteristic foresight to hold the Ephrussi clan in the Jewish section of the Vienna cemetery, and where he had his father, the patriarch Joachim, reinterred. Very biblical, I think, to be buried with your father, and to leave space for your sons. In his will he left legacies to seventeen of his servants, from his valet Sigmund Donnebaum (1,380 crowns) and the butler Josef (720 crowns) to the porter Alois (480 crowns) and the maids Adelheid and Emma (140 crowns). He asked Viktor to choose a picture for his nephew Charles from his collection, and suddenly I see a tenderness here, a remembrance from an uncle of his young bookish nephew and his notebooks forty years before. I wonder what Viktor found amongst all the heavy gilt frames.

And so Viktor, with his new young wife, inherited the Ephrussi bank, responsibilities that laced Vienna together with Odessa and St Petersburg and London and Paris. Included in this inheritance was the Palais Ephrussi, sundry buildings in Vienna, a huge art collection, a golden dinner service engraved with the double E, and the responsibility for the seventeen servants who worked in the Palais.

Emmy was shown round her new apartment, the *Nobelstock*, by Viktor. Her comment was to the point. 'It looks,' she said, 'like the foyer of the Opera.' The couple decided to stay upstairs on the second great floor of the Palais, a floor with fewer painted ceilings, less marble around the doors. Ignace's rooms were kept for the occasional party.

The newly married couple, my great-grandparents, have a balcony view onto the Ringstrasse, a balcony view for the new century. And the netsuke – my sleeping monk flat over his begging bowl and the deer scratching his ear – have a new home.

The vitrine needs to go somewhere. The couple have decided to leave the *Nobelstock* as a monument to Ignace; and Viktor's mother Emilie, thank God, has decided to go back to her grand hotel in Vichy where she can take the waters and be horrible to her maids. So they have a whole floor of the Palais for themselves. It is already full of pictures and furniture, of course, and there are the servants – including Emmy's new maid, a Viennese girl called Anna – but it is their own.

After a long honeymoon in Venice they have to make some decisions. Should these ivories go in the salon? Viktor's study isn't quite big enough. Or the library? He vetoes his library. In the corner of the dining-room next to the Boulle sideboards? Each of these places has its own problems. This is not an apartment of the 'most pure Empire', like Charles's delicate calibrations of objects and pictures in Paris. This is an accumulation of *stuff* from four decades of affluent shopping.

The great glass case of beautiful things has a particular difficulty for Viktor, as it comes from Paris, and he doesn't want it sitting and reminding him of an elsewhere, another life. The thing is that Viktor and Emmy are not quite sure about Charles's gift. They are wonderful, these little carvings, funny and intricate, and it is obvious that his favourite cousin Charles has been exceedingly generous. But the malachite-and-gilt clock and the pair of globes from cousins in Berlin, and the Madonna, can be placed straight away – salon, library, dining-room – and this great vitrine cannot. It is too odd and complicated, and it is also rather large.

Emmy at eighteen, startlingly beautiful and fabulously dressed, knows her mind. Viktor defers to her concerning where all these wedding-presents should go.

She is very slim with light-brown hair and beautiful grey eyes. She has a sort of luminosity, that rare quality of someone who is at home in the way she moves. Emmy moves beautifully. She has a good figure and wears dresses that show off the narrowness of her waist.

As a beautiful young baroness, Emmy has the full hand of social accomplishments. She has been brought up in two places, in the city and in the country, and has the skills for both. Her childhood in Vienna was in the Scheys' Palais, an austere piece of grand neo-classicism, a quick ten minutes', walk away from her new home with Viktor, facing out across to the Opera over a statue of Goethe looking extremely cross. She has a charming younger brother called Philippe, universally known as Pips, and two little sisters Eva and Gerty, who are still in the nursery.

Until she was thirteen, Emmy had a meek and biddable English governess, who was keen to keep the peace in the schoolroom. And then nothing. Her formal education is full of terra incognita as a result. There are great swathes about which she knows practically nothing – history being one – and she has a particular laugh when these things are mentioned.

What she does know are her languages. She is charming in both English and French, which she speaks interchangeably at home with her parents. She knows any number of children's poems in both languages and can quote great sections of *The Hunting of the Snark* and 'Jabberwocky'. And she has her German, of course.

Every weekday afternoon in Vienna since she was eight has included a dancing hour, and she is now a wonderful dancer, a favourite partner at balls for ardent young men, not least for that waist tied with a bright sash of silk. Emmy can skate like she dances. And she has learnt how to smile with interest as her parents' friends talk about opera and theatre at the late suppers they give, this being a household where business is not to be discussed. There are lots of cousins in their lives. Some of them, like the young writer Schnitzler, are rather avant-garde.

Emmy knows how to listen with a particular animation, sensing when to ask a question, when to laugh, when to turn away with the tilt of her head to another guest and leave her interlocutor looking at the nape of her neck. She has a lot of admirers, some of whom have experienced her sudden squalls. Emmy has a considerable temper.

For this life in Vienna she needs to know how to dress. Her mother, Evelina, only eighteen years older, also dresses impeccably and wears only white. White all year round: from her hats to the boots that she changes three times a day in the dusty summer. Clothes are a passion that her parents have indulged her in, partly because Emmy has an aptitude for them. Aptitude is too flat a description. It is more driven, more vocational, this way she has of changing one part of what she is wearing to make herself look different from other girls.

There was a lot of dressing up in Emmy's youth. I found an album from a weekend party where the girls had been photographed dressed up as characters from Old Master paintings. Emmy is Titian's Isabella d'Este in velvet and fur, while other cousins are pretty Chardin and Pieter de Hooch servant-girls. I make a note of Emmy's social dominance. Another photograph shows the handsome young

Hofmannsthal and the teenage Emmy dressed up as Renaissance Venetians at a wedding masque. There was also a party where they all dressed up as characters from a Hans Makart painting, the perfect opportunity for wide-brimmed hats with feathers.

Before and after marriage Emmy's other life is in Czechoslovakia, at the Schey country house in Kövesces, two hours by train from Vienna. Kövesces was a very large and very plain eighteenth-century house ('a large square box such as children draw', in the words of my grandmother) set in a flat landscape of fields, with belts of willows, birch forests and streams. A great river, the Vah, swept past, forming one of the boundaries to the estate. It was a landscape in which you could see storms passing far away and never even hear them. There was a swimming lake with fretted Moorish changing huts, lots of stables and lots of dogs. Emmy's mother Evelina bred Gordon setters – the first bitch arriving in a slatted crate on the *Orient-Express*, the great train stopping at the tiny halt on the estate. And there were her father's German pointers for the shooting – hares and partridge. Her mother enjoyed shooting and, as the time of a confinement grew nearer, used to go out on the partridge shoots with her midwife following her as well as the gamekeeper.

In Kövesces, Emmy rides. She stalks deer and shoots and walks with the dogs. As I struggle to bring the two parts of her life together, I am also slightly aghast. My picture of Jewish life in *fin-de-siècle* Vienna is perfectly burnished, mostly consisting of Freud and vignettes of acerbic and intellectual talk in the cafés. I'm rather in love with my 'Vienna as crucible of the twentieth century' motif, as are many curators and academics. Now I am in the Vienna part of the story, I am listening to Mahler and reading my Schnitzler and Loos, and feeling very Jewish myself.

My image of the period certainly doesn't stretch to include Jewish deer-stalking or Jewish discussion of the merits of different gun-dogs for different game. I am at sea, when my father rings me up to tell me that he has found something else to add to the growing file of photographs. I can tell that he is rather pleased with himself and his own vagabonding on this project. He comes down to my studio for lunch and produces a small white book from a supermarket bag. I'm not sure what it is, he says, but it should be in your 'archive'.

The book is bound in very soft white suede, sunned and worn away on the spine. The cover bears the dates 1878 and 1903. It is closed with a yellow silk ribbon, which we untie.

Inside are twelve beautiful pen-and-ink images of members of the family on separate cards, each edged with silver, each with its own carefully designed frame in Secessionist patterns, each with a cryptic quatrain in German or Latin or English, part of a poem or a snatch of a song. We work out that it must be a present for Baron Paul and Evelina's silver wedding anniversary from Emmy and her brother Pips. White suede for their mother who was always so particular about white: hats, gowns, pearls and white suede boots.

One of the silver anniversary pen-and-ink cards is of Pips in uniform playing Schubert at the piano: he has received the education that Emmy never had, with proper tutors. He has a wide circle of friends in the arts and the theatre, is a man around town in several capitals and is as impeccably dressed as his sister. A childhood memory of my great-uncle Iggie's was seeing into Pips's dressing-room at a hotel in Biarritz where they all spent a summer. The door of the wardrobe was open, and hanging on a rail were eight identical suits. They were all white: an epiphany, a vision of heaven.

*Pips playing the piano. An image from
Joseph Olbrich's Secessionist album, 1903*

Pips appears as the protagonist of a highly successful novel of the
time by the German Jewish novelist Jakob Wassermann, a sort of
Mitteleuropa version of Buchan's Richard Hannay in *The Thirty-
Nine Steps*. Our aesthetic hero is a pal of archdukes and manages to
outshoot anarchists. He is erudite about incunabula and Renaissance art, rescues rare jewels and is loved by everyone. The book is
viscous with infatuation.

Another pen-and-ink sketch in this album shows Emmy dancing
at a ball, leaning back as a slim young man leads her round the floor.
A cousin, I presume, as this willowy dancer is most certainly not
Viktor. One drawing shows Paul Schey almost obscured by *Die Neue
Freie Presse*, an owl sitting in deep reserve behind him on his chair.
Evelina skating. A pair of legs in striped bathing shorts disappearing

into the swimming lake at Kövesces. Each picture also contains a little image of a bottle of eau-de-vie or wine or schnapps and a few bars of music.

The cards are the work of Josef Olbrich. He was the artist at the heart of the radical Secession movement and designer of its Pavilion in Vienna with an owl relief and a golden dome of laurel leaves, a quiet, elegant place of refuge with walls that he described as 'white and gleaming, holy and chaste'. Since we are in Vienna where everything is subject to intense scrutiny, it also receives vitriol. It is the Grave of the Mahdi, say the wags, The Crematorium. That filigree dome is 'a head of cabbage'. I give Olbrich's album suitable scrutiny, but it is a lost acrostic puzzle, utterly unknowable. Why the eau-de-vie, why that piece of music? It is very Viennese, an urbane view of their country life in Kövesces. It is a window into Emmy's world, a whole warm world of family jokes.

How could you possibly not know you had this? I ask my father. What else have you got in the suitcase under your bed?

## 16. 'LIBERTY HALL'

I feel confident that there will be less to puzzle over in Emmy von Ephrussi's married life in Vienna. This is city life with a very different kind of family and with its own unshakeable rhythm, just ten minutes' walk away from her childhood home in the other Palais.

The new rhythm started soon after the return from honeymoon, when Emmy discovered she was pregnant. Elisabeth, my grandmother, was born nine months after the wedding. Viktor's mother Emilie – in my portrait, suave and implacable in her pearls – died in Vichy soon after, at the age of sixty-four. She was buried in Vichy, rather than returning to Ignace's great mausoleum, and I wonder if she planned this final separation.

After Elisabeth comes Gisela, born three years later, and Ignace – young Iggie – is the third. They are carefully named Viennese children from careful Jewish parents. Elisabeth is named after the late adored Empress, Gisela after the Archduchess Gisela, the Emperor's daughter. Iggie is the son and that is straightforward. Ignace Leon is named after his late grandfather and after his rich, childless, duellist Parisian uncle, and after his late great-uncle Leon. The Parisians have only had daughters. Thank God there is a son for the Ephrussi at last. And that the Palais is big enough to have nurseries and schoolrooms out of earshot.

The Palais has its diurnal pace, quickening and slackening for the servants. There is lots of carrying up and down the corridors. Endless carrying of hot water to the dressing-room, coals to the study, break-fast to the morning-room, the morning newspaper to the study, covered dishes, laundry, telegrams, post three times a day, messages, candlesticks for dinner, the evening newspaper delivered to Viktor's dressing-room.

There is a pattern too for Anna, Emmy's lady's maid. It starts when she brings the silver can of warm water at half-past seven and the tray of English tea to Emmy's bedroom. It only ends late at night when she has brushed Emmy's hair and fetched her a glass of water and a plate of charcoal biscuits.

In the courtyard of the Palais a fiacre stands attendant all day with a coachman in livery. There are two black carriage horses, Rinalda and Arabella. A second carriage waits to take the children to the Prater or the Schönbrunn. The coachmen wait. The porter, Alois, stands by the huge doors to the Ringstrasse ready to open the gates.

Vienna means dinner parties. There are endless discussions of placement. Every afternoon the butler and an assistant footman lay the table with a tape measure. There are discussions of whether it is safe to get ducks from Paris, if they come crated the day before on the *Orient-Express*. There are florists, a dinner with a row of small orange trees in pots bearing hollowed-out oranges filled with parfait. The children are allowed to watch through a peephole as all the guests arrive.

There are afternoons at home receiving guests, with a tea table on which a silver samovar steams on a large silver tray: teapot, cream jug and sugar basin to hand, and trays of open sandwiches and iced cakes from Demel's, the palace of confectionery in Kohlmarkt near the Hofburg. Ladies leave their furs in the hall, and the officers their képis and swords, and gentlemen carry their top hats and their gloves and place them on the floor next to their chairs.

There is a pattern to the year too.

January is a chance to get away from wintry Vienna. Nice or Monte Carlo with Viktor. The children are left behind. They visit Viktor's uncle Maurice and aunt Beatrice Ephrussi in the new pink Villa Ile-de-France in Cap Ferrat – now the Villa Ephrussi-Rothschild. Admire the collections of French pictures, French Empire furniture, French porcelain. Admire the improvements in the gardens, where parts of the hillside are being removed and a canal is being dug in imitation of the Alhambra. The twenty gardeners all wear white.

April is Paris with Viktor. The children are left behind. They stay chez Fanny in the Hôtel Ephrussi in the place d'Iéna, and there is lots of shopping for Emmy and days at the offices of Ephrussi et Cie for Viktor. Paris is not the same.

Charles Ephrussi, beloved owner of the *Gazette,* Chevalier of the *Légion d'honneur*, supporter of artists, friend of poets, collector of the netsuke, Viktor's favourite cousin, has died on 30th September 1905 at the age of fifty-five.

The notice in the newspapers begs those who have not received an invitation not to come to the funeral. The pall-bearers – his brothers, Theodore Reinach, the Marquis de Cheveniers – were in tears. There have been numerous obituaries, talking of his '*délicatesse naturelle*' and his uprightness and sense of propriety. The *Gazette* has published a memorial obituary surrounded by a black border:

It was with stupor and profound chagrin that all those who knew him learnt – at the end of last September – of the sudden illness and then the death of the lovable and good man, of the highest of intelligence that was Charles Ephrussi. In Parisian society, particularly in the world of arts and letters, he had developed numerous friendships with people who succumbed quite naturally to the charm and certainty of his manner, the elevation of his spirit and the gentleness of his heart. Anybody who knocked at his door witnessed his good charming grace, welcoming young artists as he did their elders, he had befriended – we can affirm it without a single demur – all those who had approached him.

Proust writes his condolences to the obituarist. On reading this obituary in the *Gazette*, 'those who did not know M. Ephrussi will come to love him, and those who did know him will be full of recollections'. Charles has left Emmy a golden necklace in his will. He has left a pearl collar to Louise, and his estate to his niece Fanny Reinach, who is married to the Hellenist scholar.

And, shockingly, Charles's brother Ignace Ephrussi, *mondain*, dueller, *amateur de la femme*, has also died of a poor heart at the age of sixty. He is remembered as a perfect rider, to be seen on his grey early in the morning in the Bois de Boulogne saddled *à la russe*. Generous and punctilious, he has left the three young Ephrussi children, Elisabeth, Gisela and Iggie, 30,000 francs each in his will and he has even left Emmy's younger sisters, Gerty and Eva, something too. The brothers have been buried together in Montmartre in the family tomb alongside their long-dead parents and their beloved sister.

Soon after visiting Paris – much emptier without the animation of Charles and Ignace – comes the summer. This starts in July with the Gutmanns, Jewish financiers and philanthropists, Viktor and Emmy's closest friends. They have five children, so Elisabeth, Gisela and Iggie are invited for several weeks to their country house, Schloss Jaidhof, fifty miles from Vienna. Viktor stays put in Vienna.

August is Switzerland at the Chalet Ephrussi with the Parisian cousins Jules and Fanny. Take the children and Viktor. Do very little. Try to keep the children quiet. Hear about Paris. Take the boat out onto Lake Lucerne from the boathouse where the Russian imperial flag flies, with one of the footmen to do the rowing. Go to the Concours Hippique in Lucerne with Jules in the motor-car to see the show-jumping, with ices at Hugeni afterwards.

September and October are at Kövesces with the children and parents, Pips and lots of cousins. Viktor comes for a few days at a time. Swim, walk, ride, shoot.

At Kövesces there is an eccentric collection of people gathered together to educate Emmy's sisters, Gerty and Eva, twelve and fifteen years junior to her. These now include a French lady's maid to give them a proper Parisian accent, an elderly schoolmaster to teach them the three Rs, a governess from Trieste for German and Italian, and finally a failed concert pianist (Mr Minotti) to teach them music and chess. Emmy's mother gives them English dictation and reads Shakespeare with them. There is also the elderly Viennese bootmaker who makes the white suede boots about which Evelina is so very particular. Struck low, he comes to convalesce on the estate, is given a pleasant sunny room and stays for the rest of his life, keeping her in footwear and taking charge of the dogs.

The traveller Patrick Leigh Fermor stayed in Kövesces on his walk across Europe in the 1930s and described it as still having the atmosphere of an English rectory, with piles of books in all possible languages and desks cluttered with odd objects made from antlers and silver. It was 'Liberty Hall', said Pips, welcoming him in his perfect English to the library. Kövesces radiated the sense of self-sufficiency that comes about when there are lots of children in a big house. In my father's blue paper folder there is a yellowing manuscript of a play called *Der Grossherzog* (*The Archduke*) put on one summer before the First World War by all the cousins in the drawing-room. Babies under two and dogs are strictly forbidden.

Mr Minotti plays the piano each night after dinner. The children play 'Kim's game'. Objects – a card case, pince-nez, a shell and once, thrillingly, Pips's revolver – are placed on a tray and brought in uncovered for thirty seconds. The linen is replaced and you then write down what you can recall. Elisabeth, boringly, wins every single time.

Pips invites his cosmopolitan friends to stay.

December is Vienna and Christmas. Though they are Jewish, they celebrate with lots of presents.

And Emmy's life seems set, not exactly in stone, but in amber. It seems preserved, the series of period stories, both generic and precious, that I promised myself I would escape from when I set out a year ago. The netsuke seem so far away as I keep circling the Palais.

I extend my stay in Vienna at the Pension Baronesse. They have kindly fixed my glasses, but the world is still slightly askew. I can't shake off my anxiety. My uncle in London has been searching for information for me and has produced twelve pages of a memoir that my grandmother Elisabeth wrote about growing up in the Palais, and I have brought them to read *in situ*. It is a sunny morning of breath-catching cold and I take them to the Café Central, with light streaming through the Gothic windows. There is a model of the writer Peter Altenberg holding the menu, and everything is very clean and carefully presented. This was Viktor's second café, I think, before it all went so wrong.

The café, this street, Vienna itself is a theme park: a *fin-de-siècle* film-set, glitteringly Secessionist. Fiacres trundling round with coachmen in greatcoats. The waiters have period moustaches. Strauss is everywhere, seeping from the chocolate shops. I keep expecting Mahler to walk in, or Klimt to start an argument. I keep thinking of a dreadful film I saw years ago when I was at university. It was set in Paris, and Picasso kept walking past, and Gertrude Stein and James Joyce were discussing Modernism over their Pernod. This is the problem I'm having here, I realise, assailed by one cliché after another. My Vienna has thinned into other people's Vienna.

I've been reading the seventeen novels of Joseph Roth, the Austrian Jewish novelist, some set in Vienna during the last years of the Hapsburg Empire. It is in the unimpeachable Efrussi Bank – Roth spells it in the Russian manner – that Trotta deposits his wealth in *The Radetzky March*. Ignace Ephrussi himself is sketched as a rich jeweller in *The Spider's Web*: 'lank and tall, and always [wearing] black, with a high collared coat which just revealed a black silk stock pinned by a pearl the size of a hazelnut'. His wife, the beautiful Frau Efrussi, is 'a lady: Jewish: but a lady'. Everyone had an easy life, says Theodor, the young and bitter Gentile protagonist, employed by the family as a tutor, 'the Efrussis the easiest of all . . . Pictures in gold frames hung in the hall and a footman in green and gold livery bowed as he escorted you in.'

The real keeps slipping out of my hands. The lives of my family in Vienna were refracted into books, just like Charles in Proust's Paris. The dislike of the Ephrussi keeps turning up in novels.

I stumble. I realise that I do not understand what it means to be part of an assimilated, acculturated Jewish family. I simply don't understand. I know what they didn't do: they never went to synagogue, but their births and marriages are recorded here by the Rabbinate. I know that they paid their dues to the Israelitische Kultusgemeinde, gave money to Jewish charities. I've been to see Joachim and Ignace's mausoleum in the Jewish section of the cemetery, and worried about its broken cast-iron gate and whether I should pay to get it fixed. Zionism didn't seem to hold many attractions, for them. I remember those rude comments from Herzl when he wrote to them for donations and got brushed off. The Ephrussi, speculators. I wonder whether it was plain embarrassment at the fervent Jewishness of the enterprise and not wanting to attract attention to themselves. Or whether it was a symptom of their confidence in their new homeland here on Zionstrasse, or on the rue de Monceau. They simply didn't see why others needed another Zion.

Does assimilation mean that they never came up against naked prejudice? Does it mean that you understood where the limits of your social world were and you stuck to them? There is a Jockey Club in Vienna, as in Paris, and Viktor was a member, but Jews weren't allowed to hold office. Did this matter to him in the slightest? It was understood that married Gentile women never visited Jewish households, never came to leave a card, never visited on one of the interminable afternoons. Vienna meant that only Gentile bachelors, Count Mensdorf, Count Lubienski, the young Prince Montenuovo, left cards and were then invited. Once married they never came, no matter how good the dinners were, or how pretty the hostess. Did this matter at all? These seem such gossamer threads of rudeness.

I spend my last morning of this visit in the records of the Vienna Jewish community next to the synagogue off Judengasse. There are police nearby. In the latest elections the far right has just won a third of the popular vote, and no one knows if the synagogue is a target. There have been so many threats that I must pass through a complex security system. Finally inside, I watch as the archivist pulls out the folio records, one striped volume after another, and lays them on the lectern. Each birth and marriage and death, each conversion, the whole of Jewish Vienna faithfully recorded.

In 1899 Vienna has its own Jewish orphanages and hospitals, schools and libraries, newspapers and journals. It has twenty-two synagogues. And, I realise, I know nothing about any of them: the Ephrussi family are so perfectly assimilated they have disappeared into Vienna.

Elisabeth's memoir is a tonic: twelve unsentimental pages written for her sons in the 1970s. 'The house I was born in stood, and still stands, outwardly unaltered, on the corner of the Ring . . .' She gives details of the running of the household, she gives the names of the horses, and she walks me through the rooms in the Palais. Finally, I think, I will find out where Emmy has hidden the netsuke.

If Emmy turns right out of the nursery and goes along the corridor she enters the sides of the courtyard with the kitchens and sculleries, the pantry and the silver-room – where the light burns all day – and then on to the butler's room and the servants' hall. At the end of this corridor are all the maids' rooms, rooms whose windows open only into the courtyard, some yellow light filtering in through the glassed roof, but no fresh air. Her maid Anna's room is down there somewhere.

When Emmy turns left she is in her drawing-room. She has hung it with pale-green silk brocade. The carpets are a very pale yellow. Her furniture is Louis XV, chairs and *fauteuils* of inlaid woods with bronze mounts and fat striped silk cushions. There are occasional tables, each with their little set-piece of bibelots, and a larger table on which she could perform the intricacies of making tea. There is a grand piano that is never played and a Renaissance Italian cabinet with folding doors, painted on the inside, and very small drawers that the children aren't meant to play with, but do. When Elisabeth reached between the tiny gilded twisty columns on either side of an arch and pressed upwards, a tiny secret drawer came out with an exhaled breath.

There is light in these rooms, trembling reflections and glints of silver and porcelain and polished fruitwood, and shadows from the linden trees. In the spring flowers are sent up each week from Kövesces. It is a perfect place to display a vitrine with cousin Charles' netsuke, but they are not here.

On from the drawing-room is the library, the largest room on this floor of the Palais. It is painted black and red, like Ignace's great suite of rooms on the floor below, with a black-and-red Turkey carpet and huge ebony bookshelves lining the walls and large tobacco-coloured leather armchairs and sofas. A large brass chandelier hangs over an ebony table inlaid with ivory flanked by the pair of globes. This is Viktor's room, thousands of his books running over the walls, his Latin and Greek histories and his German literature and his poetry and his lexicons. Some of the bookcases have a fine golden mesh over them and are locked with a key that he keeps on his watch chain. Still no vitrine.

And on from the library is the dining-room, with walls covered in Gobelin tapestries of the hunt, bought by Ignace in Paris, and windows overlooking the courtyard, but with the curtains drawn, so that the room is in perpetual gloom. This must be the dining table where the gold dinner service is set out, each plate and bowl engraved with ears of corn and a double Ephrussi E slap-bang in the middle, the boat with its puffed-out sails skimming across a golden sea.

The gold dinner service must have been Ignace's idea. His furniture is everywhere. Renaissance cabinets, carved baroque chests, a huge Boulle desk that could only be kept in the ballroom downstairs. His pictures are everywhere, too. Lots of Old Masters, a Holy Family, a Florentine Madonna. There are seventeenth-century Dutch pictures by some quite good artists: Wouwermans, Cuyp, something after Frans Hals. There were also lots and lots of *Junge Frau*, some by Hans Makart; interchangeable young ladies in interchangeable frocks in rooms surrounded by 'velvets, carpets, genius, panther skins, knickknacks, peacock feathers, chests, and lutes' (Musil in acidic mood). All of them framed in heavy gold or heavy black. No Parisian vitrine full of netsuke amongst these pictures, this spectacular, theatrical display, this treasure-house.

Everything here, each grandiloquent picture and cabinet, seems immovable in the light that filters in from the glassed-in courtyard. Musil understood this atmosphere. In great old houses there is a muddle where hideous new furniture stands carelessly alongside magnificent old, inherited pieces. In the rooms of the Palais belonging to the ostentatious nouveaux riches, everything is too defined, there is 'some hardly perceptible widening of the space between the pieces of furniture or the dominant position of a painting on a wall, the tender, clear echo of a great sound that had faded away'.

I think of Charles with all his treasures, and know that it was his passion for them that kept them moving. Charles could not resist the world of things: touching them; studying them; buying them; rearranging them. The vitrine of netsuke that he has given to Viktor and Emmy made a space in his salon for something new. He kept his rooms in flux.

The Palais Ephrussi is the exact opposite. Under the grey-glassed roof, the whole house is like a vitrine that you cannot escape.

At either end of the long enfilade are Viktor and Emmy's private rooms. Viktor's dressing-room has his cupboards and chests of drawers and a long mirror. There is a life-size plaster bust of his tutor, Herr Wessel, 'whom he had very much loved. Herr Wessel had been a Prussian and a great admirer of Bismarck and of all things German.' The other great thing in the room, never discussed, is a very large – and highly unsuitable – Italian painting of *Leda and the Swan*. In her memoir Elisabeth wrote that she 'used to stare at it – it was huge – every time I went in to see my father change into a stiff shirt and dinner jacket for going out in the evening, and could never discover what the objection might be'. Viktor has already explained that there is no space for knick-knacks here.

Emmy's dressing-room is at the other end of the corridor, a corner room with windows looking out across the Ring to the Votivkirche and onto the Schottengasse. It has the beautiful Louis XVI desk given to the couple by Jules and Fanny, with its gently bowed legs with ormolu mounts ending in gilt hooves, and drawers that are lined with soft leather in which Emmy keeps her writing paper and letters tied up in ribbons. And she has a full-length mirror hinged in three parts so that she can see herself properly when dressing. It takes up most of the room. And a dressing-table and washstand with a silver-rimmed glass basin and a matching glass jug with a silver top.

And here at last we find the black lacquer cabinet – 'as tall as a tall man' in Iggie's memory – with its green velvet-lined shelves. Emmy has put the vitrine in her dressing-room, with its mirrored back and all 264 netsuke from cousin Charles. This is where my brindled wolf has ended up.

This makes so much sense, and yet it makes no sense at all. Who comes into a dressing-room? It is hardly a social space, and certainly not a salon. If the boxwood turtles and the persimmon and the cracked little ivory of the girl in her bath are kept here on their green velvet shelves, this means that they do not have to be explained at Emmy's at-homes. They do not have to be mentioned at all by Viktor. Could it be embarrassment that brings the vitrine here?

Or was the decision to take the netsuke away from the public gaze intentional, away from all that Makart pomposity; putting them into the one room that was completely Emmy's own because she was intrigued by them? Was it to save them from the dead hand of *Ringstrassenstil*? There was not much in these Ephrussi parade grounds of gilt furniture and ormolu that you might want to have near you. The netsuke are intimate objects for an intimate room. Did Emmy want something that was simply – and literally – untouched by her father-in-law Ignace? A little bit of Parisian glamour?

This is her room. She spent a great deal of time in it. She changed three times a day – sometimes more. Putting on a hat to go to the races, with lots of little curls pinned one by one to the underside of the hat's wide brim, took forty minutes. To put on the long embroidered ballgown with a hussar's jacket, intricate with frogging, took for ever. There was dressing up for parties, for shopping, dinner, visiting, riding to the Prater and balls. Each hour in this dressing-room was a calibration of corset, dress, gloves and hat with the day, the shrugging-off of one self and the lacing into another. She has to be sewn into some dresses, Anna, kneeling at her feet, producing thread, needle, thimble from the pocket of her apron. Emmy has furs, sable trimming to a hem, an arctic fox around her neck in one photograph, a six-foot stole of bear looped over a gown in another. An hour could pass with Anna fetching different gloves.

*Emmy and the Archduke, Vienna, 1906*

Emmy dresses to go out. It is winter 1906 in a Viennese street and she is talking to an archduke. They are smiling as she hands him some primroses. She is wearing a pin-striped costume: an A-line skirt with a deep panel at the hem cut across the grain and a matching close-cut Zouave jacket. It is a *walking costume*. To dress for that walk down Herrengasse would have taken an hour and a half: pantalettes, chemise in fine batiste or crêpe de Chine, corset to nip in the waist, stockings, garters, button boots, skirt with hooks up the plaquette, then either a blouse or a chemisette – so no bulk on her arms – with a high-stand collar and lace jabot, then the jacket done up with a false front, then her small purse – a reticule – hanging on a chain, jewellery, fur hat with striped taffeta bow to echo the costume, white gloves, flowers. And no scent; she does not wear it.

The vitrine in the dressing-room is sentinel to a ritual that took place twice a year in spring and autumn, the ritual of choosing a wardrobe for the coming season. Ladies did not go to a dressmaker to inspect the new models; the models were brought to them. The head of a dressmaker's would go to Paris and select gowns that came carefully packed in several huge boxes, with an elderly white-haired, black-suited gentleman, Herr Schuster. His boxes were piled up in the passage, where he sat with them; they were carried into Emmy's dressing-room one by one by Anna. When Emmy was dressed, Herr Schuster was ushered in for pronouncement. 'Of course he always approved, but if he found Mama inclined to favour one of them to the extent of wanting to try it on again, he waxed ecstatic, saying that the dress absolutely "screamed for the Baroness".' The children waited for this moment and then would race down the corridor to the nursery in panicky fits of hysterics.

There is a picture of Emmy taken in the salon soon after she married Viktor. She must be pregnant with Elisabeth already, but not showing. She is dressed like Marie Antoinette in a cropped velvet jacket over a long white skirt, a play between severity and nonchalance. Her ringlets conform to what is *au courant* in the spring of 1900: 'coiffure is less stiff than it was formerly; fringes are prohibited. The hair is first crimped into large waves, then combed back and twisted into a moderately high coil . . . locks are allowed to escape onto the forehead, left in their natural ringed form,' writes a journalist. Emmy has a black hat with feathers. One hand rests on a French marble-topped chest of drawers and the other holds a cane. She must be just down from the dressing-room and off to another ball. She looks at me confidently, aware of how gorgeous she is.

Emmy has her admirers – many admirers, according to my

great-uncle Iggie – and dressing for others is as much a pleasure as undressing. From the start of her marriage she has lovers, too.

This is not unusual in Vienna. It is slightly different from Paris. This is a city of *chambres séparées* at restaurants, where you can eat and seduce as in Schnitzler's *Reigen* or *La Ronde*: 'A private room in the restaurant "zum Riedhof". Subdued comfortable elegance. The gas fire is burning. On the table the remains of a meal – cream pastries, fruit, cheese etc. Hungarian white wine. The HUSBAND is smoking a Havana cigar, leaning back in one corner of the sofa. The SWEET YOUNG THING is sitting in an armchair beside him, spooning down whipped cream from a pastry with evident pleasure . . .' In Vienna at the turn of the century there is the cult of the *süsse Mädel*, 'simple girls who lived for flirtation with young men from good

*Emmy dressed as Marie Antoinette*
*in the salon of the Palais Ephrussi, 1900*

homes'. There is endless flirtation. Strauss's *Der Rosenkavalier* with its text by Hofmannsthal – in which changing costumes, changing lovers and changing hats are all held in suspended amusement – is new in 1911 and is wildly popular. Schnitzler has problems, he confides in his journal of his sexual congresses, in keeping up with the demands of his two mistresses.

Sex is inescapable in Vienna. Prostitutes crowd the pavements. They advertise on the back page of *Die Neue Freie Presse*. Everything and everyone is catered for. Karl Kraus quotes them in his journal *Die Fackel*: 'Travelling Companion Sought, young, congenial, Christian, independent. Replies to "Invert 69" Poste Restante Habsburgergasse'. Sex is argued over by Freud. In Otto Weininger's *Sex and Character*, the cult book of 1903, women are, by nature, amoral and in need of direction. Sex is golden in Klimt's *Judith*, *Danae*, *The Kiss*, dangerous in Schiele's tumbled bodies.

To be a modern woman in Vienna, to be *comme il faut*, it is understood that your domestic life has a little latitude. Some of Emmy's aunts and cousins have marriages of convenience: her aunt Anny, for instance. Everyone knows that Hans Count Wiltschek is the natural father of her cousins, the twin brothers Herbert and Witold von Schey von Koromla. Count Wiltschek is handsome and extremely glamorous: an explorer, the funder of Antarctic expeditions. A close friend of the late Crown Prince Rudolf, he has had islands named after him.

I've delayed my return to London – I'm finally on the track of Ignace's will and want to see how he divided his fortune. The Adler Society, the genealogical society of Vienna, is only open to members and their guests on Wednesday evenings after six o'clock. The society offices are through a grand hall on the second floor of a house just down from Freud's apartment. I duck through a lowish door and into a long corridor hung with portraits of Vienna's mayors. Bookcases with box-files of deaths and obituaries to the left, aristocrats, runs of *Debrett's* and the *Almanach de Gotha* to the right. Everything else and everyone else, straight on. At last I see people at work on their projects, carrying files, copying ledgers. I'm not sure what genealogical societies are usually like, but this one has completely unexpected roars of laughter and scholars calling out across the floor, requesting help in deciphering difficult handwriting.

I ask very delicately about the friendships of my great-grandmother Emmy von Ephrussi, née Schey von Koromla, circa 1900. There is much collegiate joshing. Emmy's friendships of a hundred years ago are no secret, all her former lovers are known: someone mentions a cavalry officer, another a Hungarian roué, a prince. Was it Ephrussi who kept identical clothes in two different households so that she could start her day either with her husband or her lover? The gossip is still so alive: the Viennese seem to have no secrets at all. It makes me feel painfully English.

I think of Viktor, son of one sexually insatiable man, brother of another, and I see him opening a brown parcel of books from his dealer in Berlin with a silver paper knife at his library table. I see him reaching into his waistcoat pocket for the thin matches he keeps there for lighting his cigars. I see the ebb and flow of energy through the house, like water running into pools and out again. What I cannot see is Viktor in Emmy's dressing-room looking down into the vitrine, unlocking it and picking out a netsuke. I'm not sure that he is even a man who would sit and talk to Emmy as she got dressed, with Anna fussing around her. I'm not sure what they really talk about at all. Cicero? Hats?

I see him moving his hand across his face as he readjusts himself before he goes every morning to his office. Viktor goes out onto the Ring, turns right, first right into the Schottengasse, first left and he is there. He has begun to take his valet Franz with him. Franz sits at a desk in the outer office, so that Viktor can read undisturbed inside. Thank God for clerks who can tabulate all those banking columns correctly, as Viktor makes notes on history in his beautiful slanting handwriting. He is a middle-aged Jewish man, in love with his young and beautiful wife.

There is no gossip about Viktor in the Adler.

I think of Emmy at eighteen, newly installed with her vitrine of ivories in the great glassed-in house on the corner of the Ring; I remember Walter Benjamin's description of a woman in a nineteenth-century interior. 'It encased her so deeply in the dwelling's interior,' he wrote, 'that one might be reminded of a compass case where the instrument with all its accessories lies embedded in deep, usually violet, folds of velvet.'

The children in the Palais Ephrussi have nurses and nannies. The nurses are Viennese and kind, and the nannies are English. Because the nannies are English, their breakfast is English and there is always porridge and toast. There is a large lunch with pudding, and then there is afternoon tea, with bread and butter and jam and small cakes, and after that is supper, with milk and stewed fruit 'to keep them regular'.

On special days the children are required to be part of Emmy's at-homes. Elisabeth and Gisela are dressed in starched muslin dresses with sashes, while poor Iggie, who is on the plump side, has to wear a black velvet Little Lord Fauntleroy suit with an Irish lace collar. Gisela has big blue eyes. She is a particular pet of the visiting ladies, and Charles's little Renoir gypsy when they visit the Chalet Ephrussi, so pretty that Emmy (tactless) has her portrait done in red chalk, and Baron Albert Rothschild, an amateur photographer, asks for her to be brought to his studio to be photographed. The children are driven in the carriage for a daily walk with the English nannies in the Prater, where the air is less dusty than on the Ringstrasse. A footman comes too, walking behind in a fawn greatcoat and wearing a top hat with an Ephrussi badge stuck into it.

There are two set times when the children see their mother: dressing for dinner and Sunday mornings. Half-past ten on a Sunday morning marks the moment when the English nanny and governess leave for morning service at the English church and Mama visits the nursery. In her brief memoir, Elisabeth described 'Those two divine Sunday morning hours . . . She had made haste that morning with her toilette and was dressed very simply in a black skirt, down to the ground of course, and a green shirt-waist with a high stiff white collar and white cuffs, her hair beautifully piled up on top of her head. She was lovely and she smelt divinely . . .'

Together, they would take down the heavy picture books with their rich maroon covers: Edmund Dulac's *Midsummer Night's Dream, Sleeping Beauty* and, best of all, *Beauty and the Beast* with its figures of horror. Each Christmas brought the new *Fairy Book* of Andrew Lang, ordered from London by the children's English grandmother: Grey, Violet, Crimson, Brown, Orange, Olive and Rose. A book could last a year. Each child would choose a favourite story:

*Gisela and Elisabeth, 1906*

'The White Wolf', 'The Queen of the Flowery Isles', 'The Boy Who Found Fear at Last', 'What Came of Picking Flowers', 'The Limping Fox', 'The Street Musician'.

Read aloud, a story from the *Fairy Books* is less than half an hour long. Each story starts with 'Once upon a time'. Some stories have a cottage on the edge of the forest, like the birch and pine forests at Kövesces. Some of the stories include the white wolf, like the one shot by the gamekeeper near the house, and shown to the children and their cousins on an early autumn morning in the stable yard. Or the bronze wolf's head on the door of the Palais Schey, whose muzzle gets rubbed every time they pass it.

There are strange meetings in these stories, encounters with the bird-charmer with a flock of finches on his hat and arms – like the one you see standing in a circle of children on the Ringstrasse outside the gates of the Volksgarten. Or with pedlars. Like the *Schnorrer* with his basket of buttons and pencils and postcards hanging from his black coat, who stands by the gates out onto Franzenring and to whom they have been told by their father they must be polite.

Lots of stories include the Princess getting dressed in her gown and tiara to go to the ball, like Mama. Lots of stories have a magic palace in them with a ballroom, like the room downstairs that you see lit with candles at Christmas. All the stories finish with 'The End' and a kiss from Mama, and then no more stories for another whole week. Emmy was a wonderful story-teller, said Iggie.

The other time that the children regularly see her is when she is dressing to go out and they are allowed into her dressing-room.

Emmy would change out of her day-clothes, in which she had received or visited friends, into her clothes for dinner at home or, the opera, or a party or, best of all, a ball. Dresses would be laid out over the chaise longue and there would be a lengthy discussion with the expert Anna over which one to wear. The eyes of my great-uncle Iggie used to fire as he described her animation. If Viktor had Ovid and Tacitus – and his *Leda* – at one end of the corridor, then at the other end Emmy could describe dresses that her mother had worn season by season, how lengths were changing, how the weight and fall of a gown altered the way you moved, the differences between a muslin, gauze or tulle scarf across your shoulders in the evening. She knows about Paris fashion and what is *à la mode* in Vienna, and how to play the two. She is especially good on hats: a velvet hat with a huge ribbon on it to meet the Emperor; a fur toque with an ostrich feather, worn with a column dress trimmed in black fur; the best hat in the line of Jewish ladies at a charity do in a small ballroom somewhere. Something very wide indeed with a hydrangea on its brim. From Kövesces, Emmy sends to her mother a postcard of herself wearing a dark Makart hat: 'Tascha shot a buck today. How is your cold? Do you like my newest affected pictures?'

Dressing is the hour when Anna brushes her hair and laces corsets, fastens innumerable hooks and eyes, fetches variant gloves and shawls and hats, when Emmy chooses her jewellery and stands in front of the three great panels of mirror.

And this is when the children are allowed to play with the netsuke. The key is turned in the black lacquer cabinet and the door is opened.

## 19. TYPES OF THE OLD CITY

The children in the dressing-room choose their favourite carving and play with it on the pale-yellow carpet. Gisela loved the Japanese dancer, holding her fan against the brocade gown, caught in mid-step. Iggie loved the wolf, a tight dark tangle of limbs, faint markings all along its flanks, gleaming eyes and a snarl. And he loved the bundle of kindling tied up with rope, and the beggar who has fallen asleep over his begging bowl so that all you see is the top of his bald head. There is also a dried fish, all scales and shrunken eyes, with a small rat scuttling over it proprietorially; its eyes are inlaid jet. And there is the mad old man with his bony back and bulging eyes, gnawing on a fish with an octopus in his other hand. Elisabeth, contrary, loved the masks with their abstracted memory of faces.

You could arrange these carvings, ivory and wood, all the fourteen rats in one long row, the three tigers, the beggars over there, the children, the masks, the shells, the fruits.

You could arrange them by colour, all the way from the dark-brown medlar to the gleaming ivory deer. Or by size. The smallest is the single rat with black inlaid eyes chewing his tail, little bigger than the magenta stamp issued to celebrate the sixtieth year of the Emperor's reign.

Or you muddled them up, so that your sister can't find the girl in her brocade robes. Or you could stockade the dog and her puppies with all the tigers, and she would have to get out – and she did.

Or you could find the one of the woman washing herself in the wooden bathtub, and the even more intriguing one that looked like a mussel shell, until you opened it up and discovered the man and woman with no clothes on. Or you could scare your brother with the one of the boy trapped in the bell by the witch-snake, with her long black hair trailing round and round.

And you tell stories about these carvings to your mother, and she chooses one and starts a story about it to you. She picks up the netsuke of the child and the mask. She is good with stories.

There are so many that you can never really count them, never know that you have seen them all. And that is the point of these toys in their mirrored cabinet, extending onwards and onwards. They are a complete world, a complete space to play in, until the time comes to put them back again, until Mama is dressed and choosing her fan and her shawl, and then she gives you a goodnight kiss and you have to put the netsuke back now.

They go back into the vitrine, the samurai with the sword half out of the scabbard as the guard at the front, and the small key is turned in the lock of the cabinet. Anna rearranges the fur tippet around Emmy's neck and fusses at the fall of her sleeves. The nursemaid comes to take you down to the nursery.

And while the netsuke are playthings in this room in Vienna, they are being taken very seriously elsewhere. They are being collected across Europe. The first collections put together by the pioneer collectors are being auctioned for substantial amounts at the Hôtel Drouot. The dealer Siegfried Bing, now a force in Paris with his galleries, Maison de l'Art Nouveau, is putting netsuke into the best possible hands. He is the expert, the writer of prefaces to the sales catalogues of the collections of the late Philippe

Burty (140 netsuke), the late Edmond de Goncourt (140 netsuke), the late M. Garie (200 netsuke).

The first German history of netsuke, with illustrations and advice on how to care for them and even how to display them, is published in Leipzig in 1905. The best policy is never to display them at all, and to put them under lock and key and bring them out occasionally. But then, says the author, plaintively, we must have friends to share our interests, friends who can devote a few hours to art. This is not possible in Europe. So if you must have netsuke so that you can see them, then you should have a shallow glass case in which you can put two rows of netsuke, and a mirror or green plush should be placed in the back of the cabinet. Without knowing it, the vitrine in the dressing-room overlooking the Ringstrasse obeys many of the strictures of Herr Albert Brockhaus in his huge and magisterial book. 'It is advisable,' he writes:

to keep them from being exposed to dust by putting them into glass cases with glass edges. Dust fills up the holes, makes the raised work coarse, kills the gloss and takes away from the carving a great deal of the charm. When Netsukes are placed together with curios, trinkets and other objects on the mantel pieces, there is a danger of their being broken by careless domestics, swept away, or even carried to an unknown destination in the folds of a woman's dress upon the occasion of a friendly visit. One of my Netsukes one evening made such a trip unbeknown to the lady who carried it through the streets until she finally discovered it and returned it to me.

The netsuke could not feel safer than they are here. Careless domestics do not last long in Emmy's Palais: she snaps at the girl who spills the cream jug on the tray. A broken Harlequin in the salon means dismissal. In her dressing-room one of the other servants dusts the furniture, but only Anna is allowed to open the vitrine for the children, before she lays out her mistress's clothes for the evening.

The netsuke are no longer part of salon life, no longer part of a game of sharpened wit. No one is going to comment on the quality of their carving or the pallor of their patina. They have lost any connection to Japan, lost their *Japonisme*, are suspended from critique. They have become true toys, true bibelots: they are not so small when they are picked up by a child. Here, in this dressing-room, they are part of the intimacy of Emmy's life. This is the space where she undresses with the help of Anna, and dresses for the next engagement with Viktor, a friend, a lover. It has its own kind of threshold.

The longer Emmy lives with the netsuke and sees her children playing with them, the more she realises that they are too intimate a gift to have on display. Her closest friend, Marianne Gutmann, has a few of these netsuke – eleven, to be exact – but only in her country house. They have laughed about them together. But how could you explain the sheer number of these unconventional and rather overwhelming foreign carvings to the ladies from the Israelitische Kultusgemeinde committee, the IKG – all wearing a small dark ribbon on their dress – who gather to help Galician girls from the shtetls get honest jobs. It would be impossible.

It is April again and I am back in the Palais. I look out of the window of Emmy's dressing-room through the bare branches of the lindens, past the Votivkirche, along Währinger Strasse, and it is the fifth turning to Dr Freud's house at Berggasse 19, where he is writing up the notes on Emmy's late great-aunt Anna von Lieben as the case of Cacilie M., a woman with a 'hysterical psychosis of denial', severe facial pains and memory lapses, sent to him 'because no one knew what do with her'. For five years she had been in his care, talking so much that he had to persuade her to start writing: she was his *Lehrmeisterin*, his professor in the study of hysteria.

There are all the cases and cases of antiquities behind his back, as he writes. Rosewood and mahogany and Biedermeier vitrines with wooden shelves and glass shelves, with Etruscan mirrors and Egyptian scarabs and mummy portraits and Roman death-masks, wreathed in cigar smoke. I realise at this point that I am beginning to obsess hopelessly about what is fast becoming my very special subject, the vitrines of the *fin de siècle*. On Freud's desk is a netsuke in the form of a *shishi*, a lion.

My time-management skills are seriously awry. I spent a week reading Adolf Loos on Japanese style as the 'abandonment of symmetry', and how it flattens objects and people: they 'depict flowers, but they are pressed flowers'. I find that he designed the Secessionist exhibition of 1900, which included a huge collection of Japanese artefacts. Japan, I think, is inescapable in Vienna.

Then I decided that I needed to look at the polemical Karl Kraus in detail. I bought a copy of *Die Fackel* from an antiquarian bookshop in order to look at the particular colour of its cover. It was red, as any fierce, satirical magazine calling itself *The Torch* should be. But I worried that the red had faded over ninety years.

I keep hoping that the netsuke will be a key that unlocks the whole of Viennese intellectual life. I worry that I am becoming a Casaubon, and will spend my life writing lists and notes. I know that the Viennese intelligentsia like puzzling objects, and that looking intensely at one thing is a particular pleasure. At the moment that this vitrine is being opened every night by the children as Emmy dresses, Loos is agonising over the design of a salt-cellar, Kraus is obsessing over an advert in the newspaper, a phrase from an editorial in *Die Neue Zeitung*, Freud about a slip of the tongue. But there is no escaping the facts that Emmy is not a reader of Adolf Loos, that she managed to dislike Klimt ('a bear with the manners of a bear') and Mahler ('a racket'), and that she did not buy anything from the Wiener Werkstätte at all ('tat'). She 'never took us to an exhibition', says my grandmother's memoir.

I do know that in 1910 small things, fragments, are very *now*, and Emmy is very Viennese. What does she think of the netsuke? She has not collected them, she is not going to add to them. There are other things, of course, to pick up and move around in Emmy's world. There are the bibelots in the drawing-room, the Meissen cups and saucers, bits of Russian silver and malachite on the mantelpieces. This is amateur stuff for the Ephrussi, background noise to go with the putti hovering like plump partridges overhead, not like aunt Beatrice Ephrussi-Rothschild commissioning clocks from Fabergé for her villa in Cap Ferrat.

Emmy, however, loves stories, and the netsuke are small, quick, ivory stories. She is thirty: it is only twenty years since she was in a nursery further round the Ringstrasse, her mother reading her fairy stories of her own. Today she reads the lower part of *Die Neue Freie Presse*, the daily feuilleton.

Above the ruled line is the news, the news from Budapest, the latest pronouncement from the mayor Dr Karl Lueger, the *Herrgott von Wien*, the Lord God of Vienna. Below the fold is the feuilleton. Every day there is a charmingly phrased and sonorous essay. It could be on the opera or operetta, or about a particular building that is being demolished. It could be an arch memorialising of folk characters from old Vienna. Frau Sopherl, the Nachsmarkt seller of fruit, Herr Adabei the gossip-monger, walk-on parts in a Potemkin city. Every day there it is, mild and narcissistic, one filigree phrase twining around another, as adjectivally sweet as Demel's pastries. Herzl, who starts out writing them, talked of the feuilletonist 'falling in love with his own spirit, and thus of losing any standard of judging himself or others', and you can see this happening. They are so perfect, a riff of humour, a throw-away, glancing look at Vienna, 'a matter of injecting experience – as it were, intravenously – with the poison of sensation . . . the feuil-letonist turns this to account. He renders the city strange to its inhabitants,' in the words of Walter Benjamin. In Vienna the feuil-letonist renders the city back to itself as a perfect, sensationalised fiction.

I think of the netsuke as part of this Vienna. Many of the net-suke are Japanese feuilletons in themselves. They depict the kind of Japanese characters written about in lyrical laments by visitors to Japan. Lafcadio Hearn, an American-Greek journalist, writes about them in *Glimpses of Unfamiliar Japan, Gleanings in Buddha-Fields* and *Shadowings*, each short glimpse or gleaning essay a poetic evo-cation: 'the cries of the earliest itinerant vendors begin – "Daikoyai! kabuya-kabu!" – the sellers of daikon and other strange vegetables. "Moyaya-moya!" – the plaintive call of the women who sell thin slips of kindling-wood for the lighting of charcoal fires.'

In the vitrine in Emmy's dressing-room are the barrel-maker framed by the arc of his half-finished barrel; the street-wrestlers in a sweaty, tumbling embrace of dark chestnut wood; the old, drunk monk with his robes awry; the servant girl cleaning the floor; the rat-catcher with his basket open. When picked out and held, the netsuke are Types of

Old Edo, just like the Types of the Old City who walk onto Vienna's stage every day below the ruled line in *Die Neue Freie Presse*.

As they sit on their green velvet shelves in Emmy's dressing-room, these daily feuilletons are doing what Vienna likes to do, telling stories about itself.

And fractious as this beautiful woman in this absurd pink Palais is, she can glance out of her window into the Schottengasse and start a story for her children about the elderly driver of the shabby fiacre, the flower-seller and the student. The netsuke are now part of a childhood, part of the children's world of things. This world is made of things they can touch and things they cannot touch. There are things that they can touch sometimes and things they can touch every day. There are things that are theirs, for ever, and things that are theirs but that will be passed on to a sister or brother.

The children are not allowed into the silver-room where the foot-men polish the silver, and they are not allowed into the dining-room if there is going to be a dinner. They must not touch their father's glass in its silver holder, out of which he drinks black tea *à la Russe* – it was grandfather's. Lots of things in the Palais were grandfather's, but this is special. Father's books are placed on the library table when they arrive from Frankfurt and London and Paris in their brown paper parcels tied up with string. They are not allowed to touch the sharp silver paper-knife that also lies there. Later they are given the stamps from the parcels for their album.

There are things in this world that the children hear, but whose sounds oscillate below an adult's sense of pitch. They hear the green-and-gold clock in the salon (which has mermaids on it) tick every slow second as they sit in starched immobility during visits from great-aunts. They can hear the shuffle of the carriage horses in the courtyard, which means they are finally off to the park. There is the sound of the rain on the glass roof over the courtyard, which means they are not.

There are things that the children smell that are part of their landscape: the smell of their father's cigar smoke in the library, their mother, or the smell of schnitzel on covered dishes as it is carried past the nursery for lunch. The smell behind the itchy tapestries in the dining-room when they creep behind them to hide. And the smell of hot chocolate after skating. Emmy makes this for them sometimes. Chocolate is brought in on a porcelain dish, and then they are allowed to break it into pieces the size of a krone and these dark shards are melted in a little silver saucepan by Emmy over a purple flame. Then, when it is glaucous, warm milk is poured over it and sugar stirred in.

There are things that they see with complete clarity – the clarity of an object seen through a lens. There are also things that they see as a blur: the corridors chased along, corridors that go on for ever, one gilded flash of a picture after another, one marble table after another. There are eighteen doors if you run all the way round the courtyard corridor.

The netsuke have moved from a world of Gustave Moreau in Paris to the world of a Dulac children's book in Vienna. They build their own echoes, they are part of those Sunday mornings' story-telling, part of *The Arabian Nights*, the travels of Sinbad the Sailor and the *Rubáiyát of Omar Khayyám*. They are locked into their vitrine, behind the dressing-room door, which is along the corridor and up the long stairs from the courtyard, which is behind the double oak doors with the porter waiting, which is in the fairytale castle of a Palais on a street that is part of *The Thousand and One Nights*.

The century is fourteen years old, and so is Elisabeth, a serious young girl who is allowed to sit at dinner with the grown-ups. These are 'men of distinction, high civil servants, professors and high-ranking officers in the army' and she listens to the talk of politics, but is told not to talk herself unless she is talked to. She walks with her father to the bank each morning. She is building up her own library in her bedroom: each new book has a neat EE in pencil and a number.

Gisela is a pretty young girl of ten who enjoys clothes. Iggie is a boy of nine who is slightly overweight and self-conscious about it; he isn't good at maths, but likes drawing very much indeed.

Summer arrives, and the children travel to Kövesces with Emmy. She has ordered a new costume, black with pleating to the blouse, for riding Contra, her favourite bay.

On Sunday 28th June 1914 the Archduke Franz Ferdinand, heir to the Hapsburg Empire, is assassinated in Sarajevo by a young Serbian nationalist. On Thursday *Die Neue Freie Presse* writes that 'the political consequences of this act are being greatly exaggerated'.

On the following Saturday, Elisabeth writes a postcard to Vienna:

4th July 1914

Dearest Papa

Thank you so much for arranging about the Professors for next term. Today it was very warm in the morning so we could all go swimming in the lake but now it is colder and it may rain. I went to Pistzan with Gerty and Eva and Witold but I didn't like it very much. Toni has had nine puppies, one has died and we have to feed them with a bottle. Gisela likes her new clothes. A thousand kisses.

Your Elisabeth

On Sunday 5th July the Kaiser promises German support for Austria against Serbia, and Gisela and Iggie write a postcard of the river at Kövesces: 'Darling Papa, My dresses fit very well. We swim every day as it is so hot. All well. Love and kisses from Gisela and Iggie.'

On Monday 6th July it is cold at Kövesces and they don't swim. 'I painted a flower today. Love and heaps of kisses from Gisela.'

On Saturday 18th July mother and children return to Vienna from Kövesces. On Monday 20th July the British Ambassador, Sir Maurice de Bunsen, reports to Whitehall that the Russian Ambassador to

*The bathing lake at Kövesces*

Vienna has left for a fortnight's holiday. That same day the Ephrussi leave for Switzerland: for their 'long month'.

The Russian imperial flag still flies from the boathouse roof. Viktor, worried that his son will grow up and have to do military service in Russia, has petitioned the Tsar to change his citizenship. This year Viktor has become a subject of his Majesty Franz Josef, the eighty-four-year-old Emperor of Austria, King of Hungary and Bohemia, King of Lombardy-Venetia, of Dalmatia, Croatia, Slavonia, Galicia, Lodomeria and Illyria, Grand Duke of Tuscany, King of Jerusalem and Duke of Auschwitz.

On 28th July Austria declares war on Serbia. On 29th July the Emperor declares: 'I put my faith in my peoples, who have always gathered round my throne, in unity and loyalty, through every tempest, who have always been ready for the heaviest sacrifices for the honour, the majesty, the power of the Fatherland.' On 1st August Germany declares war on Russia. On the 3rd Germany declares war on France, and then the following day invades neutral Belgium. And the whole pack of cards falls: alliances are invoked and Britain declares war on Germany. On 6th August Austria declares war on Russia.

Mobilisation letters are sent out in all the languages of the Empire from Vienna. Trains are requisitioned. All Jules and Fanny Ephrussi's young French footmen, careful around the porcelain and good at rowing on the lake, are called up. The Ephrussi are stuck in the wrong country.

Emmy travels to Zurich to enlist the help of the Austrian Consul General, Theophil von Jäger – a lover of hers – to get the household back to Vienna. There are a lot of telegrams. Nannies, maids and trunks need sorting out. The trains are too crowded and there is too much luggage, and the railway timetable – the implacable *k & k* Railway, as certain as Spanish court ritual, as regular as the Vienna City Corps marching past the nursery window at half-past ten every morning – is suddenly useless.

There is cruelty in all of this. The French, Austrian and German cousins, Russian citizens, English aunts, all the dreaded consanguinity, all the territoriality, all that nomadic lack of love of country, is consigned to sides. How many sides can one family be on at once? Uncle Pips is called up, handsome in his uniform with its astrakhan collar, to fight against his French and English cousins.

In Vienna there is fervent support for this war, this cleansing of the country of its apathy and stupor. The British Ambassador notes that 'the entire people and press clamour impatiently for immediate and condign punishment of the hated Serbian race'. Writers join in the excitement. Thomas Mann writes an essay '*Gedanken im Kriege*', 'Thanks Be for War'; the poet Rilke celebrates the resurrection of the Gods of War in his *Fünf Gesänge*; Hofmannsthal publishes a patriotic poem in *Die Neue Freie Presse*.

Schnitzler disagrees. He writes simply on 5th August: 'World war. World ruin. Karl Kraus wishes the Emperor "a good end of the world".'

Vienna was *en fête*: young men in twos and threes with sprigs of flowers in their hats on their way to recruit; military bands playing in the parks. The Jewish community in Vienna was cheerful. The monthly newsletter of the Austrian-Israelite Union, for July and August, declaimed: 'In this hour of danger we consider ourselves to be fully entitled citizens of the state . . . We want to thank the Kaiser with the blood of our children and with our possessions for making us free; we want to prove to the state that we are its true citizens, as good as anyone . . . After this war, with all its horrors, there cannot be any more anti-Semitic agitation . . . we will be able to claim full equality.' Germany would free the Jews.

Viktor thought otherwise. It was a suicidal catastrophe. He had dustsheets put over all the furniture in the Palais, sent the servants home on board wages, sent the family to the house of Gustav Springer, a friend, near the Schönbrunn, then on to cousins in the mountains near Bad Ischl, and took himself to the Hotel Sacher to see out the war with his books on history. There is a bank to run, something that is difficult when you at war with France (Ephrussi et Cie, rue de l'Arcade, Paris 8), England (Ephrussi and Co., King Street, London) and Russia (Efrussi, Petrograd).

'This Empire's had it,' says the Count in Joseph Roth's novel *The Radetzky March*:

As soon as the Emperor says goodnight, we'll break up into a hundred pieces. The Balkans will be more powerful than we will. All the peoples will set up their own dirty little statelets, and even the Jews will proclaim a king in Palestine. Vienna stinks of the sweat of democrats, I can't stand to be on the Ringstrasse any more . . . In the Burgtheater, they put on Jewish garbage, and they ennoble one Hungarian toilet-manufacturer a week. I tell you, gentlemen, unless we start shooting, it's all up. In our lifetime, I tell you.

There were lots of proclamations that autumn in Vienna. Now that the war is properly under way, the Emperor addresses the children of his Empire. The newspapers print *'Der Brief Sr. Majestät unseres allergnädigsten Kaisers Franz Josef I an die Kinder im Weltkriege'*, a letter from His Majesty, our all-loving Franz Josef I, to the children in the time of the World War: 'You children are the jewels of all the peoples of mine, the blessing of their future conferred a thousand times.'

After six weeks Viktor realises the war is not going to end and returns from the Hotel Sacher. Emmy and the children are eventually brought back from Bad Ischl. The dustcovers are taken off the furniture. There is a lot of activity in the street outside the nursery window. There is so much noise from the demonstrating students – Musil notes 'the ugliness of the singing in the cafés' in his journal – from the marching soldiers, with their bands, that Emmy considers moving the children's rooms altogether to a quieter part of the house. This does not happen. The house is poorly designed for families, she says – we are all on show here in one glass box, we might as well be living on the street itself, for all that your father does about it.

The students' chants change week by week. They start with 'Serbien muss sterben', 'Serbia must die!' Then the Russians get it: 'One Round, One Russian!' Then the French. And it gets more colourful by the week. Emmy is worried by the war of course, but she is also worried by the effect of all this shouting on the children. They have their meals now on a little table in the music room, which opens onto the Schottengasse and is a bit quieter.

Iggie attends the Schottengymnasium. This is a *very good school* run by the Benedictines round the corner, one of the *two best schools* in Vienna, he told me. The plaque on the wall that lists famous former poets indicates this. Though the teachers are Brothers, many of the pupils are Jewish. The school lays particular stress on the Classics, but there are also mathematics, algebra, calculus, history and geography classes. Languages are studied as well. Learning these is irrelevant for these three children, who switch between English and

French with their mother and German with their father. They know only a smattering of Russian and No Yiddish. The children are told to speak only German outside the house. All foreign-sounding shops in Vienna have had their names pasted over by men on ladders.

Girls are not taught at the Schottengymnasium. Gisela is taught at home by her governess in the schoolroom, next to Emmy's dressing-room. Elisabeth has negotiated with Viktor and now has a private tutor. Emmy is opposed to this. She is so angry about this inappropriate, complicated arrangement for her daughter that Iggie hears her shouting and then breaking something, possibly porcelain, in the salon. Elisabeth scrupulously follows the same curriculum as the one boys her age are taught at the Schottengymnasium, and is allowed to go to the school laboratory in the afternoons and have a lesson by herself with one of the teachers. She knows that if she wants to go to the university, then she has to pass the final examination from this school. Elisabeth has known since she was ten that she must get from this room, her schoolroom with its yellow carpet, across the Franzenring to that room, the lecture hall of the university. It is only 200 yards away – but for a girl, it might as well be a thousand miles. There are more than 9,000 students this year, and just 120 of them are female. You can't see into the hall from Elisabeth's room. I've tried. But you can see its window, and imagine the tiered seating and a professor leaning over the lectern at the front. He is talking to you. Your hand moves in a dream across your notes.

Iggie attends the Schottengymnasium reluctantly. You can run there in three minutes, though I haven't tried this with a satchel. There is a class photograph from 1914, third form: thirty boys in grey-flannel suits with ties, or sailor suits, leaning on their desks.

Two windows are open onto the five-storey central courtyard. There is one idiot pulling faces. The teacher is implacable at the back in his monastic robes. On the reverse of the photograph are all their signatures – all the Georgs, Fritzs, Ottos, Maxs, Oskars and Ernsts. Iggie has signed in a beautiful italic hand: Ignace v. Ephrussi.

On the back wall is a blackboard scrawled over with geometry proofs. Today they have been studying how to work out the surface area of a cone. Iggie comes home each day with homework. He detests it. He is poor at algebra and calculus and hates mathematics. Seventy years on, he could give me the names of each Brother and what they tried unsuccessfully to teach him.

And he comes home with rhymes:

> *Heil Wien! Heil Berlin!*
> *In 14 Tagen*
> *In Petersburg drinn!*

> (Hail Vienna! Hail Berlin!
> In 14 days
> We'll be in Petersburg!)

There are ruder ones than this. These do not go down well with Viktor, who loves St Petersburg and is Russian-born, though he is now, of course, Austrian and loves Vienna.

For Iggie, the war means playing soldiers. It is their cousin Piz – Marie-Louise von Motesiczky – who proves to be a particularly good soldier. There is a servants' staircase in the corner of the Palais, tucked away behind a false door. It is a wide nautilus spiral of 136 steps that goes up to the roof and, if you pull the door towards you, then you are suddenly above the caryatids and acanthus leaves and you can see everything, the whole of Vienna. Turn slowly clockwise from the university, then the Votivkirche, then St Stephen's, all the way back through the towers and domes of the Opera and Burgtheater and Rathaus to the university again. And you can dare each other to crawl right up to the edge of the parapet and peer down through the glass into the courtyard below, or you can shoot all the tiny scurrying burghers and their ladies in the Franzenring or in the Schottengasse. For this you use cherry stones and a roll of stiff paper and a good blow. There is a café directly below with wide canvas awnings, which is a particularly appealing target. The waiters in their black aprons look up and shout, and you have to dodge.

And you can climb onto the roofs of the Liebens' Palais next door, where more cousins live.

Or you are spies and can go down the staircase into the cellars – barrel-vaulted – where there is a tunnel that takes you all the way across Vienna to the Schönbrunn. Or all the way to the Parliament. Or into the other secret tunnels that you have been told about, a network that you can get into from the advertising kiosks on the Ringstrasse. This is where the *Kanalstrotter* are meant to live – furtive, shadowy people who exist on the coins that drop from pockets through the gratings in the pavements.

The household and the family make their sacrifices during the war. In 1915 uncle Pips is serving as an imperial liaison officer with the German high command in Berlin, where he has been instrumental in helping Rilke get a desk job away from the Front. Papa is fifty-four and exempt. The manservants in the Palais have disappeared, apart from the butler Josef, who is too old to be called up. A small bevy of maids is kept on and a cook and Anna, who has now been with the family for fifteen years and seems to be able to anticipate everyone's needs and has an ability to calm tempers. She knows everything. There are no secrets from your maid, when you come back home after luncheon and need to change your day-dress.

The house is a lot quieter these days. Viktor used to invite friends of the servants who were between positions to come on Sunday and share the midday meal of boiled and roast meats. This no longer happens: the servants' hall is in ebb. There are no grooms or coach-men, no carriage-horses, so if you want to go to the Prater you take one of the fiacres from the stand in the Schottengasse or even go by tram. There are 'no parties'. This actually means that there are far fewer parties, and that the parties are different. You cannot be seen in a ball dress, but you can still go out to dinner and to the Opera. In her memoir Elisabeth writes that 'Mama entertained at tea only, and played bridge.' Demel's still sells its cakes, but you must not be seen to have too many on display at your at-homes.

Emmy still dresses up every evening, because it is important not to let standards slip. Herr Schuster is unable to make his annual visit to Paris to buy gowns for his Baroness, but Anna knows her so well that she is adept at managing the wardrobe and reworking gowns with assiduous study of the latest journals. There is a photograph of Emmy this spring. She is wearing a very long black gown and a sort of black bearskin pillbox hat – a colbac – with a white egret feather and a rope of pearls to her waist, and if there wasn't a date on the back you wouldn't believe that Vienna was at war. I wonder if this is a last-season dress and how I could possibly find out.

As ever, Gisela and Iggie come and talk to Emmy in her dressing-room in the evening. They are allowed to unlock the vitrine themselves. You don't play with the netsuke on the carpet if you are a girl of ten and a boy of eight, as that is rather childish, but you still reach deep into the glass to find the bundle of kindling and the puppies, if it has been a bad day and you have been shouted at by Brother Georg.

There are many, many people on the streets. There are Jews – 100,000 refugees just from Galicia alone – who have been driven out in terrible mass expulsions by the Russian army. Some are put up in barracks where there are basic amenities, but these are inadequate for families. Many find their way into Leopoldstadt and live in appalling conditions. Many are begging. They are not pedlars with a scant tray of postcards and ribbons. They have nothing to sell. The Israelitische Kultusgemeinde, IKG, organises relief efforts.

The more assimilated Jews worry about these newcomers: they are felt to be rather vulgar in their manners; their speech and dress and customs are not aligned to the *Bildung* of the Viennese. There is anxiety about whether they will impede assimilation. 'It is terribly hard to be an Eastern Jew; there is no harder lot than that of the Eastern Jew newly arrived in Vienna,' writes Joseph Roth about these Jews. 'No-one will do anything for them. Their cousins and coreligionists, with their feet safely pushed under desks in the First District, have already gone "native". They don't want to be associated with Eastern Jews, much less taken for them.' Maybe, I think, this is anxiety from the recently arrived towards the very newly arrived. They are still in transit.

The streets are different. The Ringstrasse is meant for strolling along. It is meant for chance encounters, casual cups of coffee outside the Café Landtmann, hailing friends, hoped-for assignations on the Corso. It is an easy stream of flowing people.

But Vienna now seems to have two speeds. One is the pace of marching soldiers, children racing alongside, and the other is standstill. You notice that there are people queuing outside the shops for food, for cigarettes, for news. Everyone talks of this phenomenon of *anstellen,* standing in line. The police note when queues start for different commodities. In the autumn of 1914 it is for flour and bread. In early 1915 it is milk and potatoes. In autumn 1915 it is oil. In March 1916 it is coffee. The next month it is sugar. The next month it is eggs. In July 1916 it is soap. Then it is everything. The city is sclerotic.

The circulation of things in the city is changing, too. There are stories of hoarding, rich men with rooms stacked high with boxes and boxes of food. There is profiteering, according to the rumours, by 'coffee-house types'. The only people who are doing well are those with food, these 'types', or farmers. To get food, you part with more and more. Objects are loosened from your home and become currency. There are stories about farmers wearing the tailcoats of the Viennese bourgeois, of their wives in silk gowns. Farmhouses are stuffed with pianos, porcelain and bibelots and Turkish carpets. Piano teachers, say the rumours, are moving out of Vienna to follow their new pupils into the country.

The parks are different. There are fewer park keepers and sweepers. The man who waters the paths first thing, in the park across the Ring, is no longer there. The paths have always been dusty, but now are dustier.

Elisabeth is almost sixteen. She is now allowed to get her books bound in half-morocco with marbled covers when Viktor gets his books bound for the library. This is a rite of passage, a way of marking that her reading has significance. It is a way of simultaneously separating her books from her father's – these go into my library, these into yours – and joining them together. On visits home from Berlin, uncle Pips gives her a job of copying out letters for him from his theatre director friend, Max Reinhardt.

Gisela is eleven and starts drawing lessons in the morning-room. She is very good. Iggie is nine and is not allowed in. He knows the uniforms of imperial regiments ('pale blue trousers of the infantry, the blood red fezzes on the heads of the pale blue Bosnians') and sketches the colours of their tunics in his little leather notebooks tied up with purple silk. In the dressing-room, with the cabinet of netsuke forgotten, Emmy calls him her adviser on dress.

He starts to draw dresses. Furtively.

Iggie writes a story in an octavo Manila book with a boat on the cover. It is February 1916.

Fisherman Jack. A story by I.L.E.

Dedication. To darling Mama this little volume is very lovingly dedicated.

Preface. This story is not perfect in any way, I am sure, but one thing is well done, I think: I have described the characters of the book clearly.

Chap.1. Jack and his life. Jack had not been a fisherman all his short life, at least not until his father died . . .

In March the IKG writes an open letter to the Jews of Vienna: 'Jewish Fellow Citizens! In fulfilment of their obvious duty, our fathers, brothers and sons devote their blood and their lives as brave soldiers in our glorious army. With similar consciousness of duty, those who remain at home also have happily sacrificed their property on the altar of their beloved fatherland. Thus now again the call of the state should arouse a patriotic echo in all of us!' The Jews of Vienna contribute another 500,000 crowns to the war loans.

Rumours are endemic. Kraus: 'What do you say about the rumours?/I'm worried./The rumour circulating in Vienna is that there are rumours circulating in Austria. They're even going from mouth to mouth, but nobody can tell you.'

In April in Vienna a group of soldiers on leave, survivors of the battle of Uscieczko, appear on the stage of a Viennese theatre and re-enact the events of the battle. Kraus, splenetic at this reduction of real events to spectacle, lets fly with an attack on the increasing theatricality of the war. The problem is: '*die Sphären fliesen ineinander*' – the spheres have become blurred, flow together. Boundaries are indistinct in Vienna during the war.

This means that there is plenty for the children to see. Their balcony is a splendid vantage point.

On 11th May Elisabeth goes to the Opera to hear Wagner's *Die Meistersinger* with her cousin. '*Heilige Deutsche Kunst*' – 'sacred German art' – she writes in her little green book in which she records the concerts and theatres she attends. She patriotically underlines *Deutsche*.

In July the children are taken by Viktor to the Vienna War Exhibition in the Prater. This has been organised to focus the war effort at home: it will raise morale and money. Best of all is a dog show in which army Dobermanns go through their routines. There are numerous display halls in which the children can see captured artillery pieces. There is a realistic mountain panorama of a battle

| Titel des dramatischen oder musikalischen Werkes | Autor oder Komponist | Wo aufgeführt | Wann gelesen oder gehört | | Bemerkungen |
|---|---|---|---|---|---|
| Onkel Bernhard | L. Fulda u. L. Kötter | Neue Wiener Bühne | 21/I | 1916 | Mama, Papa |
| Nathan der Weise | Lessing | Volkstheater | 24/I | 1916 | Herr, Frau, Madeleine und Georg von Kuh |
| König Richard der Dritte | Shakespeare | Burg | 1/I | 1916 | Daisy, Arthur, René, Leo |
| Der Verschwender | Raimund | Burg | 16/I | 1916 | Irmgard u. Professor Taigner, Gisela, Adolf |
| Maria Stuart | Schiller | Burg | 18/II | 1916 | Mama, Adolf, Madeleine u Georg v. Kuh |
| Vortrag Küllner | Goethe-Schiller-Rilke | Mittl. Konzert Saal | 20/II | 1916 | Alma (großartig Alice Rilke!) |
| Doktor Klaus | Adolf L'Arronge | Burg | 13/IV | 1916 | Mama, Papa |
| Vortrag, Wie wir aus im Kriege verändern | Friedrich Naumann | Gr. Konz. Saal | 28/IV | 1916 | Dr. Taigner. |
| Vortrag Küllner | Goethe-Schiller-Lessing | Gr. Mus. Vereins | 2/I | 1916 | Gisela |
| Die Meistersinger | Wagner | Oper | 11/V | 1916 | Herr, Frau, Madeleine u Georg v. Kuh |
| König Lear (Küllner) | Shakespeare | Burg | 8/VI | 1916 | Mama, Papa, Gertrud Stummer |
| Coppelia | Leon Delibes | | | | |

*Elisabeth's opera and theatre notebook, 1916*

site, so that they can imagine the boys fighting on the borders with Italy. There are concerts given by soldiers who have lost their limbs, tuba-players with prosthetic legs. As you leave, there is a cigarette room in which you can donate tobacco for the soldiers.

There is the first showing of a true-to-life trench. It is advertised, notes Kraus acidly, as showing 'life in the trenches with striking realism'.

On 8th August, staying at Kövesces, Elisabeth is given a dark-green book of poems written by her maternal grandmother Evelina, first published in Vienna in 1907. It is inscribed by her: 'These old songs have faded away from me. Since they are resonating for you, they also resonate to me again.'

Viktor is doing his bit at the bank, a thankless task in wartime, with most of the young, competent men away at the Front. He is generous and patriotic in his financial support. He buys lots of government War Bonds. Then he buys some more. Though he is advised by Gutmann and other friends at the Wiener Club to move his money to Switzerland, as they are doing, he will not so. It would be unpatriotic. At dinner he moves his hand over his face, brow to chin, as he says that in every crisis there are opportunities for those who look for them.

When Viktor arrives home, he spends more time in his study. 'A library,' he says, quoting Victor Hugo, 'is an act of faith.' Fewer books arrive for him: nothing from Petersburg, Paris, London, Florence. He is disappointed in the quality of a volume sent from a new dealer in Berlin. Who knows what he is reading in there, smoking his cigars? Sometimes a supper tray is prepared and taken in. Things are not so good between him and Emmy, and the children hear her raised voice more often.

Before the war every summer there was an operation with ladders and buckets and mops over the courtyard roof. Because there are no manservants, the glass over the courtyard has not been cleaned for two years. The light coming in is greyer than ever before.

Boundaries become indistinct. As a child, your patriotism is simultaneously unequivocal and confused. On the streets and at school you hear of 'British envy, French thirst for revenge and Russian rapacity'. Where you can go diminishes by the month, for all the family networks are in suspension. There are letters, but you cannot see your English or French cousins, cannot travel as you used to.

In the summer the family cannot go to the Chalet Ephrussi in Lucerne, so they go to Kövesces for the whole long holiday. This means that at least they can eat properly. There is roast hare, game pies and plum dumplings, to be eaten hot *mit Schlag*, with whipped cream. In September there is a shooting party, when cousins who are on leave from the shooting at the Front come to shoot partridge.

On 26th October the Prime Minister Karl von Stürgkh is assassinated in a restaurant at the Meissel & Schadn Hotel on Kärntner

Strasse. There are two points of general interest. First, that his assassin is the radical socialist Fritz Adler, son of the Social Democrat leader Viktor Adler. Second, that he had eaten a lunch of mushroom soup, boiled beef with mashed turnips and a pudding. He had been drinking a wine spritzer. There is an ancillary point of interest that excites the children greatly: it is at this *very* restaurant that they had eaten *Ischler Torte,* chocolate cake with almond and cherry filling, with their parents earlier in the summer.

On 21st November 1916 Franz Josef I dies.

All the newspapers have black borders: Death of our Emperor, Kaiser Franz Josef, The Emperor – dead! Several have engravings of him with his characteristic mistrustful look. *Die Neue Freie Presse* carries no feuilleton. *Wiener Zeitung* has the most satisfyingly graphic response, a death-notice on a blank white page. All the weeklies follow suit, apart from *Die Bombe*, which has a picture of a girl surprised in her bed by a gentleman.

Franz Josef was eighty-six and had been on the throne since 1848. On a wintry day there is a massive funeral cortège through Vienna. The streets are lined with soldiers. His coffin is on a hearse pulled by eight horses with black plumes. On either side march aged archdukes with chests of medals and representatives of all the imperial guards. Behind him walk the young, new Emperor Karl and his wife Zita, in a veil to the ground, and between them their four year-old son Otto wearing white with a black sash. The funeral takes place in the cathedral with the Kings of Bulgaria, Bavaria, Saxony and Württemberg present, fifty archdukes and duchesses and forty other princes and princesses. Then the cortège winds its way to the Capuchin church in the Neue Markt close to the Hofburg palace. The destination is the *Kaisergruft*, the imperial tomb.

There is the drama of admittance to the church – the guards knock three times and are refused twice – and then Franz Josef is buried between his wife Elisabeth and his long-dead eldest son, the suicide Rudolf.

The children are taken to the Meissel & Schadn Hotel on a corner of Kärntner Strasse, where they had that delicious cake, to watch the cortège from a first-floor window. It is extremely cold.

Viktor remembers the Makart spectacle with all the floppy hats with plumes, thirty-seven years before; his father being ennobled, forty-six years previously. It is a generation since Franz Josef opened the Ringstrasse, the Votivkirche, the Parliament, the Opera House, the City Hall, the Burgtheater.

The children think about all the other processions that the Emperor has taken part in, the countless times they have seen him in his carriage in Vienna and in Bad Ischl. They remember him riding with Mrs Schratt, his companion, when she waved to them, a small discreet wave from a gloved right hand. They remember the family joke to be repeated after visiting grim great-aunt Anna von Herzenreid, the witch. When you have got safely away from her and her questioning, you have to repeat the Emperor's old saying *'Es war sehr schön, es hat mich sehr gefreut'* – It has been very nice, I've enjoyed myself – before anyone else can say it.

In early December there is a serious meeting in the dressing-room. Elisabeth is to be allowed to choose the style of her own dress for the first time. She has had many dresses made for her before, but this is the first time she is allowed to make the decisions. This is a moment that has been much anticipated by Emmy and Gisela and Iggie, all of whom love clothes, and by Anna, who looks after them. In the dressing-room on the dressing-table is a book of swatches of fabrics and Elisabeth comes up with an idea for a dress that has a spider's-web pattern over the bodice.

Iggie is absolutely appalled. Seventy years later in Tokyo he recounts how there was complete silence when she described what she wanted: 'She simply had no taste at all.'

On 17th January 1917 there is a new edict, which states that the names of convicted profiteers will be printed in a list in the newspaper and on notice-boards in home districts. There has been some pressure to bring back the stocks. There are many names for profiteer, but increasingly they elide: *hoarder, usurer, Ostjude, Galician, Jew.*

In March Emperor Karl institutes a new school holiday to be held on 21st November to commemorate the passing of Franz Josef and his own ascension to the throne.

In April Emmy goes to a reception at the Schönbrunn given for a committee of women who organise something to do with widows of soldiers who have fallen in defence of the Empire. It is unclear to me exactly what is going on. But there is a splendid photograph of this gathering of a hundred women in their best in the State Ballroom, a great arc of hats under the rococo plasterwork and mirrors.

In May there is an exhibition of 180,000 toy soldiers in Vienna. All summer everything in the city is *helden*, heroic. All year there are white spaces in the newspapers where the censors have struck out information or comment.

The corridor between Emmy's dressing-room, the room with the netsuke, and Viktor's dressing-room seems to get longer and longer. Sometimes Emmy does not appear at the dining-table at one o'clock and her place has to be removed by a maid while everyone pretends not to notice. Sometimes it is removed again at eight o'clock.

Food is an increasing problem. There have been queues for bread and milk and potatoes for two years, but there are now queues for cabbage and plums and beer. Housewives are exhorted to use their imaginations. Kraus pictures an efficient Teutonic wife: 'Today we were well provided for . . . There were all kinds of things. We had a wholesome broth made with the Excelsior brand of Hindenburg cocoa-cream soup cubes, a tasty ersatz false hare with ersatz kohlrabi, potato pancakes made of paraffin . . .'

Coins change. Before the war, gold krone were minted, or silver ones. After three years of war they are copper. This summer they are iron.

Emperor Karl receives fervent acclaim in the Jewish press. The Jews, says *Bloch's Wochenschrift,* are 'not only the most loyal supporters of his empire, but the only unconditional Austrians'.

In the summer of 1917 Elisabeth stays in Alt-Ausee at the country house of Baroness Oppenheimer with her best friend Fanny. Fanny Loewenstein has spent her childhood living all over Europe and speaks the same run of languages as Elisabeth. They are both seventeen and very keen on poetry: they write constantly. To their great excitement, both the poet Hugo von Hofmannsthal and the composer Richard Strauss are staying too, as are Hofmannsthal's two sons. The other house-guests include the historian Joseph Redlich, who, Elisabeth wrote sixty years later, 'impressed us very unfavourably with his predictions of the impending defeat of Austria and Germany while Fanny and I still believed the official communiqués of a victorious outcome'.

In October the *Reichspost* claims that there is an international conspiracy against Austria–Hungary and that Lenin and Kerensky and Lord Northcliffe are all Jews. President Woodrow Wilson is also acting 'under the influence' of the Jews.

On 21st November, the anniversary of the late Emperor's demise, all schoolchildren get a day off.

In the spring of 1918 things are very difficult indeed. Emmy, 'the dazzling centre of a distinguished society circle', according to Kraus in *Die Fackel*, is more dazzling than ever. She has a new lover, a young count in one of the cavalry regiments. This young count is the son of family friends, a regular guest at Kövesces, where he brings his own horses. He is also extremely good-looking and is far closer to Emmy in age than to Viktor.

In the spring a book is published for the schoolchildren of the Empire, *Unser Kaiserpaar*. It describes the new Emperor and his wife and son at the funeral of Franz Josef. 'The illustrious parental couple arranged it that their first-born child was introduced at the hand of his mother. From this picture arose quite magically a bond of understanding between the ruling pair and the people: the tender gesture of the mother captivated the empire.'

On 18th April Elisabeth and Emmy go to see *Hamlet* at the Burgtheater with the impossibly handsome Alexander Moissi in the title role. '*Der grösste Eindruck meines Lebens*' – the greatest experience of my life – Elisabeth notes in her green notebook. Emmy is thirty-eight and two months pregnant.

It is in this spring that there is good family news. Both Emmy's younger sisters are engaged to be married. Gerty, twenty-seven, is to be married to Tibor, a Hungarian aristocrat with the family name of Thuróczy de Alsó-Körösteg et Turócz-Szent-Mihály. Eva, twenty-five, is to be married to Jenö, the less fantastically named Baron Weiss von Weiss und Horstenstein.

In June there is a wave of strikes. The flour ration is now just 35 grams a day, enough to fill a coffee-cup. Numerous bread trucks are ambushed by large crowds of women and children. In July milk disappears. It is meant to be saved for nursing mothers and the chronically sick, but even they find it difficult to get hold of. Many Viennese can only survive by foraging for potatoes in the fields out side the city. The government debates the carrying of rucksacks. Should city dwellers be allowed to carry them? If they do, should they be searched at the rail stations?

There are rats in the courtyard. These are not ivory rats with amber eyes.

There are also increasing numbers of demonstrations against the Jews. On 16th June there is a German People's Assembly that meets in Vienna to swear fealty to the Kaiser and reaffirm the goal of pan-German unity. One speaker has a solution to the problems: a pogrom to heal the wounds of the State.

On 18th June the Prefect of Police asks permission of Viktor to station men in the courtyard of the Palais, where the car stands, unused for want of petrol. The police will be on hand in the case of unrest, but out of sight. Viktor agrees.

Desertions multiply. More of the Hapsburg army surrender than want to fight: 2,200,000 soldiers are taken prisoner. This is seventeen times the number of British soldiers who are prisoners of war.

On 28th June Elisabeth receives her end-of-year report from the Schottengymnasium. Seven *'sehr gut'* for religious study, German, Latin, Greek, geography and history, philosophy and physics. One *'gut'* for mathematics. On 2nd July she gets her matriculation certificate, stamped with the head of the old Emperor. The printed word 'he' is crossed out and 'she' has been inscribed in blue ink.

It is hot. Emmy is five months pregnant, with the summer ahead of her. A baby will be loved and cherished, of course – but the bother of it.

August in Kövesces. There are only two old men to tend the gardens, and the roses on the long veranda are unkempt. On 22nd September Gisela, Elisabeth and aunt Gerty go to hear *Fidelio* at the Opera. On 25th they go to see *Hildebrand* at the Burgtheater and Elisabeth notes the Archduke in the audience. Brazil declares war on Austria. On 18th October the Czechs seize Prague, renounce the rule of the Hapsburgs and declare independence. On 29th October Austria petitions Italy for an armistice. On 2nd November at ten in the evening there is news that there has been a breakout of violent Italian POWs from an internment camp outside Vienna and that they are swarming into the city. At 10.15 the news becomes more graphic – there are 10,000 or 13,000 of them, and they have been joined by the Russian prisoners. Messengers start appearing in the cafés along the Ringstrasse ordering officers to report to police headquarters. Many do so. Two officers shout to those leaving the Opera to return home and lock their doors. At eleven o'clock the police chief consults with the military about defending Vienna. By midnight the Minister of Interior announces that reports have been greatly exaggerated. By dawn it is admitted that it was another rumour.

On 3rd November the Austro-Hungarian Empire is dissolved. The next day Austria signs the armistice with the Allies. Elisabeth goes to the Burgtheater and sees *Antigone* with cousin Fritz von Lieben. On 9th November Kaiser Wilhelm abdicates. On 12th November Emperor Karl flees to Switzerland, and Austria becomes a republic. There are crowds surging past the Palais all day, many with red flags and banners, converging on the Parliament.

On 19th November Emmy gives birth to a son.

He is blond and blue-eyed and they call him Rudolf Josef. It is difficult to think of a more elegiac name to give a boy just as the Hapsburg Empire crashes around them.

It is very, very difficult. The influenza is raging, and there is no milk to be had. Emmy is ill: it is twelve years since Iggie was born, eighteen years since her first child. Being pregnant during a war is not easy. Viktor is fifty-eight and surprised by fatherhood again. Amongst all the complexities and the surprise at this little boy being born – and these complexities are manifold – Elisabeth is mortified to find that most people think the baby is hers. She is eighteen after all, and her mother and grandmother had children early. There are rumours. The Ephrussi are keeping up appearances.

In her short memoir of the period she writes of the unrest, 'I remember very little of the details, only our great anxiety and fear.'

But, 'Meanwhile,' she adds in the final, triumphant line, 'I had registered at the university.' She had escaped. She had made it from one side of the Ringstrasse to the other.

It was a particularly cold winter in Vienna in 1918 and the white porcelain stove in the corner of the salon was the only fire that could be kept going all day and night. Everywhere else – the dining-room, library, bedrooms and the dressing-room with the netsuke – was freezing. Acetylene lamps gave off a noxious smell. That winter Viennese were seen cutting trees in the woods for tinder. Rudolf was barely a fortnight old when *Die Neue Freie Presse* reported that 'Only the merest shimmer of light can be seen behind some of the windows. The city lies in darkness.' Almost unthinkably, there was no coffee, 'only an unnameable mixture tasting of . . . meat extract and liquorice. Tea, milkless and lemon-less, of course, is slightly better if you can accustom yourself to the permanent taste of tin.' Viktor refused to drink it.

When I try to imagine life in the family in the weeks after the defeat, I see the paper blowing along the streets. Vienna had always been so tidy. Now there were posters and placards, leaflets and demonstrations. Before the war, Iggie remembered dropping the paper wrapping from an ice-cream cone on the gravel walks in the Prater and being scolded by his nanny and reprimanded by a succession of men with epaulettes. Now he kicked his way to school through the detritus of this convulsive, noisy, hectoring city. The advertising kiosks, cylinders ten feet high topped with a small turret, had become places where the fractious Viennese would tack up letters to the Christian Inhabitants of Vienna, to Fellow Citizens, to Brothers and Sisters in the Struggle. And all these screeds would be torn down and replaced. Vienna was anxious and loud.

Emmy, with her new baby, struggled in these first weeks and both she and Rudolf became weaker and weaker. The English economist William Beveridge, visiting Vienna six weeks after the Austrian defeat, wrote that 'A heroic effort is being made by the mothers in nursing their own children to keep them alive for their first year, but this is now done only at the expense of the mothers' own health, and is largely done in vain.' There was talk of trying to get Emmy and Rudolf out of the city and away to Kövesces, even of taking Gisela and Iggie away too, but there was no petrol for the car and the trains were in chaos. So they stayed in the Palais in the marginally quieter rooms with their backs to the Ringstrasse.

At the start of the war the house had felt very exposed, a private house surrounded by public spaces. Now, the peace seemed more frightening than the war: it was not clear who was fighting who, and it was not clear whether or not there was going to be a revolution. Demobilised soldiers and prisoners of war returned to Vienna with first-hand accounts of the revolutions in Russia and of the workers' protests in Berlin. There was plenty of 'free firing' – random gunfire – at night. The new flag of Austria was red, white and red, and some of the younger and more riotous element found that, with a quick rip and stitch, you could make a good red flag.

From every corner of the old Empire imperial civil servants with no country came to Vienna to find that whole imperial ministries to which they had sent their careful reports had closed. There were many *Zitterer* on the streets – men trembling and shaking from shell shock – as well as amputees with medals pinned to their chests.

Captains and majors were to be seen selling wooden toys on the streets. Meanwhile large bundles of imperial monogrammed linen somehow found their way into the households of burghers; imperial saddles and harnesses were found in the markets; and, it was said, security detachments had found their way into the cellars of the palace and were drinking with decreasing speed through the Hapsburg wine-vaults.

Vienna, with just under two million inhabitants, had gone from being the capital of an empire of fifty-two million subjects to a tiny country with six million citizens: it simply could not accommodate the cataclysm. Much of the talk was whether Austria was *lebensfähig*, viable, as an independent state. Viability was not just an issue of economics, it was psychological. Austria seemed not to know how to cope with its diminishment. The 'Carthaginian Peace' – harsh and punitive – formalised in the Treaty of Saint-Germain-en-Laye of 1919 meant the dismemberment of the Empire. It sanctified the independence of Hungary, Czechoslovakia, Poland and Yugoslavia and the State of Slovenes, Croats and Serbs. Istria went. Trieste went. Several Dalmatian islands were lopped off and Austria–Hungary became Austria, a country 500 miles long. There were punitive reparations. The army was reconstituted as 30,000 volunteers. Vienna, went the bitter joke, was a *Wasserkopf*, the hydrocephalic head of a shrunken body.

Many things changed, including names and addresses. In the spirit of the times, all imperial titles were to be abolished – there were to be no more von, no more Ritter, Baron, Graf, Fürst, Herzog. Every member of the post office and worker on the railways, had been able to add *k & k* (imperial and royal) to their title, but this had now ended. Of course, this being Austria, a country deeply devoted to title, other titles proliferated. You might be penniless, but you expected to be addressed as *Dozent, Professor, Hofrat, Schulrat, Diplomkaufmann, Direktor*. Or *Frau Dozent, Frau Professor*.

Streets changed, too. The von Ephrussi family no longer lived at 24 Franzenring, Wien 1, named for the Hapsburg Emperor. The Ephrussi now lived at 24 Der Ring des Zwölften Novembers, Wien 1, renamed after the day of liberation from the Hapsburg emperors. Emmy complained that this renaming business was a bit French, that they were going to end up on rue de la République.

Anything might happen. The value of the krone was so diminished that there was speculation that the new government might sell the imperial art collections for food for the starving Viennese. The Schönbrunn 'is to be sold to a foreign consortium and turned into a gambling palace'. The Botanical Gardens are to be 'razed for the building of apartments'.

With the collapse in the economy, 'loud-voiced people were arriving from all parts of the world to buy banks, factories, jewels, carpets, works of art or landed estates, and the Jews were not the last ones to come. Foreign sharks, swindlers and forgers poured into Vienna and a pest of lice came with them.' This is the backdrop to the 1925 silent film *Die Freundlose Gasse* (*Lonely Street*). Car headlights rake along the night-time queue outside a butcher's shop. 'After waiting all night many are turned away empty-handed.' A hook-nosed 'International Speculator' plots to destroy the value of the stock of a mining company, while a widowed civil servant (could there be a more pitiable Viennese stereotype?) cashes in his pension to buy shares and loses everything. His daughter, played by Greta Garbo, hollow-eyed, faint with hunger, is forced to work in a cabaret. Rescue comes from a handsome Red Cross official, a gentleman, the bearer of tinned food.

Anti-Semitism gained even more ground in Vienna during those years. You could hear the echo of the demonstrations, of course, with their rants against the 'plague of Eastern Jews', but Iggie remembered that they used to laugh at those, as they laughed at the mass displays of youth groups in their proud uniforms and of Austrians in peasant costumes of dirndl and lederhosen. There were lots and lots of these parades.

What was particularly terrifying were the *Krawalle,* brawls of savage ferocity, that took place on the steps of the university between the newly resurrected pan-German student fraternities, the Bummel, and Jewish and socialist students. Iggie remembered his father white with anger when he and Gisela were caught watching one of these bloody fights from the window of the salon. 'Don't let them see you watching,' he shouted – and this from a man who did not shout.

Under the slogan of 'Keeping the Austrian Alps clean of Jews', the German–Austrian Alpine Club expelled all their Jewish members. It was the club that provided access to hundreds of the mountain cabins in which you could spend the night and make coffee over a stove.

Like many of their peers, Iggie and Gisela hiked in the mountains during the early summer. They would take a train to Gmunden and then set off with a rucksack each, a walking stick and a sleeping bag, chocolate and a screw of coffee and sugar in brown paper: you could get milk and hard rolls and a crescent slice of yellow cheese from farmers. It was exhilarating to be free of the city. And once, said Iggie to me, hiking with a friend of Gisela's, we were caught out at dusk high in the Alps. It was already cold, but there was a hut, full of students round the stove and cheerful noise. They asked us for our cards and then us told to get out, told us that Jews polluted the mountain air.

We were okay, said Iggie, we found a barn lower down the valley in the dark, but our friend, Franzi, had a card and stayed in the hut. We never talked about it.

Not talking about anti-Semitism was possible; not hearing about it was impossible. There was no political consensus on what politicians could say in Vienna. This was tested by the publication in 1922, by the novelist and provocateur Hugo Bettauer, of *The City Without Jews: A Novel about the Day after Tomorrow*. In this unnerving novel he tells the story of Vienna racked by post-war poverty and the rise of a demagogue – a dead-ringer for Dr Karl Lueger, named Dr Karl Schwertfeger – who binds the populace together in one easy way: 'Let us look at our little Austria today. In whose hands is the press, and therefore public opinion? In the hands of the Jew! Who has piled billions upon billions since the ill-starred year 1914? The Jew! Who controls the tremendous circulation of our money, who sits at the director's desk in the great banks, who is the head of practically all industries? The Jew! Who owns our theatre? The Jew! . . .' The Mayor has a solution, a simple solution: Austria will throw out the Jews. All of them, including the children of mixed marriages, will be deported in orderly ways on trains. Those Jews who attempt to continue staying secretly in Vienna will do so under pain of death. 'At one o'clock in the afternoon whistles proclaimed that the last trainload of Jews had left Vienna, and at six o'clock . . . all the church bells rang to announce that there were no more Jews in Austria.'

And this novel, with its chilling descriptions of the painful break-ups of families, desperate scenes at railway stations as closed carriages take away the Jews, is counterpointed with the descent of Vienna into a drab, provincial backwater as the Jews who animated it leave. There is no theatre, no newspaper, no gossip, no fashion and no money until Vienna finally invites the Jews back.

Bettauer was assassinated by a young Nazi in 1925. He was defended at his trial by the leader of the Austrian National Socialists, giving the party some prestige amongst the fissile politics of Vienna. That summer, eighty young Nazis attacked a crowded restaurant shouting '*Juden Hinaus!*'

Part of the wretchedness of these years was the effect of inflation. It was said that if you passed the building of the Austro-Hungarian Bank in Bankgasse in the early hours of the morning you could hear the printing presses clattering away printing more money. You were passed banknotes with their ink still damp. Perhaps, say some bankers, we should change our currency totally and start again. Schillings are talked of.

'An entire winter of denominations and zeroes snows down from the sky. Hundreds of thousands, millions, but every flake, every thousand melts in your hand,' wrote the Viennese novelist Stefan Zweig about the year 1919 in his novel *The Post-Office Girl*. 'Money dissolves while you're sleeping, it flies away while you're changing your shoes (coming apart, with wooden heels) to run to the market for a second time; you never stop moving, but you're always late. Life becomes mathematics, addition, multiplication, a mad whirl of figures and numbers, a vortex that snatches the last of your possessions into its black insatiable vacuum . . .'

Viktor looked into his own vacuum: in the safe at the office off the Schottengasse were stacks of files of deeds and bonds and share-certificates. They were worthless. As the citizen of a defeated power, all his assets in London and in Paris, the accounts that had been building over forty years, the office building in one city, the share of Ephrussi et Cie in another, had been confiscated under the Allied terms of the punitive settlement after the war. In the Bolshevik conflagration the Russian fortune – the gold held in St Petersburg, the shares in the Baku oilfields, the railways and the banks and the property Viktor still owned in Odessa – had disappeared. That was not just a spectacular loss of money, it was the loss of several fortunes.

And, more personally, at the height of the war in 1915 Jules Ephrussi, Charles's elder brother and owner of the Chalet, had died. Because of the hostilities his vast fortune, long promised to Viktor, had been left to the French cousins. So no suites of Empire furniture. Or the Monet of willows overhanging a river bank. 'Poor Mama,' wrote Elisabeth 'all those long Swiss evenings in vain.'

In 1914, before the war, Viktor had a fortune of twenty-five million crowns, several buildings scattered around Vienna, the Palais Ephrussi, the art collection of '100 old paintings' and an annual income of several hundred thousand crowns. It was the equivalent of $400 million today. Now even the two floors of the Palais that he rented out for 50,000 crowns did not bring in any more income. And his decision to leave his money in Austria had proved catastrophic. This newly-minted patriotic Austrian citizen had invested massively in war bonds late into 1917. They were worthless, too.

Viktor admitted the severity of all this in crisis meetings on 6th and 8th March 1921 with his old friend, the financier Rudolf Gutmann. 'On the Borse the Ephrussi have the best reputation in Vienna,' wrote Gutmann to another German banker, one Herr Siepel, on 4th April. The Ephrussi bank was still fundamentally viable and its reach across the Balkans made it a useful business partner. The Gutmanns took part of the bank, putting in twenty-five million crowns, and the Berlin Bank (a predecessor of the Deutsche Bank) put up seventy-five million crowns. Viktor now owned only half the family bank.

Lodged in the archives of Deutsche Bank are files and files of these documents, the careful toing and froing about percentages, the reports of conversations with Viktor, the deals. But through the Manila shadings you can still hear the faint oscillation of Viktor's voice, his weariness, in those tumbling consonants. The business was '*buchstäblich gleich Null*'. It was 'literally zero'.

This feeling of loss, of having failed to preserve an inheritance, affected Viktor profoundly. He was the heir: it was his legacy and he had lost it. Each part of his world had closed down – his life in Odessa, St Petersburg, Paris and London was finished and only Vienna was left, the hydrocephalic Palais on the Ringstrasse.

Emmy, the children and little Rudolf weren't exactly destitute. Nothing had to be sold for food or fuel. But what they possessed comprised the contents of this vast house. The netsuke still lay in their lacquer cabinet in the dressing-room, and were still dusted by Anna when she came in to arrange the flowers on Emmy's dressing-table. The walls still held their Gobelin tapestries, their Dutch Old Masters. The French furniture was still polished, clocks still wound, the wicks of candles still trimmed. The Sèvres still lay stacked in the china closet next to the silver-room, service by service on the linen-covered shelves. The gold dinner-service with its double E and the proud little boat with its full sails were still in the safe. There was still a motor-car in the courtyard. But the life of objects within the Palais was less mobile. The world had undergone an *Umsturz*, an over-turning, and this led to a kind of heaviness in the things that made up their lives. Things now had to be preserved, sometimes even cherished, where before they had been just a background, a gilt-and-varnish blur to a busy social life. The uncounted and the unmeasured started at last to be counted very accurately.

There was a huge falling away; things were so much better and fuller before. Perhaps this was when there were the very first intimations of nostalgia. I begin to think that keeping things and losing them are not polar opposites. You keep this silver snuff-box, a token for standing as second in a duel, a lifetime ago. You keep the bracelet given by a lover. Viktor and Emmy kept everything – all these possessions, all these drawers full of things, these walls full of pictures – but they lost their sense of a future of manifold possibilities. This was how they were diminished.

Vienna is sticky with nostalgia. It has breached the heavy oak door of their house.

## 22. YOU MUST CHANGE YOUR LIFE

Elisabeth's first term at university was chaotic. The financial situation of Vienna University had become so critical that an appeal was was made to Austria in general, and Vienna in particular, for help. 'If assistance is not promptly forthcoming the University will inevitably sink to the level of a little Hochschule. The Professors are on starvation salaries . . . the library is not able to function.' The annual income of a professor, commented a visiting scholar, was inadequate to buy a suit and undergarments for himself and clothes for his wife and child. In January 1919, lectures were cancelled as there was no fuel for the lecture-halls. Against this rose the incendiary academic climate of possibility. It was, perversely, a fantastic time to study: there were Austrian – or Viennese – schools of economics, theoretical physics and philosophy, law, psychoanalysis (under Freud and Adler), history and art history. Each of these schools represented extraordinary scholarship coupled with intense rivalry.

Elisabeth had chosen to study philosophy, law and economics. It was, in one sense, a very Jewish choice: all three disciplines had strong Jewish presences in the faculty. One-third of the legal faculty was Jewish. To be a lawyer, an *Advokat*, in Vienna meant being an intellectual. And that is what she was, a plain, fierce, focused intellectual eighteen-year-old in her white crépe-de-Chine blouse with a black bow at the neck. It was a way of making absolute the division between her and the emotional intermittencies of her mother. And the slowly resurgent domestic life in the Palais, the nursery, her noisy new infant brother, the fuss.

Elisabeth chose to study under a fearsome economist, Ludwig von Mises, a man known in the university as *der Liberale,* Mr Libertarian. Mises was a young economist out to make his reputation through his stress on the implausibility of the socialist state. There might be communists on the streets of Vienna, but Mises was going to find the economic arguments to prove them wrong. He started a small seminar circle, 'privatissimum', in which his selected disciples would give a paper. On 26th November 1918, a week after Rudolf was born, Elisabeth gave the first talk on 'Carver's theory of interest'. Mises's students remembered the intensity of the scrutiny in these seminars, the genesis of a famous school of free-market economics. I have her student essays on '*Inflation und Geldknappkeit*' (fifteen pages of small italic handwriting), on '*Kapital*' (thirty-two of the same) and 'John Henry Newman' (thirty-eight pages).

But Elisabeth's passion was for poetry. She sent her poems to her grandmother and to her friend Fanny Lowenstein-Schaffeneck, now working in an exciting contemporary art gallery selling the paintings of Egon Schiele.

Elisabeth and Fanny were in love with the lyric poetry of Rainer Maria Rilke. It consumed them: they knew the two volumes of his *Neue Gedichte* (*New Poems*) by heart and waited impatiently for the next poem to be published: his silence was unbearable. Rilke had been Rodin's amanuensis in Paris, and after the war the girls had travelled with their copies of Rilke's book on the sculptor to pay homage in the Musée Rodin. Elisabeth marked their excitement in the margins in pencilled rushes.

Rilke was the great radical poet of the day. He combined direct-
ness of expression with intense sensuousness in his *Dinggedichte*,
'thing poems'. 'The *thing* is definite, the *art-thing* must be still more
definite, removed from all accident, reft away from obscurity . . .',
Rilke wrote. His poems are full of epiphanies, moments when things
come alive – a dancer's first movement is the flare of a sulphur
match. Or of moments when there is a change in the summer
weather, a catch in mood when you see someone as if for the first
time.

And his poems are full of danger, 'all art is the result of one's
having been in danger, of having gone through an experience all the
way to the end, where no one can go any further'. This is what it is
like to be an artist, he says, breath-catchingly. You are unsteady on
the edge of life, like a swan, before an 'anxious launching of him-
self/On the floods where he is gently caught'.

'You must change your life,' Rilke wrote in his poem on the
'Archaic Torso of Apollo'. Could any instruction be more thrilling?

It was not until after Elisabeth died, aged ninety-two, that I
realised how important Rilke was to her. I knew there were some letters, but they were a rumour, a muffled roll of splendour. It was
when I stood in front of the statue of Apollo with his lyre in the
courtyard of the Palais Ephrussi on a winter's afternoon and haltingly
tried to remember Rilke's poem, the marble glistening like 'a preda-
tor's coat', that I knew I had to find them.

Elisabeth had been given an introduction to Rilke by her uncle.
Pips had helped Rilke when he was stranded in Germany by the out-
break of war. Now he wrote to invite Rilke to Kövesces: 'this house is
always open for you. You would make us all very happy if you would
announce yourself "sans ceremonie".' And Pips begs permission for his

favourite niece to send some poems. Elisabeth wrote – breathlessly – to Rilke in the summer of 1921, enclosing 'Michelangelo', a verse-drama, and asking him whether she might dedicate it to him. There was a long delay until the spring – a delay occasioned by his finishing the *Duino Elegies* – but then he wrote back a five-page letter and they began to correspond, the twenty-year-old student in Vienna and the fifty-year-old poet in Switzerland.

The correspondence started with a refusal. He resisted a dedication. The best outcome would be to have the poem published, then the book 'would represent a lasting link to me . . . It will be a pleasure to accept being a mentor in your first "Erstling", but only if you don't name me.' But, continues the letter, I would be interested to see what you are writing. They wrote to each other for five years.

*Dr Elisabeth Ephrussi, poet and lawyer, 1922*

Twelve very long letters from Rilke, sixty pages interspersed with manuscript copies of his recent poems and translations, and many volumes of his verse with warm dedications of his own.

If you stand in a library and look at Rilke's collected works, the yard or so of volumes, most of them are letters, and most of these seem to be to 'titled, disappointed ladies', to borrow John Berryman's penetrating phrase. Elisabeth was a young poetic baroness, and so not unusual amongst many of his correspondents. But Rilke was a great letter-writer, and these in particular are wonderful letters, exhortatory, lyrical, funny and engaged, a testament to what he called 'a writing friendship'. They have never been translated and only recently transcribed by a Rilke scholar working in England. I move my pots to one side and cover the tables with photocopies of these letters. I spend a happy couple of weeks trying out possible translations of these sinuous, rhythmical sentences with a German PhD student.

Translating the work of his friend, the French poet Paul Valéry, Rilke writes about his 'great silence', the years when Valéry didn't write poetry at all. Rilke encloses the translation he has just finished. He writes about Paris and how the recent death of Proust has affected him, made him think of his years there, working as Rodin's secretary, makes him wish to return and study again. Has Elisabeth read Proust? She should do so.

And he is very careful and particular about Elisabeth's situation in Vienna. He is intrigued by the contrast between her academic studies at the university where she is studying law and her poetry:

Be that as it may, dear friend, I am not anxious for your artistic abilities, to which I attach such a great importance . . . Even though I cannot foresee which path you will decide to take with your law doctorate, I find the great contrast between your two occupations positive; the more diverse the life of the mind, the better the chances are that your inspiration will be protected, the inspiration which cannot be predicted, that which is motivated from within.'

Rilke reads her recent poems 'A January Evening', 'Roman Night' and 'King Oedipus': 'all three good, however I tend to put Oedipus over the rest'. In this poem she writes about the King leaving the city into his exile, his hands over his eyes, wrapped in a cloak, and that 'the others went back to the Palace, and all the lights were extinguished one by one'. She has spent enough time with her father and his *Aeneid* for exile to provoke powerful emotion in her.

If Elisabeth has time at the end of her studies, she *could* read literature, but Rilke's advice is 'to look into the blue of the hyacinths. And the spring!' He gives her specific advice about her poems and about translation; after all, 'it is not the gardener who is encouraging and caring who helps, but the one with the pruning-shears and spade; the rebuke!' He shares his emotions about what it is like to have finished a great work. You feel a dangerous buoyancy, writes Rilke, as if you could float away.

In these letters he becomes lyrical:

I believe that in Vienna, when the dragging wind is not cutting through you, you can sense the spring. Cities often feel things in anticipation, a paleness in the light, an unexpected softness in the shadows, a gleam in the windows – a slight feeling of embarrassment of being a city . . . in my own experience only Paris and (in a naïve way) Moscow absorb the whole nature of the spring into them as if they were a landscape . . .

And then he signs off: 'Farewell to you for now: I deeply appreciated the warmth and friendship of your letter. May you keep well! Your true friend RM Rilke.'

Just think what it must have been like to get that letter from him. Imagine seeing his slightly right-sloping and looping handwriting on the envelope from Switzerland as the post is brought into the breakfast-room in the Palais, your father at one end opening the beige book-catalogues from Berlin, your mother at the other with the feuilleton, your brother and sister arguing quietly. Imagine slitting open the envelope and finding that Rilke has sent you one of his 'Sonnets to Orpheus' and a transcription of a poem of Valéry. 'It is like a fairytale. I cannot believe it belongs to me,' she writes back that night from her desk pushed up against the window looking onto the Ring.

They planned to meet. 'Let it not be a short hour, but a real moment of time,' he writes, but they were unable to meet each other in Vienna, and then Elisabeth got the time wrong for their meeting in Paris and had to leave before he arrived. I find their telegrams. Rilke at the Hôtel Lorius in Montreux, 11H 15 to Mademoiselle Elisabeth Ephrussi, 3 rue Rabelais Paris (*Réponse Payee*), and her response forty minutes later and his the next morning.

Then he was ill and couldn't travel, and there is a hiatus while Rilke is in the sanatorium where they are trying to treat him; then a final letter a fortnight before his death. And later a package from Rilke's widow in Switzerland returning Elisabeth's letters to him, reuniting the correspondence into one envelope, carefully marked and carefully put away in one drawer and then another over Elisabeth's long life.

As a present 'for my dear niece Elisabeth', uncle Pips had

'Michelangelo' written and illuminated by a scribe in Berlin on vellum, like a medieval missal, and bound in green buckram. It is a gentle echo of an early volume of Rilke's *The Book of Hours*, where each stanza is initialled in carmine. This is one of the books my father remembered having, and looked out and brought down to my studio. I have it on my desk now. I open it up and there is the epigraph from Rilke and then her poem. It is quite good, I think, this poem about a sculptor making things. It is properly Rilkean.

When she was eighty, and I was fourteen or so, I started sending her my schoolboy poetry and would get in return careful critiques and suggestions of what to read. I read poetry all the time. I had a passionate, silent longing for the girl in the bookshop where on Saturday afternoons I would spend my pocket money on slim volumes of Faber poets. I carried poetry in my pocket at all times.

Elisabeth's criticism was direct. She hated sentimentality, 'emotional inexactitude'. She thought there was no point in having formal poetic structures if they didn't scan. No points for my sonnet sequence on the dark-haired girl in the bookshop then. But her greatest scorn was for the indefinite, a blurring of the real in rushes of emotion.

When she died I inherited many of her books of poetry. Her personal numbering system means that Rilke's *Das Stundenbuch* is no. 26, his book on Rodin no. 28, Stefan George is EE no. 36 and her grandmother's books of poems are nos 63 and 64. I send my father off to a university library that has some of her books to check when she read them, and I have to stop as I find myself late at night looking through Elisabeth's copies of French poetry, the twelve volumes of Proust, early editions of Rilke, for comments in the margins, scraps of forgotten lyric, a lost letter. I remember Saul Bellow's

Herzog spending his nights shaking out banknotes that he had left in volumes as bookmarks.

When I do find things, I wish I hadn't. I find a transcription by her of a poem by Rilke written on the back of a page from a desk diary from *Sonntag Juli 6*, black and red like a missal. There is a translucent gentian marking a page in Rilke's *Ephemeriden*; the address of a Herr Pannwitz in Vienna tucked into Valéry's *Charmes*; a photograph of the sitting-room at Kövesces in *Du Côté de chez Swann*. And I feel like a bookseller judging the sunning of the cover of a book, marking the annotations, assessing its possible interest. It is not only a trespass on her reading, which feels strange and inappropriate, but close to a cliché. I am turning real encounters into dried flowers.

I remember that Elisabeth didn't really have much feel for the world of objects, netsuke and porcelain, just as she disliked the fuss and bother around which clothes you put on in the morning. In her last flat she had a great wall of books, and only a narrow white shelf on which were balanced a small Chinese terracotta of a dog and three lidded jars. She was supportive of my making pots – and wrote me a handsome cheque once when I was trying to build my first kiln – but was mildly amused by the idea of me making things for a living. But what she loved was poetry, the world of things, hard and defined and alive, made lyrical. She would have hated my fetishising of her books.

In Vienna in the Palais Ephrussi there are three rooms in a row. On one side is Elisabeth's room, a sort of library, where she sits and writes poetry and essays and letters to her poetic grandmother Evelina, to Fanny and to Rilke. On the other is Viktor's library. In the centre is Emmy's dressing-room with its great mirror and dressing-table with its posy of flowers from Kövesces and the vitrine of netsuke. It is opened less often.

These are hard years for Emmy. She is in her early forties, with children who need her attention but who turn away. They all worry her in different ways, and they no longer come to sit and talk and confide about their days as she dresses. There is the little boy in the nursery to complicate things. She takes them to the Opera as it is neutral territory: *Tannhäuser* with Iggie on 28th May 1922, *Tosca* with Gisela on 21st September 1923, and the whole family to *Die Fledermaus* in December.

In these hard years there are not quite so many excuses for dressing up in Vienna. Anna is no less busy here – a lady's maid is always kept busy – but the room is no longer the centre of the life of the house. It is quiet.

I think of this room and remember Rilke writing of 'a vibrating stillness like that in a vitrine'.

The three older children leave the city.

Elisabeth, poet, is the first to go. She receives a doctorate in law in 1924, the first given to a woman from the University of Vienna. And then a Rockefeller Scholarship to travel to America – she is off. She is redoubtable, my grandmother, clever and focused, and she writes about American architecture and idealism for a German journal, how the ardour and fervour of skyscrapers fit with contemporary philosophy. When she returns she moves to Paris to study political science. She is in love with a Dutchman she met in Vienna, recently divorced from a cousin of hers, with a little boy from the marriage.

The beautiful Gisela is next. She marries well, a lovely Spanish banker from a rich Jewish family called Alfredo Bauer. The couple are married in the synagogue in Vienna, which causes confusion for the secular Ephrussi, who are unsure of what to do, where to sit or stand. There is a party for the young couple and the great floor of the Palais is opened up for a proper reception in the gilt ballroom under Ignace's triumphant ceilings. Gisela is effortlessly stylish in a long cardigan and a silver belt low over a print skirt, a dark black-and-white dress with a string of dark beads for going away in. She has an open smile and Alfredo is handsome and bearded. The couple move to Madrid in 1925.

Then Elisabeth sends the young Dutchman, Hendrik de Waal, a note to say that she has heard he is coming through Paris on Friday week and might they meet? Her phone number is Gobelius 12–85, if he could ring. Henk was tall with slightly thinning hair and wore very good suits – grey with the slightest of charcoal stripes – and a monocle and he smoked Russian cigarettes. He had grown up in Amsterdam on the Prinzengracht, the only son of a merchant family that imported coffee and cocoa. He was well travelled and played the violin and was charming and very funny. And he also wrote poetry. I'm not sure if my grandmother, who at twenty-seven was wearing her hair drawn back in a severe bun and had round black spectacles worthy of a Baronin Doktor Ephrussi, had ever before been wooed by such a man. She adored him.

I find their wedding notice in the archives of the Adler Society in Vienna. It is rather elegantly printed. We are *gemeinde* (compelled/led to/unable not to) announce, it reads, that Elisabeth von Ephrussi has already married Hendrik de Waal. And then Viktor and Emmy's names in one corner and the de Waal parents in the other. My grandparents – one Dutch Reformed Church, the other Jewish – were married in the Anglican church in Paris.

The genealogists are amused by this notice and this use of this word *gemeinde*, with its undercurrents of familial complexity.

Elisabeth and Henk bought an apartment in Paris in the rue Spontini in the 16th arrondissement and furnished it in the newest Art Deco taste, with armchairs and carpets by Ruhlmann and rather excitingly *moderne* metal lamps and glassware of impossible lightness from the Wiener Werkstätte. They hung large reproductions of paintings by Van Gogh and, briefly, housed a Schiele landscape in the drawing-room that they bought in Vienna from Fanny's gallery. I have a couple of photographs of this apartment, and you can sense the complete delight this couple took in creating it, the pleasures of buying new things, rather than inheriting stuff. No gilt, no *Junge Frau*, no Dutch chests. And no family portraits at all.

When things were going well, they lived in this apartment with Henk's son Robert and their two little boys, born soon after their marriage, my father Victor – known, like his grandfather Viktor, by his Russian patronymic Tascha – and my uncle Constant Hendrik. They played every day in the Bois de Boulogne. When things were going well there was a governess and a cook and a maid, and even a chauffeur, and Elisabeth wrote poetry and articles for *Le Figaro* and improved her Dutch.

Sometimes, when it was wet, she would take the boys to the gallery of the Jeu de Paume on the edge of the Tuileries gardens. Here in the long, bright rooms they would look at the Manets and Degas and Monets *coll. C. Ephrussi*, left to the museum in memory of her uncle Charles by Fanny and her husband Theodore Reinach, the clever scholar who had married into the family. There are cousins in Paris, but Charles's generation has gone, trailing benefactions to the country it adopted. The Reinachs have left the Villa Kerylos, a fabulous re-creation of a Greek temple, to France, and great-aunt Beatrice Ephrussi-Rothschild has bequeathed the rose-pink villa in Cap Ferrat to the Académie française. The Camondos have given their collections, and the Cahen d'Anvers have given their chateau outside Paris, too. It is seventy years since all these first Jewish families built their houses on the golden rue de Monceau and they are giving something back to this generous country.

In terms of religious faith it is an interesting marriage. Henk had grown up in a severe family – they look doomed in their black suits and dresses – but had converted to become Mennonite. Elisabeth, who felt completely confident of her Jewishness, was reading the

Christian mystics and talking about conversion. Not expedient conversion for marriage, or to fit in with the neighbours, or to Catholicism – I'm not sure if any Jewish girl brought up in Vienna opposite the Votivkirche would choose to do that – but to the Church of England. They go to the Anglican church in Paris.

When things did not go well with the Anglo-Batavian Trading Company, Henk lost a lot of his own money, and other people's too. He lost, inter alia, a fortune belonging to Piz, the wild cousin and childhood friend, who had become an up-and-coming Expressionist painter and was living a bohemian life in Frankfurt. Losing this amount of money was a nightmare, and the maid and the chauffeur were let go and the furniture was put into storage in Paris and there were discussions of labyrinthine complexity.

Henk's incompetence with money was different from his father-in-law Viktor's. Henk could make numbers dance. My father talks of how he could scan three columns, take away another column and conjure a (correct) total with a smile. It was just that he believed he could do the same sleight of hand with money. He believed that it was all going to come right, that the markets would move, the ships would come into port and that fortunes would click back together like his slim shagreen cigarette case. He was, simply, deluded in his abilities.

And I understand that Viktor never believed he had any control over the columns of figures at all. I wonder, very belatedly, what it was like for Elisabeth to realise that she had married a man almost as poor with money as her father.

Iggie graduated from the Schottengymnasium and was the third to leave. I have his graduation photograph and can't find him at first, until I suddenly recognise a rather portly young man in the back row in a double-breasted suit. He looks like a stockbroker. Bow-tie and handkerchief, a young man practising how to stand properly, how to look convincing. Do you, for instance, stand with one hand in your pocket? Or are two hands in pockets better? Or even, this is most endearing, one hand inside the waistcoat, a *clubman* pose.

To celebrate the end of his schooling, he went for a motoring tour with his childhood friends the Gutmanns, from Vienna to Paris the long way round through northern Italy and the Riviera in a Hispano-Suiza, an elephantine car of fabled luxury. In some cold, bright pass somewhere, three young things sit in the back with the hood down, swaddled in their motoring coats with goggles up over their motoring caps. Their luggage is piled in front of them. A chauffeur hovers. The bonnet of the car disappears to the left of the photograph and the boot of the car disappears to the right. It feels balanced on the faintest breath of a fulcrum, hovering between deep descents.

It would have been difficult to have Elisabeth as an older sister if you were academic: Iggie was not bookish. The family finances are not so rocky in these days – Emmy, an elegant forty-five, is buying clothes again – but Iggie does need to concentrate and not just spend his time watching endless looping afternoons of films in the cinemas. Viktor and Emmy are clear about his future. Iggie should join the bank, turn left and left again each morning with his father, sit at a desk under the shield with the little boat ploughing its way onwards, *Quod Honestum,* through the generations from Joachim to Ignace and Leon, and then to Viktor and Jules, and now to Iggie. Iggie was, after all, the only young man in the whole of the extended Ephrussi family, Rudolf being a rather gorgeous child of seven.

The fact that Iggie was not particularly good with his figures was swept aside. Plans were made for him to continue his studies in finance at Cologne at the university. This had the advantage of allowing Pips – now on his second marriage, this time to a glamorous film actress – to keep an avuncular eye on him. Iggie was given a tiny car as a gesture towards independent living, and he looks good in it. He survived this ordeal – three whole years of German lectures – and started work in a Frankfurt bank, which 'gave me the opportunity to acquaint myself with all phases of the banking business' as he drily put it in a letter years later.

He would not talk of these years, except to say to me that being a Jewish banker in Germany in the Depression was *unwise*. These were the years of the Nazi ascendancy when the votes for Hitler spiralled higher, when the paramilitary SA doubled its membership to 400,000, and when street battles became part of the life of cities. Hitler was appointed Chancellor on 30th January 1933 and a month later, after the Reichstag fire, thousands were taken into 'preventive detention'. The largest of these new detention camps was on the edge of Bavaria in Dachau.

In July 1933 Iggie was expected back in Vienna to start at the bank.

It was not *wise* to stay in Germany, but it was not a propitious time to return to Austria. Vienna was turbulent. The Austrian Chancellor, Engelbert Dollfuss, had suspended the constitution in the face of increasing Nazi pressure. There were violent confrontations between police and demonstrators, and some days Viktor did not even go to the bank, but waited impatiently all day for the evening papers to be brought to him in the library.

Iggie did not turn up. He ran away. The list of reasons for running away started with the bank – the smirk that the doorman always gave him – but tangled into Vienna. And then tangled further into Family:

Papa, the old cook Clara and her welcoming veal pie with potato salad, Anna fussing over his shirts, his room with its Biedermeier bed waiting for him along the familiar long corridor, past the dressing-room, the counterpane turned down at six.

Iggie ran to Paris. He began work in a 'third-rung fashion house' learning how to sketch tea-gowns. He spent nights learning how to cut in an atelier, starting to sense how the scissors slip across a billowing field of green shot-silk. Four hours' sleep on the floor of a friend's apartment and then coffee and back to drawing. Fifteen minutes for lunch, coffee, and back again.

He is poor: he learns the tricks to keeping clothes clean and smart, how to take in and hem cuffs. He has a small allowance from Vienna that continues, without comment, from his parents. And though it must be mortifying for Viktor to explain to his friends that Iggie is not joining the firm – and perhaps he mumbles when asked what Iggie is actually doing in Paris – I wonder if he has sympathy for his son. Viktor must know about running away and not running away, just as Emmy must know about staying.

Iggie is twenty-eight. As with Emmy, clothes are a vocation. All those nightly hours in the dressing-room with the netsuke and Anna and his mother, smoothing down a dress, comparing lace details at cuff or neck. All those dressing-up games with Gisela, the trunk of old gowns kept in the box-room at the far corner. The old copies of *Wiener Mode*, pored over on the parquetry floor of the salon. Iggie could tell you how the trousers of one imperial regiment differed in cut from another and how you could wear crêpe de Chine on the bias. And now, finally, he finds that he is not as good as he had hoped, but he has started.

And then, after nine hard months, he runs away again, to New

York, to boys and to fashion. This was a trinity so wonderful in its cadence that in very old age he couldn't help smilingly describing the voyage to New York as a sort of baptismal crossing from one life to another, a voyage in some way into himself.

I know a little about this from his wry attempts to make me dress better when I first stayed with him in Tokyo. It was during that hot, humid June in Iggie's apartment, earnest and gushing and rather grubby from my travels, that I first understood not that clothes mattered, but *how* they mattered. Iggie and Jiro, his friend in the interlocking apartment, took me to Mitsukoshi, the grand department store in the centre of the Ginza, to buy some proper clothes, some linen jackets for the summer and some shirts with collars. My jeans and collarless shirts were taken away by their housekeeper Mrs Nakano and returned rehemmed, folded with little pins across the cuffs and all my buttons restored to full array. Some things did not re-emerge.

On a much later visit to Tokyo, Jiro gave me a small card that he

I. LEO EPHRUSSI

takes pleasure to invite you to see his exclusive
Paris and New York Lines
of Smart Accessories
shown for the first time in California

Studio Huldschinsky
8704 Sunset Blvd.
West Hollywood
CR. 1-4066

Belts, Bags, Ceramic Jewelry
Compacts, Handknit Suits and Blouses

*Iggie's invitation, 1936*

had found: 'Baron I. Leo Ephrussi begs to announce his association with Dorothy Couteaur Inc. formerly of Molyneux, Paris'. The address is 695 Fifth Avenue and the phone number Eldorado 5-0050. It seems appropriate. Fashion was El Dorado for Iggie: he has dropped the Ignace bit for Leo, but kept the Baron in place.

For Dorothy Couteaur Inc. – a name straight out of Nabokov with its mocking, drawling version of *couture* – Iggie designed 'The Free-Swinging Coat', shown 'posed smartly over a diagonally tucked sheer crêpe frock in beige, with beige also the background color of the novelty silk crêpe coat patterned in brown swallows'. It is very brown indeed. Iggie mostly designed 'Sophisticated gowns for the smart American woman', though I did find a reference to 'Smart Accessories shown for the first time in California. Belts, Bags, Ceramic Jewelry and Compacts', which shows either his financial straits or his astuteness. In *Women's Wear Daily* for 11 March 1937 there was 'an important type of evening ensemble that makes a point of an interesting fabric alliance, the gown reflecting Grecian influence in mother-of-pearl satin jersey, the coat in the gayest red chiffon, with pin-tucks for surface decoration. The scarf can be worn as a girdle on the coat, giving a redingote suggestion.'

'An interesting fabric alliance' is a wonderful phrase. I look at the illustration for a long time for the 'redingote suggestion'.

It was only when I found his design of cruise-wear based on US Navy signal flags that I realised just how much fun Iggie was having. It shows girls dressed in shorts and skirts being run up the rigging by magnificent swarthy sailors, while the code helpfully informs us that the girls are wearing signals for 'I need to have personal communication with you', 'You are clear of all danger', 'I am on fire' and 'I cannot hold out any longer'.

New York was full of newly impoverished Russians, Austrians and Germans escaping Europe, and Iggie was one of many. His minute allowance from Vienna had finally petered to nothing and his earnings from his designs were meagre, but he was a happy man. He found his first great love: Robin Curtis, a dealer in antiques, slightly younger, slim and fair. In a domestic picture in their apartment shared with Robin's sister on the Upper East Side, with both men in pin-striped suits, Iggie perches on the arm of a chair. There are joint family photographs on their mantelpiece behind them. In other pictures they are larking around on a beach in their trunks, in Mexico, in LA: a couple.

Iggie really did get away.

Elisabeth wouldn't sanction moving back to Vienna. But when the finances became intolerable – clients had let Henk down, promises had not been fulfilled, et cetera – she took the boys off to a farmhouse in Oberbozen, a beautiful village in the Italian Tyrol. The village had its own cacophonous band of drums on feast days, and meadows of gentians. It was beautiful, and the air was marvellous for the children's complexion, but above all it was very, very cheap with none of the expenses of a Parisian lifestyle. The children went briefly to the local school, before she decided to teach them herself. Henk stayed in Paris and London trying to retrieve the losses of his Trading Company. 'When he came to see us,' my father recalled, 'we were told to be very quiet as he was very, very tired.'

Sometimes Elisabeth took the children back to Vienna to see their grandparents and their uncle Rudolf, now a teenager. The chauffeur took Viktor and the grandchildren out in the back of the long black car.

Emmy was not terribly well – a heart condition – and had started to take pills. She looks much older in the few pictures of her from these years, and slightly surprised by middle age, but is still beautifully dressed in a black cloak with a white collar, a hat pinned at an angle to her grey curls, one hand on my father and another on my uncle's shoulder. Anna must be looking after her well. And she still falls in love.

She says she is not ready to be a grandmother, but she sends my father a series of colourful postcards from the stories of Hans Christian Anderson, 'The Swineherd', 'The Princess and the Pea', 'Jack and the Beanstalk'. Dozens of cards each with a short message, one every week without fail, each one signed 'with a thousand kisses from Your Grandmother'. Emmy still cannot resist telling stories.

Rudolf, growing up at home, without his sisters or his brother from one year to the next, is tall and handsome and in one picture he is dressed in riding breeches and an army greatcoat, framed by a doorway in the salon of the Palais. He plays the saxophone. Its echo must have sounded glorious in the increasingly empty rooms.

Elisabeth and the boys spent a fortnight in Vienna at the Palais in July 1934, the weeks in which there was an attempted coup led by the Austrian SS, in which Chancellor Dollfuss was assassinated in his office, the signal for a Nazi uprising. It was put down with heavy casualties, and the new Chancellor Kurt Schuschnigg was sworn in against a real fear of civil war. My father remembers waking in the nursery in the Palais and running to the window to see a fire-truck rattling down the Ring with its bells ringing. I have tried to get him to remember more (Nazi demonstrations? armed police? crisis?), but he is not suggestible. A fire-truck is the alpha and omega of his 1934 Vienna.

Viktor hardly pretends to be a banker any more. Perhaps as a consequence of this, or the competence of his deputy, Herr Stein-hausser, the bank is doing well. He still goes to the bank every day, where he studies long, closely printed catalogues from Leipzig and Heidelberg. He has taken up collecting incunabula, early printed books, and his particular passion – more intense since the crumbling of the Empire – is for Roman history. The books are kept in the library overlooking the Schottengasse in a tall bookcase with a mesh door, and the key is kept on his watch chain. Early printed Latin histories seem a characteristically abstruse thing – and an expensive thing – to collect, but he is interested in empires.

Viktor and Emmy holiday together at Kövesces, but since the death of her parents it is a strangely diminished place, with only a couple of horses in the stables and fewer gamekeepers and no great weekend shoots any more. Emmy walks down to the bend in the river, past the willows where you can get the breeze, and back before dinner as she used to with the children, but with her heart problem she is quite slow. The swimming lake has been let go. Its edges are susurrating reeds.

The Ephrussi children are dispersed. Elisabeth is still in the Alps, but has moved to Ascona in Switzerland and comes to Vienna with her boys when she can. Anna makes a great fuss of them. Iggie is now designing cruise-wear in Hollywood. And Gisela and her family have had to leave Madrid for Mexico because of the Spanish Civil War.

By 1938 Emmy is fifty-eight years old and is still very handsome, her rope of pearls looping around her neck and down to her waist. Vienna is a chaotic place to be living in, but life in the Palais is strangely immobile. There are eight servants to keep this stasis perfect. Nothing really happens, though the table is set in the dining-room for one o'clock, and again for dinner at eight, but this time it is Rudolf who does not appear. He is out, she says, at all hours.

Viktor is seventy-eight and looks exactly like *his* father – and like the portrait of his cousin Charles printed with his obituary. I think of Swann in his old age, when all his features have become larger: the Ephrussi nose is resplendent. I look at a picture of Viktor with his neatly trimmed beard and realise that he looks like *my* father does now, and wonder how long I've got before I too start to look like this.

Viktor is so anxious that he reads several of the papers each day. He is right to be anxious. There have been years of overt pressure and covert funding by Germany of the Austrian National Socialists. Hitler has now demanded that the Austrian Chancellor, Schuschnigg, release members of the Nazi Party from prison and let them participate in government. Schuschnigg has complied. The pressure has increased and now he has had enough. He has decided to hold a plebiscite on Austria's independence from the Nazi Reich on 13th March.

When Viktor goes to the Wiener Club on the Kärtner Ring on Thursday 10th March for lunch with his Jewish friends (out the door, turn left, 500 yards on the left) the afternoon disappears in smoky debate about what is happening. History is not helping Viktor.

*Part Three*

VIENNA, KÖVESCES, TUNBRIDGE WELLS, VIENNA 1938–1947

On 10th March 1938 the hopes for the plebiscite were high. The previous evening in Innsbruck the Austrian Chancellor had given a ringing speech invoking an old Tyrolean hero: 'Men – the hour has struck!' It was a gorgeous winter day, bright and clear. There were leaflets everywhere, scattered from trucks, and posters illustrated with a dramatic '*Ja!*' on them. 'With Schuschnigg for a free Austria!' There were the crosses of the Fatherland Front painted in white on the walls of buildings and on pavements. There were crowds in the streets and columns of youth groups chanting '*Heil Schuschnigg! Heil Liberty!*' And 'Red-White-Red until Death!' The radio played endless broadcasts of Schuschnigg's speech. The Israelitische Kultusgemeinde put up the huge sum of 500,000 schillings – $80,000 – to help towards the campaign of support: the plebiscite was a bastion for the Jews of Vienna.

Before dawn on Friday 11th the head of the Vienna police woke Schuschnigg to tell him of troop movements on the German border. Rail traffic had been stopped. It was another bright and sunny morning. It was the last day of Austria, a day of ultimata from Berlin, desperate attempts from Vienna to see if London or Paris, or Rome, would support them against the increasing German demands for the Chancellor to resign in favour of a pro-Hitler minister, Artur von Seyss-Inquart.

On 11th March the IKG added an extra 300,000 schillings to Schuschnigg's campaign. There were rumours that columns of troops had crossed over the border from Germany, rumours that the plebiscite might be postponed.

The radio – a huge English radio – brown and impressive, with a dial with names of capital cities on it, is kept in the library, and Viktor and Emmy spend the afternoon there, listening. Even Rudolf joins them. At half-past four Anna brings in Viktor's tea in a glass with the porcelain dish bearing a slice of lemon and the sugar, and Emmy her English tea and the little blue Meissen box with the pills for her heart condition. There is coffee for Rudolf, who is nineteen and contrary. Anna puts the tray on the library table with its book rest. At seven o'clock Radio Vienna reveals the postponement of the plebiscite and then, a few minutes later, the resignation of the entire cabinet except for the Nazi-sympathising Seyss-Inquart, who is to stay on as Interior Minister.

At ten to eight Schuschnigg broadcasts: 'Austrian men and women! This day has brought us face to face with a serious and decisive situation . . . The Government of the German Reich presented an ultimatum to the Federal President demanding that he choose a candidate chosen by the Reich Government to the office of Chancellor . . . or . . . German troops would begin to cross our frontiers this very hour . . . We have, because even in this solemn hour we are not willing to spill German blood, ordered our army, in case an invasion is carried out, to pull back without any substantial resistance to await the decisions of the next few hours. So in this hour I take my leave of the Austrian people with a German word and a heartfelt wish: God protect Austria.' *Gott schütze Österreich*. And then the music plays for the *'Gott erhalte'*, the Austrian national anthem.

It is as if a switch has been thrown. There are runnels of noise down the street, the Schottengasse echoing with voices. They are shouting,

'*Ein Volk, ein Reich, ein Führer*' and '*Heil Hitler, Sieg Heil*'. And they are screaming '*Jude Verreke!*' – perish Judah! Death to the Jews!

It is a flood of brown shirts. There are taxi horns blaring and there are men with weapons on the streets, and somehow the police have swastika armbands. There are trucks rushing along the Ring, past the house, past the university towards the Town Hall. And the trucks have swastikas on them, and the trams have swastikas on them, and there are young men and boys hanging off them, shouting and waving.

And someone turns out the lights in the library, as if being in the dark will make them invisible, but the noise reaches into the house, into the room, into their lungs. Someone is being beaten in the street below. What are they going to do? How long can you pretend this is not happening?

Some friends pack a suitcase and go out into the street, push through these swirling, eddying masses of ecstatic citizens of Vienna to get to the Westbahnhof. The night train to Prague leaves at 11.15, but by nine it is completely packed. Men in uniforms swarm through the train and pull people off.

By 11.15 Nazi flags are hanging from the parapets of government ministries. At half-past midnight President Miklas gives in and approves the cabinet. At 1.08 a.m. a Major Klausner announces from the balcony 'with deep emotion in this festive hour that Austria is free, that Austria is National Socialist'.

There are queues of people on foot or in cars at the Czech frontier. The radio is now playing the Badenweiler and the Hofenfriedberger, German military marches. These are interspersed with slogans. The first Jewish shop windows are broken.

And it is on that first night that the sounds of the street become shouting in the Ephrussi courtyard, echoing around the walls and off the roof. Then there are feet pounding up the stairs, the thirty-three shallow steps to the apartment on the second floor.

There are fists on the door, someone leaning on the bell, and there are eight or ten, a knot of them in some sort of uniform – some with swastika armbands, some familiar. Some are still boys. It is one o'clock in the morning and no one is asleep, everyone is dressed. Viktor and Emmy and Rudolf are pushed into the library.

This first night they swarm through the apartment. There are shouts from across the courtyard, as a couple of them have found the salon with its French ensembles of furniture and porcelain. There is laughter from someone as Emmy's closet is ransacked. Someone bangs out a tune on the piano keys. Some men are in the study pulling out drawers, roughing up the desks, pushing the folios off the stand in the corner. They come into the library and tip the globes from their stands. This convulsive disordering, messing up, sweeping off is barely looting; it is a stretching of muscles, a cracking of the knuckles, a loosening up. The people in the corridors are checking, looking, exploring, working out what is here.

They take the silver candlesticks held up by slightly drunken fauns from the dining-room, small animals in malachite from mantelpieces, silver cigarette boxes, money held in a clip from a desk in Viktor's study. A small Russian clock, pink enamel and gold, that rang the hours in the salon. And the large clock from the library with its golden dome held up by columns.

They have walked past this house for years, glimpsed faces at windows, seen into the courtyard as the doorman holds the gate open while the fiacre trots in. They are inside now, at last. This is how the Jews live, how the Jews used our money – room after room stacked

with stuff, opulence. These are a few souvenirs, a bit of redistribu-
tion. It is a start.

The last door they reach is Emmy's dressing-room in the corner,
the room with the vitrine containing the netsuke, and they sweep
everything off the desk she uses as a dressing-table: the small mirror
and the porcelain and the silver boxes and the flowers sent up from
the meadows in Kövesces that Anna arranges in the vase, and they
drag the desk out into the corridor.

They push Emmy and Viktor and Rudolf against the wall, and
three of them heave the desk and send it crashing over the handrail
until, with a sound of splintering wood and gilt and marquetry, it
hits the stone flags of the courtyard below.

This desk – the wedding-present from Fanny and Jules, from
Paris – takes a long time to fall. The sounds ricochet off the glass
roof. The broken drawers scatter letters across the courtyard.

You think you own us, you fucking foreign *shit*. You'll be fucking next, you shit, you *fucking* Jews.

This is a *Wilde*, unsanctioned Aryanisation. No sanction is needed.

The sound of things breaking is the reward for waiting for so
long. This night is full of these rewards. It has been a long time
coming. This night is the story told by grandparents to grandchildren, the story of how one night the Jews will finally be held
accountable for all they have done, for all they have robbed off the
poor; of how the streets will be cleaned, how light will be shone into
all the dark places. Because it is all about dirt, about the pollution
the Jews brought to the imperial city from their stinking hovels, the
way they took what was ours.

All across Vienna doors are broken down, as children hide behind
their parents, under beds, in cupboards – anywhere to get away from

the noise as fathers and brothers are arrested and beaten up and pulled outside into trucks, as mothers and sisters are abused. And across Vienna people help themselves to what should be theirs, is theirs by right.

It is not that you cannot sleep. You cannot go to bed. When these men go, when these men and boys finally go, they say that they'll be back, and you know they mean it. Emmy is wearing her pearls and they take them off. They take her rings. Someone pauses to spit handsomely at your feet. And they clatter down the stairs, shouting until they reach the courtyard. One takes a run to kick the debris, and they are out through the doors onto the Ring, a large clock under an overcoated arm.

Snow is on its way.

In that grey dawn, on Sunday 13th March, when there should have been the plebiscite for a free, German, independent, social, Christian and united Austria, there are neighbours on their hands and knees scrubbing away at the streets of Vienna – kids and the elderly, the man who owned the newspaper kiosk on the Ring, the orthodox, the liberal, the pious and the radical, the old men who knew their Goethe and believed in *Bildung*, the violin teacher and her mother – surrounded by SS, by Gestapo and by NSDAP (Nazi Party Members), by policemen and by the people they have lived next to for years and years. Jeered at, spat at, shouted at, beaten, bruised. Scrubbing away at the Schuschnigg plebiscite slogans, making Vienna clean again, making Vienna ready. We thank our Führer. He's created work for the Jews.

In a photograph a young man in his shiny jacket oversees the middle-aged women on their knees in the soapy water. And he has rolled up his trouser legs to make sure they do not get damp. It is all about the dirty and the clean.

The house has been breached. And that morning, as my great-grandmother and great-grandfather sit in silence in the library, there is Anna picking up the photographs of cousins from the floor, sweeping the broken fragments of porcelain and marquetry away, straightening pictures, trying to get the carpets clean, trying to close the door that has been opened.

All that day squadrons of Luftwaffe planes fly low over Vienna. Viktor and Emmy do not know what to do. They do not know where to go, as that Sunday morning the first German troops cross the border to be met with flowers and crowds. The story is that Hitler is returning home to visit the grave of his mother.

All that day there are arrests – arrests of anyone who has supported any previous political party, prominent journalists, financiers, civil servants, Jews. Schuschnigg is in solitary confinement. That evening there is a torchlit procession through the city led by the NSDAP. There is the din of '*Deutschland, Deutschland über Alles*' sung in the bars. It takes Hitler six hours to make the journey from Linz to Vienna. It takes this long because of the crowds.

On Monday 14th March Hitler arrives: '. . . before the shadows of the evening sank over Vienna, when the wind died down and the many flags fell silent in festive rigidity, the great hour became reality and the Führer of the united German people entered the capital of the Ostmark'.

The Cardinal of Vienna has ordered the bells of Austria to ring, and the bells of the Votivkirche opposite the Palais Ephrussi start pealing in the afternoon, and the noise of the *Wehrmacht* as it grinds round the Ring makes the house shake. There are flags: flags with swastikas and old Austrian flags with swastikas painted on them. There are kids climbing the linden trees. There are already maps in the bookshop windows showing the new Europe: one solid German nation stretching from Alsace-Lorraine to the Sudetenland to the Baltic to the Tyrol. Half the map is Germany.

On Tuesday 15th March the crowds start early past the Schottengasse, past the Palais Ephrussi, along the Ring, all going in one direction, towards the Heldenplatz, the Place of Heroes, the huge square outside the Hofburg; 200,000 people are jammed into the square and the streets. They cling to the statues, to the branches of trees, to railings. There are figures on the parapets silhouetted against the sky. At eleven o'clock Hitler comes onto the balcony. He can hardly be heard. As he comes to his peroration, the noise prevents him speaking for minutes on end. You can hear it all the way to the Schottengasse. Then: 'In this hour I can report to the German people the greatest accomplishment of my life, as Führer and Chancellor of the German nation and the Reich, I can announce before history the entry of my homeland into the German Reich.' 'The scenes of infatuation at Hitler's arrival defy description,' writes the *Neue Basler Zeitung*.

The Ring is made for this, the massed crowds, the parade ground of emotion, the uniforms. As a student in 1908, Hitler had planned two huge arches to complete the Heldenplatz, an architectural climax: 'an ideal spot for mass marches'. Long ago he had watched the imperial pageantry of the Hapsburgs. And now once again the Ringstrasse becomes 'an enchantment out of "The Thousand-and-One-Nights"', but one of those stories where someone is transfigured before your eyes into something terrible, morphing out of control as you say the wrong words.

At half-past one Hitler returns to review the massive display of marching soldiers and trucks, while 400 planes fly overhead. It is announced that there will be a plebiscite – another one, this time legitimate. 'Do you acknowledge Adolf Hitler as our Führer and the reunion of Austria with the German Reich which was effected on 13th March 1938?' On the pale-pink ballot there is a huge circle for *Ja* and a diminutive one for *Nein*. To encourage Vienna to think hard about this vote, trams are sheathed in red bunting, and St Stephen's Cathedral is draped in red, and Leopoldstadt, the old Jewish quarter, is shrouded in Nazi flags. In this *proper* plebiscite, Jews are ineligible to vote.

There is terror. People are picked up off the streets and bundled into trucks. Several thousand activists, Jews, troublemakers are sent to Dachau. In these first few days there are messages from friends who are leaving, desperate phone-calls about people who have been arrested. Emmy's cousins Frank and Mitzi Wooster have left. Their closest friends, the Gutmanns, have gone, leaving on the 13th. The

*Vienna, 14th March 1938. View along the Ringstrasse from the Parliament and Opera towards the Palais Ephrussi*

Rothschilds have gone. Bernhardt Altmann, a business colleague of Viktor's, a friend from countless dinner-parties, has left already: it takes something to walk out your door and leave everything.

Sometimes it is possible to get people out of police-stations with money. Viktor helps a couple of cousins who need to get across the border to Czechoslovakia, but he and Emmy seem incapable of a decision. Friends tell them to go. It is Viktor who has frozen. He cannot leave this house, his father's and grandfather's house. He cannot leave the bank. He cannot just leave his library.

Others have left the household. Who wants to be associated with the Jews? There are three servants left. The cook and Anna, who make sure that there is still coffee for the Baron and Baroness, and the porter, Herr Kirchner, who has the little room by the gate and no known family.

The city is metamorphosing hour by hour as more German army personnel appear, men in uniforms on every street corner. The currency is now the Reichsmark. *Jude* is painted on Jewish-owned shops, and customers are targeted if they are seen going in or coming out. The huge Schiffmann department store, owned by four Jewish brothers, is systematically emptied by the SA as crowds look on.

People are disappearing. It is increasingly difficult to know where anyone is. On Wednesday 16th March, Pips's old friend, the writer Egon Friedell, jumps out of the window of his flat when he sees storm-troopers arrive and question the porter in his apartment building. There are 160 suicides of Jews in March and April. Jews are dismissed from theatres and orchestras. All state and municipal employees have been sacked; 183 Jewish teachers have lost their jobs. All Jewish lawyers and public prosecutors are relieved of office.

In these days, the wild quality of release, the helping yourself to

Jewish property, the random beatings of Jews on the streets change into something more steely. It becomes clear that there has been a lot of planning and that there are orders. On Friday 18th March, two days after his arrival in Vienna, the young SS lieutenant Adolf Eichmann takes matters personally in hand by participating in a raid on the IKG in the Seitenstettgasse during which documents linking the Jewish community to the Schuschnigg plebiscite campaign are confiscated. This is followed by the confiscation of the IKG library and archive itself. Eichmann is concerned to get the best material of Judaica and Hebraica for the planned Institute for Research into the Jewish Question.

It becomes clear that there are plans for the Jews of Vienna. On 31st March Jewish organisations are no longer recognised under public law. The chaplain of the little English church is baptising Jews. If you convert, you may have more options for escape. There are queues outside the presbytery. He curtails instruction into the Christian faith to ten minutes to help more desperate people.

On 9th April Hitler returns to Vienna. His motorcade goes through the city and onto the Ring. At noon Goebbels steps out onto the balcony of the Rathaus, the Town Hall that now stands in Adolf Hitler Platz, to declaim the results of the plebiscite. 'I proclaim the day of the Greater German Reich': 99.75 per cent have voted yes to legitimise the *Anschluss*.

On 23rd April a boycott of Jewish shops is announced. That same day the Gestapo arrive at the Palais Ephrussi.

How can I write about this time? I read memoirs, the journals of Musil, look at the photographs of the crowds on this day, the following day, the day after that. I read the Vienna newspapers. On Tuesday the Hermansky bakery is baking Aryan bread. On Wednesday Jewish lawyers are sacked. On Thursday non-Aryans are excluded from the football club Schwarz-Rot. Goebbels gives out free radios on Friday. Aryan razor blades are on sale.

I have Viktor's passport with its stamps and a thin shake of letters between members of the family, and I put these out on my long desk. I read them again and again, willing them to tell me what it was like, what Viktor and Emmy feel as they sit in their house on the Ring. I have folders of notes from the archives. But I realise that I can't do this from London, from a library. So I go back to Vienna, to the Palais.

I stand on the balcony of the second floor. I have bought a netsuke back with me, the pale-brown one of three chestnuts with the small white grub in ivory, and I realise that I'm worrying away at it in my pocket, tumbling it round and round. I hold the balcony rail hard and look down to the marble floor and think of Emmy's dressing-table falling. I think of the netsuke undisturbed in their vitrine.

And I hear a group of businessmen come in down the passageway from the Ringstrasse for a meeting in the offices, a knot of talk and laughter, and I hear how the faintest echo of the street comes in with them. It is those voices that make me remember Iggie. He said that the old doorkeeper, Herr Kirchner, who used to swing the gates of the Palais Ephrussi open with a flourish and a low bow to amuse the children, had conveniently gone out and left the gates to the Ringstrasse wide open on the day the Nazis came.

Six members of the Gestapo, in perfect uniforms, walk straight in.

They start out quite polite. They have orders to search the apartment as they have reason to believe that the Jew Ephrussi has supported the Schuschnigg campaign.

Searching. Searching means this: every single drawer is wrenched open, the contents of every cupboard pulled out, every single ornament is scrutinised. Do you know how much stuff there is in this house, how many drawers in how many rooms? The Gestapo are methodical. They are in no hurry. This is no *Wilde*. The drawers in the little tables in the salon are rifled through, papers scattered. The study is taken apart. The filed catalogues of incunabula are swept through for evidence, letters winnowed. Every drawer in the Italian cabinet is probed. Books are pulled off the shelves in the library and examined and dropped. They reach deep into the linen closets. Pictures are taken off walls and the stretchers are checked. The tapestries in the dining-room where the children used to hide are jerked away from the wall.

After they have searched the twenty-four rooms in the family apartment, the kitchens and the servants' hall, the Gestapo request the keys to the safe, to the silver-room and to the porcelain store where the plates are stacked, service by service. They need the key to the boxroom in the corner, where all the hatboxes, the trunks, the crates with the children's toys, the nursery books, the old Andrew

Lang fairy stories are kept. They need the keys for the cabinet in Viktor's dressing-room where he keeps his letters from Emmy, from his father, from his old tutor Herr Wessel, the good Prussian, the man who taught him about German values, made him read Schiller. They take Viktor's keys to the office at the bank.

And all these things, a world of things – a family geography stretching from Odessa, from holidays in Petersburg, in Switzerland, in the South of France, Paris, Kövesces, London, everything – is gone through and noted down. Every object, every incident, is suspect. This is a scrutiny that every Jewish family in Vienna is undergoing.

At the end of these long hours there is a cursory consultation and the Jew Viktor Ephrussi is accused of having contributed 5,000 schillings to the Schuschnigg campaign and this has made him an enemy of the State. He and Rudolf are arrested. They are taken away.

Emmy is allowed two rooms at the back of the house. I go into these rooms. They are small and high and very dark, and an opaque window above the door lets in a little light from the courtyard. She is not allowed to use the main staircase, not allowed to go into their old rooms. She has no servants. She has – at this moment – only her clothes.

I do not know where Viktor and Rudolf were taken. I cannot find the records. I never asked Elisabeth or Iggie.

It is possible that they were taken to the Hotel Metropole, which has been sequestered as the headquarters of the Gestapo. There are many other lock-ups for this flood of Jews. They are beaten, of course; but they are also forbidden to shave or wash so that they look even more degenerate. This is because it is important to address the old affront of Jews not looking like Jews. This process of stripping away your respectability, taking away your watch-chain, or your shoes or your belt, so that you stumble to hold up your trousers with one hand, is a way of returning everyone to the shtetl, stripping you back to your essential character – wandering, unshaven, bowed with your possessions on your back. You are supposed to end up looking like a cartoon from *Die Stürmer*, Streicher's tabloid that is now sold on the streets of Vienna. They take away your reading glasses.

For three days father and son are in prison somewhere in Vienna. The Gestapo need a signature, there is a form that you sign, or you and your son get sent to Dachau. Viktor signs it away, the Palais and its contents and all his other properties in Vienna, the accumulation of all the diligence of the family, a hundred years of possessions. And then they are allowed to return to the Palais Ephrussi, walk in through the open gates, across the courtyard to the servants' staircase in the corner and up to the second floor to these two rooms that are now their home.

And on 27th April it is declared that the property at number 14 Dr Karl Lueger Ring, Vienna 1, formerly the Palais Ephrussi, has been fully Aryanised. It is one of the first to receive such an accolade.

As I stand outside the rooms that they were given, on the other side of the courtyard, the dressing-room and the library seem impossibly close. This is the moment, I think, that is the beginning of exile, the moment when home is with you and is very, very far away.

The house wasn't theirs any more. It was full of people, some in uniforms and some in suits. People counting rooms, making lists of objects and pictures, taking things away. Anna is in there somewhere. She has been ordered to help with this packing-up into boxes and crates, told that she should be ashamed of working for the Jews.

And it not just their art, not just the bibelots, all the gilded stuff from tables and mantelpieces, but their clothes, Emmy's winter coats, a crate of domestic china, a lamp, a bundle of umbrellas and walking-sticks. Everything that has taken decades to come into this house, settling in drawers and chests and vitrines and trunks, wedding-presents and birthday-presents and souvenirs, is now being carried out again. This is the strange undoing of a collection, of a house and of a family. It is the moment of fissure when grand things are taken and when family objects, known and handled and loved, become stuff.

To assess the value of art objects belonging to Jews, appraisal officers are appointed by the Property Transactions Office, who will methodically facilitate the stripping-out of pictures, books, furniture, objects from the houses of Jews. Experts from the museums appraise what is of value. In these early weeks of the *Anschluss* the museums and the galleries hum to the sounds of busy, focused work as letters have to be written and copied, lists created, queries entered about provenance or attribution, and every picture, every piece of furniture, every *objet* ranked. For every single thing there are competing levels of interest.

As I read these documents I think of Charles as he was in Paris. *Amateur de l'art*, passionate and diligent in his searching out and his listing, his life of scholarship, his vagabonding to piece together knowledge about his loved painters, his lacquer, his netsuke collection.

Never have art historians been so useful, their opinions attended to so seriously, than in Vienna in the spring of 1938. And because the *Anschluss* means that all Jews lose their jobs in official institutions, there are exciting opportunities for the right candidates. Two days after the *Anschluss*, Fritz Dworshak, previously the keeper of medals, is made the Director of the Kunsthistorisches Museum. The distribution of all this seized artwork, he announces, is a 'singular, never-to-be-repeated opportunity for expansion . . . in a great number of areas'.

He is correct. Most art objects are to be sold on or auctioned off to raise money for the Reich. Some items are to be bartered with dealers for other objects; some items are to be given to the Führer for his new museum that is being planned for his birthplace of Linz; others to the National Museums. Berlin closely monitors the situation. 'The Führer plans to personally decide on the use of the property after its seizure. He is considering putting artwork first and foremost at the disposal of small Austrian towns for their collections.' Some pictures, some books, some furniture are earmarked for the collections of the Nazi leadership.

In the Palais Ephrussi this process of assessment is now under way. Everything in this great treasure-house is held up to the light and examined. This is what collectors do. In the grey light from the glassed-in courtyard all these objects from this Jewish family are held accountable.

The Gestapo write rather acidly about the taste behind the collections, but note that thirty of the Ephrussi pictures are 'museum-ready'. Three Old Masters are given directly to the 'gallery for painting' at the Kunsthistorisches Museum, six to the Austrian Gallery, one Old Master is sold to a dealer, two terracottas and three paintings traded to a collector, ten sold to another dealer in the Michaelerplatz for 10,000 schillings. And so on and on and on.

Numerous 'artistic and high-quality pieces that are unsuitable for office purposes' go to the Kunsthistorisches Museum (the Museum of Art History) and the Naturhistorisches Museum (the Natural History Museum). All other 'unsuitable' objects are taken to the 'Depot of Moveables', a huge storage depot from which other organisations can come and take their pick.

The very, very best pictures in Vienna are photographed and pasted into ten leather-bound albums, and then these albums are sent to Berlin to be looked over by Hitler.

And in a letter from (initials illegible) Reference: RK 19694 B, from Berlin on 13th October 1938, there is a note that 'The Reichs Fuehrer SS and Chief of the German [sic] submits with letter of 10 August 1938, received here 26 September 1938, 7 inventories concerning property and objects of art confiscated and sequestered respectively in Austria, also 10 albums of photographs and the catalogue are available in the office, the inventories and the certificate are attached.' And apart from the 'Palace including grounds and forest of the Jew Rudolf Gutmann' and '7 estates of the family property of the House Habsburg and Lothringen as well as 4 villas and 1 palace of Otto V. Habsburg', there are the art objects sequestered in Vienna, including the property of: 'Viktor V. Ephrussi, No. 57, 71, 81–87, 116–118 and 120–122 ... Confiscation has been made in favour of various offices: Austria, Reichs Fuehrer SS, NSDAP, Armed Forces, Lebensborn and others.'

While Hitler looks over the albums and chooses what he wants, and while these matters are being discussed and the difference between confiscation and sequestration is mulled over, Viktor's library is taken away: his history books, the Greek and Latin poetry, his Ovid and Virgil, the Tacitus, the runs of English, German and French novels, the huge morocco-leather edition of Dante with the illustrations by Doré that so scared the children, the dictionaries and atlases, Charles's books sent from Paris, the incunabula. Books bought in Odessa and Vienna, sent from his dealers in London and Zurich, his lifetime of reading, are taken off the library's shelves and sorted and packed into wooden crates, and then the crates are nailed shut and are carried down the stairs into the courtyard and heaved onto the back of a lorry. Someone – initials illegible – scrawls a signature across a document, and the lorry coughs and starts up and drives through the oak doors onto the Ring and disappears.

There is a special organisation that identifies particular libraries belonging to Jews. When I go through the membership booklet for the Wiener Club for 1935 – President Viktor v. Ephrussi – I see that eleven of his friends have their libraries taken.

Some of these crates are taken to the National Library. Here the books are picked over by librarians and scholars and then they are dispersed. As with the art historians, these are busy days for librarians and scholars. Some of these books are to stay in Vienna, some end up in Berlin. Others are destined for the '*Führerbibliothek*' planned for Linz, still others for Hitler's private library. And some are earmarked for Alfred Rosenberg's Centre. Rosenberg, the early ideologue of Nazism, is a power in the Reich. 'The essence of the contemporary world revolution lies in the awakening of the racial type,' wrote Rosenberg grandiloquently in his books, 'for Germany the Jewish Question is only solved when the Last Jew has left the Greater German space.' These books, choked with rhetoric, sold in their hundreds of thousands with a popularity second only to *Mein Kampf*. One of the duties of his office became the confiscation of research material from 'ownerless Jewish property' in France, Belgium and Holland.

All across Vienna this is happening. Sometimes Jews are forced to sell things for next to nothing to raise money for the *Reichsflucht* tax in order to be permitted to leave. Sometimes things are just taken. Sometimes taken with violence, sometimes without, but always accompanied by a penumbra of official language, a piece of paper to sign, an admission of guilt, of involvement in activities that run counter to the legality of the Reich. There is lots of documentation: the list of the Gutmanns' collection runs over page after page. The Gestapo take Marianne's eleven netsuke of the boy playing and the dog and the monkey and the tortoise, the ones that she showed to Emmy a lifetime before.

How long does this separation of people and where they have lived take? The Dorotheum, Vienna's auction house, runs one sale after another. Every day there are sales of sequestered property. Every day all these things find people willing to buy them cheap, collectors willing to add to their collections. The sale of the Altmann collection takes five days. It begins on Friday 17th June 1938 at three o'clock, with an English grandfather clock with Westminster chimes. It sells for only thirty reichsmarks. Each day is neatly enumerated to reach an impressive 250 entries.

So this is how it is to be done. It is clear that in the *Ostmark*, the eastern region of the Reich, objects are now to be handled with care. Every silver candlestick is to be weighed. Every fork and spoon is to be counted. Every vitrine is to be opened. The marks on the base of every porcelain figurine will be noted. A scholarly question mark is to be appended to a description of an Old Master drawing; the dimensions of a picture will be measured correctly. And while this is going on, their erstwhile owners are having their ribs broken and teeth knocked out.

Jews matter less than what they once possessed. It is a trial of how to look after objects properly, care for them and give them a proper German home. It is a trial of how to run a society without Jews. Vienna is once again 'an experimental station for the end of the world'.

Three days after Viktor and Rudolf come out of prison, the Gestapo assign the family apartment to the *Amt für Wildbach und Lawinenverbauung*, the Office for Flood and Avalanche Control. Bedrooms become offices. The grand floor of the Palais, Ignace's apartment of gold and marble and painted ceilings, is handed over to the *Amt Rosenberg*, the Office of Alfred Rosenberg, the Plenipotentiary of the Führer for the Supervision of all Intellectual and Ideological Education and Indoctrination in the National Socialist Party.

I picture Rosenberg, slight and well dressed, leaning on the huge Boulle table in Ignace's salon overlooking the Ring, his papers arrayed in front of him. His office is responsible for coordinating the intellectual direction of the Reich, and there is so much to do. Archaeologists, literary men, scholars all need his imprimatur. It is April and the linden trees are showing their first leaves. Out of the three windows in front of him, across the fresh green canopy, there are swastika flags flying from the university, and from the new flagpole that has just been erected in front of the Votivkirche.

Rosenberg is installed in his new Viennese office with Ignace's carefully calibrated hymn to Jewish pride in Zion – his lifetime bet on assimilation – above his head: the grandiose, gilded picture of Esther crowned as Queen of Israel. Above him to his left is the painting of the destruction of the enemies of Zion. But there are to be no Jews in Zionstrasse.

On 25th April there is a ceremonial reopening of the university. Students in lederhosen flank the steps up to the main entrance as Gauleiter Joseph Bürckel arrives. A quota system has been introduced. Only 2 per cent of the university students and faculty will be allowed to be Jewish: from now on, Jewish students can only enter with a permit; 153 of the Medical School's faculty of 197 have been dismissed.

On 26th April Hermann Göring commences his 'transfer-the-wealth' campaign. Every Jew with assets of more than 5,000 Reichsmarks is obligated to tell the authorities or be arrested.

The next morning the Gestapo arrive at the Ephrussi Bank. They spend three days looking at the bank's records. Under the new regulations – regulations that are now thirty-six hours old – the business has to be offered first to any Aryan shareholders. The business also has to be offered at a discount. This means that Herr Steinhausser, Viktor's colleague for twenty-eight years, is asked if he wants to buy out his Jewish colleagues.

It is only six weeks since the planned plebiscite.

Yes, he says, in a post-war interview on his role at the bank, of course he bought them out. 'They needed cash for the "Reichsflucht-steuer", the Reich flight tax . . . they offered me their shares urgently, because this was the fastest way to get cash. The price, Ephrussi and Wiener's price to get out, was "totally appropriate" . . . it was 508,000 Reichsmarks . . . plus the 40,000 Aryanisation tax of course.'

So, on 12th August 1938, Ephrussi and Co. is taken off the business register. In the records it says, singularly, ERASED. Three months later the name is changed to Bankhaus CA Steinhausser. Under its new name it is revalued, and under its new Gentile ownership is worth six times as much as under Jewish ownership.

There is no longer a Palais Ephrussi and there is no longer an Ephrussi Bank in Vienna. The Ephrussi family has been cleansed from the city.

It is on this visit that I go to the Jewish archive in Vienna, the one seized by Eichmann, to check up on the details of a marriage. I look through a ledger to find Viktor, and there is an official red stamp across his first name. It reads 'Israel'. An edict decreed that all Jews had to take new names. Someone has gone through every single name in the lists of Viennese Jews and stamped them: 'Israel' for the men, 'Sara' for the women.

I am wrong. The family is not erased, but written over. And, finally, it is this that makes me cry.

## 26. 'GOOD FOR A SINGLE JOURNEY'

What do Viktor and Emmy and Rudolf need to do to leave the *Ostmark* of the German Reich? They can queue outside as many embassies or consulates as they like – the answer is the same. Quotas have already been filled. There are enough refugees, émigrés, needy Jews in England to keep the lists closed for years to come. These queues are dangerous because they are patrolled by SS, by local police, by those who might hold a grudge. There is the endless pulse of fear that any of those police trucks could pick you up and take you to Dachau.

They need enough money to pay all the inventive taxes, pay for the many punitive permits to emigrate. They need to have an assets declaration of what they owned on 27th April 1938. This is collected by the Jewish Property Declaration Office. They have to declare all domestic and foreign assets, any real estate, business assets, savings, income, pensions, valuables, art objects. Then they have to go to the Finance Ministry to prove that they do not owe any inheritance or building taxes, and then show evidence of income, commercial turnover and pension.

And so Viktor, seventy-eight years old, begins his tour of historical Vienna, visiting one office after another, rebuffed from one place, unable to get into another, queuing in order to get to offices at which he has to queue again. All the desks in front of which he has to stand, the questions barked at him, the stamp resting on the pad of red ink that allows him to leave or not, and the taxes, edicts and protocols that he needs to understand. It is only six weeks since the *Anschluss*, and with all these new laws and new men behind desks anxious to get noticed, anxious to prove themselves in the *Ostmark*, it is mayhem.

Eichmann sets up the Central Office for Jewish Emigration in the Aryanised Rothschild palace in Prinz-Eugen-Strasse to process Jews more quickly. He is learning about how to run an organisation efficiently. His superiors are hugely impressed. This new office will show that it is possible to go in with your wealth and citizenship and depart a few hours later with only a permit to leave.

People are becoming the shadow of their documents. They are waiting for their papers to be validated, waiting for letters of support from overseas, waiting for promises of a position. People who are already out of the country are begged for favours, for money, for evidence of kinship, for chimerical ventures, for anything written on any headed paper at all.

On 1st May the nineteen-year-old Rudolf gets permission to emigrate to the US: a friend has secured him a job in the Bertig Cotton company in Paragould, Arkansas. Viktor and Emmy are left alone in the old house. All the servants have now left except Anna. These three people are not moving towards complete stasis: they are there already, frozen. Viktor goes down the unaccustomed steps to the courtyard, passes the statue of Apollo, avoids the looks of the new officials, and the looks of his old tenants, out of the gateway, past the SA guard on duty, onto the Ring. And where can he go?

He cannot go to his café, to his office, to his club, to his cousins. He has no café, no office, no club, no cousins. He cannot sit on a public bench any more: the benches in the park outside the

Votivkirche have *Juden verboten* stencilled on them. He cannot go into the Sacher, he cannot go into the café Griensteidl, he cannot go into the Central, or go to the Prater, or to his bookshop, cannot go to the barber, cannot walk through the park. He cannot go on a tram: Jews and those who look Jewish have been thrown off. He cannot go to the cinema. And he cannot go to the Opera. Even if he could, he would not hear music written by Jews, played by Jews or sung by Jews. No Mahler and no Mendelssohn. Opera has been Aryanised. There are SA men stationed at the end of the tram line at Neuwaldegg to prevent Jews strolling in the Vienna Woods.

Where can he go? How can they get out?

As everyone tries to leave, Elisabeth returns. She has a Dutch passport, a possible shield against her arrest as a Jewish intellectual and undesirable, but this is a remarkably dangerous thing to do. And she is indefatigable: she sorts out permits for her parents, pretends to be a member of the Gestapo to get an interview with one particular official, finds ways to pay the *Reichsflucht* taxes, negotiates with departments. She refuses to be cowed by the language of these new legislators: she is a lawyer and she is going to do this right. You want to be official, I can be official.

Viktor's passport shows him inching towards departure. On 13th May the stamp *Passinhaber ist Auswanderer*, 'Passport holder is an emigrant', is signed by Dr Raffergerst. Five days later, on 18th May, is the stamp *Einmalige Ausreise nach CSR*, 'good for a single journey'. That night there are reports of German troop movements on the border and a partial mobilisation of the Czechoslovakian army. On 20th May the Nuremberg Laws come into force in Austria. These laws, in existence for three years in Germany, classify Jewishness. If three out of four of your grandparents are Jewish, then you are a

Jew. You are not allowed to marry a Gentile, have sex with a Gentile or display the flag of the Reich. You are not allowed to have a Gentile servant under the age of forty-five.

Anna is a middle-aged Gentile servant who has worked for the Jews since she was fourteen, for Emmy and Viktor and their four children. She has to stay in Vienna. She has to find new employers.

On 20th May the Grenzpolizeikommissariat Wien, the border control in Vienna, gives Viktor and Emmy their final clearance.

On the morning of the 21st Elisabeth and her parents go out of the oak door and turn left onto the Ring. They have to go to the station on foot. They each carry a suitcase. *Die Neue Freie Presse* reports that the weather is a clement fourteen degrees Celsius. It is a route they have done a thousand times along the Ring. Elisabeth leaves them at the station. She has to return to the children in Switzerland.

When Viktor and Emmy reach the border, it is almost impossible to cross into Czechoslovakia as there are fears of an imminent German invasion. They are detained. 'Detained' means that they are taken off the train and kept standing in a waiting-room for hours while telephone calls are made and papers consulted, before they are robbed of 150 Swiss francs and one of their suitcases. Then they are allowed to cross. Later that day Emmy and Viktor arrive at Kövesces.

Kövesces is close to many borders. This has always been one of its attractions, a good meeting point for friends and family from across Europe, a shooting-box, a liberty-hall for writers and musicians.

In the summer of 1938 Kövesces looks much the same as it has done, a jumble of grand and informal. You can see the summer storms approaching across the plains, the bands of willows buffeted by the winds on the edge of the river. The roses are more unkempt,

*Viktor and Emmy at Kövesces,*
*18th August 1938*

in a photo from that month, and Emmy leans into Viktor. It is the only picture I have where they are touching.

The house is much emptier. The four children are dispersed: Elisabeth is in Switzerland, Gisela in Mexico, and Iggie and Rudolf are in America. And you wait for the post each day, wait for a newspaper, wait.

The borders are under review and Czechoslovakia is fissile, and Kövesces is just too close to danger. That summer there is the crisis in the Sudetenland, the area on the western edge of the country: Hitler demands that the German population be allowed to secede to the Reich. There is increasing disruption, the threat of war. In

London, Chamberlain attempts to be emollient, to be tactical and to persuade Hitler that his aspirations can be met.

For nine days in July there is an international conference at Evian on the refugee crisis: thirty-two countries, including the United States, meet and fail to pass a resolution condemning Germany. The Swiss police, wishing to stem the influx of refugees from Austria, have asked the German government to introduce a symbol of some kind so that they can identify Jews at border checkpoints. This has been agreed. Jews' passports are now nullified, must be sent to police stations and will be returned to them stamped with a letter J.

In the early morning of 30th September, Chamberlain, Mussolini and the French Premier Edouard Daladier sign the Munich Accord with Hitler: war has been averted. The lightly shaded areas on the map of Czechoslovakia are to be handed over by 1st October 1938 and the darker areas are to be granted plebiscites. The government in Prague is not present as their country is dismembered. On this day Czech frontier guards leave their posts and Austrian and German refugees are ordered to depart. There are the first Jewish persecutions. There is chaos. Hitler enters the Sudetenland to cheering acclamation two days later. On the 6th there is the formation of a pro-Hitler Slovak government. The new border is just twenty-two miles from the house. On the 10th Germany completes its annexation.

It is only four months since they walked onto the Ring in Vienna to make their way to the station to escape. And now there are German soldiers on every border.

Emmy dies on 12th October.

Neither Elisabeth nor Iggie used the word 'suicide' to me, but they both said she could not go on, that she did not want to go any further. She died in the night. Emmy took too many of her heart pills, the ones she kept in the porcelain box of robin's-egg blue.

In the file of documents is her death certificate, folded into four. A maroon Republic of Czechoslovakia five-krone stamp with a rampant lion is fixed and stamped, though today, the day on which it is filled in, Czechoslovakia no longer exists. On 12th October 1938, it says in Slovak, Emmy Ephrussi von Schey, wife of Viktor Ephrussi, daughter of Paul Schey and Evelina Landauer, died aged fifty-nine. The cause of death was a fault with her heart. It is signed 'Frederik Skipsa, *matrikar*'. And there is a handwritten note in the bottom left-hand corner. The deceased was a citizen of the Reich and these records are according to the laws of the Reich.

I think of her suicide. I think that she did not want to be a citizen of the Reich and to live in the Reich. I wonder whether it was too much for Emmy – that beautiful and funny and angry woman – that the one place in her life in which she had been completely free had become another trap.

Elisabeth heard the news in a telegram two days later. Iggie and Rudolf three days after that in America. Emmy was buried in the churchyard of the hamlet near Kövesces. And my great-grandfather Viktor was alone.

I lay out my thin trail of blue letters from 1938 on the long table in my studio. There are eighteen or so, a scant trail across the winter. They are mostly between Elisabeth, her uncle Pips and cousins in Paris, attempting to track where everyone is, how to gain permission for people to leave, suggestions of how to raise money as surety. How could they get Viktor out of Slovakia? All his property had been sequestered and he was stranded in the middle of the countryside, with an Austrian passport that should have been valid until 1940, but now has negligible value as Austria no longer exists as a separate country. As Viktor had been expelled he could not apply at a German consulate for a German passport. He had started to apply for Czech citizenship, but then that country too disappeared. All he has is a document showing him to be a citizen of Vienna and another document concerning his renunciation of Russian citizenship and acquisition of Austrian citizenship in 1911. But that was in the Hapsburg era.

On 7th November a young Jew walked into the German Embassy in Paris and shot a German diplomat, Ernst von Rath. On the 8th collective punishments against the Jews were announced: Jewish children were no longer to attend Aryan schools, Jewish newspapers were banned. On the evening of the 9th von Rath died in Paris. Hitler decided that the spontaneous demonstrations should be unchecked, that the police should be withdrawn.

Kristallnacht is a night of terror: 680 Jews commit suicide in Vienna: twenty-seven are murdered. Synagogues are burnt across Austria and Germany, shops are looted, Jews are beaten and rounded up for prison and the camps.

The letters, flimsy airmail letters, are increasingly desperate. Pips writes from Switzerland, 'My correspondence has become a kind of clearing-house for friends and relatives who can't write to one another . . . I am terribly worried about them as I hear from reliable sources that sooner or later all Jewish men are to be sent to the so-called "preserve" in Poland.' He begs friends to intercede for Viktor's admission to England. And Elisabeth writes to the British authorities:

As a result of the radical political changes in Cechoslavaquia, and quite especially in Slovaquia in which his present residence is situated, his situation can no longer be deemed safe. Arbitrary measures against Jews, inhabitants as well as immigrants, have already been taken, and the entire subservience of the country to German domination is sufficient justification for apprehending 'legal' measures against Jews in a very short time.

On 1st March 1939 Viktor receives his visa, 'Good for a Single Journey', from British passport control in Prague. The same day Elisabeth and the boys leave Switzerland. They take the train to Calais and the ferry to Dover. On 4th March Viktor arrives at Croydon airport, south of London. Elisabeth is there to meet him and takes him to the St Ermin's Hotel in Madeira Park, Tunbridge Wells, where Henk has booked rooms for them all.

Viktor has one suitcase. He is wearing the same suit Elisabeth had seen him wear to the railway station in Vienna. She notices that on his watch-chain he still carries the key to the bookcase in the library in the Palais, the bookcase of his early printed books of history.

He is an émigré. His land of *Dichter* and *Denker*, poets and thinkers, had become the land of *Richter* and *Henker*, judges and hangmen.

## 27. THE TEARS OF THINGS

Viktor lived in Tunbridge Wells with my grandparents and father and uncles in a rented suburban house, called St David's. A herringbone brick path ran from a wooden gate between two privet hedges up to a porch. It was a sturdy house with gables. There were rose beds and a vegetable garden. It was an ordinary house in an ordinary Kentish town, thirty miles south of London, safe and rather staid.

They went to the church of King Charles the Martyr for morning service on Sundays. The boys – eight, ten and fourteen years old – were sent to schools where they were not teased for their foreign accents, on the strict instructions of the headmaster. They collected shrapnel and soldiers' buttons and made elaborate castles and boats out of cardboard. They went for walks in the beech woods at the weekends.

Elisabeth, who had never cooked in her life, learnt to prepare meals. Her former cook, now living in England, sent her letters that ran to pages, with recipes for *Salzburger Nockerln* and schnitzel, and meticulous instructions: 'the honoured lady slowly *tilts* the frying pan'.

She tutored neighbours' children in Latin for housekeeping money, and translated to make enough to buy the boys their bicycles, £8 each. She tried to write poetry again, but found she could not. In 1940 she wrote an essay on Socrates and Nazism – three pages of fury – and sent it to her friend the philosopher Eric Voegelin in America. She continued her correspondence with her scattered family. Gisela and Alfredo and her boys were in Mexico. Rudolf was still in small-town Arkansas: he sends her a cutting from *The Paragould Soliphone* about 'Rudolf Ephrussi, Baron Ephrussi as he would have been in the old country, a long, good-looking lad, teasing the latest tunes out of his saxophone'. Pips and Olga were in Switzerland. Aunt Gerty had escaped from Czechoslavakia and now lived in London, but there was still no news of Elisabeth's aunt Eva or uncle Jenö, last seen in Kövesces.

Henk, my grandfather, commuted up to London on the 8.18 and was involved in helping to sort out where the Dutch merchant shipping fleet was, and where it should have been.

And Viktor sat in a chair by the kitchen range, the only warm place in the house. He followed the news of the war in *The Times* every day and took the *Kentish Gazette* on Thursdays. He read Ovid, particularly *Tristia*, his poems of exile. When he read, he ran his hand over his face so that the children couldn't see what the poet did to him. He read for most of the day, apart from a short walk up Blatchingdon Road and back, and a nap. Occasionally he walked all the way into the centre of the town to Hall's second-hand bookshop, where the bookseller Mr Pratley was particularly kind to Viktor as he ran his hands along the shelves of Galsworthy, Sinclair Lewis and H. G. Wells.

Sometimes when the boys came back from school he told them about Aeneas and his return to Carthage. There, on the walls, are scenes of Troy. It is only then, confronted by the image of what he has lost, that Aeneas finally weeps. *Sunt lacrimae rerum*, Aeneas says. These are the tears of things, he reads, at the kitchen table as the boys try to finish their algebra, 'Write a Day in the Life of a Pencil', note 'The Dissolution of the Monasteries: Triumph or Tragedy?'

Viktor missed the flat matches that you could buy in Vienna that fitted his waistcoat pocket. He missed his small cigars. He had his black tea in a glass, Russian-style. He poured sugar into it. Once he poured in the family's ration for the week and stirred it round, as everyone sat open-mouthed.

In February 1944, to everyone's delight, Iggie turns up in Tunbridge Wells in his American uniform, an Intelligence Officer with the 7th Corps Headquarters. A childhood switching between English, French and German has made him valuable. Both of the brothers have taken American citizenship to enlist in the army,

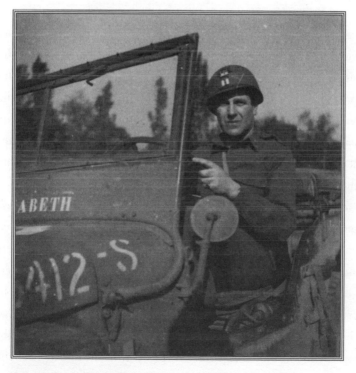

*Iggie during the Normandy campaign, 1944*

Rudolf in Virginia in July 1941 and Iggie in California in January 1942, a month after Pearl Harbor.

The next they know of Iggie is a photograph on the front of *The Times* on 27th June 1944, three weeks after the Allied landings in France. It shows the surrender of a German admiral and a German general at Cherbourg. They stand in sodden greatcoats across from a now-slightly-balding Captain I. L. Ephrussi and the dapper American Major General J. Lawton Collins. There are maps of Normandy pinned to the walls, a tidy desk. And everyone is canted slightly forward to catch Iggie's interpretation of General Collins's terms.

Viktor died on 12th March 1945, a month before Vienna was liberated by the Russians and two months before the unconditional surrender of the German High Command. He was eighty-four. 'Born Odessa, Died Tunbridge Wells' reads his death certificate. Lived, I add as I read it, in Vienna, the centre of Europe. His grave in the municipal cemetery in Charing is far away from his mother in Vichy. And far away from his father and grandfather in the Doric-pillared mausoleum in Vienna, built with all that self-confidence to house the dynastic Ephrussi clan for ever in their new imperial Austrian-Hungarian homeland. It is furthest from Kövesces.

Soon after the war ended Elisabeth received a long letter from uncle Tibor, typed in German. It was sent on from Pips in Switzerland in October. It was on paper that was nearly transparent and it contained dreadful news.

I do not want to repeat everything, but have to write about Jenö and Eva once more. It is terrible to think about the distress under which they died. Jenö already had the certificate in his hand before they were deported from Komarom into the Reich, since he was allowed to go home. He did not want to leave Eva since he believed that they would still be allowed to remain together, but they were immediately separated at the German border and all the better clothes they wore were taken from them too. Both died in January.

Eva, Jewish, had been taken on to the concentration camp at Theresienstadt, where she died of typhus; and Jenö, Gentile, was sent to a labour camp. He died of exhaustion.

Tibor goes on to tell news of neighbours at Kövesces, listing the names of family friends and of cousins of whom I know nothing: Samu, Herr Siebert, the whole Erwin Strasser family, the widow of János Thuróczy, 'a second son who is missing since this time' deported during the war or disappeared into the camps. He writes of the devastation around him, the burnt-out villages, the starvation, the inflation. There are no deer left in the countryside. The estate next to Kövesces, Tavarnok, 'is empty and has burned. Everyone has left, only the old lady is in Tapolcány. I only possess what I am wearing.'

Tibor had been to Vienna to the Palais Ephrussi: 'In Vienna a few things were saved . . . The picture of Anna Herz (Makart) is still there, a portrait of Emmy (Angeli) and the picture of Tascha's mother (I think also Angeli's), a few pieces of furniture, vases etc. Almost all of your father's and my books have disappeared, we found a few of them, some with Wassermann's dedication.' A few family portraits, a few inscribed books and some furniture. No mention of who is there.

In December 1945 Elisabeth decides that she has to return to Vienna to find out who and what remains. And to rescue the picture of her mother and bring it home.

Elisabeth wrote a novel about her journey. It is unpublished. And unpublishable, I think, as I appraise it in typescript, 261 pages with painstaking tippexed corrections. The rawness of its emotion makes for uncomfortable reading. In it she appears as a fictionalised Jewish Professor, Kuno Adler, returning to Vienna from America for the first time since leaving at the *Anschluss*.

It is a book about encounters. She writes of her character's visceral reaction to an official on the train at the border, when asked for a passport:

It was the voice, the intonation that hit a nerve somewhere in Kuno Adler's throat; no, below the throat, where breath and nourishment plunge into the depths of the body, a non-conscious, ungovernable nerve, in the solar plexus probably. It was the quality of that voice, of that accent, soft and yet rough, ingratiating and slightly vulgar, sensible to the ear as a certain kind of stone is to the touch – the soap-stone that is coarse-grained and spongy and slightly oily on the surface – an Austrian voice. 'Austrian passport-control.'

The exiled professor arrives at the bombed-out station and wanders, trying to accommodate himself to the squalor, the rapacity of the poor inhabitants and the ruined landmarks. The Opera, the Stock Exchange, the Academy of Fine Arts – all destroyed. St Stephen's a burnt-out shell.

Outside the Palais Ephrussi the professor stops:

Finally, there he was, on the Ring: the massive pile of the Natural History Museum on his right, the ramp of the Parliament building on his left, beyond it the spire of the Town Hall, and in front of him the railings of the Volksgarten and the Burgplatz. There he was, and there it all was; though the once tree-bordered footpaths across the roadway were stripped, treeless, only a few naked trunks still standing. Otherwise it was all there. And suddenly the dislocation of time which had been dizzying him with illusions and delusions snapped into focus, and he was real, everything was real, incontrovertible fact. He was there. Only the trees were not there, and this comparatively trivial sign of destruction, for which he had not been prepared, caused him incommensurate grief. Hurriedly he crossed the road, entered the park gates, sat down on a bench in a deserted avenue and wept.

Elisabeth's childhood was spent looking through the canopy of the linden trees in front of the house. In May her bedroom was full of the scent of the flowers.

On 8th December 1945, six and a half years since she was last there, Elisabeth walks into her old home. The enormous gates are hanging off their hinges. It is now the offices of the American occupying authorities: the American Headquarters/Legal Council Property Control Sub-Section. Motorbikes and jeeps are parked in the courtyard. Most panes of the glazed roof are smashed: a bomb had landed on the building next door, destroying much of its façade and taking the Palais' caryatids, behind which the children had hidden. There are puddles on the floor. Apollo is still there, on his plinth, paused with his lyre.

Elisabeth climbs the thirty-three steps, the family stairs, to the apartment, and she knocks and is shown in by a charming lieutenant from Virginia.

The apartment is now a series of offices, each room with desks and filing cabinets and stenographers. Lists and memoranda are tacked up on the walls. In the library a huge map of occupied Vienna is hanging above the fireplace, with the Russian, American and Allied zones marked in different colours. There is a pall of cigarette-smoke, the sound of talk and typewriters. She is taken around the offices with interest and sympathy and an air of slight disbelief that this – all this – had been a family home. The American office has simply been floated on top of the last Nazi office.

There are a few pictures still on the walls, the *Junge Frau* in their heavy gilt frames, some studies of Austrian landscapes in mist and the three portraits of Emmy, a grandmother and a great-aunt. The heaviest furniture is still in place, the dining-table and its chairs, a secretaire, wardrobes, beds, the vast armchairs. A few vases. What is still there seems random. Her father's desk is still there in the library. There are some carpets on the floors. But it is still an empty house. More exactly, it is an *emptied* house.

The boxroom is empty. The mantelpieces are empty. The silver-room is empty and so is the safe. There is no piano. There is no Italian cabinet. No little tables inlaid with mosaic. In the library there are empty shelves. The globes are gone, the clocks are gone, the French chairs are gone. Her mother's dressing-room is dusty. It contains a filing cabinet.

There is no desk or mirror, but there is a black-lacquer vitrine and it is empty too.

The kindly lieutenant wants to help and is chatty when he finds that Elisabeth studied in New York. Take your time, he says, look around, find what you can. I'm not sure what we can do for you. It is very cold, and he offers her a cigarette and mentions that there is an old lady who still lives here – he waves his hand – who might know more. A corporal is sent off to find the old woman.

Her name is Anna.

## 28. ANNA'S POCKET

There are two women, one of them older. The younger is now middle-aged with grey hair.

They meet again after a war. It has been eight years since they last met.

They meet in one of the old rooms, now an office full of the clatter of filing. Or they meet in the damp courtyard. All I can see is two women, each of whom has a story.

27th April. Six weeks after the *Anschluss*, the day the doors to the Ringstrasse were left open by Otto Kirchner and the Gestapo came in. It was the start of Aryanisation. Anna was told she could no longer work for Jews, and that she was to work for her country. She was to make herself useful and help sort out the belongings of the previous occupiers, pack them into wooden crates. They had lots to do, and she should start by packing up the silver in the silver-room.

There were crates everywhere, and the Gestapo made lists. Once she'd wrapped something, it was ticked off. After the silver it was porcelain. All around her people were busy taking the apartment to pieces. It was the day Viktor and Rudolf were arrested and taken away, and Emmy was barred from the apartment and sent to the rooms on the other side of the courtyard.

They were taking the silver. 'And your mother's jewellery, the porcelain, your mother's dresses.' And the clocks that Anna had wound (library, hall, salon, the Baron's dressing-room every week), the books from the library, the lovely porcelain figures of the clowns in the salon. Everything. She had looked to see what she could save for Emmy and the children.

'I couldn't carry anything precious away for you. So I would slip three or four of the little figures from the Baroness's dressing-room, the little toys you played with when you were children – you remember – and I put them into the pocket of my apron whenever I was passing, and I took them to my room. I hid them in the mattress of my bed. It took me two weeks to get them all out of the big glass case. You remember how many there were!

'And they didn't notice. They were so busy. They were busy with all the grand things – the Baron's paintings and the gold service from the safe, and the cabinets from the drawing-room, and the statues and all your mother's jewellery. And all the Baron's old books that he loved so much. They didn't notice the little figures.

'So I just took them. And I put them in my mattress and I slept on them. Now you are back, I have something to return to you.'

In December 1945 Anna gave Elisabeth 264 Japanese netsuke.

This is the third resting-place in the story of the netsuke.

From Charles and Louise in Paris, the vitrine in the lambent yellow room with all those Impressionist pictures, to Emmy and her children in Vienna, the interweaving of stories and dressing up, childhood and make-believe, to this strange bedding-down with Anna in her room.

The netsuke had been moved around before. Ever since they had arrived from Japan they had been appraised: picked up, examined, weighed in the hand, placed again. That is what dealers do. It is what collectors do, and it is what children do. But when I think of the netsuke in Anna's apron pocket with a duster or a spool of thread, I think that these netsuke have never received so much care. It is April 1938 and, with the *Anschluss* still giddy with proclamations, the art historians are working dedicatedly on the inventories, pasting photographs into the Gestapo folders to be sent to Berlin, and the librarians are marking up their lists of books so diligently. They are preserving art for their country. And Rosenberg needs Judaica to prove his theories on the animality of the Jews for his institute. Everyone is working so hard, but none of them come near the dedication and diligence of Anna. With Anna sleeping on them, the netsuke are looked after with more respect than anyone has ever shown them. She has survived the hunger and the looting, and the fires and the Russian invasion.

Netsuke are small and hard. They are hard to chip, hard to break: each one is made to be knocked around in the world. 'A netsuke must be devised so as not to be a nuisance to the user,' says a guide. They hold themselves inwards: a deer tucking its legs beneath its body; the barrel-maker crouching inside his half-finished barrel; the rats a tumble around the hazelnut. Or my favourite, a monk asleep over his alms bowl; one continuous line of back. They can be painful: the end of the ivory bean-pod is as sharp as a knife. I think of them inside a mattress, a strange mattress where boxwood and ivory from Japan meet Austrian horsehair.

Touch is not only through the fingers, but through the whole body, too.

Each one of these netsuke for Anna is a resistance to the sapping of memory. Each one carried out is a resistance against the news, a story recalled, a future held on to. Here that Viennese cult of *Gemütlichkeit* – the easy tears over sentimental stories, the wrapping of everything in pastry and cream, the melancholy falling away from happiness, those candied pictures of servant girls and their beaux – meets a place of adamantine hardness. I think of Herr Brockhaus and his imprecations against the carelessness of servants, and I think of how wrong he was.

There is no sentimentality, no nostalgia. It is something much harder, literally harder. It is a kind of trust.

I heard Anna's story a long time ago. I heard it in Tokyo, the first time I saw the netsuke lit up in a long glass vitrine held between bookcases. Iggie had made me a gin and tonic, and himself a Scotch and soda, and he said – in passing, under his breath – that they were a hidden story. By which he meant, I think now, not that he was hesitant of telling the story, but that the story was about hiddenness.

I knew the story. I didn't *feel* the story until my third visit to Vienna, when I was standing in the courtyard of the Palais with a man from the offices of Casino Austria who asked me if I wanted to see the secret floor.

We went up the Opera Stairs and he pushed part of the panelling on the left and we ducked through into a whole floor, room after room with no windows to the outside: when you stand on the Ring, the eye moves unimpeded from street level to Ignace's grand floor. It maps the great rooms above, but each of these is compressed. There are only small, opaque square windows into the courtyard, insignificant enough to be disguised as part of the treatment of the wall. The only way on or off the floor is either through the door disguised as a panel of marble that leads onto the grand stairs or via the servants' stair in the corner to the courtyard. It is the floor of servants' rooms.

The place where Anna slept is now the company cafeteria. Standing amongst the bustle of a workday lunchtime in Vienna, I feel that lurch of something not being right – that lurch when you have turned a page and find yourself reading without understanding. You have to go back and start again, and the words seem even more unfamiliar and sound strangely in your head.

And, said the man responsible for the house, warming to his project, have you noticed the way that light is brought into the house? How do you think the Opera Stairs have light? So we climb up the servants' spiral staircase and push open a little door to a whole roof-landscape of iron bridges and ladders. We cross to the parapet above the caryatids and peer down so that I can see that: yes, there are hidden lightwells, too. He fetches the plans and shows me the way in which the house is connected to its neighbours, and how the subterranean passages into the cellars meant that you could bring fodder and straw in for the horses without using the front gates.

This whole solid house, inlaid and overlaid and gessoed and painted, marble and gold, was as light as a toy theatre, a run of hidden spaces behind a façade. *Potemkinische.* This marble wall is scagliola, lath and plaster.

It is a house of hidden children's toys, hidden games on the parapets above the Palais, hide-and-seek in the tunnels and the cellars, secret drawers in cabinets with lovers' letters to Emmy. But it was also a house of unseen people and unknown lives. Food appearing from hidden kitchens, linen disappearing into hidden laundries. People sleeping in airless rooms tucked between floors.

It was a place to hide where you have come from. It was a place to hide things in.

I started the journey with my files of family letters, a sketch-map of sorts. More than a year has passed and I keep finding hidden things. Not just forgotten things: the Gestapo lists and diaries, journals, novels and poems and press-cuttings. The wills and the shipping manifests. The interviews with bankers. The overheard comments in a back room in Paris, and the swatches of cloth for dresses made for turn-of-the-century cousins in Vienna. The pictures and the furniture. I can find the lists of who came to a party a hundred years ago.

I know too much about the traces of my gilded family, but I cannot find out any more about Anna.

She is not written about, refracted into stories. She is not left money in Emmy's will: there is no will. She does not leave traces in the ledgers of dealers or of dress-makers.

I am compelled to keep looking. In libraries, I stumble across things that lead onwards, sideways. I am looking to check a fact – the date of the yellow carpet of the winds, from Charles's salon, something on the painter of the ceilings in the Palais Ephrussi – when I see a footnote and then a note in an appendix. I am winded to find that Louise's house in the rue Bassano, the one opposite Jules and Fanny's house, up the street from Charles's last house, all golden stone and curlicues, was used by the Nazis as one of their Paris detention camps. It was one of three annexes of the Drancy concentration camp where Jewish inmates had to sort, clean and repair furniture and objects stolen by Rosenberg's organisation for the functionaries of the Reich.

Then, terribly, there is a note in brackets that the girl in the blue dress in Renoir's double portrait of the daughters of Louise Cahen d'Anvers – the commission so endlessly and anxiously fussed over by Charles to raise money for Renoir – had been deported and had died in Auschwitz. And then I find that Fanny and Theodore Reinach's son Leon and his wife Beatrice Camondo and their two children were deported. This family died in Auschwitz in 1944.

All those old calumnies, venomous diatribes against the Jewish families on that golden hill, had their late and appalling flowering in Paris.

Here, in this house, I am wrong-footed. The survival of the netsuke in Anna's pocket, in her mattress, is an affront. I cannot bear for it to slip into symbolism. Why should they have got through this war in a hiding-place, when so many hidden people did not? I can't make people and places and things fit together any more. These stories unravel me.

And there are things that I have been searching for ever since I heard the story almost thirty years ago when I first met Iggie in Japan. There is a space around Anna, like that around a figure in a fresco. She was a Gentile. She had worked for Emmy since she got married. 'She was always there,' Iggie would say.

She gave the netsuke to Elisabeth in 1945, and Elisabeth put the persimmon and the ivory stag and the rats and the rat-catcher and the masks that she had loved when she was six, and all the rest of this world, into a little leather attaché case to take back to England. They can expand to fill a huge vitrine in a Paris salon or a dressing-room in Vienna, but they also fit into next to nothing.

I do not even know Anna's whole name, or what happened to her. I never thought to ask, when I could have asked. She was, simply, Anna.

## 29. 'ALL QUITE OPENLY, PUBLICLY AND LEGALLY'


Elisabeth took the little attaché case with the jumble of netsuke home. England was home now: there was no question that she would take the family to live in Vienna. Iggie, demobbed from the American army and searching for work, felt the same. Returning to Vienna was something that very few Jews would do. There were 185,000 Jews in Austria at the time of the *Anschluss*. Of these only 4,500 returned; 65,459 Austrian Jews had been killed.

Nobody was called to account. The new democratic Austrian Republic established after the war gave an amnesty to 90 per cent of members of the Nazi Party in 1948, and to the SS and Gestapo by 1957.

The return of émigrés was felt to be harassment of those who had stayed. My grandmother's novel of return to Vienna helps me understand how she felt. There is one moment of confrontation in Elisabeth's novel that is particularly revealing. The Jewish professor is challenged as to why he returned, what he was expecting out of Austria: 'You did choose to leave a little early. I mean you resigned before you could be dismissed – and you left the country.' This is the key, powerful question: What do you want by coming back? Have you come back to take something from us? Have you come back as an accuser? Have you come back to show us up? And, as a tremor beneath these other questions: Could your war have been worse than our war?

Restitution was difficult for those who survived. Elisabeth fictionalises this in one of the strangest moments in the novel, when a collector, Kanakis, notices 'two dark, heavily-framed pictures hanging on the wall just opposite his chair, and a faint smile creased his eyelids'.

'Do you really recognise those pictures?' exclaims the new owner. 'They did in fact belong to a gentleman who was surely an acquaintance of your family, Baron E. You might possibly have seen them at his house. Baron E unfortunately died abroad, in England, I believe. His heirs, after they had recovered what could be traced of his property, had it all sold at auction, having no use for this old-fashioned stuff in their modern homes, I suppose. I acquired them in the auction-rooms, as well as most of the things you see in this room. All quite openly, publicly and legally, you understand. There is no great demand for this period.'

'There is no need to apologise, Herr Doktor,' replies Kanakis, 'I can only congratulate you on your bargains.'

'All quite openly, publicly and legally' were words that Elisabeth was to hear repeated back to her. She discovered that, on the list of priorities in a shattered society, the restitution of property to those from whom it had been sequestered came near the bottom. Many of those who had appropriated Jewish property were now respected citizens of the new Austrian Republic. This was also a government that rejected reparations, because in their view Austria had been an occupied country between 1938 and 1945: Austria had become the 'first victim', rather than an agent in the war.

As the 'first victim', Austria had to hold out against those who would damage it. Dr Karl Renner, a lawyer and post-war president of Austria, was clear about this. He wrote in April 1945:

Restitution of property stolen from Jews . . . [should be] not to the individual victims, but to a collective restitution fund. The establishment of such and the following foreseeable arrangements is necessary in order to prevent a massive, sudden flood of returning exiles . . . A circumstance, that for many reasons must be paid very close attention to . . . Basically the entire nation should be made not liable for damages to Jews.

When, on 15th May 1946, the Republic of Austria passed a law which declared that any transactions that had made use of discriminatory Nazi ideology were to be deemed null and void, it seemed that the path was open. But the law was strangely unenforceable. If your property had been sold under the policy of forced Aryanisation, then you might be asked to buy it back. If an artwork was returned to you that was considered significant to Austria's cultural heritage, then its export was blocked. But if you donated works to the museum, then a permit for other lesser artworks might be forthcoming.

In deciding what to return and what not to return, the government agencies used the documents to hand that held the most authority. These were those put together by the Gestapo, who were noted for their thoroughness.

One file, on the appropriation of Viktor's collection of books, noted that a library was handed over to the Gestapo, but 'there is no record describing its full content. However, there can only have been a small number of works, given that the document confirming the takeover mentions the content of two large and two small boxes as well as of a rotating bookshelf.'

So, on 31st March 1948, 191 books are returned from the Austrian National Library to the heirs of Viktor Ephrussi; 191 books are a couple of shelves full, a few yards out of the hundreds that made up his room.

And so it goes. Where are the records Herr Ephrussi kept? He is still held culpable, even after death. Viktor's life of books is lost because of a document with its initials illegible.

Another file is on the appropriation of the art collection. It contains a letter between the directors of two museums. They have an inventory made by the Gestapo, and they have to sort out what happened to the pictures 'of the banker Ephrussi, Wien I , Lueggerring 14. The inventory does not form a particularly valuable arts collection but the wall decoration from the apartment of a wealthy man. From the style it seems clearly to have been put together according to the taste of the 1870s.'

There are no receipts, but the 'only paintings, which were not sold, were the absolutely not sellable ones'. The implication is that there is not much one can really do.

Reading these letters, I feel idiotically angry. It is not that it matters that these art historians don't like the taste of 'the banker Ephrussi' and his wall decoration, though the phrase is far too close to the Gestapo's 'Jew Ephrussi' for comfort. It is the way in which the archives are used to close down the past: there is no receipt for this, we cannot read that signature. It was only nine years ago, I think, and these transactions were by your colleagues. Vienna is a small city. How many calls would it take to sort this out?

My father's childhood was punctuated by Elisabeth writing letter after letter against the backdrop of failing expectations that the family would get their fortune returned. She wrote partly from anger at the way in which pseudo-legalistic measures were put up to dissuade claimants. She was a lawyer, after all. But mostly because all four siblings were in real financial need and she was the only one in Europe.

Whenever a picture was retrieved, it was sold and the money split. The Gobelin tapestries were recovered in 1949 and sold for school fees. Five years after the war the Palais Ephrussi was returned to Elisabeth. It was not a good time to sell a war-damaged Palais in a city still under control of four armies, and it raised just $30,000. After that Elisabeth gave up.

Herr Steinhausser, Viktor's former business partner who had become President of the Association of Austrian Banks, was asked in 1952 if he knew anything of the history of the Ephrussi Bank that he had Aryanised. It was believed that the following year, 1953, would be the centenary of its foundation in Vienna. 'Know nothing of it,' he writes back. 'Won't be celebrated.'

The Ephrussi legatees received 50,000 schillings on agreeing to a renunciation of any further claim. It was the equivalent of about $5,000 at the time.

I find all this stuff about restitution exhausting. I can see how you could spend your life tracking something down, your energy sapping away with all these rules and letters and legalities. You know that on someone else's mantelpiece is chiming the clock from the salon, with the mermaids twined liquidly around its base. You open a sales catalogue and see two ships in a gale, and suddenly you are standing by the door to the stairs with nanny wrapping a muffler around your neck ready for your walk along the Ring. For one held breath you can piece together a life, a broken setting for a diasporic family.

It was a family that could not put itself back together. Elisabeth provided a kind of centre in Tunbridge Wells, writing and relating news, sending on photographs of nieces and nephews. After the war Henk started a good job in London working for the UN relief association and they were more comfortably off. Gisela was in Mexico. She had lean times and worked as a cleaner to support the family. Rudolf was demobbed and living in Virginia. And fashion had 'given up' on Iggie – as he put it. He could not face working on gowns again: the thread from Vienna to Paris to New York had been broken by his battle experiences in 1944 in France.

He was now working for Bunge, an international grain exporter, an unintentional return to the patriarch's roots in Odessa. His first assignment had been a long year in Léopoldville in the Belgian Congo, hated for both its heat and its brutality.

In October 1947 Iggie visited England between postings. He had been offered placements back in the Congo or in Japan, neither of which appealed. He travelled to Tunbridge Wells to see Elisabeth and Henk and his nephews, and to visit his father's grave for the first time. Then he planned to make a decision about his future.

It was after supper. The boys had done their homework and were in bed. Elisabeth opened the attaché case and showed him the netsuke.

A melee of rats. The fox with inlaid eyes. The monkey wrapped around the gourd. His brindled wolf. They take a few out and put them on the kitchen table of the suburban house.

We didn't say anything, Iggie told me. We had last looked at them together in our mother's dressing-room, thirty years before, sitting on the yellow carpet.

It's Japan, he said. I'll take them back.

*Part Four*

# TOKYO 1947–1991

## 30. TAKENOKO

On 1st December 1947 Iggie received Military Permit no. 4351 for entry to Japan G1 GHQ FEC, Tokyo. Six days later he arrived in the occupied city.

Coming in from Haneda airport, the taxi swerved around the worst of the potholes in the roads, swerved to avoid the children, the bicyclists and the women in their baggy patterned trousers trudging towards the city. Tokyo was a strange landscape. The first thing to notice were the looping calligraphies of telephone wires and power cables stretching in every featureless direction over the red of the rusted iron roofing on the shacks. Then, in the winter light, Mount Fuji rose up in the south-west.

The Americans had bombed Tokyo for three years, but the raids of 10th March 1945 were cataclysmic. There were walls of flame from the incendiary bombs, 'sowing the sky with fire': 100,000 people were killed and sixteen square miles of the city were destroyed.

All but a handful of buildings were flattened or incinerated. Those that survived included the Imperial Palace behind its grey ramparts of boulders and its wide moats, the few built from stone or concrete, the odd *kura*, the storehouse in which merchant families kept their treasures, and the Imperial Hotel. This had been designed by Frank Lloyd Wright in 1923, a fantastic, brash confection of concrete temples around a series of pools, a slightly Aztec version of *Japonisme*. It had also survived the earthquake of 1923 and was grazed, but mostly intact.

So were the Japanese parliament building, the Diet, some government ministries, the American Embassy and office buildings in the Marunouchi business district opposite the palace.

All had been requisitioned for the Occupation authorities. The journalist James Morris, later Jan Morris, wrote of this strange area in his 1947 travelogue *The Phoenix Cup*: 'Marunouchi is a small American island surrounded by a Japanese sea of ashes, rubble and rusted cans. Walking around the blocks, discordant music, from the Armed Forces Radio Station, batters on the eardrums, and ruminating G.I.s off duty stand propped against the nearest convenient wall . . . one might be in Denver . . .'

It was here, in the grandest of these buildings, the Dai-Ichi (Number One) Building, that General MacArthur had his headquarters. The Supreme Commander Allied Powers (SCAP). The Yankee Daimyo.

Iggie arrived two years after the Emperor had broadcast his declaration of defeat in his high falsetto, using a diction and locution unknown outside the court, warning that 'the hardships and sufferings to which our nation is to be subjected will be great . . .' In the months since, Tokyo had become used to its army of occupation. The Americans had declared that they would rule with sensitivity.

In the photograph of the General and the Emperor in the US Embassy in Tokyo the relationship was made clear. MacArthur is in khaki uniform, an open-necked shirt and boots. He has his hands on his hips, a 'big, ribbonless American soldier', as *Life* puts it. The Emperor is alongside. He is slight, immaculate, in a black suit with his wing collar and striped tie, caught in convention. Sensitivity and manners, states the photograph, are up for negotiation now. The Japanese press refuse to publish the picture. SCAP makes sure it is published. The day after the photograph is taken, the Empress sends

Mrs MacArthur a bouquet of flowers grown in the palace grounds. And a few days later a lacquer box with the imperial crest. Cautious, anxious communications are started with gifts.

Iggie's taxi took him to the Teito Hotel opposite the Palace. It was not only difficult to get papers to get into Japan and permission to stay; it was then difficult to get lodgings when you arrived, because the Teito was one of only two hotels standing. The non-military expatriate community was tiny. Apart from the diplomatic corps and the press, there were only a handful of businessmen like Iggie and a scattering of academics. He had arrived as the trials of war criminals, including Hideki Tojo and Ryuchi Tanaka, head of the secret police, were just starting at the International Military Tribunal for the Far East. Tojo, according to the Western press, had 'the unearthly smugness of the samurai'.

There were constant edicts from SCAP concerning everything from the minutiae of civic life to how Japan was to be ruled, and these often reflected American sensitivities. MacArthur had decided that there was to be a separation between the Shinto religion – deeply implicated in the rise of nationalism of the last fifteen years – and the government. He also wanted the great industrial and commercial conglomerates broken up:

The emperor is the head of the state . . . his duties and powers will be exercised in accordance with the new constitution and responsible to the basic will of the people as provided therein . . . War as a sovereign right of the nation is abolished . . . The feudal system of Japan will cease . . . No patent of nobility will from this time forth embody within itself any national or civic power of government.

MacArthur had also decided that women should get the vote for the first time in Japan's history and that the twelve-hour day in factories should be reduced to eight. Democracy had come to Japan, SCAP announced. The local and foreign press were censored.

The American army in Tokyo had their newspapers and magazines, as well as their radio blaring out from sentry boxes. They had their brothels (the RAA, or Recreation and Amusement Association) and their sanctioned pick-up joints (the Oasis of Ginza, with girls dressed in 'shoddy imitations of long, afternoon frocks', in the words of one American commentator). There were special carriages on trains reserved for members of the Occupation Army. A theatre had been requisitioned and had become the 'Ernie Pyle', where soldiers could see films or revues, go to a library or to one of 'several large lounges'. And there were the Occupation-only stores, the OSS (Overseas Supply Store) and the PX, which stocked American and European food, cigarettes, household utensils and liquor. They accepted only dollars or MFC: military payment certificates, military scrip.

As this was an occupied country, everything had an acronym – opaque to both the defeated and to newcomers.

In this strange defeated city, street names had been removed, so that there was now an A Avenue and a 10th Street. Alongside the military jeeps and General MacArthur's 1941 black Cadillac, with a master sergeant at the wheel and an escort of white MP jeeps sweeping through the streets en route to his office, were Japanese vans and trucks burning coal or wood for propulsion, spewing out smoke, and three-wheeler taxis, the *bata-bata*, getting stuck in the cavernous potholes. There were still notices up outside Ueno station asking for information on lost relatives, soldiers returning from abroad.

The poverty of those years was extreme. The destruction of 60 per cent of the city meant overcrowding in the ramshackle houses that had been rebuilt out of any materials to hand. The American army had commandeered most building materials in the first eighteen months. But it also meant that workers had to struggle for hours to get in from countryside billets on horrific trains. New clothing was very difficult to buy, and it was common for years after the war to see decommissioned men still in their uniforms, stripped of their badges, and women in *mompei*, the baggy trousers that used to be worn in the fields.

There was not enough fuel. Everyone was cold. The baths charged black-market rates for the first hour before the water temperature dropped. Offices were barely heated, but workers were 'not in a hurry to leave the office, since they have nothing much else to do. Most of the offices have some sort of heating in winter, and the workers can keep warm as long as they stay there.' In one bad winter, train officials said that they would silence the whistles of locomotives to save coal.

Above all, there simply was not enough food. This meant leaving before dawn on crowded trains to barter in the country for rice. There were rumours that farmers had stacks of money a foot high. Or it meant going to the blue-sky black markets that had sprung up near the railway stations in Tokyo, where you could buy and sell and barter anything in the open air under the disinterested eyes of the army. There was an American Lane in the market near the Ueno station to cater for goods that had been appropriated or bartered from Occupation forces. American army blankets were particularly sought after. 'As the trees shed their leaves, Japanese shed their kimonos, one by one, to sell for food. They even devised an ironic name for their wretched existence: *takenoko,* after the bamboo sprout which peels, layer after layer.' Faced with this hardship, the phrase of the moment was *Shikata ga nai*. It means 'Nothing can be done about it', with a strong undercurrent of 'and don't complain'.

Many of these American goods, the spam and the Ritz biscuits and the Lucky Strikes, were taken to the black market by the *panpan* girls, the 'squalid tribe of harpies . . . girls who go with soldiers for food . . . In the daytime, they stroll about in cheap, smart dresses from the PX, noisily talking and laughing, almost invariably chewing gum, or enraging hungry citizens in trains and buses by a display of their ill-gotten gains.'

There was much discussion of these girls and what they meant for Japan. There had been so much fear about the American army that the *panpan* were seen as a sacrificial way of preserving the decency of the majority of Japanese women. This was allied to horror at their lipstick, their clothes and the way they kissed in public. Kissing became symbolic of the release from conventions that the Occupation had brought.

There were also gay bars – what Yukio Mishima called *gei pati* in his novel *Kinjiki* (*Forbidden Colours*), serialised in the early 1950s. *Gei* was written in roman script, indicating that it was already in common usage. Hibiya Park was a popular pick-up spot. I only have the unreliable Mishima as a guide: 'He entered the dim, clammy lamplight of the rest room, and saw what is called an "office" among the fellowship. (There are four or five such important places in Tokyo.) It was an office where the tacit procedure is based on winks instead of documents, tiny gestures instead of print, code communication in place of a telephone.'

There was a need to be entrepreneurial. This young generation was known colloquially as *Apure, 'après-guerre'*. An *Apure* is a 'college student who frequents dance-halls, passes examinations by hiring a proxy, and may engage in un-orthodox money-making activities'. The key was their unorthodox way of surviving, as much as their aspirations to achieve an American standard of life. They had managed to disrupt norms concerning how to work. 'Since the war tardiness has become the norm,' wrote one Japanese commentator of these *Apure*. They might be late to work, dishonest in exams, yet they were also known as hustlers, able to make money out of nothing. Hustling meant being able to wear aloha shirts, nylon belts or even rubber-soled shoes, called the 'three sacred regalia' in an ironic reference to the three sacred symbols associated with the Emperor. In the years after the defeat there was a slew of new magazines aimed at young men, with articles on 'How to save Y1,000,000' or 'How to Become a Millionaire from Scratch'.

In Tokyo in the summer of 1948 the hit song was 'Tokyo boogie-woogie'. It blared out from loudspeakers on the streets and from nightclubs advertising themselves. 'Tokyo boogie-woogie/Rhythm ookie-ookie/Kokoro zookie-zookie/Waku-waku.' This is the start, says the press, of *kasutori*, pulp culture: it will overwhelm us. Vulgar and brash, hedonistic, limitless.

Shops spill into the streets. There are white-robed veterans begging on the streets, unscrewed tin legs or arms in front of them, a sign out with a list of the campaigns they had fought in. Children roam everywhere. War orphans with stories of parents dead of typhus in Manchuria, begging, stealing, feral. School kids shouting out for *chocoretto* or cigarettes, or the phrases they have learnt from page one of the *Japanese–English Conversation Manual*:

Thank you!
Thank you, awfully!
How do you do?

Or, as they have learnt it in phonetic form: *San kyu! San kyu ofuri! Hau dei dou?*

The sounds of the pachinko parlours, the cacophonous cascading din of thousands of small metal balls ricocheting around the machines. You could buy twenty-five for the equivalent of a shilling and, with dexterity, could sit for several hours under the strip-lights feeding them in. The prizes – cigarettes, razor blades, soap and canned food – can be sold back to the owner for another cupful of balls, another few hours of oblivion.

Street life, the sprawl on the pavement outside a bar of drunken salarymen in their thin black suits with their thin ties over woollen overshirts. The peeing in the streets, the spitting. The comments as to your height, or hair colour. The everyday litany of the kids calling *gai-jin, gai-jin*, 'foreigner, foreigner' after you. Then there is the other Tokyo street life: the blind masseuses, tatami-mat makers, pickle-sellers, the crippled elderly women, the monks. Then the sellers of skewers of pork and pepper, ochrous tea, fat chestnut sweets, salted fish and seaweed snacks, the smells of grilling fish over charcoal braziers. Street life means being accosted by shoe-shine boys, flower-sellers, itinerant artists, bar touts, as well as smells and noise.

If you were a foreigner, you were not allowed to fraternise. You were not allowed to enter the homes of Japanese, or to go to a Japanese restaurant. But in the streets, you were part of a noisy, jostling world.

Iggie had a small attaché case filled with ivory monks, craftsmen and beggars, but he knew nothing about this country.

## 31. KODACHROME

Iggie told me that before he arrived he had read only one book on Japan, *The Chrysanthemum and the Sword: Patterns of Japanese Culture,* bought en route in Honolulu. It was written by the ethnographer Ruth Benedict at the invitation of the American Office of War Information, pieced together through research into press clippings, literature in translation and interviews with internees. Its clarity is due, perhaps, to the fact that Benedict had no direct experience of Japan. There is a pleasingly simple polarity in the book between the samurai sword of self-responsibility and the chrysanthemum, trained into its aesthetic shape only by means of hidden wires. Her famous thesis that the Japanese had a culture of shame rather than a culture of guilt was hugely influential amongst the American officers in central Tokyo planning the shape of Japanese education, law and political life. Benedict's book was translated into Japanese in 1948 and was enormously popular. Of course it was. What could be more intriguing than to see how the Americans saw Japan? And how a woman saw Japan at that.

Iggie's copy of Benedict is in front of me as I write. His meticulous pencil notes – mostly exclamation marks – stop seventy pages before the end and the final chapters on self-discipline and childhood. Perhaps his plane had landed.

Iggie's first office was in the business district of Marunouchi, with its dull, wide streets. In summer it became impossibly hot, but his memories were of the cold of that first winter of 1947. There was a little *hibachi*, the stove fed by charcoal, in each office, but these only give a vague impression of heat. They acknowledge the possibility, but without warming you properly. You would need to put one under your jacket to make any difference.

It is night outside. The offices are lit up beyond the fire escape. Heads down over the typewriters, the arms of their white shirts folded back twice, these young men are busy with the Japanese miracle. Cigarettes and abacuses lie amongst their papers. They have swivel chairs. Iggie is partly out of view, standing with a sheaf of papers, in an office with opaque glass and a telephone (rare).

The office knows it is the end of the day when Iggie disappears down the corridor just before five o clock. To shave you need hot water, so he would heat up the kettle on the office *hibachi*. And he must shave before going out.

Iggie hated living in the hotel in the Denver-like part of Tokyo and within weeks had moved to his first house. It was in Senzoku, on the edge of Senzoku Lake, in the south-eastern part of the city. It was more of a pond, he told me – and, anxious to make it clear, a large Thoreau pond, not a small English pond. He moved in winter, and had been told about the cherry trees that grew in the garden and round the water, but was still unprepared for the effect when spring came. The drama built over the weeks in front of him, until there was such abundance of blossom that he said it was like a blinding white cloud across your retina. You lost foreground or background or distance and floated.

After so many years of living with only the contents of a suitcase or two, this was Iggie's first house. He was forty-two and had lived in Vienna and Frankfurt and Paris and New York and Hollywood,

*A summer party in Senzoku, Tokyo, 1951*

and in army billets across France and Germany – and in Léopoldville – but had never been able to shut a door in his own house until this first liberated, exhilarating spring in Japan.

The house had been built in the 1920s, with an octagonal dining-room and a balcony overlooking the lake, perfect for drinks parties. You stepped out of the sitting-room onto a large, flat boulder and then down into the garden with its clipped pines and azaleas, a terrace of stones arranged in a careful random pattern, and a moss garden. It was the kind of house that the young Japanese diplomat Ichiro Kawasaki described: 'In pre-war years a university professor or army colonel could afford to build such a house and live there himself. Today the owners find these houses so expensive to maintain that they must either sell them or rent them to foreigners.'

I'm looking at the clutch of small, round-cornered Kodachrome prints of this first house of Iggie's in Tokyo. 'Zoning is a subject to which Japanese city planners have given little thought. It is quite common to find a group of slummy wooden shacks of labourers immediately adjacent to the palatial residence of a millionaire.' That is the case here, though the rebuilding of the shacks to the left and the right are being done in concrete rather than wood and paper. This neighbourhood is starting again: temples and shrines, the local market, the bicycle-repair man and the cluster of shops at the end of the road – more a track than a road – where you can buy fat white daikon radishes laid out in rows, and cabbages, and little else.

We start on the front doorstep with Iggie, hand in pocket, tie clip glinting on a green silk tie. He is a broad man now, given to keeping a handkerchief in his jacket pocket. This is something that the youngsters in his office have started to copy, the coordinating pocket handkerchief–necktie combo. Today he is in brogues. He looks a little squirearchical. He could be in the Cotswolds if it was not for the pruned pines that flank him and the green tiles of the roof. We move inside into a long corridor and turn left, where the cook Mr Haneda is in his whites, eyes closed against the flash, leaning on the new cooker, chef's hat set jauntily on the back of his head. A bottle of Heinz ketchup is the only food in view, Kodachrome scarlet against all the blindingly clean enamel.

Back in the corridor we move through an open doorway, under a Noh mask and into the sitting-room. The ceiling is of slatted wood. All the lamps are on. Objects are displayed on spare, dark, clean-lined Korean and Chinese furniture alongside comfortable low sofas, occasional tables and lamps, and ashtrays and cigarette boxes. A wooden Buddha from Kyoto sits on a Korean chest, a hand raised in blessing.

The bamboo bar holds an impressive quantity of liquor, none of which I can identify. It is a house made for parties. Parties with small children on their knees, and women in kimonos, and presents. Parties with men in dark suits seated round small tables, loquacious with whisky. Parties at New Year with cut boughs of pine trees hanging from the ceiling, and parties under the cherry trees, and once – in a spirit of poetry – a firefly-viewing party.

There is lots and lots of fraternisation here: Japanese and American and European friends, sushi and beer served by Mrs Kaneko, the maid in her uniform. It is Liberty Hall, again.

It is also a house with panache. There is none of the clutter of his childhood in the Palais: it is a dramatic interior of golden screens and scrolls, paintings and Chinese pots created as a new home for the netsuke.

For right in the centre of this house, in the centre of Iggie's life, are the netsuke. Iggie designed a glass case for them. It has a patterned paper on the walls behind it, a pale-blue pattern of chrysanthemums. Not only are the 264 netsuke back in Japan, but they are back on show in a salon. They are placed by Iggie on three long glass shelves. There are hidden lights so that at dusk the vitrine glows with all the gradations of cream, bone and ivory. At night they can light the whole room.

Here the netsuke became Japanese again.

They lose their strangeness. They are surprisingly accurate renditions of the food you eat: clams, octopus, peaches, persimmon, bamboo shoots. The bundle of kindling that is kept by the kitchen door is knotted like this netsuke carved by Soko. The slow, emphatic turtles climbing over each other on the edge of the temple pond are your Tomokazu netsuke. You are not, perhaps, meeting monks and pedlars and fishermen, let alone tigers, on the way to your office in Marunouchi, but the man at the noodle-stand at the train station has the same permanent scowl as the disappointed rat-catcher.

The netsuke share their imagery with the Japanese scrolls and gilded screens across the room. They have something to talk with in this room, unlike Charles's Moreaus and Renoirs, or Emmy's silver and glass scent bottles on her dressing-table. They have always been objects to be picked up and handled – now they become part of another world of handled objects. Not only are they familiar in material (ivory and boxwood are gripped every day as chopsticks), but their shapes are deeply embedded. One whole type of netsuke, the *manju* netsuke, is named after the small, rounded beancurd sweet cakes eaten daily with tea or given as *o-miyagi*, the small gifts you present if you go anywhere in Japan. *Manju* are dense and surprisingly heavy, but they give slightly as you pick them up. When you pick up a *manju* netsuke your thumb expects the same sensation.

Many of Iggie's Japanese friends had never seen netsuke before, let alone handled them. Jiro just remembered his grandfather, the entrepreneur, dressed in his dark dense grey kimono for weddings and funerals. Five heraldic motifs on neck and cuffs and sleeves, white split-toed socks and *geta* or wooden clogs, the wide obi belt in its stiff knot round his waist, and a netsuke – some animal? a rat? – hanging on its cord. But netsuke had disappeared from daily use eighty years beforehand in the early Meiji period, when kimonos for men had been discouraged. At Iggie's parties, with glasses of whisky and plates of edamame, crunchy green-bean pods, scattered on the tables, the cases were opened. Netsuke were picked up again, exclaimed over, handed round and enjoyed. And friends explain them to you. As it is 1951, the Year of the Hare in the zodiac, you hold the netsuke made from the clearest ivory in the whole collection, and it is explained that it gleams because it is a lunar hare racing across the waves, illuminated by moonlight.

The last time netsuke had been handled in this social way was in Paris by Edmond de Goncourt, by Degas and Renoir in Charles Ephrussi's salon of contemporary good taste, a conversation between an eroticised otherness and new art.

Now they are back home in Japan, the netsuke are a memory of conversations with grandparents about calligraphy, or poetry, or the shamisen. For Iggie's Japanese guests, they are part of a lost world, made more astringent by the bleakness of post-war life. Look, the netsuke reprove, at this wealth of time there used to be.

Here they are also part of a new version of *Japonisme*. Iggie's house has its counterpart in 1950s international-design magazines with their emphasis on the layering of Japanese style into the contemporary home. Japan can be referenced by a signature Buddha, a screen, a rough country jar in the new folk-craft trend. *Architectural Digest* is full of residences in America with these objects alongside the gold leaf in the hall, a wall of mirrors, the use of raw silk on the walls, vast plate-glass windows and abstract paintings.

In this Tokyo house of an adopted American there is a tokonama, the alcove that is so important in traditional houses, a space held apart from the rest of the house by a pillar of untreated timber. Country grasses are arranged in a basket near a scroll painting and a Japanese bowl. Contemporary Japanese pictures of etiolated figures and horses by Fukui, a favourite young painter, hang on the walls. Iggie's catholic collection of books on Japanese art, Proust up against James Thurber and stacks and stacks of American crime, range the shelves.

But here amongst the Japanese art are also a few paintings from the Palais Ephrussi in Vienna, collected by his grandfather in the heady years of the family's ascendancy during the 1870s. A picture of an Arab boy by a painter whom Ignace supported on his travels around the Middle East. A couple of Austrian landscapes. A little Dutch painting of some contented cows that once hung on a back corridor. In his dining-room, above a sideboard, is a melancholy picture of a soldier with a musket in a penumbrous wood, which used to be in his father's dressing-room at the end of the corridor alongside the vast *Leda and the Swan* and the bust of Herr Wessel.

Here are the bits of restitution wrung out of Vienna by Elisabeth, hanging alongside Iggie's Japanese scrolls. This, too, is a bit of fraternisation: *Ringstrassenstil* in Japan.

These photographs are vivid: they radiate happiness. Iggie had a capacity to get along, wherever he was – there are even snaps of him and soldier friends during the war, playing with an adopted puppy in a ruined bunker. In Japan he is expansive to his Japanese and Western friends in this eclectic setting.

His happiness was compounded when he moved to another beautiful house and garden in a more convenient location in Azabu. He hated the idea of this area – a *gaijin* colony full of diplomats – but the house was high up, with a series of interconnecting rooms and with a garden falling away in front of it, full of white camellias.

It was big enough to build a separate apartment for his young friend Jiro Sugiyama. They had met in July 1952. 'I ran into an old classmate outside the Marunouchi building who introduced me to his boss Leo Ephrussi . . . Two weeks after that, I had a call from Leo – I always called him Leo – inviting me to have dinner with him. We had lobster thermidor on the roof garden of the Tokyo

Kaikan . . . and through him I got a job at an old Mitsui company, Sumitomo.' They were to be together for forty-one years.

Jiro was twenty-six, slight and handsome, fluent in English and a lover of Fats Waller and Brahms. When they met he had just returned from three years studying at an American university on a scholarship. His passport from the Administration Office Occupation Forces was stamped no. 19. Jiro remembered his anxiety about how he would be treated in America, and how the newspapers wrote it up: 'a young Japanese boy off to America in a grey flannel suit and white Oxford shirt'.

Jiro had grown up as the middle child of five siblings in a merchant family that made lacquered wooden clogs in Shizuoka, the city between Tokyo and Yokohama: 'our family made the very best, painted *geta* with *urushi* lacquer on them. My grandfather Tokujiro made our fortune out of *geta* . . . We had a large traditional house with ten people working in the shop, and they all had quarters to live in.' They were a prosperous and entrepreneurial family, and in 1944 Jiro, aged eighteen, had been sent to the preparatory school for Waseda University in Tokyo and then on to the university itself. Too young to fight, he had seen Tokyo obliterated around him.

Jiro, my Japanese uncle, has been part of my life for as long as Iggie. We sat together in the study of his Tokyo apartment and he talked of those early days together. They would leave the city on Friday nights and 'have our weekends around Tokyo, in Hakone, Ise, Kyoto, Nikko, or stay in *ryokan* and *onsen* and have good food. He had a yellow DeSoto convertible with a black top. The first thing after leaving our luggage at the *ryokan* Leo always wanted to do, was to go to antique shops – Chinese pots, Japanese pots, furniture . . .' And during the week they would meet up after work. 'He'd say "Meet me at the Shiseido restaurant for beef curry rice, or for crabmeat croquette." Or we'd meet at the bar of the Imperial. There were so many parties at home. We'd have whisky together late at night after everyone had gone, with opera on the gramophone.'

Their life was Kodachrome – I can see that yellow-and-black car glistening like a hornet on a dusty road in the Japanese alps, the pinkness of the croquette framed on white.

They explored Japan together, travelling to an inn that specialised in river trout one weekend; to a town on the coast for an autumn *matsuri*, a jostling parade of red-and-gold festival floats. They went to exhibitions of Japanese art at the museums in Ueno Park. And to the first travelling exhibitions of Impressionism from European museums, where the queues stretched from the entrance to the gates. They came out from seeing Pissarro, and Tokyo looked like Paris in the rain.

But music was closest to the heart of their life together.

*Iggie and Jiro on a boat in the Inland Sea, Japan, 1954*

Beethoven's Ninth Symphony had become extremely popular during the war. The Ninth – *Dai-ku* as it was known colloquially – became an entrenched part of New Year, with huge choirs singing the 'Ode to Joy'. Under the Occupation, the Tokyo Symphony Orchestra had been partly sponsored by the authorities with programmes selected from requests by the troops. And now, in the early 1950s, there were regional orchestras across Japan. Schoolchildren with satchels on their backs clutched violin cases. Foreign orchestras started to visit, and Jiro and Iggie would go to one concert after another: Rossini, Wagner and Brahms. They saw *Rigoletto* together, and Iggie recalled that it was the first opera he had seen with his mother in their box in Vienna during the First World War, and that she had cried at the final curtain.

And so this is the fourth resting-place of the netsuke. It is a vitrine in a sitting-room in post-war Tokyo looking out across a bed of clipped camellias, where the netsuke are washed late at night by waves of Gounod's *Faust*, played loud.

The arrival of the Americans meant that Japan had, once again, become a country to plunder, a country full of attractive objects, pairs of Satsuma vases, kimono robes, lacquer and gilt swords, folding screens with peonies, chests with bronze handles. Japanese stuff was so cheap, so abundant. *Newsweek*'s first report on Occupied Japan on 24th September 1945 was headlined 'Yanks Start Kimono Hunt, Learn What Geishas Doesn't' (*sic*). That blunt and cryptic headline, joining souvenirs and girls, sums up the Occupation. The *New York Times* later that year reported 'A Sailor Goes on a Shopping Spree': if you were a GI there was very little else to buy, after you had spent what you could on cigarettes, beer and girls.

A successful *après-guerre* opened a small money-exchange booth on the pier at Yokohama, converting dollars into yen for the first American soldiers. He also bought and resold American cigarettes. But, crucially, the third part of his business was selling 'cheap Japanese bric-a-brac, such as bronze Buddha images. Brass candleholders, and incense burners, which he had salvaged from bombed-out areas. Being great novelties in those days, these curio items sold like proverbial hotcakes.'

How did you know what to buy? All soldiers 'had to suffer an hour in combat subjects [such] as Japanese flower arrangement, incense burning, marriage, dress, tea ceremonies, and fishing with cormorants,' John LaCerda acidly commented in *The Conqueror*

*Comes to Tea: Japan under MacArthur*, published in 1946. For the more serious there were the new guides to Japanese arts and craft, printed on grey paper so thin that it feels like tissue. The Japan Travel Bureau published its guides 'to give to the passing tourists and other foreigners interested in Japan a basic knowledge of various phases of Japanese culture'. They included, amongst other subjects: *Floral Art of Japan*, *Hiroshige*, *Kimono (Japanese Dress)*, *Tea Cult of Japan*, *Bonsai (Miniature Potted Trees)*. And, of course, *Netsuke: A Miniature Art of Japan*.

From the bric-a-brac salesmen on the pier at Yokohama to the men with a handful of lacquers on a white cloth sitting outside a temple, it was difficult not to encounter Japan for sale. Everything was old, or labelled as old. You could buy an ashtray, a lighter or tea towel with images of geisha, Mount Fuji, wisteria. Japan was a series of snapshots, of postcards coloured like brocade, cherry blossom as pink as candy-floss. Madame Butterfly and Pinkerton, cliché jumbled up against cliché. But you could just as easily buy an 'exotic remnant of the Age of the Daimyos'. As *Time* put it in the article 'Yen for Art', writing about the Hauge brothers, who had amassed an exceptional collection of Japanese art:

Of the countless GIs who spent a tour of duty in Japan, few failed to load up on souvenirs. But only a handful of Americans realised what a collector's paradise was within their reach . . . The Hauges got off to a flying start with the whirlwind of inflation that swept the Japanese yen from 15 all the way to 360 to the dollar. At the same time the Hauges were reaping a paper harvest of yen, Japanese families, hit with postwar taxes, were living an 'onionskin' existence, peeling off long-treasured art works to stay afloat.

Onionskin, bamboo shoots. They were images of vulnerability, tenderness and tears. They were also images of undressing. It paralleled the stories so avidly told and retold by Philippe Sichel and the de Goncourts in Paris during the first febrile rush of *Japonisme* of how you could buy anything, how you could buy anyone.

Iggie might be expatriate, but he was still an Ephrussi. He too started to collect. On his trips with Jiro he bought Chinese ceramics – a pair of Tang Dynasty horses with arching backs, celadon-green dishes with swimming fish, fifteenth-century blue-and-white porcelain. He bought Japanese golden screens with crimson peonies, scrolls with misty landscapes, early Buddhist sculpture. You could buy a Ming Dynasty bowl for a carton of Lucky Strikes, Iggie told me, guiltily. He showed it to me. It has a perfect high ring, if you tap it gently. It has peonies painted in blue under a milky glaze. I wonder who had to sell it.

It was during these years of the Occupation that netsuke became 'collectables'. The Japan Travel Bureau guide on netsuke, published in 1951, records 'valuable help given by Rear Admiral Beton W. Dekker, former commander of the US Fleet Activities at Yokosuka, Japan and a most devoted connoisseur of Netsuke'. This guide, in print for thirty years, gave its view of netsuke in the clearest way:

The Japanese are by nature clever with their fingers. This deftness may be attributed to their inclination to small things, developed in them because they live in a small insular country, and are not continental in character. Their habit of eating their meals with chopsticks, which they learn to handle cleverly from early childhood, may also be regarded as one of the causes that made them thus deft-handed. Such a special characteristic is responsible at once for the merits and demerits of Japanese art. The people lack an aptitude for producing anything on a large scale or deep and substantial. But they display their nature in finishing their work with delicate skill and scrupulous execution.

The way that Japanese objects were talked of had not changed in the eighty years since Charles bought them in Paris. Netsuke were still to be enjoyed for all those positive attributes given to precocious children, the ability to finish, scrupulousness.

It is a bitter thing to be compared to a child. It was made even more painful when this was publicly expressed by General MacArthur. Sacked by President Truman on the grounds of insubordination over the Korean War, the General left Tokyo for Haneda airport on 16th April 1951: 'escorted by a cavalcade of military police motorcyclists . . . Lining the route there were American troops, the Japanese police and Japanese people. School children were given time off from classes to line the road; public servants in post offices, hospitals or administrations were given the opportunity to attend also. The Tokyo police estimated that 230,000 persons had witnessed MacArthur's departure. It was a quiet crowd,' wrote the *New York Times*, 'which gave little outward sign of emotion . . .' At the Senate hearings on his return, MacArthur compared the Japanese to a twelve-year-old boy in comparison to a forty-five-year-old Anglo-Saxon adult: 'You can plant basic concepts there. They [are] close enough to origin to be elastic and acceptable to new concepts.'

It felt like public, global humiliation for a country free after seven years of Occupation. Since the war Japan had been substantially rebuilt, partly through American subsidies, but substantially by their own entrepreneurial skills. Sony, for instance, started as a radio repair shop in a bombed-out department store in Nihonbashi in 1945. It created one new product after another – electrically heated cushions in 1946, Japan's first tape recorder the following year – by hiring young scientists and buying materials on the black market.

If you walked along the Ginza, the central shopping boulevard in Tokyo, in the summer of 1951 you would pass one well-stocked store after another: Japan was making its way in the modern world. You would also pass Takumi, a long thin shop with dark bowls and cups stacked on shelves alongside bolts of indigo cloth from folk-craft weavers. In 1950 the Japanese government introduced the category of the National Living Treasure, someone – usually an elderly man – whose skill in lacquer or dying or pottery was rewarded with a pension and fame.

Taste had swung round towards the gestural, intuitive, ineffable. Anything made in a remote village became 'traditional' and was marketed as intrinsically Japanese. These years saw the start of Japanese tourism, with booklets published by the Japanese Department of Railways: *Some Suggestions for Souvenir Seekers*. 'Travel of any kind would not be complete without some souvenirs to take home.' You should return with the right *o-miyagi*, or gift. It could be a sweetmeat, a kind of biscuit or dumpling specific to one village, a box of tea, a pickled fish. Or it could be a handicraft, a sheaf of paper, a teabowl from a village kiln, an embroidery. But it must have its regional specificity pulsing behind its paper-and-cord wrapping, its calligraphic tag: there is a mapping of Japan, a geography of appropriate gifts. Not to bring an *o-miyagi* is an affront in some way to the idea of travelling itself.

Netsuke now belonged to the age of the Meiji and the opening up of Japan. In the hierarchies of knowledge, netsuke were now rather looked down on as *over-skilled*: they carried the slightly stale air of *Japonisme* with them, of the marketing of Japan to the West. They were just too deft.

No matter how many calligraphies were shown – a single explosive brushstroke of black by some monk, a concentration of decades into four seconds of control – show something small and ivory, 'a group of Kiyohimi and a dragon circling the temple bell within which the monk Anchin hides' and everyone marvelled. Not at the idea, or the composition, but at the possibility of concentrating for so long on such a small thing. How did Tanaka Minko carve the monk inside the bell through that tiny, tiny hole? Netsuke were too popular with Americans.

Iggie wrote about his netsuke in an article published in Japanese in the *Nihon Keiza Shimbun*, the Tokyo equivalent of the *Wall Street Journal*. He described his memories of them as a child in Vienna

*The vitrine of netsuke in Iggie's house in Azabu, Tokyo, 1961*

and their escape from the Palais, under the noses of the Nazis in the pocket of a maid. And he wrote of them returning to Japan. Good fortune had brought them back to Japan after three generations in Europe. He had, he said, asked Mr Yuzuru Okada of the Tokyo National Museum in Ueno, the writer on netsuke, to come and examine the collection. Poor Mr Okada, I think, trailing out to a *gaijin*'s house to smile over another collection of Westerner's bric-a-brac evening after evening. 'He met me very reluctantly – I did not know why – and he glanced at about three hundred netsuke spread out on a table as if he were sick of seeing them . . . Mr Okada picked up one of my netsuke. Then he began to carefully examine the second one with his magnifier. At last, after he had examined the third one for a long time, he suddenly stood up and asked me where I got them . . .'

These were great examples of Japanese art. They might be currently out of fashion – in Okada's museum in Ueno Park in Tokyo's National Museum of Japanese art, a visitor would find only a single vitrine of netsuke amongst the chilly halls of ink-paintings – but here was real sculpture for the hand.

Ninety years after they first left Yokohama, someone picks up a netsuke and knows who made it.

## 33. THE REAL JAPAN

By the early 1960s Iggie was a 'long-term Tokyo resident'. European and American friends came on three-year postings and were gone. Iggie had seen off the Occupation. He was still in Tokyo.

He had a tutor for Japanese and now spoke it beautifully, with fluency and subtlety. Every foreigner who can stammer a few apologetic phrases in Japanese is complimented on their extraordinary skills. *Jozu desu ne*: my, but how skilled you are! My own Japanese, wrenchingly clumsy, full of strange longueurs and rushed ascents, has been praised enough for me to know how this works. But I heard Iggie in deep conversation and know he could speak Japanese well.

He loved Tokyo. He loved the way the skyline changed, the rust-red Tokyo Tower built at the end of the 1950s to emulate the Eiffel Tower; the new apartment blocks hard against the smoky yakitori booths. He identified with the city's capacity for reinvention. The chance to reinvent himself was one that seemed godsent. There was a strange correlation between Vienna in 1919 and Tokyo in 1947, he said. If you haven't been so low, you don't know how you can build something, you can't measure what you've built. You will always think it is due to someone else.

How can you bear to stay in this place? Iggie was asked repeatedly by expatriates. Don't you get bored doing the same old things?

Iggie told me what qualified as expatriate Tokyo life, the eight brittle hours held between your orders to the maid and cook after breakfast and the first cocktail at half-past five. If you were a man of business in Japan, you had your office and then you socialised. Sometimes there would be geisha parties of such length and tediousness and cost that Iggie cursed leaving Léopoldville. Every night, cleanly shaven, he had drinks with clients. The first bar was at the Imperial, dark mahogany and velvet, whisky sours, a pianist. Drinks at the American Club, the Press Club, International House. Then, perhaps, another bar. D. J. Enright, a visiting English poet, listed his favourites: the Bar Renoir, Bar Rimbaud, La Vie en Rose, Sous les Toits de Tokyo and, best of all, La Peste.

If you had no work, you had those eight hours to fill. What could you do? Go to Kikokuniya in the Ginza to see if they have any new Western novels and magazines or to Maruzen bookshop with its pre-war stock of lives of clerics, which have been on their shelves for thirty years? Or to one of the cafés on the top floors of the department stores?

You have visitors. But how many times do you take visitors to see the great Buddha at Kamakura, or to the shrines for the Tokugawa Shoguns at Nikko – red lacquer and gold climbing up a hillside of cryptomeria? Outside the temples in Kyoto, or the shrine at Nikko, or the steps up to the Buddha at Kamakura are the kiosks of souvenir-sellers, the prayer-hawkers, the *o-miyagi*-pushers. There are the 'take your photograph' merchants under a red umbrella, by the lacquer bridge, next to the Golden Pavilion, by the side of a simpering girl dressed in an ersatz costume with white make-up and a comb in her hair.

How often can your bear kabuki? Or, worse, three hours of the Noh drama? How often do you go to an *onsen*, the hot-water springs, before the prospect of relaxing chest-high in a pool comes to be one of horror?

You can go to the lectures at the British Council by visiting poets, or to an exhibition at the department stores of ceramics, or you can learn flower-arranging – ikebana. To be a women in this expatriate environment is to be made aware of your fragile status. You are encouraged to learn what Enright wrote was one of the 'humiliatingly "simplified" art-crafty cults' like the tea-ceremony, newly resurgent in Japan.

Because this is what it was about: Getting to the Real Japan. 'I must try to see something in the country that was whole and untouched,' writes one desperate traveller after a month of Tokyo in 1955. Getting to the whole and untouched means getting out of Tokyo: Japan starts where the sounds of the city end. Ideally it means going to a place where no Westerner has visited before. This makes it increasingly competitive to find authentic experiences. It is cultural one-upmanship, this sensitivity in comparison with others. Do you write haiku? Do brush-painting? Make pots? Meditate? Do you drink green tea from choice?

Getting to the real Japan depends on your schedule. If you have a fortnight, this would mean Kyoto and a day-trip to see some cormorant fishermen, maybe a day-trip to a pottery village, a tea ceremony with its attendant longueurs. A month would mean a visit to Kyushu in the south of the country. A year and you could write a book. Dozens did. Japan – my, what an odd country! A country in transition. Vanishing traditions. Enduring traditions. Essential verities. Seasons in. Myopia of the Japanese. Love of detail of. Dexterity. Self-sufficiency of. Childishness of. Inscrutability of.

Elizabeth Gray Vining, the American tutor to the Crown Prince for four years and author of *Windows for the Crown Prince*, wrote in a sequel of the 'many books about Japan written by Americans who have lost their hearts to their former foes'. There were travelogues by the English too: William Empson, Sacheverell Sitwell, Bernard Leach, William Plomer. *It's Better with Your Shoes Off* – cartoons telling what it's really like to live in Japan – *The Japanese Are Like That, An Introduction to Japan, This Scorching Earth, A Potter in Japan, Four Gentlemen of Japan*. A gush of books interchangeably called *Behind the Fan, Behind the Screen, Behind the Mask, Bridge of the Brocade Sash*. There is Honor Tracy's *Kakemono: A Sketch Book of Post-War Japan*, with its dislike of 'young men with their stickily pomaded hair and girls with garish make-up circling the floor, an expression of near imbecility on their faces . . .' Enright wryly remarked that he harboured an ambition to belong to that small and select band of people who have lived in Japan without writing a book about it, in his introduction to his own book on the subject, *The World of Dew*.

Writing about Japan means that you have to show a visceral dislike of (Western) lipstick smeared across a beautiful (oriental) cheek, the ways in which modernisation disfigures the country. Or you try to make it funny, like the special issue of *Life* on Japan for 11th September 1964, with a geisha in full get-up launching a bowling ball on the cover. The new Americanised country tastes like the flatness of *pan*, the doughy white bread that had been made in Japan since the end of the nineteenth century, and a sort of processed cheese of incomparable soapiness, yellower than a marigold. This you compare to the spikiness of Japanese pickles, radishes, the bite of wasabi in a piece of sushi. In doing so you are mirroring the views of travellers eighty years before. You all share in Lafcadio Hearn's lyrical falling lament.

And this is where Iggie was different. He might open a black lacquer bento box, with its rice and pickled plums and fish neatly arranged on vermilion for lunch. But it would be châteaubriand with Jiro and his Japanese friends in the evening at a restaurant near the Ginza Crossing where the new neon signs flashed Toshiba, Sony, Honda. And on to a film by Teshigahara and then back home for a whisky, with the netsuke cabinet open and Stan Getz on the gramophone. Iggie and Jiro's life was lived in another kind of Real Japan.

After twenty years of false starts and comparative hardship in Paris, New York, Hollywood and the army, Iggie had now lived in Tokyo longer than he had in Vienna: he was starting to belong. He had competence in the world, he was making something of himself, earning enough to support himself and his friends. He helped his siblings and his nephews and nieces.

By the mid-1960s Rudolf was married with five young children. Gisela was flourishing in Mexico. And Elisabeth in Tunbridge Wells, walking to 9.30 matins at the parish church on Sundays in her sensible coat, seemed completely English. Henk is retired and reads the *Financial Times*, hopefully. Their two sons are doing well. My father has been ordained as a priest in the Church of England, has married a vicar's daughter, a historian, and has become a university chaplain in Nottingham. They have four sons – including me. My uncle Constant Hendrik (Henry), a successful barrister in London, has joined the Parliamentary Law Office and is married with two sons. The Reverend Victor de Waal and his brother Henry are professional Englishmen, speaking English at home, continental only in the slight roll to their Rs.

Iggie had turned himself into a businessman, becoming the kind of man, he said once, poignantly, that his father would recognise. Partly because I don't understand money, I see him in a similar way to Viktor, the great man of business hiding slightly behind his desk, a book of poetry surreptitiously hidden amongst the ledgers, looking forward to his release of the end of the day. In fact, unlike his father, who had presided over a spectacular series of downfalls, Iggie proved to be good with money. 'Suffice it to say,' he types in a copy of a 1964 Private & Confidential letter to the General Manager of Swiss Bank Corp, Zurich – used as a bookmark in his copy of *Our Man In Havana* – 'that I started in Japan from scratch and have been able over the years to build up an organisation with a yearly turnover of over 100 million yen. We maintain two offices in Japan, in Tokyo and Osaka, employing some 45 people and I am Vice President and Japan manager . . .' 100 million yen was a fair amount.

Iggie became a banker after all, a hundred years after his grandfather Ignace opened the bank in Vienna off the Schottengasse. He became the representative of Swiss Bank in Tokyo – the *ne plus ultra* of banks, he explained to me. He acquired a bigger office – this one with a secretary behind a desk in the reception area, with an ikebana arrangement of a pine branch and iris. From the sixth-floor windows he could look west across the blocky new landscape of cranes and aerials of Tokyo, and east to the pines of the Imperial Palace and down to the streams of yellow taxis below in Otemachi. He was growing into himself, too. In 1964 he was fifty-eight, with a firmly knotted tie under a dark-grey suit, a hand in a pocket as in his Viennese graduation photograph. His hair was receding, but Iggie knew enough about himself to avoid a comb-over.

Jiro, a handsome thirty-eight, had a new career working for CBS negotiating to bring American TV programmes into Japan. 'And,' said Jiro, 'I was responsible for bringing the Viennese concert for New Year to Japan for NHK. No one wanted it! The wild reaction!

You know the adoration of Japanese for Viennese music, for Strauss? They asked Iggie in the taxi "Where are you from?" He'd reply "Wien, Austria" and then they start la-la-la-ing the Blue Danube Waltz.'

In 1970 the couple bought some land on the Ito peninsula, seventy miles south of Tokyo, enough space for a cottage. In a photograph there is a veranda for evening drinks. The ground falls away in front of you and, framed by bamboos, there is a glimpse of sea.

And they bought a plot for a grave in the grounds of the temple where one of their closest friends had his family tomb. Iggie was here to stay.

And then in 1972 they moved to Takanawa, to apartments in a new building in a good location. 'Higashi-Ginza, Shimbashi, Daimon, Mita' sings the voice on the subway, and then 'Senkaku-ji', and you alight and walk up the hill to home, on this quiet street next to the walls of the palace of Prince Takamatsu. Tokyo can be very quiet. I once sat waiting for them to come home, sitting on the low green railing opposite, and in an hour only two old ladies came past and a hopeful yellow taxi.

They were not large apartments, but very convenient: they were thinking ahead. Separate front doors, but adjoining, with a door from one dressing-room to another. Iggie put one mirrored wall in his hall and lined the other with squares of gold leaf. There was a little stool on which you could sit to slip your shoes off, and a tutelary Buddha from some long-forgotten raid in Kyoto. Some of the Vienna pictures migrated to Jiro's side, and some of Jiro's Japanese porcelain ended up on Iggie's shelves. A photograph of Emmy stood next to a photograph of Jiro's mother on the little shrine. From

Iggie's dressing-room, with its library of jackets, you looked over the Prince's gardens. From the drawing-room with its vitrine you could see all the way to Tokyo Bay.

Iggie and Jiro went on holidays together. Venice, Florence, Paris, London, Honolulu. And in 1973 they went to Vienna. It was the first time Iggie had been back since 1936.

Iggie takes Jiro to stand outside the Palais where he had been born. They go to the Burgtheater, to the Sacher, to his father's old café. And when they return, Iggie makes two decisions. They are connected. The first is to adopt Jiro as his son. Jiro becomes Jiro Ephrussi Sugiyama. The second is to revoke his American citizenship. I asked him about this return to Vienna, and his return to becoming an Austrian citizen, thinking of Elisabeth's journey round the Ring from the station to find the broken lindens outside their childhood house. 'I couldn't bear Nixon' was all he said, catching Jiro's eye, changing the subject, moving the conversation as far away as he could.

It makes me wonder what belonging to a place means. Charles died a Russian in Paris. Viktor called it wrong and was a Russian in Vienna for fifty years, then Austrian, then a citizen of the Reich, and then stateless. Elisabeth kept Dutch citizenship in England for fifty years. And Iggie was Austrian, then American, then an Austrian living in Japan.

You assimilate, but you need somewhere else to go. You keep your passport to hand. You keep something private.

## 34. ON POLISH

It must have been in the 1970s that Iggie pasted little numbers onto the netsuke, drew up a list of what they all were and had them assessed. They were surprisingly valuable. The tiger was the star.

This is finally when the netsuke carvers regain their names and start to become people with families, craftsmen in a particular landscape. The stories start to settle around them:

Early in the nineteenth century there lived in Gifu a carver named Tomokazu, who excelled in making netsuke animal figures. One day he left home lightly clad as if he were going to the public bath, and nothing was heard of him for three or four days. His family and the neighbours were greatly concerned about what had become of him, when suddenly he returned. He explained the reason for his disappearance, saying that he had intended to carve a netsuke of a deer and had gone into the depths of the mountains, where he watched intently the way these animals lived, eating nothing during the whole time. He is said to have accomplished the intended work, based on his observations in the mountains . . . It was not rare that a month or even two months were spent in making a single netsuke . . .

When I go to my cabinet I find four small tortoises climbing on each other's backs. I look up the number on Iggie's list and it is by Tomokazu. It is made from boxwood, the colour of a *caffè macchiato*.

It is very small, and has been carved so that when you roll it in your hands you feel the slippery tortoises struggling over one another, round and round and round. As I hold it, I know that this man did look at tortoises.

Iggie made notes on the queries by scholars and by a dealer or two who came to see the collection. Why should anyone think that signing a piece simplifies matters? Signing is the start of questions of Byzantine complexity. Are the strokes done with authority or are they hesitant? How many strokes have gone into a character? Is it enclosed within a border? If so, what is the shape of the cartouche? What about alternative readings of the characters? And, my favourite, a question of almost scholastic profundity: what is the relationship between a great carver and a poor signature?

I can't cope with this, so I look at the patination. And then I read up on it:

To Occidentals it may seem that a difference in polish is only a matter of formula and application. In point of fact, polish is a very important process in the creation of a fine netsuke. It comprises a series of boilings, dryings and rubbings with various ingredients and materials that are carefully guarded secrets. A fine polish requires three or four days of laborious patience and conscientious care. The thick, rich, brown polish of the younger Toyozaku, although fine, is not of such eclipsing excellence.

So I take out my tiger with the yellow-horn inlaid eyes by the younger Toyokazu of the Tamba school. This carver worked in fine, dense boxwood and was well known for the mobility he achieved in his animals. Mine has a striped tail that is a whiplash up his back. I take it out for a day or two, and once, stupidly, leave it on my notes in the fifth-floor stacks (Biography K–S) at the London Library while I go for coffee. But he is still there when I get back, my non-eclipsing tiger with his glowing eyes in his rich, brown scowling face.

He is pure menace. He has seen off the other readers.

*Coda*

# TOKYO, ODESSA, LONDON 2001–2009

## 35. JIRO

I am back in Tokyo, walking up from the underground station past the isotonic drink machines. It is September and I haven't been here for a couple of years. The machines are new. Some things change slowly in Tokyo. There are still the few raggedy wooden houses with their washing pegged out next to the silvery condominiums. Mrs X at the sushi restaurant is cleaning the steps.

I stay with Jiro, as I always do. He is in his early eighties, busy. He goes to the Opera, of course, and the theatre. And he has spent a few years going to a pottery class and making tea-bowls and small dishes for soy sauce. Jiro has left Iggie's apartment unchanged since he died fifteen years ago. The pens are still in their holder and the blotter is still central on the desk. This is where I'm staying.

I've brought a tape-recorder and we fiddle with it for a while and then give up, watch the news and have a drink and some toast and pâté. I am here for three days to ask him more about his life with Iggie, and check that I have not remembered anything incorrectly in the story of the netsuke. I want to make sure that I have the story of Iggie and Jiro's first meeting correct, the name of the street where they had their first house together. It is one of those conversations that needs to happen, but I'm worried about its formality.

I'm jet-lagged and awake at three-thirty in the morning. I make myself coffee. I run my hands along Iggie's bookcases, the old children's books from Vienna, complete runs of Len Deighton next to

Proust, trying to find something to read. I take down some old copies of *Architectural Digest*, which I love for their glamorous adverts for Chryslers and Chivas Regal whisky, and I find sandwiched between June and July 1966 an envelope containing very old documents, official-looking, in Russian. I walk round and round. I'm not sure I can cope with any more surprising envelopes.

I look up at the pictures salvaged from the Palais, which used to hang in Viktor's study at the end of the corridor, and at the gold screen with the irises on it that Iggie bought in Kyoto in the 1950s. I pick up an old Chinese bowl with deeply carved petals. The incisions hold the green glaze. I suppose I've known it for thirty years now and it still feels good.

This whole room has been part of my life for so long that I can't watch it, distance myself from it. I can't inventory it, as I did Charles's rooms in the rue de Monceau and the avenue d'Iéna, or Emmy's dressing-room in Vienna.

I fall asleep at dawn.

Jiro makes good breakfasts. We have excellent coffee and pawpaw and tiny *pains au chocolat* from one of the Ginza bakeries. And then we take a deep breath and he starts to tell me for the first time about the day the war ended, how on 15th August 1945 he was recuperating from a slight case of pleurisy and was bored. He had come up to Tokyo to see a friend and they were going home on the afternoon train to Izu. 'It was not easy to get train tickets, and we were chatting on the train when we saw women wearing very colourful clothes. And we couldn't believe it. We hadn't seen colour for years and years. And we heard the news that a few hours earlier there had been the declaration of surrender.'

We talk through the journeys I've been on in search of the

history of the netsuke, all the vagabonding. We look at the photo-graphs I've taken in Paris and Vienna and I show him a clipping from last week's newspaper. A pink and gold Fabergé egg that opens to reveal a diamond-studded cockerel – commissioned by Iggie's great-aunt Beatrice Ephrussi-Rothschild – has just become the most expensive Russian object ever auctioned. And because we are in Iggie's old apartment, Jiro opens up the vitrine once again and reaches in to pick up a netsuke.

And then he suggests that we go out tonight. There is a new restaurant he has heard good things of, and we could see a film.

## 36. AN ASTROLABE, A MENZULA, A GLOBE

It is November and I need to go to Odessa. It is nearly two years since I began this journey and I've been everywhere else but the city where the Ephrussi family started. I want to see the Black Sea and imagine the grain warehouses on the edge of the seaport. And perhaps, if I stand in the house where Charles and my great-grandfather Viktor were born, I will understand. I am not sure what I will understand. Why they left? What it means to leave? I think I'm looking for a beginning.

I meet Thomas, my youngest brother, and the tallest, who has travelled from Moldova by taxi. He is an expert on conflict in the Caucasus. It is a journey that has taken him five hours. Thomas, who is writing on Odessa and speaks Russian, is blasé about borders. He has been held up, laughs that it's always a problem whether to bribe or not. I worry about visas: he doesn't. We haven't been on a trip together for twenty-five years, since we were students and went off around the Greek islands. He speaks Greek, too. He was pretty competent then, I remember suddenly. Andrei, the Moldovan taxi driver, sets off.

We bump along the outskirts of ravaged apartment blocks and decaying factories, overtaken by huge black 4x4s with tinted windows and by old Fiats, until we meet the wide avenues of old Odessa. No one told me, I tell Thomas petulantly, that it was so beautiful, that there were catalpa trees alongside the pavements, that there were courtyards glimpsed through open doors, shallow oak steps, that there were balconies. Some of Odessa is being restored, plasterwork

repaired and stucco repainted, while other buildings sink in Pira-
nesian squalor with looping cables, sagging roofs, gates off their
hinges and missing capitals to the pillars.

We come to a full stop outside the Hotel Londonskya, a Belle
Epoque palazzo of gilt and marble on the Primorsky Boulevard.
Queen is playing softly in the foyer. The Boulevard is a great prom-
enade, a run of classical buildings washed in yellows and pale blues.
It stretches an either side of the Potemkin Steps, made famous in
Eisenstein's film *The Battleship Potemkin*. There are 192 steps with
ten landings, designed so that when you look down you see only
landings, and when you look up you see only steps.

Climb these steps slowly. When you reach the top, avoid the
predatory hawkers of Soviet navy hats, the begging sailor with the
poem round his neck, and the man dressed as Peter the Great who
wants you to pay for a photograph with him. To the front is the
statue of the Duc de Richelieu, the early nineteenth-century governor of the region brought in from France to plan the city, in his
toga. Walk past him and on through the curved arcs of golden buildings, two perfect parentheses, and you reach Catherine the Great
surrounded by her favourites. For fifty years there was a Soviet statue
here, but now Catherine is being restored to her old position, courtesy of a local oligarch. Granite setts are being laid around her feet.

Turn right at the top of the steps and the Promenade runs
between two avenues of chestnut trees and dusty flowerbeds until the
punctum of the Governor's Palace, the site of famous parties. It is
severe and Doric.

Each view is calibrated. There are landmarks to walk between:
the Pushkin statue commemorating his stay here, a cannon captured
from the British during the Crimean War. This is where the evening

*passeggiata* would take place, 'the twilight walking to and fro, gossiping and even . . . liberal amounts of flirting'. Higher up is the Opera House modelled on Vienna, where Jewish and Greek factions supporting this season's new Italian singers would take their name – the 'Montechellisti', 'the Carraristi' – and fight. This is not a city around a cathedral or a fortress. It is a Hellenic city of merchants and poets, and this is its bourgeois agora.

In a junk shop in an arcade I buy some Soviet medals for my kids and a couple of nineteenth-century postcards. In one it is high summer, perhaps July, late in the century. It is the middle of the day, as the shadows of the chestnut trees are short. The Promenade was 'cool even at noon in the heat of midsummer', said an Odessan poet. A woman with a parasol moves down the Promenade away from the Pushkin statue, while a nanny pushes an enormous black perambulator. You can just see the dome of the funicular railway that carries people up and down

*Postcard of the promenade in Odessa in 1880. The bank and Ephrussi mansion are the second and third buildings on the left*

to the port. Beyond that there is a line of the masts of ships in the bay.

Turn left at the top of the steps and you look all the way down to the Stock Exchange, a Corinthian villa in which to conduct your business. It is now the Hôtel de Ville and a banner welcomes a Belgian delegation. It is early November and so mild that we walk down the street in our shirt-sleeves. We pass some mansions, then the Hôtel, and three buildings down is the Ephrussi bank, with the family house next door. This is where Jules and Ignace and Charles were born. It is where Viktor was born. We go round the back.

It is a mess. The stucco is coming off in great gouts, the balconies are shedding, there is a bit of slippage amongst the putti. When I come up close I see it has been refaced too, replastered, and those are certainly not original windows. But right at the top is a single balcony in which the double E of the family hangs on.

I hesitate. Thomas, who is good at this, fearless, walks through the broken gates under the arch into the yard behind the Ephrussi house. Here are the stable blocks with their floors of dark stone. It is ballast, he says over his shoulder, lava from Sicily brought in on the grain ships. Grain out. Lava back. A dozen men, suddenly silent, drinking tea, a Citroën 2CV up on blocks. There is a chained Alsatian barking. The yard is full of dust. It has three skips full of timber and plaster and broken stone. He finds the foreman in a shiny leather jacket. Yes, you can go in – you're lucky, it is just being renovated, new everything, beautifully done, a real success, on schedule, a quality job. We have just put laboratories into the basement, fire doors and a sprinkler system. It is the offices next. We had to get rid of all of the old house, it was shot, hopeless. You should have seen it a month ago!

I should have. I am too late. What can I touch here in this stripped-out hulk? It has no ceilings, only steel girders and electric cabling. It has no floors, only concrete screed. The walls have just been plastered, the windows have been reglazed. Some ironwork is up for partitions. They have taken out all the doors, except for one in oak, destined for the skips tomorrow. The only thing left is the volume, the scale of these rooms, sixteen feet high.

There is nothing here.

Thomas and the shiny man are racing ahead, talking Russian. 'This house was the headquarters of the steamship company since the Revolution. Before that? God knows! Now? The headquarters of the Marine Hygiene Inspection Office. That's why we've put in the laboratories.' They are fast. I have to keep moving.

We are almost out the door and into the dusty yard when I double back. I am wrong. I am back up the staircase and I put my hand on the cast-iron balustrade, each column topped with a blackened ear of wheat of the Efrussi, the wheat from the granary of the black soil of the Ukraine that made them rich. And while my brother calls up, I go and stand next to a window and look out across the Promenade through the double avenue of chestnut trees, the dusty paths and the benches to the Black Sea.

The Efrussi boys are still here.

Some traces are fugitive. The Efrussi live in the stories of Isaac Babel, the Jewish chronicler of downtown life, the gangs of the slums. An Efrussi bribes his way into the gymnasium ahead of an abler, poorer student. They are in the Yiddish tales of Sholem Aleichem. A poor man from the shtetl treks to Odessa to beg for help from Efrussi the banker. And the banker refuses. There is a Yiddish saying, *lebn vi Got in Odes* – 'to live like God in Odessa' – and the Efrussi live like gods on their Zionstrasse.

Some traces are archival. Below the Opera is the Angliisky Klub, the English Club where Charles's father Leon was elected 'by acclamation' to be the first Jewish member, a move so radical and unexpected that it receives a mention in the newspaper. This is the place on the Boulevard where an aggrieved merchant pulled a revolver on Ignace outside his house, and was overpowered by passers-by. A gift of 500 roubles contributes to the statue of the governor whose great palace stands beyond the Potemkin steps. Somewhere down that street between the catalpa trees is where the disinherited Stefan, banished from Vienna, poorer by the month, lodged with his new wife, his father's mistress.

Some traces are more concrete. After one of the pogroms the brothers founded an Efrussi orphanage. There is the Efrussi School for Jewish children, endowed by Ignace in honour of his father, the patriarch, and supported over thirty years by new endowments from Charles and Jules and Viktor. It is still there on the edge of a dusty park with feral dogs and ripped-up benches, two low buildings slung together alongside the tram line. In 1892 the school reports the receipt of 1,200 roubles donated by the Efrussi brothers. The school authorities have bought from St Petersburg an astrolabe, a menzula, a globe, a steel knife for cutting glass, a skeleton and a demountable model of an eye. In an Odessan bookshop they have spent 533 roubles and sixty-four kopeks and bought 280 volumes by Beecher Stowe, Swift, Tolstoy, Cowper, Thackeray and Scott. With the remainder there is money to purchase coats, blouses and trousers for twenty-five poor Jewish boys, so that they can read *Ivanhoe* or *Vanity Fair* without shivering, covered up from the Odessan dust.

The dust in Paris on the rue Monceau, the dust in Vienna as they build the Ringstrasse: nothing compares to this dust. 'The dust lies like a universal shroud of some two or three inches thick,' writes

Shirley Brooks in *The Russians of the South* in 1854. 'The slightest breeze flings it over the town in clouds, the lightest footstep sends it flying high in dense heaps. When I tell you that hundreds of the carriages driven at high speed . . . are perpetually racing about, and that the sea breezes are as perpetually rushing through the streets, the statement that Odessa lives in a cloud is no figure of speech.' It was a city on the make: 'a stirring, business-look about the streets and the stores; fast walkers; a familiar *new* look about the houses and everything, yes, and a driving and smothering dust . . .' according to Mark Twain. It makes sense to me, suddenly, that the Efrussi children grow up with dust.

Thomas and I arrange to meet Sasha, a small dapper academic in his seventies. On the corner he bumps into an old friend, a professor of comparative literature, so we all stroll up to the school together, Tom and Sasha talking in Russian and the professor and I talking in English about the International Shakespearian Institute. When we get to the school the professor peels off and the three of us sit in the park café drinking sweet coffee, glared at by the three prostitutes at the bar who periodically juke-box us. I tell Sasha why we've come, that I'm writing a book about – I stumble to a halt. I no longer know if this book is about my family, or memory, or myself, or is still a book about small Japanese things.

He tells me politely that Gorky collected netsuke. We drink more coffee. I have brought the envelope of documents that I found in Iggie's flat in Tokyo between the old copies of *Architectural Digest*. Sasha is appalled that I've brought the originals, and not copies, but as I watch him he is like a pianist, playing with the different papers.

There are records of the fearsome Ignace, the builder of the Palais, as Consul in Odessa for the Swedish and Norwegian crown, an imperial notification from the Tsar that he is allowed to wear a Bessarabian medal, papers from the Rabbinate. This is the old paper, Sasha says, they changed this in 1870; that is the stamp, that is the fee. Here is the signature of the governor, always so emphatic – look, it has almost gone through the paper. Look at the address of this one, the corner of X and Y! It is very Odessan. This is a clerk's copy, poor writing.

As Sasha handles the desiccated records and they flicker into life, I look at the envelope for the first time. It is addressed in Viktor's handwriting, sent out from Kövesces to Elisabeth in September 1938. This bundle of documents meant something to Viktor and to Iggie. It was the family archive. I place them carefully back.

On the way back to the hotel we duck into a synagogue. The Odessan Jews are so worldly, it was said, that they stubbed out their cigarettes on its walls. There is a circle of hell put aside just for them. It is busy in here today. There is a school run by young men from Tel Aviv in progress. They are restoring part of the building, and one of the students comes over to greet us in English. We look in, not wanting to disturb them, and there up on the left neat to the front, is the yellow armchair. It is a Seder chair, the chair for the elect, the special chair set apart.

Charles's yellow armchair was invisible in plain sight. It was so obvious that it disappeared when placed among the Degas and the Moreaus and the cabinet of netsuke in his Parisian salon. It is a pun, a Jewish joke.

As I stand in front of the museum with its statue of a wrestling Laocoön, the one that Charles drew for Viktor, I realise how wrong I've been. I thought the boys left Odessa to get their education in Vienna and in Paris. I thought that Charles went off on his Grand Tour in order to broaden his horizons, to get away from the provinces and learn about the Classics. But this whole city is a classical world balancing above the port. Here, a hundred yards from their house on the boulevard, was a museum that held rooms and rooms of antiquities, the Greek artefacts that were dug up as the town became a city, doubling in size every decade. Of course Odessa had scholars and collectors. Just because Odessa was a dusty city, with its stevedores and sailors, stokers, fishermen, divers, smugglers, adventurers, swindlers, and their grandfather Joachim, the great chancer in his Palais, did not mean that it was not full of writers and artists too.

Does it start here on the edge of the sea? Perhaps that up-and-off entrepreneurial spirit is Odessan; their vagabonding after old books or Dürer or adventures in love or the next good grain deal. Odessa is certainly a good place to ship out from. You can turn east or you can turn west. It is wry, avid, polyglot.

It is a good place to change your name. 'Jewish names are unpleasant to the ear': this is where their grandmother Balbina became Belle, and where their grandfather Chaim became Joachim, and then Charles Joachim. This is where Eizak became Ignace and where Leib became Leon. And Efrussi became Ephrussi. This is where the memory of Berdichev, the shtetl in the eastern Ukraine on the edge of Poland where Chaim came from, was walled up behind the pale-yellow plaster of their first Palais on the Promenade.

This is where they became the Ephrussi from Odessa.

This is a good place to put something in your pocket and start a journey. I want to go to see what the sky looks like in Berdichev, but I have to go home. From the chestnut trees outside the house I look out for a conker to put in my pocket. I walk the whole promenade twice, but I am a month too late with this as well. They have gone. I hope some children have picked them up.

## 37. YELLOW/GOLD/RED

As I fly home from Odessa I feel exhausted by the whole year. I correct myself. It is not a single year, it has become close to two years of looking at the scribbles in the margins of books, the letters used as bookmarks, the photographs of nineteenth-century cousins, the Odessan patents of this and that, the envelopes at the backs of drawers with their few sad aerogrammes. Two years of tracing routes across cities, an old map in one hand, lost.

My fingers are tacky from old papers and from dust. My father keeps finding things. How can he keep finding things in his tiny flat in his courtyard of retired clergymen? He has just found a diary in unreadable German from the 1870s that I need to get translated. A week goes by in an archive and all I have is a list of unread newspapers, a note to look up some correspondence, a question mark about Berlin. My studio is full of novels and books on *Japonisme*, and I miss my children and I haven't made any porcelain for months and months. I'm anxious about what I'll make when I finally sit down at my wheel with a lump of clay.

A few days in Odessa and now there are more questions than before. Where did Gorky buy his netsuke? What was the library like in Odessa in the 1870s? Berdichev was destroyed in the war, but perhaps I should go there too and see what it looks like. Conrad came from Berdichev: perhaps I should read Conrad. Did he write about dust?

My tiger netsuke comes from Tamba, a village in the mountains west of Kyoto. I remember an endless bus journey thirty years ago to visit an old potter on a dusty street straggling up a hillside. Perhaps I should trace my tiger home. There must be a cultural history of dust.

My notebook is made up of lists of lists. *Yellow / Gold / Red /* Yellow armchair / Yellow cover *Gazette* / Yellow Palais / Golden lacquer box / Titian gold Louise's hair / Renoir: *La Bohémienne /* Vermeer's View of Delft.

My competent brother is home already. In Prague airport, where I change planes and have three hours to kill, I sit with my notebooks and a bottle of beer, and then another, and worry about Berdichev. I remember that Charles, that graceful dancer, was called *Le Polonais*, the Pole, both by his brother Ignace and by the dandy Robert de Montesquieu, a great friend of Proust's. And that Painter, the early biographer of Proust, picked this up and made Charles barbarous and uncouth. I thought he had simply got it wrong. Perhaps, I think over my beer, he was making a point about where you start from: Poland, not Russia. I realise that in all my enthusiasm about tactile responses to Odessa I have mislaid its reputation as a city of pogroms, a city you might wish to leave behind.

And I have the slightly clammy feeling of biography, the sense of living on the edges of other people's lives without their permission. Let it go. Let it lie. Stop looking and stop picking things up, the voice says insistently. Just go home and leave these stories be.

But leaving be is hard. I remember the hesitancies when talking to Iggie in old age; hesitancies that trembled into silences, silences that marked places of loss. I remember Charles in his final illness, and the death of Swann and the opening of his heart like a vitrine, his taking out one memory after another. 'Even when one is no longer attached to things, it's still something to have been attached to them; because it was always for reasons which other people didn't grasp . . .' There are the places in memory you do not wish to go with others. In the 1960s, my grandmother Elisabeth, so assiduous in her letter-writing, such an advocate for the letter ('write again, write more fully'), burnt the hundreds of letters and notes she had received from her poetic grandmother Evelina.

Not 'Who would be interested?' But 'Don't come near this. This is private.'

In very old age she would not talk of her mother at all. She would talk about politics and French poetry. She did not mention Emmy until she was surprised by a photograph falling out of her prayer book. My father picked it up and she, matter-of-factly, told him that it was one of her mother's lovers and started to talk about the difficulty of those love-affairs, how compromised she felt by them. And then silence again. There is something about that burning of all those letters that gives me pause: why should everything be made clear and be brought into the light? Why keep things, archive your intimacies? Why not let thirty years of shared conversation go spiralling in ash up into the air of Tunbridge Wells? Just because you have it does not mean you have to pass it on. Losing things can sometimes gain you a space in which to live. I don't miss Vienna, Elisabeth would say, with a lightness in her voice. It was claustrophobic. It was very dark.

She was over ninety when she mentioned that she had received rabbinical instruction as a child: 'I asked my father for permission. He was surprised.' She was matter-of-fact, as if I already knew.

When she died two years later my father, the clergyman in the Church of England, born in Amsterdam with a childhood everywhere in Europe, stood in his Benedictine-black, rabbinical-black cassock and recited the Kaddish for his mother in the parish church near her nursing home.

The problem is that I am in the wrong century to burn things. I am the wrong generation to let it go. I think of a library carefully sorted into boxes. I think of all those careful burnings by others, the systematic erasing of stories, the separations between people and their possessions, and then of people from their families and families from their neighbourhoods. And then from their country.

I think of someone checking a list to make sure that these people were still alive and resident in Vienna, before stamping 'Sara' or 'Israel' in red over the record of their birth. I think, of course, of all the listings of families in the manifests, for deportations.

If others can be so careful over things that are so important, then I must be careful over these objects and their stories. I must get it right, go back and check it again, walk it again.

'Don't you think those netsuke should stay in Japan?' said a stern neighbour of mine in London. And I find I am shaking as I answer, because this matters.

I tell her that there are plenty of netsuke in the world, sitting in velvet-lined trays in dealers' cabinets off Bond Street or Madison Avenue, Keizergracht or the Ginza. Then I get a bit side-tracked onto the Silk Road, and then onto Alexander the Great's coins still being in circulation in the Hindu Kush in the nineteenth century. I tell her about travelling with my partner Sue in Ethiopia, and finding an old Chinese jar covered in dust in a market town and trying to work out how it had got there.

No, I answer. Objects have always been carried, sold, bartered, stolen, retrieved and lost. People have always given gifts. It is how you tell their stories that matters.

It is the counterpart of the question that I am often asked: 'Don't you hate to see things leave your studio?' Well, no, I don't hate it. I make my living from letting things go. You just hope, if you make things as I do, that they can make their way in the world and have some longevity.

It is not just things that carry stories with them. Stories are a kind of thing, too. Stories and objects share something, a patina. I thought I had this clear, two years ago before I started, but I am no longer sure how this works. Perhaps patina is a process of rubbing back so that the essential is revealed, the way that a striated stone tumbled in a river feels irreducible, the way that this netsuke of a fox has become little more than a memory of a nose and a tail. But it also seems additive, in the way that a piece of oak furniture gains over years and years of polishing, and the way the leaves of my medlar shine.

You take an object from your pocket and put it down in front of you and you start. You begin to tell a story.

When I hold them I find myself looking for the wear, the fine cracks that run alongside the grain of some of the ivories. It is not just that I want the split in these wrestlers – a tangle of hopelessly thrashing ivory limbs – to have come from being been dropped onto Charles's golden carpet of the winds by someone famous (a poet, a painter, Proust) in a moment of grand *fin-de-siècle* excitement. Or that the deeply ingrained dust lodged under the wings of a cicada resting on a walnut shell comes from being hidden in a Viennese mattress. It probably doesn't.

The collection's latest resting-place is in London. The Victoria and Albert Museum is getting rid of some of its old vitrines to make way for new displays. I buy one.

Because my work as a potter is seen as minimalist – rows of pale celadon blue-grey porcelain vessels – it is assumed that my wife and our three children live in some temple to minimalism, with a concrete floor perhaps, or a wall of glass, some Danish furniture. We don't. We live in an Edwardian house in a pleasant London street with plane trees out the front, and a hall that contained – this morning – a cello and a French horn, some wellington boots, a wooden fort that the boys have outgrown and that has been on its way to a charity shop for three months, a heap of coats and shoes, and Ella, our aged, loved gun-dog – beyond the hall it gets messy. But I want our three kids to have the chance to get to know the netsuke as those children did a hundred years ago.

So, with great effort, we haul in this decommissioned vitrine. It takes four of us and a lot of swearing. It is seven feet high on its mahogany base and is made of bronze. It has three glass shelves. It is only as it is being fixed to the wall that I remember my own childhood collections. I collected bones, a mouse skin, shells, a tiger's claw, the sloughed scales of a snake, clay pipes and oyster shells, and Victorian pennies from the archaeological dig that my elder brother John and I started one summer in Lincoln, forty years ago, marking out the ground with string into a grid before getting bored. My father was Chancellor of the Cathedral and we lived opposite its great Gothic east window in the Chancery, a medieval house with a spiral staircase and a chapel at the very end of a long corridor. An archdeacon in the Close passed on his collection of fossils dug up during an Edwardian childhood in Norfolk, some still marked with the day and place they were found. When I was seven the cathedral library was getting rid of mahogany cases, and so half my room was taken over by a vitrine – my first – in which I would arrange and rearrange my objects, turn the key and open up the case on request. It was my *Wunderkammer*, my world of things, my secret history of touch.

This latest vitrine I think will be a good place for the netsuke. It is next to the piano, and unlocked so that the children can open the door if they wish to.

I put some of the netsuke out on display – the wolf, the medlar, the hare with amber eyes, a dozen more – and when I next look they have been moved around. A rat, curled up asleep, has been pushed to the front. I open the glass door and pick it up. I slip it into my pocket, put the dog on the lead and leave for work. I have pots to make.

The netsuke begin again.

# ACKNOWLEDGEMENTS

This book has been long in its gestation. I first told this story in 2005 and thank you to the three people, Michael Goldfarb, Joe Earle and Christopher Benfey, who told me to stop talking and start writing.

Firstly, I want to thank my brother Thomas for his great encouragement, his practical help and his companionship. My uncle and aunt Constant and Julia de Waal have been very supportive throughout. Thank you to all those who have helped with research and translation, in particular Georgina Wilson, Hannah James, Tom Otter, Susannah Otter, Chantal Riekel and Aurogeeta Das. Dr Jo Catling of the University of East Anglia has been invaluable for her work on the Rilke/Ephrussi papers and Mark Hinton of Christies was a great help in elucidating signatures on the netsuke. Carys Davis, my studio manager, has kept the world at bay, and been a tremendous interlocutor day by day.

I would like to thank Giselle de Bogarde Scantlebury, the late Marie-Louise von Motesiczky, Francis Spufford, Jenny Turner, Madeleine Bessborough, Anthony Sinclair, Brian Dillon, James Harding, Lydia Syson, Mark Jones, A.S. Byatt, Charles Saumerez-Smith, Ruth Saunders, Amanda Renshaw, Tim Barringer, Jorunn Veiteberg, Rosie Thomas, Vikram Seth and Joram ten Brink. I am particularly grateful to Martina Margetts, Philip Watson and Fiona MacCarthy, all of whom have kept faith with this book.

Thank you to the staff at the London Library, the National Art Library at the Victoria and Albert Museum, the British Library, Cambridge University Library, Courtauld Institute, Goethe Institute,

Musée d'Orsay, Louvre, Bibliothèque Nationale, National Library Tokyo, Israelitische Kultusgemeinde, Adler Society of Vienna. In Vienna, I would like to thank Sophie Lillie for all her pioneering work on restitution, to Anna Staudacher and Wolf-Erich Eckstein at the Israelitische Kultusgemeinde, to Georg Gaugusch and Christopher Wentworth-Stanley for help on genealogies, and thanks go to Martin Drschka of Casinos Austria for his welcome to the Palais Ephrussi. In Odessa, Mark Naidorf, Anna Misyuk and Alexander (Sasha) Rozenboim guided me through some of the history of the Efrussi.

Felicity Bryan has been the most wonderful agent and encourager. I want to record my gratitude to her and her colleagues at the Felicity Bryan Agency, and to Zoe Pagnamenta, and all the staff at Andrew Nurnberg Associates. I'd also like to thank Juliet Brooke and Kate Bland at Chatto. Jonathan Galassi at Farrar, Straus and Giroux has been a marvellous advocate from the start.

I have been overwhelmed by the care, dedication and imagination which my two editors have taken. Clara Farmer at Chatto wrote to me asking if the book existed. She and Courtney Hodell at FSG have made this book happen and I am deeply indebted to them both.

Above all I want to record my love and gratitude to my late grandmother Elisabeth and my late great-uncle Iggie, to my mother Esther de Waal, to my father Victor de Waal and to Jiro Sugiyama.

I could not have written this book without the sustaining generosity of my wife Sue Chandler. It is for our children Ben, Matthew and Anna.

© Hannah Jones

Edmund de Waal's porcelain is shown in many museum collections round the world and he has recently made installations for the V&A and Tate Britain. He was apprenticed as a potter, studied in Japan and read English at Cambridge. He is Professor of Ceramics at the University of Westminster and lives in London with his family.

# A TASTE OF SIN

# A TASTE OF SIN

BY

MAGGIE COX

First published in Great Britain 2015
by Mills & Boon, an imprint of Harlequin (UK) Limited,
Large Print edition 2015
Eton House, 18-24 Paradise Road,
Richmond, Surrey, TW9 1SR

© 2015 Maggie Cox

ISBN: 978-0-263-25695-6

C46348377B

Harlequin (UK) Limited's policy is to use papers that
are natural, renewable and recyclable products and made
from wood grown in sustainable forests. The logging
and manufacturing processes conform to the legal
environmental regulations of the country of origin.

Printed and bound in Great Britain
by CPI Antony Rowe, Chippenham, Wiltshire

To Karen Middlemiss at the MS Therapy Centre.

Whenever we speak you help me make peace
with this condition and remind me that life
is for living, whatever our challenge.

With love and blessings, Maggie x

# CHAPTER ONE

ROSE WAS STANDING by the window, mesmerised by the steady rain that hadn't let up all morning, when a gleaming black Mercedes drew up in front of the antiques shop and effortlessly glided to a stop.

It was just like a scene from a movie and she was immediately riveted. Inside her chest her heart thumped hard, because she knew it was the visitor she'd nervously been anticipating... *Eugene Bonnaire.*

Even the name gave her chills. He was one of the country's wealthiest restaurateurs, with an uncompromising reputation for getting what he wanted, and when Rose's boss, Philip, had put the beautiful Thames-side antiques shop he owned up for sale the businessman had wasted no time in declaring his interest.

Not for the first time that morning she wished Philip could be there alongside her, but sadly his already failing health had deteriorated and he was now in hospital. In his absence, he had asked Rose to handle the property's sale on his behalf.

The responsibility was a bittersweet one. Not just because he was ill, and she feared he might not recover, but because she'd nurtured a secret hope to take over the business herself one day. Having spent ten enjoyable years working with Philip, and training as a dealer, she'd honestly grown to love the place. Consequently, she wasn't predisposed to warming to their potential buyer.

Her first glimpse of the man, after his chauffeur had opened his door and he'd stepped out into the rain, was of a pair of classy Italian brogues, followed by a flawless charcoal suit that was no less than stunningly perfect. Rose caught her breath. As soon as she saw his arrestingly sculpted features, the cut-glass jaw and crystalline blue eyes that were frequently described by the press as 'unflinchingly piercing', she had the disturbing sense that she was coming face to face with her greatest fear and—*inexplicably*—her greatest desire…

She irritably chided herself for the thought. Snapping out of the near trance she'd fallen into watching him, she smoothed her hands down her smart navy dress and made herself walk calmly to the door. It was then she saw that the business-man's height dwarfed hers.

Lifting her head to gaze up at him, she said, 'Eugene Bonnaire? Please come in. I'm Mr Houghton's assistant—Rose Heathcote. I've been asked to conduct the meeting with you on Mr Houghton's behalf.'

The handsome Frenchman stepped inside. Charmingly polite, he shook Rose's hand with a slight bow of his head and she immediately sensed the reined-in strength he exuded.

'I am delighted to meet you, Miss Heathcote.

But I have to confess I was sorry to hear that your boss has been taken ill. Might I ask how he is?'

Before answering, Rose pulled the door shut behind him and adjusted the sign that hung inside the glass to read 'closed'. She was glad of the chance to compose herself before she turned round again. Not only had his firm handshake made her far too aware of him as a man, but the deep bass timbre of his arrestingly attractive voice made her skin feel as though he'd brushed it with gossamer. She prayed that the blood that had heatedly rushed into her face didn't too obviously reveal the fact…

'I wish I could say he was a little better, but the doctors tell me it's going to be a while before we see any improvement.'

'*C'est la vie*. It is the way of things…but I wish him well.'

'Thank you. I'll tell him you said so. Anyway, would you like to come with me into the office, Mr Bonnaire, and we can start our meeting?'

'Before we discuss anything I would like you

to show me round the building, Miss Heathcote. After all, that is the reason I am here.'

Although there was a faultlessly charming smile on his lips to accompany this statement, Rose realised that here was a man who wouldn't be diverted by small talk, however polite and concerned. Nothing would take precedence over pursuing his goals, and his goal today was clearly deciding whether he wanted to buy the antiques shop or not…

'Of course,' she replied. 'It will be my pleasure.'

Rose led him upstairs to one of the three spacious rooms that, although elegantly arranged, were stacked to the rafters with a mixture of antiques and collectables. The air smelled faintly musty because there was a generous amount of furniture on display, although it was tempered somewhat by the scent of beeswax.

While the sound of the rain against the leaded windows made for a cosy ambience it was a little chilly too, and the dress she wore was sleeveless.

Wishing she'd collected her cardigan from the office, she briskly rubbed her arms to warm them.

'The rooms are generously sized, considering it's such an old building,' she remarked, 'which is why we can house so many antiques. I hope you like what you see, Mr Bonnaire.'

Looking faintly amused, her visitor lifted his gaze.

Rose privately attested to spending the most electrifying few seconds of her life as her glance met his. It struck her that she could have chosen her words better. Not in a million years would she invite a man like Eugene Bonnaire to look at her. Did he think that she *would*? He had a reputation for liking exceptionally beautiful women, and Rose knew she was a long way from being in that particular category.

'So far...I like what I see very much, Miss Heathcote,' he answered, not moving his gaze.

Now she really *did* feel hot and bothered. 'I'm...I'm glad. Take as much time as you want, looking over things.'

'Trust me, I will do exactly that.'

'Good.'

Hastily averting her glance, she crossed her arms over her chest, not wanting to draw any more attention. But it wasn't long before she found herself surreptitiously observing him as he walked round, his keen-eyed gaze carefully examining the layout and proportions of the room, every so often dropping down into a crouch to examine the durability and condition of the timbered walls and crevices. It was fascinating to watch him stroking his large but slim hands over the wood and occasionally tapping it with his knuckles.

Whilst Rose understood that it was important the man knew what he would be getting for his investment, he didn't give the impression that the room's contents interested him at all, and she began to be concerned. Philip had told her it was imperative he sell the business as a going concern, because his poor health meant that he now had to retire, as well as pay for his aftercare when he left the hospital.

He had added sadly, 'I'm afraid that pensions aren't worth a light these days...'

The weight of the responsibility she'd taken on in agreeing to make the sale for him hit Rose even harder.

She was still frowning when the preoccupied Frenchman pivoted and remarked, 'Forgive me, but I saw you shiver a couple of times. Are you cold? Perhaps you'd like to go and get your jacket, Rose?'

Even as he asked another small shiver ran up her spine. But it wasn't due to the less than comfortable temperature...it was because it had sounded disturbingly intimate when he'd used her name.

Last night, ahead of her interview with him, she had looked up Eugene Bonnaire on the internet, and as well as reading about the numerous plaudits he had earned in his career thus far she had also learned that he could be quite ruthless in his dealings and had an insatiable appetite for success. He was cited as a man who went after the very best of everything, no matter what the cost, and his penchant for stunning women suggested he was quite the playboy.

Rose knew she couldn't afford to let her guard down round him for an instant. She didn't want to be persuaded to agree to the sale of the business against her better judgement just because he was so attractive.

Deciding that she couldn't and *wouldn't* let that happen—she knew from bitter experience the danger that men like him could pose—she unwaveringly returned his gaze and said, 'I think I *will* go and get my cardigan. If you want to look at the other rooms on this floor, be my guest. I'll be back in a minute.'

With a polite but inarguably *knowing* nod, Eugene Bonnaire glanced away.

A short while later she returned upstairs to find that he'd gone into the furthest room at the back. This was where the more valuable items were displayed and where jewellery was housed behind secure custom-made glass cabinets. Much to Rose's surprise, she found Eugene staring transfixed into one of the cabinets and wondered if she'd misjudged him. Maybe he *did* admire some of the artefacts and maybe he *would* buy the business as well as the building?

She couldn't help but smile as she stepped up beside him, curious to see what he was examining so avidly. When she saw that he was staring at the exquisite pearl and diamond ring from the nineteenth century that was the centrepiece of the display, her curiosity was even more piqued.

'It's pretty, isn't it?' she commented.

'Yes, it is. It looks very similar to the ring my father bought my mother when their business first started to take off.' He was lost in thought for a moment. Then, with a heartfelt sigh, he turned towards her. 'But the pearls and the diamonds weren't real. They were just costume jewellery… He couldn't afford to buy her anything expensive back then.'

There was definitely a glimmer of pain in his eyes as he related this, and Rose found herself warming to him probably more than was wise, because he suddenly seemed oddly vulnerable.

'I'm sure your mum loved the ring just as much as if it were the genuine article. Surely it's what it represented, not how much it cost?' When Eugene failed to comment, and turned back to examine the jewel broodingly, she said softly, 'You might be interested to know that this ring was given to a girl who was a nurse in the Crimean War by the grateful family of a wounded soldier.'

His crystal blue gaze meandered interestedly across her features. Then he gazed deeply into her eyes. Rose's mouth went dry as a sun-bleached plain… She was glad she was wearing her navy wool cardigan so he wouldn't see her shiver again.

'Every picture tells a story, so they say,' he mused. 'No doubt it's the same for jewellery. But let me ask you this: do you think the nurse who was gifted it was very pretty and the wounded soldier a handsome officer?'

The roguish twinkle that accompanied his question took her by surprise and all but made Rose's knees buckle. Flooded with heat, she congratulated herself on quickly regaining her equilibrium and not glancing away too soon. Instead, she made herself steadily hold his gaze and her lips curved in a gentle smile.

'Whether he was handsome or not, shortly after they met he died from his wounds. It's a terribly sad story, isn't it? Whether the two of them had feelings for each other we can only wonder, but the giving of the ring was documented in the soldier's family archives. That's how we were able to trace its provenance.'

'I am guessing that you like to imagine the couple *did* have feelings for each other, Rose.' Eugene's expression was suddenly intense.

Feeling strangely as if she was under siege, she shrugged. 'Why not? Who could begrudge them the little bit of happiness they may have had in the midst of such a terrible situation? But the truth is we'll never know what really happened.'

What Rose *did* know was that she had to engineer some space between her and Eugene. She might at one point have felt a chill, but now she was definitely warmer…*too* warm.

'If you've finished having a look round up here we should go downstairs and have that meeting… don't you think?'

'I agree. Perhaps you could make us some coffee?'

'Of course… How do you take it?'

'How do you *think* I might take it, Rose? Humour me.'

If his tactic was to disarm her and lull her into a false sense of security because he'd decided to be playful, Rose couldn't deny that on another day she might have succumbed to his charm. After all, what woman *wouldn't* feel flattered by his exclusive attention? But today she wouldn't be so easily swayed. Not when she had an important task to fulfil. She had to sell the antiques shop on her boss's behalf and secure the very best deal she could. Nothing could distract her from that goal.

Leading the way back downstairs, in an attempt to let Eugene see that she wasn't rattled by his friendly repartee, she breezily threw over her shoulder, 'Okay, then. I'm guessing you probably like it strong and black. But I'm also guessing you like a couple of spoons of sugar to sweeten it. Am I right?'

'I'm impressed. But be careful not to assume you know what I like in any other respect, Rose... You might find that you've bitten off a little bit more than you can chew.'

Even though she'd heard a smile in his voice, Rose didn't doubt the comment carried a warning. No man became as successful as Eugene Bonnaire without carefully assessing anyone who might put obstacles in the way of him getting what he wanted...

When she returned to the office with the tray of coffee she'd made Eugene had his back to her, and she couldn't help but let her gaze linger for a moment on the impressive breadth of his shoulders. In the better lit room she also saw that his hair was a rich dark brown, with dulled gold lights glinting here and there.

As if that wasn't enough to capture her attention, the scent of his classy cologne drifted beguilingly on the air and made her insides turn over. With the tip of her tongue she moistened her suddenly dry lips and placed the tray on the gracious Victorian desk in front of him. Then she walked round to the beautifully carved chair that her boss usually occupied.

Coming face to face with Eugene's features again was not something any woman with a pulse would soon forget… He was chisel-jawed and handsome as a Michelangelo sculpture. But she was perturbed when she saw that his dazzling blue eyes didn't seem as warm as they had upstairs, when she'd met his gaze over the jewellery cabinet and he'd shared that touching story about the fake pearl and diamond ring his father had bought his mother.

In fact, as they swept over her they brought to mind a once sunlit ocean frozen under ice. A little alarmed, Rose sensed hot colour flooding into her cheeks. *Was he assessing the way she looked?*

Having never considered herself a beauty, she was painfully disconcerted at being scrutinised by the businessman so penetratingly. Friends had often remarked that her best features were her eyes and her cheekbones, but other than that she knew she was quite ordinary. Disturbed that she should waste even a second fretting over what the man's opinion of her might be her instinct was to be doubly wary of him.

But the restaurateur's carved lips curved in another disconcerting smile. 'Would you like to pour the coffee for us? Then we can proceed. I have a particularly heavy schedule today, and would like to settle our business as quickly as possible.'

'You sound as though you've made a decision?'

'I have. Having seen the interior of the building, I'd like to make you an offer.'

Straight away Rose noted that he'd said 'the building'—not the antiques business. Her stomach plunged like a stone.

'I'd really like to tie up the sale of the property today,' he added smoothly, bringing his hands together with his long fingers forming a steeple.

His words suggested it was a given that she would agree to the sale. Maybe he didn't think she could possibly refuse him because she was only standing in for the owner? Perhaps he imagined his wealth and status would intimidate her?

If she was right, then his arrogance beggared belief. Biting her lip, she decided to delay commenting and garner her thoughts.

Reaching for the cafetière, she carefully poured out his coffee. 'It's two sugars, isn't it?' she checked, aware that his intense gaze was closely surveying everything she did and resenting it mightily.

'That's right.'

Passing him the beverage, Rose made a particular point of *not* meeting his gaze. After pouring her own drink she sat down, but in truth she
knew any hopes she might have had of remaining
calm throughout the meeting had fled as soon as
her glance had encountered the Frenchman's...

'Can I just clarify something? You said that
you wanted to tie up the sale of "the property"
today?'

'That's correct'

'Forgive me, but I thought my boss had made
it clear that he wanted to sell the business as a
going concern, Mr Bonnaire? You can't separate
it from the property and just purchase the building. Do I take it that you're not interested in running the antiques shop at all?'

'That's right, Rose—but, please, call me Gene.
You may or may not know, but I already run a
very successful worldwide restaurant business
and I'd like to install one of my most prestigious
restaurants here. The location is perfect. And,

although I do also have other successful businesses, to be frank with you I'm afraid that antiques don't interest me in the slightest. I'm sure you must have learned from your boss that people just aren't as interested in them these days as they used to be. Anyone in business wants to make money. No interest in the product, equals no profit. Isn't that the reason why he wants to sell?'

Rose felt as if her face had suddenly been seared by an iron. She was both embarrassed and furious. 'You don't have to be so brutal—'

'Business *is* brutal, *ma chère*...make no mistake about that.'

'Well, Philip is selling because he's ill and no longer has the energy to run the business. This antiques shop has always been his pride and joy, and if he was well I can assure you it wouldn't be up for sale at all.'

It was Gene's turn to sigh. 'But I'm guessing the fact is, due to his poor health, he's decided to take the opportunity to make as much money

as he can on his asset while he is still in a position to do so. Is that not so?'

She flushed again, and twisted her hands in her
lap to still their trembling. She couldn't make a
proper decision about anything if her emotions
got in the way. But Gene, as he seemed to prefer
being called, had guessed right. Because of his
failing health Philip *needed* to make this sale.
But she knew that he'd fervently hoped to sell
the business along with the building, and if Rose
didn't manage to do that for him then she would
have failed the man who was not just her boss
and mentor, but who had been her father's dearest friend...

She came to the only decision that could possibly be right. Now calmer, she met the Frenchman's gaze across the desk. 'It's true that Mr
Houghton needs to make this sale, Mr Bonnaire—Gene—but, since you've just admitted
that antiques don't interest you in the slightest,
and that you're not interested in running the business and only want the building, I'm afraid I can't

agree to sell it to you. It just wouldn't be right. I realise it's not the decision you hoped for, but I'm sorry. I hope you understand?'

'No. I do *not* understand. I have told you that it's the building I'm interested in and I'm willing to pay what I know to be the going rate for the property…no question. How many interested buyers has your boss seen since he put the shop up for sale?'

Gene Bonnaire's glare was steely.

'In the current economic climate my guess is not many… Maybe I'm the only one? If I were you, Rose, I would take my offer on your employer's behalf and congratulate yourself. Trust me… the only regret he would have is if you should be foolish enough to turn me down. Do you *really* want to put yourself in such an untenable position and lose the faith and trust he has obviously accorded you?'

As a helpless tide of defensive anger surged through her Rose set her eyes on the man she now considered to be not quite so charming. He

might not be as heartless as she'd first thought—
the story about the fake pearl and diamond ring
his father had bought his mother demonstrated
that he had the capacity to feel things deeply—
but she knew that he was determined to secure
the desirable Thames-side building at all costs.
And he was plainly willing to risk Rose not liking him if he became too insistent.

'I think you've said quite enough, Mr Bonnaire.
I've given you my decision and you're just going
to have to accept it.'

'Is that so? Do you imagine that any businessman or woman worth their salt who is determined to seal a deal should give up so easily
merely because you tell them that they *should*?'

His tone was sardonic, and Gene's glance swept
over Rose as if she was a foolish little girl.

Swallowing down her fury that anybody could
be so reprehensible, she stiffly folded her arms.
'I wouldn't dream of advising anyone what's best
for them, because I clearly don't know. I'm not a
businesswoman…I'm an antiques dealer. How-

ever, I *do* know my boss Philip, and how much this antiques business means to him. He's impressed upon me more than once that he wants to sell it as a going concern, so I would be failing in my duty if I didn't adhere to that. On his behalf, I thank you for your interest but our meeting is over. I'll see you to the door.'

'Not so fast.'

As he rose immediately to his feet it wasn't hard for Rose to detect that Gene Bonnaire was more than a little thrown off balance by her refusal to sell. He was holding on to his temper by a thread.

The expensive cologne he wore again stirred the air, reminding her that the moneyed and elite world he inhabited was light years away from hers and that he hadn't expected an argument. But on this occasion, Rose was determined to stand her ground...

'Look, I didn't come here to waste my time or yours,' he went on. 'I came here for one reason and one reason only: to purchase a listed build-

ing that I understood was up for sale. If you won't
sell the premises to me then perhaps you'd reconsider your decision if I agree to purchase the antiques as well? I don't doubt some of them might
be valuable to an ardent collector.'

The comment was hardly encouraging. He
might just as well have referred to the collector
as misguided rather than ardent. Rose didn't have
to guess how appalled Philip would be if he knew
that Gene didn't want to purchase the antiques for
their beauty and historical significance, or even
because he might be considering continuing the
business after all, but only because he was thinking about their monetary worth.

'Indeed, some of them are extremely valuable,'
she confirmed. 'But unfortunately your remark
illustrates to me exactly what you asserted earlier…you have no interest whatsoever in antiques.
That being the case, I'm not inclined to consider
your offer any further, Mr Bonnaire.'

Extracting a leather wallet from the inside
pocket of the impeccably tailored jacket he wore,

the businessman took out a card and threw it down onto the desk. The blue eyes that Rose had noted could be icy had turned even more glacial.

'When you've had some time to think things over—meaning when you can make a far less *emotional* decision about the matter, Rose—I don't doubt you'll want to get in touch with me to discuss a sale. In the meantime, I'll say *au revoir.*'

As he spoke Rose found herself yet again uncomfortably captured by his mocking glance, and she thanked her lucky stars that the man was going. Yet as her gaze followed him to the door in truth she didn't know whether or not to be pleased she'd stood her ground—whether the decision she'd made was the right one or not…

Back in his Mayfair office, after the tedious round of meetings he'd chaired that afternoon, Gene asked his secretary to get him some coffee and sank down into his high-backed leather chair to mull over the day's events. He didn't think he had ever felt more irritable and out of sorts, and it was all down to his offer being refused on that damn property.

He'd admired the architecture of the Thames-side building for years, and had often thought it would make the most fantastic restaurant should he buy it. He didn't envisage it as an addition to the more commercial restaurants he already owned, but saw it as the kind of exclusive place that the glitterati liked to frequent. Just like the two esteemed establishments he owned in New York and Paris.

Recalling his meeting with Rose Heathcote, Gene mused that it was beyond his understanding how she couldn't see what a gold-edged opportunity to capitalise on his assets he had given her boss. Most people would have ripped his arm off to take it. But one thing had become eminently clear to him… Just as she had said, Rose was no businesswoman. Her attitude had really irked him. Especially when he'd seen that she wasn't going to be easily influenced by any amount of charm he might utilise. Yet part of him admired the brunette for her determination to stand firm even though he knew she was wrong.

And there was something else about her that had caught his attention. *She had the most startlingly beautiful violet eyes.* Her glossy black hair and ivory-coloured skin made them even more captivating. The passion he'd seen in their mesmerising depths had intrigued him and made him want to get to know her, even though she'd denied him the chance to purchase the property. But, as was his modus operandi when faced with situations or outcomes he didn't like, Gene knew he would immediately work to turn it to his advantage.

Yes…he would step right back into the breach and make his purchase of the building a foregone conclusion. He wouldn't be satisfied until it was his. Rose could take a couple of days' sober reflection on what a mistake she'd made in turning him down, then Gene would get back to her with an offer that he knew her boss simply *couldn't* refuse.

If he could have some more time with her and assure her that he was respectful of the gracious building's admirable history, had always admired it and only sought to elevate it by housing his restaurant there, he didn't doubt he could persuade her to convince Philip Houghton that selling the building to one of the country's richest entrepreneurs wasn't just a good idea…it was the *only* one that would take it off his hands and make him enough money to see him right for the rest of his life.

But just then, somewhere deep inside him, Gene couldn't help feeling disturbed that he'd so easily dismissed the other man's welfare in the belief that money was the answer to his problems. Even his parents had counselled him on that once.

*'Son, you can't always fix someone's pain by throwing money at the problem. No amount of money or good fortune made it any easier for us to endure the devastation of your sister's death. Don't forget that.'*

The memory jolted him, and for a few disturbing seconds he felt as if a grenade had been thrown into the room. But now wasn't the time to reflect on how much his sister's death had nearly broken him…

He squared his shoulders. He and his parents saw life very differently. Gene saw practical solutions to adversity while they succumbed to their emotions and allowed their feelings to dictate how they responded… The idea of behaving in the same way was anathema to him. He'd heard his parents' stories about their poor upbringings, how their own parents and siblings had suffered terribly when there hadn't been the means to put food on the table or to have adequate heat and light, and how many nights they had gone to bed hungry… From a tender age he'd intuited how essential it was to have money, and as he'd grown older, having discovered that he had a talent for making it with ease, he wasn't about to relinquish it—not for *anyone*.

Pleased that he'd come up with a plan to help

him win the beautiful old property—a plan he was convinced would work because he never, *never* entertained the possibility of failure— Gene got to his feet, straightened his tie and strode out through the door.

Stopping at the desk of his blonde, statuesque secretary, Simone, whose cousin was an up-and-coming Parisian designer—and frankly that was why he'd given her the job…because it always paid to utilise his assets—he flashed her a warmer smile than usual and said, 'Forget the coffee, *ma chère,* and book me a table for dinner at my club for eight o'clock.'

'Will you be taking a guest with you, Mr Bonnaire?'

'No, Simone. Not tonight.'

'Then I will ring the *maître d'* straight away and arrange for you to have your favourite table.'

'Thank you.'

'You are most welcome. It always makes me glad when I can do something to please you and make your life a little easier.'

The woman's glossy pink lips curved in a smile that was definitely inviting.

Gene's fleetingly good mood instantly vanished. Scowling, he said, 'In that case you won't mind doing some overtime tonight, will you? I've left a "to do" list on my desk for you. Goodnight, Simone. I will see you in the morning.'

He was more irritated than usual with the blonde's obsequious manner. She hadn't been working for him for very long, but he didn't need to be a genius to know that she was only too aware of how to use *her* best assets…especially as she clearly thought it was only a matter of time before he would bed her… Just yesterday he had overheard her stating the fact, not very discreetly, to someone on her mobile.

Waiting impatiently for the elevator to arrive, he muttered savagely beneath his breath, 'God save me from predatory women!'

# CHAPTER TWO

LONG AFTER HER MEETING, and still stinging from her encounter with the mercurial force of nature that was Gene Bonnaire, Rose couldn't help but be interested in what drove the man to be the way he was. He clearly hadn't liked her decision not to sell the shop to him. Her refusal had really grated on him, because he obviously wasn't used to being denied when he'd set his sights on something that he wanted.

Knowing that he was a restaurateur, and that he wanted the building for one of his establishments, that night she went home and did some more research.

Rose discovered that Gene was one of the richest men in Europe and had made his fortune by turning a once small French restaurant in East

London called Mangez Bien into a well-known chain that had spread across the globe. The original restaurant had been owned by Gene's parents. They were both French immigrants, who'd settled in London when they were young and had turned their love of cooking and food into owning a much loved eatery that had been patronised by a devoted local clientele.

By the time their son had turned seventeen, so the story went, he was already a fine chef whose ambitions far exceeded his parents' own. He had progressed from being Head Chef at one of London's finest hotels to becoming an astute entrepreneur who had started to establish restaurants of his own. But as he'd begun to build an empire of affordable French restaurants he had also acquired a reputation for being quite ruthless in his business dealings.

*Rose already knew he didn't like being denied...*

Leaning back in her chair, she studied the photograph that her computer had helpfully supplied.

It had been taken at a prestigious awards ceremony in LA, and even though the picture of him couldn't help but be flattering, to her mind it didn't depict any pleasure at his being at the event, nor at having received an award. Instead, the man's immense dissatisfaction was clear. It emanated from Gene's steely blue eyes in forbidding icy waves...

*He doesn't look even remotely pleased,* she mused. And he was probably even less pleased since she'd turned down his offer.

The headline of the article onscreen read, *The man who has everything once again strikes gold.*

'Hmph,' Rose muttered out loud. 'That doesn't mean that any of what he's got makes him happy. *Something* must be bugging him...something he doesn't like to talk about.'

Was it anything to do with his father not being able to afford a *real* diamond and pearl ring for his mother in the early days when they were starting to establish their business? Why else had he told Rose that it was only costume jewellery?

Had it made him feel insecure? She remembered the flicker of pain that had accompanied his remark. But surely he wasn't still burdened by the memory? Was he sad that once upon a time his parents had struggled…that not everything had been as easy for them as it had for their son?

Wearily dragging her fingers through her pixie cut short hair, she sighed. Why was Gene Bonnaire at the forefront of her thoughts when she still had to face her boss and tell him that she'd turned down the Frenchman's offer?

She would have done anything to spare him the disappointment and distress the news would undoubtedly bring him, and could only hope he would see that her motivation had been to do what was right by him. After all, he'd been there for her when her father had passed away, staying by his bedside with Rose until he breathed his last breath… The last thing he needed now, when he was so ill, was to be put under pressure to sell the antiques shop to someone who didn't have the first idea about what it meant to him…

Switching off her computer, she stood up and stretched. Annoyed that she'd wasted even more time thinking about Gene Bonnaire, she went into her living room to collect the book she'd been reading. It was a hefty tome all about the Aztecs, with a fascinating chapter on the magnificent jewellery worn by the emperors. There had recently been a momentous find in northern Mexico, and straight away it had fuelled Rose's interest. She'd have loved to go and see the treasure that the archaeologists had uncovered, but she'd have to wait until it finally went on display in a prestigious gallery or museum.

Going to bed, she fell asleep with the book on her chest and dreamt disturbingly of an Aztec emperor who uncannily resembled Gene Bonnaire...

Just like an addict, desperate to buy his next fix, Gene sat in the café across the street from the antiques store and couldn't turn his mind to anything else other than fulfilling his desire to own the gracious building he was staring at… The coffee he'd ordered had long gone cold as he restlessly contemplated going in and demanding that Rose Heathcote came to her senses and accepted the offer he'd made.

It had been three days since their meeting, and no phone call had been forthcoming to tell him that she'd had second thoughts. Maybe her boss had had a better offer from someone else? The very idea made him feel nauseous. He wanted that building as much as he wanted his next breath, and he deplored the notion that he might not get it.

Glancing down at his Rolex, he saw that he'd been sitting in the café for nigh on half an hour, hoping to catch Rose unawares. Catching someone off-guard often paid dividends, he'd found. If he'd seen her then he would have asked her out to dinner, so that they could talk amicably outside of work and get to know each other a little better. If he was able to get her to trust him then he didn't doubt he could persuade her to sell the building to him.

But she hadn't stepped outside even once, and in truth he was taking an unnecessary risk, sitting in the café in front of the window. Any minute now the paparazzi might turn up—and that really *would* ruin his day, because they were frequently on a mission to expose him as ruthless and uncaring...

Even in the early days, when he'd started to have some success, he'd realised there were more people in the world who were jealous of his achievements rather than pleased. More to the point, they were jealous of his *wealth*... Knowing that, he knew the press was more than eager to take him down a peg or two—no doubt so that their readers could feel a bit better about their own lives.

Suddenly impatient, he glanced upwards at the now darkening skies. Any moment now it would start to rain. He shouldn't waste any more time sitting there, waiting for inspiration to dawn

about what he should do. He'd never been someone who *waited* for opportunity to strike. Gene
made his own opportunities.

His gaze settled on the old building again. The
name of the shop was The Hidden Diamond, and
to be honest he thought it a little trite. After all,
he reasoned, if it was hidden then what use was
it to anybody? Diamonds should be displayed to
denote their owner's wealth…not hidden away.

With a jaundiced sigh he got to his feet. The
promised rain began to splatter the pavement.
He was done with waiting. He was going into
the shop to present Rose with a more persuasive
offer. If she really cared so much about helping
her boss then she ought to be relieved he was
giving her a second bite of the cherry…

Rose was finishing up her bookwork when she
heard the doorbell chime. Hurriedly toeing on
her maroon leather flats, she tucked her cream
silk blouse more securely into the waistband of

her smart black skirt and left the office to deal with what she assumed was a late customer.

She should have closed up shop half an hour ago, but she'd been so immersed in cataloguing the dwindling monthly sales and wishing they were better that she hadn't noticed the time.

Her lips automatically curved into a smile, but the gesture immediately melted away when she saw that her late caller wasn't the customer she'd envisaged but Gene Bonnaire. She stared. What was *he* doing here? Forgoing a suit, he was dressed casually today, in jeans and a dove-grey T-shirt beneath a tailored black jacket. But he was no less formidable. It was raining outside, she saw, and the shoulders of his jacket glistened with moisture—as did his hair.

'Do you usually stay open this late?' he asked, clearly opting to dispense with any social nice-ties.

Tensing, Rose found herself caught in the crys-talline spotlight of his disquieting blue gaze. 'Not usually no. But I was busy doing some bookwork and didn't notice the time. What can I do for you, Mr Bonnaire? If you were hoping to persuade me to change my mind about your offer then I'm sorry. I wouldn't want you to waste your time.'

'Don't be sorry. Just let me have a few minutes with you to talk things over.'

'To what end?'

'Why don't we sit down and I'll tell you?'

Rose arched an eyebrow. 'Like I said, I gave you my decision and I see no reason in discussing it any further.' When Gene scowled she got the distinct impression that he was having considerable trouble remaining calm. His next words confirmed it.

'You really have no idea about business, do you, Rose? I'd like to know why your boss, Philip Houghton, has such faith in you… Perhaps you'd enlighten me?'

Now Rose had trouble holding on to her own temper, and she had no hesitation in replying passionately, 'Because I care about him—that's why! I have no ulterior motive other than that I want

what's best for him. And what's best for him is
to sell the antiques business as a going concern,
to someone who will love it as much as he does.'

'That's a nice thought…but hardly a realistic
one.'

'Did you come here just to tell me how inept
you think I am, Mr Bonnaire?' Incensed, she
folded her arms. 'Because if it makes you feel
any better, then you should know that I've had
sleepless nights about the whole thing. It would
be very easy to take your offer to my boss and
tell him that he'd be lucky to get another one
half as good—remind him that the antiques
trade isn't what it used to be and he should just
take what he can while the going's good. But I
couldn't be so cruel. Not when I know how much
the business means to him. If he was just interested in selling a beautiful period building in a
very desirable area then he would have done so.
But he wants the business to continue… What
do you think he'd say if I accepted your offer

and then told him you weren't remotely interested in antiques?'

Gene looked thoughtful. Then he smiled. 'I
think he'd probably feel that he can't be sentimental about it. At the end of the day, if he be-
lieves that his poor health will prohibit his return
to work, no doubt he will need the money to help
pay for his care. Surely that's the priority here?'

What he said made perfect sense and, suddenly
unsure, Rose felt tears of frustration surge into
her eyes.

Gene all but covered the distance between them
in less than a couple of strides, and as before the
air stirred hypnotically with the exotic scent of
his expensive cologne.

'You're upset. Is there anything I can do? Why
don't we go into the office and I'll get you a cup
of tea?'

'I don't want tea. All I want is… All I want is
for you to go away!' Her outburst sounded em-
barrassingly childish even to her own ears… *So*

*much for keeping her composure.* Rose wanted the ground to open up and swallow her.

But the man in front of her didn't go away. He didn't even look remotely put out. The dazzling blue eyes that she knew could turn forbiddingly cold when he was angry were now inexplicably warm…*tender*, even. He lifted his hand to touch her arm gently. Her heart thudded quietly as she felt his smooth skin brush against her own.

'Your boss gave you a tough job when he asked you to sell the business for him, Rose—perhaps *too* tough. I don't mean this as a criticism, but I can see that it's not where your skills lie…I've already learned that it's the *job* you love—being with the artefacts and learning about their history. More than that, you like discovering the personal stories behind them. You're a *people* person, Rose…not a businesswoman.'

She realised the man had an almost uncanny knack of knowing what a person was about. But she didn't want to let him see even for a second that his astute insight perturbed her. Surely Gene

Bonnaire had enough advantages without her giving him any more…namely the fact that she could so easily warm to him, when everything in her told her it would be a mistake that would undoubtedly cost her dear…

'That might be the case, and I *know* my forte isn't in the world of business—I told you that before. But my love of antiques and understanding what they mean to people also makes me understand why my boss, Philip, wants to sell the business as a going concern. I think it means even more to him since he's become ill. He's taught me so much about the trade, and that's why I want to get the best deal for him.'

'That's also why you should give me a little bit more of your time and listen to what I have to say, Rose.'

'Why? Are you going to tell me that you've decided to take on the business after all?'

Gene was already shaking his head. 'No. I'm sorry I have to disappoint you, but I won't be getting involved in that side of things. I haven't changed my mind about that.'

'Then how can I possibly be interested in listening any more to what you have to say, Mr Bonnaire?'

'If you'd do me the courtesy of having dinner with me tonight, I'll explain.'

Even as she guessed that most women would be surprised and pleased by such an invitation— not to mention immensely flattered—Rose defiantly lifted her chin to indicate that she wasn't one of them. 'Thank you, but I'm going to have to decline.'

'You have a previous engagement?'

'No, but—'

'You don't want to hear what I have to say, even though it might be to your boss's advantage?'

'How can it *possibly* be to his advantage? You've already said that you're not interested in the business…that you only want the building.'

Gene Bonnaire's steely-eyed gaze didn't waver for so much as a second as he examined her, and it was easy to guess he'd hoped to have the upper hand.

'Like I said, Rose… Have dinner with me tonight and all will be explained.'

Prickling with unease, she sensed herself flush heatedly. 'You're just playing games—and I don't trust men who play games. If you have something to say that you know for a fact my boss will be interested in, then why don't you just come right out and say it?'

'Very well, then, although I'm sad that you won't agree to dinner, and just to reassure you, Rose, I'm not playing games. It's just that it has been my experience that all the best deals are made over a cordon bleu meal and a fine bottle of wine.'

One corner of the handsome Frenchman's mouth lifted in a smile that would make most women—young, old and in between—*ache* to be close to him in the most intimate way… And even though Rose was quite aware that he was using his charm to get what he wanted, she was hardly immune to the idea.

'Is that right? Well, I'm afraid that's not been *my* experience.'

'So you won't even take a risk and try it?'

Unable to glance away from his mesmerising gaze, she felt her breath hitch. 'No…I won't…'

But even as she refused a look of heated longing drifted across his irises and she sensed her resistance indisputably melting. Underneath their polite words, somehow a much more sensual conversation was taking place. Rose couldn't deny it. That impossibly irresistible look of Gene Bonnaire's was captivating her, stirring her own longing into life, and right then all she wanted to do was to fulfil it…

Gene moved to stand in front of her, his mesmerising blue eyes smouldering like simmering fires… In the next instant the businessman had firmly caught hold of her arm and pulled her against his chest.

Rose's blood pumped hard. All she could do

was helplessly stare back at him. It was undeniable that he excited her, but his sheer physical
presence disturbed her too. It only took a glance
to see how supremely fit and strong he was.

Low-voiced, he murmured, 'God forgive me,
but…'

The time that elapsed between his words and
his next action was brief…*too* brief for her to
stop him.

His urgent, initially demanding kiss stole her
breath and made her sink against the hard wall
of his chest. *Her senses were utterly besieged
by him.* And as his hot silken mouth moved over
hers and became more and more seductive Rose
didn't have the faintest inclination to end the passionate caress.

Then somehow it filtered through to her fogged
brain just how dangerous her compliant actions
were and she came hurtling back to her senses.
Shocked and shaken, she freed herself from the
Frenchman's embrace and wiped her hand over
her already aching lips.

Staring back at him, she declared, 'Your arrogance, Mr Bonnaire, has to be seen to be believed! I don't know what you thought you were doing, but I think you'd better just leave.'

Her heart pumped even harder. The heat from his body and his velvet mouth had seared her indelibly, and she already knew she wasn't easily going to forget it.

'I didn't intend to kiss you, Rose, but somehow the desire overwhelmed me. I am as disturbed by it as you are. I apologise. If you really won't come to dinner with me then I can do no more than tell you about the amended deal I have come up with.'

He paused, as if to take a moment to straighten his thoughts. There was a slight crimson tint beneath his tan that bore out his declaration that desire had overwhelmed him. Rose didn't know what to make of it herself. She was just an ordinary girl, and he was—he was a living, breathing *Adonis*...

'I already know how much getting the best deal

for your boss means to you, and I have spent quite some time thinking about how I can make that a reality for you both. This is my new offer.'

His hand dived into the inside pocket of his jacket and he drew out a slim sheet of paper. Unfolding it, he handed it to Rose.

Her jaw all but hit the floor when she saw how much he was prepared to pay for the privilege of owning the building. His initial offer had practically *doubled*. For dizzying moments she was literally lost for words.

'This amount of money can be a real life-changer for Philip, Rose. That being the case, why on earth would you turn down the opportunity to help make things better for him? If you were to persuade him to see the sense in selling to me, then I'm sure he would be nothing but relieved. If he accepted my offer then he would have the worry of the business off his hands and earn himself a more than healthy profit. No doubt *you* would be happy too, Rose, because his ill health would undoubtedly be restored and, last but not least, I don't deny *I* would be pleased, because I'd get the property I've long desired.'

'And the name of the game is always that you get what *you* want, isn't it, Mr Bonnaire? There's nothing altruistic about this scenario, is there? You don't give a fig about my employer's health, or whether I'm happy or not happy. Why *should* you? You know nothing about us! You've seen something you want and you'll do anything… pay *any* price…to get it. Isn't that how people like you operate?'

To Rose's consternation, he chuckled. It was a rich, gravelly sound that sent shivers running up and down her spine.

'*Touché*…you've got it in one. You're a bright woman…'

'Don't patronise me!'

Sighing, he folded his arms over his chest and studied her. 'I wouldn't dream of it. I'd much rather have you on my side than make you my enemy, Rose. By the way, your eyes are an *incredible* colour… I don't doubt you've been told that many times before. What's the shade? I'd say they were violet…'

Rose was hardly prepared for his remarks suddenly to become personal, even though he'd so passionately kissed her, and for several disturbing seconds it threw her. She could hardly think, let alone come back with a retort to put him in his place.

'The colour of my eyes is neither here nor there. This conversation is completely futile. Now, I really need to close the shop and you have to go.'

'Not yet. You haven't told me what you intend to do.'

'What do you mean?'

His eyes narrowed. 'Are you going to talk to your boss about accepting my new offer?'

Rose was still holding the piece of paper he'd given her and she carefully folded it and slipped it into her skirt pocket.

Returning her gaze to his, she said, 'I'll show him what you're offering —of course I will—but if you're asking if I'll try and persuade him to take it, then, no…I won't. Philip makes his own decisions—always has and always will. I neither have nor *want* any influence over him.'

'I don't believe you.' Dropping his hands to his hips, Gene smiled. 'I can sense that you're a sensitive woman, Rose. I'm sure that Philip must appreciate that. If he knows that you care about his feelings then I'm sure he must respect any opinions you have about the matter and know that you have his best interests at heart.'

'Even so, it would feel wrong for me to persuade him to just sell the building, and some of the antiques, when he dearly wants to sell the business as a going concern.'

'But surely he must know by now that his beloved business clearly isn't viable any more?'

'Do you think I want to tell him that? When I know it's been his life's work and he's lying ill in hospital?'

'You would find a way to put it compassionately, I'm sure. You obviously care about him very much.'

'I do…'

'Then he is a lucky man.'

'*I'm* the lucky one. If he hadn't taken me on and taught me the trade I'd never have found the work that I've grown to love.'

'I'm sure he must have found it a pleasure to teach you, Rose. What sentient man *wouldn't*? Not only does he get a beautiful woman with captivating violet eyes and patrician cheekbones to work for him, but she becomes quite devoted to him too.'

Rose sensed her cheeks flush red. 'I think you've got the wrong end of the stick. Philip isn't attracted to me, if that's what you're implying, and neither am I to him. For goodness' sake— he's an elderly man, past retirement age!'

Gene was instantly apologetic. 'I'm sorry if I've caused offence. I thought he must be middle-aged, but I didn't realise he was elderly. I'm afraid I confess I was a little jealous when I heard you talk about him in such glowing terms.'

Dry-mouthed, Rose hardly knew what to say.

The way he'd complimented her looks just now was unbearably seductive, and saying that he'd been *jealous* of her admiration for Philip was crazy. Coming from a man who could have any woman he wanted, it was plainly ridiculous.

Realising that for a dangerous moment she'd been more flattered than she should, Rose gritted her teeth. Gene Bonnaire was even more of a threat than she'd thought…

'Look…I think you'd better just go. I mean it. I'll be in touch if I get any news from Mr Houghton for you.'

For a surreal moment Gene honestly forgot what he was about—because he suddenly found himself even more mesmerised by the brunette. Those violet eyes of hers were strangely bewitching, and he'd fallen into a bit of dream staring back at them.

He'd known when he kissed her that he wanted to seduce her…it was just a matter of *when*…but his sudden fierce attraction was honestly a revelation—because Rose Heathcote certainly wasn't the usual type of woman he was attracted to. She was not blonde, statuesque or shapely. She was small and slender, with black hair cut boyishly short. Yet the passionate spark in her eyes that he'd just witnessed, along with her feisty nature and her determination to protect her boss at all costs, made her surprisingly alluring.

It was another first, because Gene usually liked his women to be more compliant. *He* liked to be the one in control.

Quickly returning to his senses, he realised he was just going to have to bide his time and wait for Rose to speak to her boss.

Moving across to the door, he glanced out at the now teeming rain and then back at the diminutive brunette. 'All right, then. I won't press you any further. But tell me… Is there anything I can do for *you*, Rose? Does someone as generous as you are, with your regard for others, ever have her kindness reciprocated? For instance I'd be *very* interested to know if you have a personal heartfelt desire. If you do, then all you have to do is say the word and I'll do my utmost to help you get it.'

'Why would you want to do that? I suspect it's because you have some devious ulterior motive…'

Gene laid his hand over his heart and grinned. 'You wound me deeply.'

'If you could give me my "heartfelt desire" then you'd be much more than a mere man. Has it never occurred to you that not all heartfelt desires are material ones?' Rose challenged him.

He shrugged. 'I can't say I spend much time thinking about it. I prefer to deal with the tangible, not the abstract.'

'So in your world feelings are abstract, are they?'

'Why don't you have dinner with me and we can talk about it?'

She grimaced. 'I'd rather have dinner with a boa constrictor! At least I'd know for sure what I'd be dealing with.'

In spite of his disappointment that Rose didn't

seem to believe he might just want to give her something that pleased her, and at not immediately strengthening his chances to buy the property, Gene found her answer undeniably amusing. To his surprise, he also found it indisputably *seductive*...

'I can't say I'm flattered, Rose, but that's *funny*!'

'You should stop calling me Rose. It's Miss Heathcote to you.'

Gene smiled. 'I can see that I've really got to you, haven't I? All right, then—I'll go. But you haven't heard the last of me...not by a long chalk...*Rose*...'

He opened the door and, with a resigned grimace, walked out into the rain.

The phone rang in the early hours of the morning and a brisk-sounding nurse from the hospital informed Rose that Philip had taken a turn for the worse and asked if she could she please come in. Feeling numb with fear, she dragged

on her jeans, T-shirt and Mackintosh and practically flew out the door.

When she got to the hospital and was directed
to a ward she drew in a deep breath as she saw
him. White-faced and fragile, he was lying in
bed breathing through an oxygen mask and wired
up to the kind of medical paraphernalia that told
her this was serious.

All her worst fears crashed in on her at the
same time. It hadn't escaped her notice that her
boss had been transferred to the same ward that
her father had been in when he died. He'd had a
fatal coronary whilst in hospital for investigation
into something relatively minor, so it had come
as the most terrible shock. *Was this how Philip
was destined to leave her as well?* Rose could
hardly bear the thought.

The doctor on call had diagnosed pneumonia
and he told her that it was crucial they stabilised
the condition and that he got plenty of rest. To
that end they would be keeping him in longer

than they'd first envisaged, and would be treating him with antibiotics and extra oxygen.

As she sat by his bedside holding his hand, Philip opened his eyes just once, to acknowledge that he knew she was there, and she gently assured him that everything was going to be all right, that he wasn't to worry. But even as she said the words Rose didn't entirely believe them. Suddenly the man who had been such a firm friend to her and her father looked worryingly old and haggard...and very, very ill.

Having tried so hard to hold back the tears during her visit, as soon as she got home she threw herself onto the couch and the floodgates opened.

They weren't the last tears she cried over the testing week that followed. One day Philip was rallying encouragingly, looking a little better, and the next it seemed he was worse. Managing the shop as well as talking to an array of healthcare professionals about his aftercare, Rose was on a rollercoaster of emotion that one moment had her feeling hopeful for his full recovery and the next fearing the unthinkable…

She had all but forgotten her recent encounter with Gene Bonnaire. But one evening after work when she visited the hospital Philip told her he wanted to discuss something important. She had an uneasy feeling that the billionaire's offer to buy the antiques shop was on his mind. A couple of days earlier she had shown him Gene's offer. *She was right.* He clearly hadn't felt ready to discuss it then, but he did now.

'Rose…I want you to contact Mr Bonnaire and tell him that I'm going to agree to the sale.'

There was a flash of what looked to be deep regret in his pale blue eyes, and his expression was apologetic.

'I'm disappointed that he doesn't want to buy the business and that it won't continue as I'd hoped, but in my present situation beggars can't be choosers. Seeing as I haven't had any other offers, and I'm advised I'm going to be housebound for quite some time after this, I'll need to pay for private care. As you know, I don't have any family, but at least I have some material assets that I can realise to help me—the main one being the antiques shop. The man's offer for the building coupled with the antiques is more generous than I could have hoped for. He left me his card, didn't he? Can you contact him and arrange a meeting?'

Fighting to regain her composure at the idea that she was going to have to talk to the Frenchman again, Rose replied 'I'll do whatever you want me to do to help, Philip, but surely you can't meet with him to discuss things until you get out of hospital?'

Once more he was apologetic. 'I'm afraid I can't risk waiting that long. I need to sell the place as quickly as I can to free up some money for my care. I'm asking you to handle the sale for me, Rose. I've contacted my solicitor and he'll draw up the necessary papers. This is his name and number.'

He opened the bedside drawer, took out a single

sheet of vellum that he'd written on and handed it to her.

'Anything you need to know, he'll explain.'

'It seems that you've made up your mind, then.' Frowning, Rose felt her muscles clench tight at the idea of once again coming face to face with Gene Bonnaire and knowing that this time *he* would be the one who had the advantage and would undoubtedly use it for all he was worth...

'Yes, my dear...I have.'

'Then I'll see to things right away. In the meantime you should try and rest as much as possible. The last thing you need is to be stressed about anything.'

Smiling fondly, Philip patted her hand as it lay on the counterpane. 'I should have told you this before, Rose...I don't know how I would have managed these past ten years without you. Without question, your loyalty, friendship and hard work have been invaluable and if I had been a much younger man I don't doubt I would have fallen a little bit in love with you.'

Feeling her cheeks glow warmly, Rose smiled back—even as she remembered Gene Bonnaire's ridiculous implication that her relationship with her boss might not be just a *working* one. *What she'd give to wipe that self-satisfied smirk off his handsome face when next she saw him!* Only she couldn't. She had to be nice to him because Philip urgently needed this sale. The last thing she would do was jeopardise things just because the man had rattled her.

But then, as she recalled that he'd asked her if other people ever reciprocated her kindness to them, she knew that the man had much more sensitivity than his very public persona suggested and thought that it would be intriguing to discover more…

'It's sweet of you to say so,' she answered Philip, 'but to be frank I think I'm destined to stay single. I've only been in love once in my life and it wasn't the happiest of experiences. I'm not eager to do it again.'

'I'm sorry to hear that. Don't you believe that

it might be different the next time? Not so pain-ful, I mean?'

'No, I don't. I don't because—present company not included—I don't trust men. I think I'd be better off on my own.' She shrugged. 'Besides, I'm far too independent, and men sense that. It would take someone pretty exceptional to get me to change my mind and I haven't yet met anyone who fits that particular bill.'

'Not yet, you haven't, Rose, but you will...you will.'

With a knowing smile, the man in the hospital bed closed his eyes and, leaving him to doze, she folded the sheet of notepaper he'd given her, slipped it into her bag and discreetly left...

# CHAPTER THREE

STANDING IN ONE of his magnificent rooms,
where huge plate-glass windows overlooked the
ocean, Gene took the call from his secretary in-
forming him that Rose Heathcote had requested
a meeting. By the time he ended the call he was
feeling more than vindicated. There could only
be one reason why the feisty brunette wanted to
see him, and that must be to convey the news that
her boss had finally agreed to his offer.

He was elated. All his fantasies about owning the gracious building beside the Thames and
turning it into the finest restaurant imaginable
were becoming a dazzling reality in his mind.

He already knew the people he wanted to
hire—both to do the renovations and to create
and provide the cuisine that would be second to

none. He had the private numbers of some of the finest chefs and sommeliers in the country, and he wasn't above using his money and power to entice them away from their current exclusive establishments. Before much time had passed the place would be up and running and he would be welcoming anybody who was anybody and yet again demonstrating to the world just how far drive and ambition could take a person if they were dedicated enough.

*Make no mistake. Eugene Bonnaire was a force to be reckoned with.*

His parents had never understood his ambition and drive for more…more money, more success, *more everything…* But they had both come from humble families in France, with barely a franc to keep body and soul together—hardworking folk who had barely eked out a sustainable living.

'Our families may not have always had enough food to put on the table but there was no lack of love in our homes,' his mother had often told him.

But the very idea of not having the most basic requirements had pained their son. No matter how much love they'd had, their lives had been pretty grim when they were growing up. Was it any wonder that Gene wanted so much more, to obliterate the stain of his ancestors' impoverished past?

Yes, his parents had made an admirable success of their East London restaurant, and their teaching him to cook at a young age had been a great platform for him to hone his culinary skills—a fact for which he was eternally grateful. It was that which had led to him becoming a much lauded chef, then a successful restaurateur. Add to that some eye-popping lucrative investments and the sky was his limit… But it had always been beyond him that his parents couldn't see that they could have had so much more for *themselves*…weren't even *interested*.

Breathing out a sigh, he rubbed his hand over his chest. It had been several months now since he'd paid them a visit and he knew they must be concerned. But he guessed that they didn't want to put pressure on him in case he did the unthinkable and cut them out of his life for good. *He would never do such a thing...* God knew they'd suffered enough.

When Gene had been just nine years old they had lost his little sister, Francesca, to a stomach virus. She had been only three. That shattering experience had changed them all. His mother had used to smile so easily—but not any more... There was always the sense that something vital and irreplaceable was missing when they were together, and of course there *was*...

Ever since that time Gene had sought to compensate his parents for their loss. If he became successful, he had reasoned, they would be so proud of him, and in turn he could ensure they enjoyed a comfortable old age. But somehow his success and ambition hadn't seemed to overly impress them. It was the one area in his life where he felt a failure. Consequently, his relationship with them had begun to deteriorate.

Feeling as though he'd lost the ability to properly connect with them, he had turned in on himself to protect his emotions. Inevitably, his other relationships had suffered. Women sensed that he wasn't available emotionally, and now the only women he seemed to attract were the ones who liked his wealth and what it could buy for them... That being the case, he'd decided to keep his liaisons short and sweet. More meaningful and longer-term relationships definitely weren't on his agenda...

But as he crossed the polished parquet floor to the door unbidden he suddenly found himself recalling the incandescent violet of Rose Heathcote's eyes. Without a doubt the woman intrigued and excited him. Gene mused that perhaps she wouldn't be so averse to his company now, when she would in effect be coming to him cap in hand because Philip Houghton had finally seen the sense in agreeing to sell him the shop. In any case, it meant that Gene would have the upper hand, and the diminutive Rose would no doubt have to swallow her pride and be nice to him.

He had no intention of making things easy for her either. Having not long ago arrived at his personal retreat on a remote Scottish island—the one place where he could genuinely enjoy some respite and didn't have to contend with petty jealousies and criticism from press and public alike—he wasn't about to charge back to London to sign the papers for purchase in a hurry. *Not when the tide had just turned in his favour.* No, he would insist that Rose brought them to *him*. Although he had never even invited family or friends to this house, he would make an exception for the brunette.

In that instant Gene knew that he would make it his mission to change Rose's mind about him. He would slowly reveal more of his true nature and let her see that, despite what she might have read and heard about him, he was at his core an *honourable* man.

As he opened the door and went out he felt more than a little pleased with his decision…

Faced with the prospect of spending time in a landscape as alien to her as the moon, Rose gritted her teeth and braced herself as a friendly Scottish boatman guided a sturdy fishing boat towards the island.

As fierce waves lashed at the sides and inevitably splashed her she couldn't help praying that she was doing the right thing in adhering to Philip's heartfelt plea to take the papers to the arrogant businessman and get the deal 'done and dusted' as quickly as possible. Philip had looked so poorly when she'd last seen him in the hospital that the need to arrange some full-time care for him when he went home—at least until he had recovered more fully—had become glaringly imperative.

'This is a rare event,' the young curly-headed boatman remarked cheerfully as he steered the craft towards a landing bay carved out between the rocks. 'As far as I know the Lord of the Manor never has women visit him here… In fact, he never has *anyone*. It's his private hideaway, he told me once. He likes the remoteness of the place. 'It helps him to think straight.' Grinning, he added, 'Must like you a lot, I'd say.'

Grimacing painfully, Rose answered. 'The truth is the man doesn't like me at all. The sooner my business with him is over and I'm heading away from here, the better.'

'Well, the soonest you can leave is tomorrow, lass. The tides dictate when you can come and go. They're a stern mistress to these remote islands.'

'I can't leave until *tomorrow*?' Crestfallen at the news, Rose wrinkled her smooth brow in distress. 'You mean I'll have to stay here overnight?'

'Yes, lass. I'm sure His Lordship will have made arrangements. Here we go—give me your hand and I'll help you out.'

Once on terra firma, although it was rocky and felt less than safe underfoot, Rose couldn't deny she was relieved to be on dry land again. The small craft had negotiated the choppiest of seas on their crossing and she couldn't attest to being remotely excited by it. Give her the ground beneath her feet any day. At least there she felt some small semblance of control.

Arranging the strap of her red leather tote more securely over her shoulder, she lifted her hand to shade her eyes from a watery sun and stared. The wind was groaning with a mournful howl and as far as she could see the surrounding landscape looked relentlessly bleak. She shivered hard.

There was no welcoming party in sight to greet her—but then she wasn't exactly surprised. Although Gene Bonnaire had arranged for a luxurious sedan to pick her up and take her to the airport, and had provided a business class ticket for her to travel on the plane, Rose wasn't resting on her laurels. The two encounters she'd had with the man had been both unpredictable and unsettling, but as she'd made the effort to travel all this way to bring him the documents to sign she thought he might at least have had the decency to meet her and take her up to the house.

'Likely he's forgotten what time you were arriving…' The boatman lifted a broad shoulder in an apologetic shrug.

'Can I get a signal here to ring him on my mobile?' she asked hopefully.

The boatman shook his head. 'Sorry, but we don't have any service. I'd take you up to the house myself, but I've got to make tracks straight away or lose the tide. See that path marked out up ahead? Follow it right to the top and you'll get to Four Winds. You can't exactly miss it. The house is like some huge glass fortress from a sci-fi movie.'

'What about the other people on the island? Where do *they* live?'

'They don't. Live here, I mean. When he's here, Mr Bonnaire is the sole inhabitant.'

Rose took a deep breath in. So, not only did she have to stay on the island tonight, but she would be marooned with one of the most unpredictable and challenging men she'd ever met. Now she really *did* have to grit her teeth.

As she turned to watch the boatman get back into his craft she had a real sense of being abandoned. She knew that wasn't good for her morale. The last thing she needed to feel when she came face to face with Gene Bonnaire again was unsure. The man had too many advantages as it was. And the most disturbing of all wasn't his power and wealth, but his arrogant belief that money could get him anything he wanted—that getting what he wanted was in fact his *right,* even if it meant remorselessly manipulating people to achieve it…

She addressed the young man who'd brought her over to the island. 'Will you be collecting me tomorrow?'

'Aye, it will be me. If you could be here in the morning round eleven I'll come and get you.'

'I wish it could be sooner…'

'You'll be all right, lass. His bark is worse than his bite.'

'You're a lot more confident about that than I am. By the way, I didn't ask your name or tell you mine. I'm Rose…Rose Heathcote.'

'You can call me Rory. It's nice to meet you, Rose. Well, I'd best be on my way. Take care, won't you? Chin up—and don't worry. Just look at His Lordship with those beguiling violet eyes of yours and he'll be putty in your hands! Bye, now!'

With a cheerful salute, Rory expertly steered the craft out of the rocky bay and headed out to sea.

Warmed by his jovial assurance, Rose stood for perhaps longer than she should have, watching the boat. It very quickly disappeared, engulfed by the wind and the rain and the thrashing waves as if it had never been. Offering up a silent prayer for the young boatman's safe journey home, she turned and negotiated some rocks that had been carved into paving stones and made her way onto the path marked out on the hillside.

By the time she'd made the deceptively steep

climb to the end, even though on several occasions the icy wind had threatened to unbalance her and she'd had to watch carefully where she stepped, she was surprisingly warm, and she was more than a little out of breath when an impressive glass edifice loomed up before her.

Rory's description had been right on the money. Four Winds *was* like something out of a sci-fi movie. All that glass and chrome was a stunning contradiction, set in the bleak and yet beautiful landscape that embraced it.

Wiping away the sea spray that had moistened her face, Rose stared for what felt like an eternity, trying to make out where the entrance to the building was. Because it was a circular design, it wasn't easy to detect. There was no sign of Gene Bonnaire. How could she be sure he was even *there*?

As tense seconds turned into minutes she had a battle royal on her hands to keep her fury at bay. *What the hell did the man think he was playing at?* What if he'd changed his mind about his offer. What if he'd decided to pay her back for not agreeing to persuade Philip he should sell to him straight away and had made her come all the way out here to this remote Scottish island just because he *could*?

Her heart thumped so hard it felt as if it might burst out of her chest. If this was Gene Bonnaire's warped idea of a joke then it wasn't remotely funny…

'Well, well, well…look who the wind's blown in.'

The deeply gravelled tone almost made Rose jump out of her skin. Glancing up, she saw that part of the glass edifice had silently peeled back to reveal an entrance. Standing outside that futuristic doorway was the man she'd come to see. Dressed in fitted blue jeans that hugged his hard-muscled thighs and a black cashmere sweater, he had his arms casually folded across his impressive chest, giving the impression that it was the most natural thing in the world for him to come outside and find her standing there.

Clearly she wasn't going to receive an apology for his not meeting her off the boat...just his usual mockery. Her warmed hands had quickly turned icily cold while she'd been searching for the doorway, and now she gripped the strap of her tote hard as she fought to counter his cavalier treatment.

'You're lucky I'm here at all. I could have been blown off that hillside into the sea more than once on the way up here and you would have been none the wiser. Is this the way you usually treat your visitors?'

'No... It isn't...'

She had the briefest glimpse of what looked like regret in his fierce blue eyes—almost as if the idea had genuinely hurt him.

'I don't have any visitors here,' he stated. 'This is my private retreat and that's usually the way I like it. I've accorded *you* the privilege of coming here, Rose, because you have something that I very much want...and we both know what that is. However, I'm sincerely sorry that I wasn't down on the shore to meet you—I was busy with some work and simply forgot the time. I trust your journey wasn't too arduous?'

Rose suddenly felt ridiculously guilty. The Frenchman had sent a car to pick her up and take her to the station, and on the plane he'd arranged for her to travel first class. She had no complaints about the journey...

'It wasn't arduous at all. It's not every day that I get to travel business class. It was very pleasant, in fact.'

'Good. Well, you'd better come inside and get warm. And, by the way, there was no danger of you being blown off the hillside.' The corners of his eyes crinkled in amusement. 'You were too far inland for that.'

Biting back an irritable retort, Rose hurriedly moved past him into a curved entrance hall. A sublime wave of welcoming heat enveloped her. Dropping her tote onto the pristine oak floor, she rubbed her hands together to restore their circulation.

Her reluctant host joined her and the chrome and glass wall behind him slid elegantly closed. She had a disturbing moment of fear, realising she didn't know how to open them again. Were the controls some kind of heat-sensitive mechanism that only recognised the house's owner?

Swallowing hard, she turned round to face him. 'The boatman Rory told me I'd have to stay here until tomorrow because of the tides. I don't want to inconvenience you, but I wish you'd told your secretary to tell me that before I travelled.'

'Would you still have come if I had?'

'Of course I would. I'm doing this purely to help Philip, Mr Bonnaire, so I'll do whatever is necessary.'

'Ah, Philip…' His tone suggested the idea that she should undertake what was clearly for her an unwelcome mission only because of loyalty to her boss irked him. 'How is he? Getting better, I hope?'

'As a matter of fact he's still in hospital. He took a turn for the worse. That's what has motivated him to accept your offer.' Rose's heart thumped a little harder as she was suddenly reminded of the precarious nature of her boss's health.

'I'm sorry to hear that. Please convey my wishes to him that he may get better soon. And, by the way, please call me Gene. Mr Bonnaire sounds ridiculously formal, considering the situation we're in. Why don't you come with me into the sitting room and I'll get you a hot drink?'

Rose wasn't so proud that she'd deny that was just what she longed for. The chill on that hillside and in the boat must have seeped into her bones.

'Thank you. I'd like that.'

Pushing her fingers through her short damp hair, she retrieved her holdall and followed her host through what seemed like an acreage of corridor into a wide, spacious living area furnished with state-of-the-art minimalist couches and chairs and a glass table long enough to seat a small dinner party.

The vista through the huge uncovered windows

was breathtaking. The rain was pouring from the skies in an endless stream now, and every time it lashed against the flawless glass it was accompanied by the anguished and ethereal sigh of the wind. But nothing detracted from the stunning beauty that surrounded the futuristic building. The wildness of the sea and the terrain were absolutely fitting.

Yet what was a successful entrepreneur who seemed to have an insatiable desire for everything—be it property, land, not to mention beautiful women—doing with a sanctuary in this wild, isolated place with just himself for company? Rose couldn't help feeling even more intrigued.

'What would you like? Tea, coffee, hot chocolate? Or perhaps you'd prefer something stronger?'

She swung her gaze round to meet Gene's. He looked to be studying her with interest. His intense blue eyes suggested he had the capacity to look right inside her, and the idea made her shiver. The planes and angles of his face were uncommonly perfect, yet at the same time undoubtedly proclaimed him to be powerfully Alpha. He was so handsome that she couldn't help wondering what he would look like if he *really* smiled—if he was to drop that arrogant air of his for even a moment and genuinely connected with someone for no other reason than that it was *human*…

Shrugging off the notion because she sensed it was pointless, she replied, 'Hot chocolate sounds wonderful.'

'Your wish is my command. Why don't you sit down and make yourself comfortable? You can watch the storm that's coming, knowing you're sitting inside safe and warm.'

'There's a storm coming?'

'Of course…' He jerked his head towards the skyline. 'See those clouds that look like purple and black bruises? They definitely herald a storm. It's likely to be a big one, so all we can do is batten down the hatches and watch the entertainment. Are you up for watching nature at its wildest, Rose?'

She hadn't missed the provocative implication in his gravelled voice. Nor had she forgotten that scorching kiss he'd given her on his second visit to the shop. More than once the memory had made her catch her breath...

Arching a brow, she responded, 'None of us can control the weather—so why not? Seeing as my stay here was unforeseen, and isn't likely to be remotely pleasurable, it might be a welcome distraction and will help the time to pass more quickly.'

To Rose's astonishment he threw back his head and laughed. It was a full-throated, hearty sound that made her pulse skitter wildly and her blood heat. She'd told him that she didn't anticipate her stay would be pleasurable but in that unexpected moment, as the aloof businessman expressed a response to something that clearly elicited delight, once again she found herself helplessly warming to him.

'Can I ask what you find so funny?'

He dropped his hands to his straight lean hips and stared at her. 'I find your determination not to like me and your desire to leave my company as quickly as possible oddly endearing, Rose. I'm not exaggerating when I tell you that most women have the opposite reaction when they receive an invitation from me.'

'I'm sure it can't be just because of your scintillating personality...'

Gene's dazzling blue eyes narrowed. 'I agree, it's not my personality or even my looks that women are drawn to. Don't you think I *know* that? They're drawn to me because I'm a very rich man. I can buy them beautiful things and take them to all the best places. When they're with me it makes them feel special. It's not hard to work out why they like me. You're frowning. Does it surprise you that I would be so frank?'

Rose shivered as an icy drip of water slid off the ends of her hair and down onto the back of her neck, but her attention didn't waver for a second as she contemplated her host's chiselled countenance.

She sighed. 'More than finding it surprising, I'm disturbed that it doesn't bother you. I mean, can you honestly say that you're comfortable with women who only want to be with you for what you can give them materially?'

Right at that moment a flash of lightning still some way off on the horizon made her flinch, and thunder grumbled ominously. Although she'd deliberately made light of anticipating the 'entertainment' that was coming, thunder and lightning had always terrified her.

'I'm a realist, Rose. At least I don't kid myself. But you might also ask me if people disappoint me when they're so obviously shallow? My answer is *yes*…they do.'

They both fell silent for a while, each immersed in their unspoken reflections about the other…

It was Gene who ended the lull in the conversation. 'Before I get you that hot chocolate I'll show you into a guestroom and you can change out of those wet clothes. Do you have a spare set with you? If not, then I'm sure I can find you something.'

Surprised that he should be so considerate, Rose shrugged. 'Yes, I do. I brought a change of clothes with me in case I had to book into a hotel before I returned. It's a long journey to do in one day.'

'Good. Then follow me.'

As he guided Rose back out into the corridor and into the expansive area that housed the guest-rooms—ironically for the guests he never in-vited—Gene knew a surprising pleasure at being able to help her to feel more comfortable. With her big violet eyes, her diminutive form and the dark hair that had been plastered to her head in the softly falling rain, she'd looked so small and delicate when he'd opened the door and found her standing there.

To his amazement, his pulse had inexplicably quickened at the sight of her. He'd never experi-enced such an unexpected reaction to a woman before and, disturbingly, he didn't think it was solely because she'd brought him the means to purchase the antiques shop building...

# CHAPTER FOUR

RELIEVED TO FIND a hairdryer in the luxurious en-suite bathroom that accompanied the spacious guestroom, Rose sat on the capacious bed drying her damp hair. As the dryer blew welcome heat onto her scalp and neck she stared out through the surrounding bank of windows at the roiling sea and the ever more threatening darkening sky, her belly clenching at the thought of the storm that would very soon envelop them. She'd already witnessed one or two bolts of forked lightning in the distance and couldn't help flinching.

'Get a grip, Rose, for God's sake!' she scolded herself. But in truth it didn't help to engender confidence when she was going to have to sit out the coming elemental furore with Gene Bonnaire. As soon as he saw that she was scared would he mock her?

Recalling that he'd referred to the gathering storm clouds as being like 'purple and black bruises', she confessed to being surprised that he would use such a poetic turn of phrase. When he'd asserted that he had no interest in antiques whatsoever, Rose had wondered why they seemed to leave him cold. Couldn't he see the beauty and artistry in their creation? It had bothered her that he couldn't. Yet why refer to storm clouds as bruises in the sky? Didn't that suggest there was something in him that saw beyond the material? Some innate sense that recognised the incomparable beauty and necessity of nature, knowing that it was the one thing nobody had any control over?

Rising to her feet, she returned the hairdryer to its rightful place in the bathroom. As she turned she caught sight of herself in the generous-sized gilt-edged mirror. Her skin looked white as alabaster and the dark blue sheen in her black hair gleamed fiercely where it caught the light. Most of all, her violet eyes looked big and *scared*.

What was *wrong* with her? Was it just the coming storm she was frightened of? Or was it the thought of spending time with Gene?

Impatient with herself, she returned to the bedroom. After hanging her Arran sweater in a mirrored wardrobe whose doors swished open when she held her hand briefly over an electronic button, as her host had demonstrated, she donned the fresh pink woollen one she'd brought as a spare. Tugging it down over her jeans, she pinched her cheeks to instil a little more colour into them and then returned to the room that Gene had first taken her to.

Rose was amazed when she found it easily. Clearly her sense of direction hadn't let her down.

She found Gene seated on one of the futuristic couches opposite the glass table, his elbows resting against his hard-muscled thighs as he stared out of the windows at the increasingly wild weather. Two steaming mugs were evident on the table as she approached.

Glancing up at her, he smiled. Startled, she fell headlong into his sublime azure gaze and forgot her own name. She'd never seen a man as beautiful... More than that, she had never experienced the forceful sense of a desire so profound that it stopped her in her tracks and—frighteningly— made it hard to breathe...

Gene's heart jolted and plunged him into a reverie of lust and longing that was unprecedented. Transfixed by the sight of the petite and pretty woman in front him, dressed in a girlish pink sweater and fitted blue jeans, all he could do was stare. What *was* it about her elfin features and ethereal eyes that made it hard to think straight when he looked at her? She wasn't a bit like any of the voluptuous women he was usually attracted to.

Suddenly aware that her appearance had rendered him momentarily dumb, he cleared his throat. Then he reached for one of the mugs of steaming hot chocolate and handed it to her. 'I see you found your way back, then? I've made your drink. You should sit down and enjoy it while it's hot.'

'Thanks. You timed it perfectly.' Accepting the proffered mug, Rose moved to the other end of the couch and sat down.

Gene's reaction at the distance she'd put between them was at first amused, then irritated. 'Why don't you come and sit closer to me? I promise I don't bite.'

Cupping her drink, she crumpled her smooth brow a little. 'That sounds like an invitation from the Big Bad Wolf…'

'Do you think of yourself as Little Red Riding Hood, then?'

'Why not? She was a very clever girl. She saw through the wolf right from the beginning. She knew he was up to no good.'

She flushed and Gene sensed his blood heatedly go south. How had he not seen just how engaging this woman was the moment he'd first set eyes on her?

Clearly unfazed by his teasing invitation to sit closer, she took an experimental sip of hot chocolate and licked her lips. The unknowingly provocative gesture had the effect of making his already entranced gaze hone in on the alluring shape of her mouth. The sight inevitably brought back the memory of the kiss he'd stolen at the antiques shop. He tightened as he remembered the luxuriant taste of her satin textured lips and the tide of molten longing that had flowed through him.

'My God, this is so good!' She smiled. 'How did you learn to make it so delicious?'

Once again Gene had to shake himself out of the trance he'd seemingly fallen into. 'My father taught me. He's a connoisseur in the art of making sinfully delicious hot chocolate. "Make this for the woman in your life, son, and she'll love you forever." That's what he used to say.'

'And do you? Make it for the woman in your life, I mean?'

He couldn't take the question lightly. Not when he'd never let a woman get close enough to engage his emotions, let alone make her his mate for life...

Disgruntled, he replied, 'No. I don't have a particular woman in my life—and neither do I want to. I believe in keeping my options open.'

'You mean you'd prefer to have a selection of women to choose from rather than just one special one?'

He sensed an aggravated muscle jerk in the side of his cheek. 'I suppose you could say that.'

Rose's violet gaze was thoughtful. 'Then I guess I'm privileged that you chose to make hot chocolate for me, Mr Bonnaire, especially when I'm not remotely interested in joining your select little harem.'

'Indeed. And I asked you to call me Gene,' he snapped, unhappy that she should dismiss him so mockingly. It was hardly flattering.

*Why on earth had he mentioned that silly comment his father had made?* Not only had it highlighted to Rose that he liked to play the field—a fact he suddenly didn't feel proud of at all—but referencing the man who had raised him made him feel wretchedly guilty that he hadn't seen him in a while. It wasn't something he wanted to dwell on.

Pushing to his feet, he moved restlessly towards the panoramic windows and was momentarily captivated by the gigantic waves crashing violently against the rocks on the shoreline.

'Storm's getting wilder...' he murmured.

'Do they bother you...storms, I mean?'

Turning to smile at the woman Gene now realised was innately curious, he felt a frisson of excitement throb through him. What else might Rose be curious about if he were to delve a little deeper? he wondered.

'They don't bother me at all. I certainly don't fear them, if that's what you're getting at. The more wild and furious they are the better, as far as I'm concerned. As you commented earlier, Rose, the unpredictable quality of nature is an ever-present reminder that people aren't in control of everything…even though some of us might like to think we are.'

His companion looked genuinely surprised. 'Forgive me, but I never guessed you could be so philosophical. You definitely gave me the impression that you're a man who likes to be firmly in control.'

For a long moment Gene contemplated the remark. Rose's deceptively calm demeanour gave no clue as to how feisty she was, or indeed how challenging she could be. Yet again he was taken aback that she dared to be so candid with her opinions. He wasn't used to that. It was true that he prided himself on being in control, but he didn't particularly enjoy it being pointed out to him. It might give his opposition an advantage. He also liked to steer the direction his conversations went in, so that they didn't stray into areas he didn't want them to go. He had a genuine fear of being exposed, of being seen as vulnerable in any way.

Biting back his irritation, he asked, 'And what about you, Rose? Do *you* like storms?'

As she set down her mug of hot chocolate on the table her expression was uneasy. 'Not particularly. To tell you the truth, they scare me. Not so much the wind and the rain, or even the thunder…it's the lightning I don't like. I've always been afraid of it. Once when I was little there was the most terrifying storm one night. Some lightning hit our greenhouse and shattered all the glass. It was like a bomb exploding. I was afraid to go back to sleep in case it happened again. No doubt that event has programmed me to be afraid of it for life. I have occasionally thought of getting some therapy…'

Finding himself intrigued, Gene moved back to the couch and sat down—but this time he deliberately positioned himself a little closer to Rose. 'It's not therapy you need, *ma chère*, but courage.'

'I'm not a coward.'

'Did I suggest that you were? Everyone has something they're afraid of. It's only human. No, what I'm saying is that you have to face your fears head-on. Expose them for what they are.'

'And what *are* they?'

Rose's voice had nervously dropped a little lower, and Gene saw the child she'd once been, too afraid to go back to sleep after lightning had shattered her greenhouse. It made him feel fiercely protective of her.

'They're just *illusions*. Thoughts in your head that don't serve you… Don't let them get the better of you or they'll dictate what you can and can't do for the rest of your life.'

'Is that how you handle *your* fears, Gene?'

For a sensually charged moment he absorbed the prickles of warmth that flared in his belly at the sound of his name on her lips, then he replied, 'Thankfully, they rarely arise for me—but, yes… that's how I handle them.'

'You mean there are no ifs or buts or maybes?'

'I don't let anything stop me from getting what I want, Rose—least of all *doubt*.'

'That's obviously why you appear to be so fearless, then?'

He didn't like it that she'd said *appear*. It suggested there was an element of doubt in her mind—that the confident image he projected wasn't all it seemed. Yet again Rose Heathcote was pushing all his hot buttons and the conversation was definitely taking a direction he didn't appreciate.

It seriously bothered him that he should be so unsettled by a woman, and he quickly sought to reassert his position.

'What you see with me is what you get, sweetheart. I don't need to resort to pretence. If you'd ever read my résumé you'd know that's a fact. My success speaks for itself. Now, as interesting as it undoubtedly is, I think we should bring this little conversation to an end. We'll both need something to eat soon, and I plan on cooking us dinner.'

Surprised, Rose quickly got to her feet. 'I don't want you to go to any trouble. A simple snack will do. I don't need a full-blown meal.'

'Say that to any top chef and they're likely to eject you from the restaurant. Food is more than just essential fuel, Rose... *Great* food is manna from heaven. A "simple snack" is not, and you won't be getting any such thing from me.'

Tucking her hair behind her ear, she felt her cheeks turn arrestingly pink. 'I meant no offence. But if you're insisting on cooking us a meal then the least I can do is help you...'

Gene immediately warmed to the idea. So much so, he couldn't suppress a grin. 'So your talents go beyond being a devoted and able assistant in the antiques trade?'

She immediately looked stung. 'I'm not just an assistant. I'm a dealer in my own right.'

'Ah... That tells me that being valued and admired for your achievements *does* matter to you. We're not so different after all, are we? Very well, you can be my sous-chef tonight. Let's go into the kitchen and we'll get started.'

Gene handed Rose a white chef's apron and rolled up his sleeves. The tanned skin of his forearms looked silky smooth, and was dusted with a fine coating of dark hair.

As the rain thundered against the roof with increasing force, and the waves at the shoreline spewed icy foam against the jagged rocks, he instructed her on where she could locate the essential items they needed. The stunningly vast 'space age' kitchen didn't reveal its secrets easily. Drawers opened with the lightest touch, or a hand held in front of a discreet sensor, and the refrigerator and freezer looked as if they'd been designed by someone who excelled in writing sci-fi.

Rose's heart knocked anxiously against her ribs at being part of a scenario she would never have envisaged in a thousand years. From their first meeting Gene Bonnaire had challenged her. His too-confident air and superior manner unsettled her more than just a little. Add to that his reputation for acquiring anything he wanted simply because his money dictated that he could, in truth there was little to commend him to Rose.

She had never been the kind of woman who was easily impressed by a man, no matter what his credentials. A good character—someone honourable and loyal—that was what she secretly wanted in a man.

She'd once foolishly fallen for a stockbroker who had professed himself to be madly in love with her and wanted to marry her. But, although briefly dazzled by his declarations of adoration and devotion, Rose had soon found out that it was all a game to him. It had stroked his ego to think that she couldn't live without him. He'd enjoyed the power he had imagined it gave him over her. But his ambition to make money and go much further in his career had been his top priority—not *her*. And when she'd found out that she wasn't the *only* woman he professed to adore

Rose had vowed never to make such a painful mistake again and had ended the relationship.

The man her mother had left her father for was also driven by money and status, and he was insufferably arrogant. Rose had not had cause to change her opinion in all the years she had known him. All she saw when she looked at David Carlisle was the man who had selfishly charmed her mother with his money and his looks just because it had stroked his ego to win over a happily married woman and—having won her—destroy her family.

When her mother, Ruth, had left it had been the first time Rose had seen her usually resolute father cry…

Gene Bonnaire was obviously cut from the same cloth as her ex *and* her mother's second husband, and she had plenty of reasons not to trust him. Hadn't he already indicated that he was an uncaring playboy—the kind of man who took what he wanted simply because his money and position allowed him to be as mercenary as he liked?

Yet here she was in his isolated sanctuary on a remote Scottish island, miles away from anywhere civilised, and until the boatman Rory met her tomorrow to take her back to the mainland she had to make the best of things. She'd sleep a whole lot better tonight if she didn't antagonise the man.

Despite all of that, she couldn't help recalling that crazily unreal moment when her gaze had locked with Gene's and molten desire had made her feel frighteningly weak. For a shocking instant there had been the urge to abandon all reason and surrender to the wild and wanton nature of it… How was any sane person able to explain such a thing?

Rose could only put it down to the fact that her guard was down after all the stress she'd endured recently. Philip was still in the hospital, and out of the blue he'd decided to sell the property to Gene.

One thing was certain: she would do every-thing in her power to make sure that a repetition of that crazy moment between them wouldn't happen. In fact she probably wouldn't rest easy until Gene had signed the documents she'd brought and deposited the funds for the sale into Philip's account. Then and only then would she be convinced that she'd done the right thing in coming here on behalf of the man who wasn't just her employer and mentor but her surrogate uncle as well.

Like many people who loved and appreciated craftsmanship in all its forms, after watching Gene effortlessly put the most sublime meal to-gether Rose had to attest that the man was a su-preme artisan.

It had been fascinating to watch him work with his hands. Whether it was slicing onions on a chopping board, rubbing spices between his fingers and sprinkling them into the food as he stood over the stove, or working the delicious ingredients he'd put together in a pan with two or three economical stirs, she'd found herself becoming more and more intrigued by the man. With his handsome profile diligently focused, he looked as if he inhabited another world when he was cooking, and the so-called commonplace activity somehow made him seem much more human…

'Should be ready soon—would you like a taste?'

In a near trance where she stood by Gene's side, Rose glanced up at him in surprise. He scooped some food from the aromatic pan onto a metal spoon and offered it to her. *She didn't need to be asked twice.*

His compellingly blue eyes glinted knowingly as she expressed her pleasure at what she'd tasted with an appreciative groan.

'That's amazing! I've never tasted anything so delicious in my life…'

'Haven't you? That makes me want to give you more delicious things to try.'

She felt her skin flame red, and a mixture of embarrassment and irritation throbbed through her.

But then Gene stepped towards her.

'You've got some sauce at the side of your mouth…let me get it for you.'

With the pad of his thumb, he wiped it away. But it was no simple gesture. The way he lingered over the task made it seem like some kind of erotic foreplay, and as he pressed his flesh against the side of Rose's lips it was as though he ignited a flame that wouldn't easily be extinguished.

There wasn't a single part of her body that didn't feel restless and hot. Trapped by his gaze, all she could do was stare helplessly. But at the same time her intuition alerted her to the danger… *What was she thinking?* Dear God, she was behaving as if she was *enjoying* his attention. One thing she was sure of: Gene Bonnaire didn't need another entranced woman pandering to his already inflated ego.

Stepping hastily away, she grabbed some kitchen towel and dabbed at her lips, unconsciously seeking to obliterate his touch.

Watching her, he released a low-voiced chuckle. 'I hope you're not feeling nervous around me, Rose? I told you I don't bite…' Levelling his chiselled jaw at her, he paused and smiled. 'That is unless you *want* me to?'

Rose's heart thundered so hard in her chest that she wondered he didn't hear it.

As adrenaline shot through her system on a dizzying white water rapid she straightened her shoulders and aimed for a withering glare. 'You know, you might think that *all* women enjoy your insincere flirtatious technique…that they should even be *grateful* for the attention…but I can assure you that *I* don't. That said, I think I should go and lay the table while you finish cooking the food.'

Opening a drawer that she'd learned was full of silver cutlery she grabbed the necessary knives and forks and closed it again. Not waiting for further comment, she strode out of the kitchen with her head held deliberately high, praying as she went through the door that she'd remember where to locate the dining room…

# CHAPTER FIVE

Bringing a bottle of Scotch whisky over to the coffee table, Gene poured some into the two waiting glass tumblers. His reluctant house guest was sitting with her shapely legs tucked beneath her on the couch, a satin cushion clutched to her belly, her transfixed gaze focused on the scene that played outside the windows as if she couldn't believe what she was seeing.

He'd witnessed a few wild storms since he'd built his sanctuary but never one quite like this. The thunder was akin to an earth-shattering sonic boom, whose power shook the walls of the futuristic dwelling he was so proud of. And the *rain*… The rain was like an enraged wild river that had burst its banks and was ruthlessly deluging everything in its wake. It was impossible to see where the sky ended and the ocean began.

And, like the most magnificent firework display ever conceived, the lightning had come.

They'd been expecting it for hours now, and had sensed the atmosphere growing thicker and thicker. It had grown so thick that *something* had to cut through it to lessen the tension.

Having arrived at last, the electrifying bolts that ripped through the atmosphere with their eerily bright light did exactly that. But the deafening noise and fury even made Eugene's heart jolt. Sensing a muscle tighten in the side of his jaw, he glanced at his companion. It was plain to see that she was more than a little jumpy.

'Rose?' Feeling an uncharacteristic sense of concern, he leant towards her and pressed a glass into her hand. 'I'd advise you to drink some of this. Not just because it's the best malt whisky in the world, and I only ever drink the best, but it might help calm your nerves.'

Although her hand shook a little, Rose tipped

the glass back and gulped down some of the contents. Almost instantly her incandescent violet eyes flooded with tears. Then she started to cough.

Gene reached round to pat her on the back, his lips shaping an amused smile. 'You drank that down a bit too quickly, sweetheart. Make the next sip a little slower, hmm…?'

Returning his wry look, she commented, 'I'll bear that in mind. It's pretty powerful stuff, isn't it?'

'This particular blend is smoky, sweet and smooth. But I don't doubt to a novice it can still pack a punch.'

Even as he was speaking a fierce display of dazzling lightning lit up the room, highlighting everything in full cinematic glory.

'Oh my God!' Visibly shocked, Rose all but threw herself against him.

Even though he knew it was purely a reflex re-action, instigated by fear, Gene was inordinately pleased that in that instant she genuinely seemed to need him. He'd never experienced anything remotely like the feeling before, and it made his heart race a little.

As the gentle scent of her summery perfume made provocative inroads into his senses he draped his hard-muscled arm round her slender shoulders and pulled her a little closer to him.

His beard-roughened jaw glanced against the silkily soft strands of her ebony hair and he murmured, 'It's all right, Rose. Nothing's going to hurt you…I promise…'

At first she stiffened at the assurance, and then she relaxed.

Relieved, Gene was glad she didn't pull away. Despite the storm raging outside, he felt strangely peaceful as he sat there with Rose. He had a distinct sense of being introduced to an aspect of his character that he'd never before suspected. The only woman he'd ever felt remotely protective towards before was his mother. His more intimate female relationships all centred round money and sex. *His* desire for sex and *their* desire for money... Genuine intimacy didn't feature. How could it when he'd allowed himself to become more and more distant from his feelings? Since his little sister had died the spectre of loss and heartbreak was ever-present, and in truth he *feared* it...

The soft weight against his arm grew a little heavier and Rose's quiet, steady breathing made Gene realise that she'd fallen asleep.

It seemed to be a day of shocks and surprises, he thought wryly. Not only had the ferocity of the storm taken him aback, but the realisation that he wasn't just *enduring* his visitor's company but was actively *enjoying* it really rattled him. His pleasure at being able to purchase the lovely old shop building hadn't dominated his thoughts half as much as he'd expected it to.

He frowned. *Why was that?*

Settling back more comfortably against the cushions, hardly aware that he was doing so, he drowsily let his eyelids drift closed...

The first thing that alerted him to the realisation that he'd fallen asleep was Rose trying to disengage his arm from her shoulders. Eugene cursed...*loudly*. The limb had cramped painfully, and in the throes of sleep he thought someone was attacking him. His primal masculine instinct was automatic.

When he sat up and grabbed his imagined attacker Rose yelped, and the shocked look on her face woke him up to the reality of what he was doing. His hands were tightly gripping her arms through her soft woollen sweater and she looked absolutely terrified. Albeit indignant...

Even as he lessened the pressure of his fingers on her arm he was suddenly mesmerised by the inviting shape of her luscious mouth. Her beautiful eyes were shining like stars. Staring back into that hypnotic violet glance was like falling into another dream...one that he was in no hurry to wake up from.

'Let go of me,' Rose breathed huskily.

Gene heard the words, but even as he registered them he was helplessly bending his head towards her. His body was heavy with desire, and only the taste of those lush tender lips would alleviate some of the insatiable erotic need he was suddenly inflamed by.

'Not yet...' he whispered, and claimed the mouth that unknowingly taunted him as if it were a choice between breathing to live and *not* breathing.

If he'd had any expectations that first time he'd kissed her, then the touch of Rose's lips beneath his had exceeded them all. Now, for the second time, the sensation was beyond wonderful. And the most pleasurable surprise came when she gasped softly, didn't resist his urgently seeking tongue as he thought she might, but instead welcomed the heated exploration as if she needed it as much as he did.

The hot satin interior of her mouth sent his temperature skyrocketing, and Gene's fingers moved through her silky hair to anchor her head and explore her flavours more deeply. Again, Rose showed no sign of protesting. His heart was galloping hard and the strangest feeling washed over him. It was an inexplicable sense that he was diving too deep ever to surface again without some serious damage having been caused...

Rose could hardly believe she was passionately kissing Gene Bonnaire. Had she unknowingly suffered some kind of bump to the head and been transported to an uncanny parallel universe where everything she'd known to be real had vanished? Who could blame her for that conclusion when the violent storm outside was growing ever more ferocious, adding to the sense that she was in some kind of twilight world? Being marooned in this isolated dwelling with a man she'd undoubtedly give a wide berth to if she met him under any other circumstances just didn't make sense. *Yet perhaps it wasn't as unbelievable as it seemed.* How could she have known that this avaricious businessman could seduce her with his unexpected displays of care and concern?

First he'd dispensed advice on dealing with her fears. Then he'd cooked a sublime French dish that had been nothing less than exquisite. And finally...*finally* he'd put his arm around her and held her against him when the lightning had looked to be heralding the end of the world and she'd been terrified.

Was that why she'd found herself willingly kissing him...? Because she was grateful for his protection? Had the feeling awakened some latent desire she'd been burying?

Her father had always sought to protect her from harm and keep her safe, and she'd trusted him more than any other man. Was she hoping to find someone similar in her romantic life? But Gene Bonnaire was nothing like her father had been. The billionaire was known to be utterly ruthless in pursuing his desires, and he had a reputation for letting nothing stand in his way. Yet when he'd held her against his powerful chest as they'd watched the storm Rose had trusted him enough to fall asleep.

*How to explain it?* All she knew was that she hadn't been able to resist him. Everything about the man seemed to dazzle her...the way he looked, the way he smelled, his sheer indomitable maleness... The realisation confused her. It also made her wary about the danger she might be inviting. She only had to remember her ex and the way he'd blatantly lied to her to get what he wanted... Gene was another man who liked the sense of power money could give him...

When Gene carefully separated his lips from hers, his long fingers stroking her hair back, he smiled down at her with a knowing glint in his piercing blue eyes and she knew it was time to end this craziness and return to some kind of normality.

When she explained to him why she'd succumbed to that kiss—she'd been stressed and worried about her boss, and scared of the lightning—hopefully he would understand and not use the minor aberration against her.

Flattening her hand against his chest, she started to move away.

Frowning, Gene reached out to pull her back. 'Where are you going?'

For a moment Rose couldn't think what to say, because his glittering blue eyes were holding her to him as securely as if they'd been bound together.

'I shouldn't have done that. I'm sorry.'

'Why? Didn't you enjoy it?'

'That's not the point. The point is I'm here solely on business. And you're not responsible for comforting me just because I'm scared of lightning.'

'Would your boyfriend have comforted you if he'd been here?'

'What's that got to do with anything?'

His eyes narrowed. *'Would* he?'

'I don't have one.' Rose lifted a shoulder in a shrug, her gaze unflinching. 'I'm not interested in having a relationship at the moment.'

'Presumably that's because you're concerned about your boss?'

'It's not just that. I want to concentrate on my career. When Philip leaves the antiques shop, so will I. I'll have to find another position.'

'Presumably that won't be difficult? You're a qualified dealer, you said.'

She lifted her chin, as if to challenge him to doubt her. 'I am. And if I can't find anything suitable back home I might go abroad for a while and work.'

It was definitely an option, but somehow she didn't feel quite ready to take such a bold leap. She'd like to think she could make things work at home first. Anyway, the thought reminded her of what was most pertinent now.

Meeting the diamond-bright glance that had barely left her since they'd kissed, she said, 'Getting back to the reason I'm here… Don't you think we'd better deal with the signing of the documents tonight rather than leave it until the morning? It's just that I want to make sure I'm ready in plenty of time to meet the boat. The sooner I get back to the hospital and see how Philip is doing, the better.'

'I won't be signing anything until I'm satisfied that everything is in order. Give me the papers and I'll look over them tonight. Then we'll see what the morning brings.'

Dry-mouthed, Rose stood up. Gene's enigmatic comment had left her feeling as though she'd just plunged down a flight of hard-edged stone steps. 'Are you suggesting that there might be a possibility you *won't* sign?'

As he got to his feet his expression was tight-lipped and serious. 'Make no mistake. I want the property. That desire hasn't changed. But it's a policy of mine never to sign anything until I'm sure.'

'You mean you got me to come all the way out here in the *belief* that you were going to buy, but now you're not *sure*? Is this some kind of warped game you're playing?' She shook her head in despair. 'I should have known as soon as I saw you that you weren't to be trusted, but it seems I never learn…'

He moved closer. So close that Rose could see the gentle indentations in his otherwise smooth skin where the dark stubble of his beard had started to grow. His warm breath drifted over her face and made her teeth clench.

'What do you mean by that? Has someone let you down, Rose? Was it an ex-boyfriend, perhaps? If that's true, then I'm sorry. But this isn't a game I'm playing…it's the way I do business. I set out my intentions, believe without a doubt that what I want is going to be mine, and then I take some time to enjoy the realisation before I finally take the prize.'

She swallowed hard as he reached out and laid his palm against her cheek. It was clear that he wasn't just referring to his purchase of the antiques shop building.

Rose felt alternately hot and cold. Did he think that she'd fall into bed with him because she'd so willingly returned his kiss? He'd caught her off guard—that was all.

It was her cue to firmly lift his hand away and engineer some distance between them. Folding her arms over her sweater, she glanced out at the scene before her. Although the storm was still evident, somehow it seemed less ferocious. Sounding more like a subdued grizzly bear now, rather than a rampaging tiger, the thunder continued to rumble but the lightning was definitely lessening. Electrical flashes of cobalt pierced the sky here and there, but they were starting to suggest a once rampaging force now spent and retreating, and she was more than a little relieved.

However, Rose was still anxious that she might not be going home with the business sold and the funds deposited into Philip's bank account after all. A sleepless night was definitely on the horizon, because it wasn't going to be easy to wait until the morning for Gene's decision.

She was quickly learning that the man was a bit of a wild card...a law unto himself. That was a challenge. If for any reason he should change his mind about buying, what could she do but walk away in defeat? The situation might grieve her, but she hardly had the power to make him reconsider, did she? And he didn't look to be the type of man who would be swayed by any sense of compassion.

Rose was dreading taking such demoralising news back to Philip. What if it caused his health to deteriorate even more? The only thing she could do now was stay as calm as possible and not let her host see how perturbed she was.

'Well, there's not much more to say, then, is there? I'll go and get the purchase documents and give them to you to look over.' Glancing down at the pretty platinum wristwatch her father had given her for her twenty-first birthday, she added, 'After that I think I'll say goodnight.'

Turning towards the door, she was stopped in her tracks by Gene's intimate gravel-voiced reply.

'If we have any more lightning during the night and you're feeling scared my room is just down the hall from yours. I'm a very light sleeper, so don't hesitate to knock and come in, will you?'

Clenching her fists down by her sides, Rose prayed for the strength not to succumb to the pure unadulterated temptation the hard-chiselled specimen of masculinity before her exuded with a mere glance...let alone the sexy bass voice that reeled her in like a fish on a hook...

'I'm sure I'll be fine,' she said airily. 'I'll simply use that technique you told me about and remember that my fears are just illusions.'

She swore she heard Gene chuckle in amusement as she walked to the door and went out...

He had another restless night. It wasn't so easy to fall asleep when he knew that Rose slept just a short walk away from him, down the corridor in one of his guestrooms. Somehow Gene couldn't shake the memory of that inflammatory kiss he'd stolen from her. All night it tempted and mocked him, until the fervent hope of a repeat performance finally lured him into sleep with its promise. But then he dreamt of holding Rose in his arms and making passionate love to her, and he woke at sunrise with his body coated in perspiration and heavy with desire.

*Why hadn't she come to him in the night as he'd*

*hoped?* The storm had returned round three a.m. and the lightning had once again been spectacular. Surely she couldn't have slept through such a display? Had stubborn pride stopped her from seeking his reassurance?

Even though he admired her tenacity, he had to find out for himself how she'd fared. Quickly showering and dressing, he glanced at the property sale documents he'd examined minutely into the early hours and took them with him into the living room. There was no sign that his guest had been there.

His stomach clenching with nervous excitement at the thought of seeing her, he left the papers he'd been studying on the coffee table then returned to the room he'd allocated to Rose. He rapped sharply on the door. She didn't answer straight away and Gene was immediately concerned.

He was about to knock again when the door opened.

'Morning...' she murmured. Paler than usual,

and distinctly bleary-eyed, her appearance suggested that she too had had trouble sleeping. Her black hair was prettily tousled but her skin looked as smooth and delicious as a peach. She was still in her nightwear—a short white satin affair, with spaghetti straps—and one of the straps had drifted down over a slim shoulder.

Gene took a moment to assemble his emotions. Once again he felt concerned and protective. It was so unlike his usual response at seeing a woman he desired that it honestly perturbed him.

'Good morning,' he greeted her. 'Don't tell me you didn't see and hear the lightning last night because I won't believe you.'

Groaning, she was already shaking her head and tunnelling her fingers through her hair. 'I'm not going to lie. I didn't sleep a wink. I wouldn't say no to some coffee if you're making it?'

'Never mind the coffee—why didn't you knock on my door like I told you to?'

Even as he asked the question Gene stepped over the door's threshold and, with no intention other than to reassure her, wound his arms round her impossibly slim waist. The act was his undoing. The combination of the silky satin nightdress and the warm, shapely body beneath his hands aroused him more than he'd ever been aroused before…to the point where he couldn't help but act on sheer primal instinct.

'I would have held you close all night…protected you…' he murmured.

In between each word of the huskily voiced affirmation he touched his lips to Rose's hair then, hearing her gasp softly, he tipped up her chin and touched them to her mouth. The irresistible fusion was hot, sultry…and almost beyond controllable…

Rose glanced up into his eyes, the flat of her hand resting lightly against his chest. But this time there was no suggestion that she wanted him to leave.

'I—I can't seem to think straight when I'm around you,' she confessed. 'I didn't come to you last night because I was afraid of what might happen.'

'What did you think might happen?'

'I feel like—like I'm under some kind of spell when I'm near you and that makes you danger-ous.'

'You think *I'm* the one who's dangerous? You're the one that's cast a spell, you little witch…'

'You should go,' she breathed, but her fingers were curling into his shirtfront and her eyes were full of longing.

Gene needed no further invitation. 'Sweet-heart, I don't think so…' he murmured.

Sweeping her up into his arms, without further ado he carried her across to the lavish double bed. As he laid her down against the rumpled silk sheets his heart beat so fast he was dizzy. Rose wasn't looking sleepy any more. She looked wide awake, her flawless complexion no longer pale, but softly rouged pink with desire…

As he started to lower the spaghetti straps of her nightgown down over her shoulders, so that the satin mounds of her breasts were more evi-dent, he couldn't resist a grin. 'If I'd known you wore such sexy nightwear I would have battered down your door and come to you last night. Honest to God, I would have,' he swore.

For answer, she made a helpless little sound of hunger and pulled his head down to hers. As they kissed Gene reached down to his back pocket and drew out the foil packet he kept there. There were no more words after that. There was no need. His whole world had narrowed down to these few heatedly charged moments, to the beautiful woman beneath him and their hungry, *insatiable* need for each other.

When he finally took her, with Rose's strong, slender thighs wrapped round his middle, he honestly thought he'd died and gone to heaven. It wasn't just her kisses and her body that were heavenly—everything about her was divine. Already he knew there was no way on earth he would be satisfied with just taking his pleasure and then setting her aside, as he usually did with the women in his life. A strong desire to *really* get to know her was building inside him.

As she quickly came to her fulfilment her thighs clamped him even tighter and she rode the wild waves that took her. Staring back into her superlative violet gaze, Gene soon followed, issuing a harsh-sounding cry that seemed to emanate from deep inside him. In the aftermath of his climax he was rendered both breathless and speechless for a while before he came back to himself. Then he lay down next to Rose and gently pulled her into his arms.

'*Tu es incroyable...*' he whispered into her ear.

Her pretty cheeks dimpled. 'I like it when you speak French. You can whisper some more to me, if you like?'

'Right now I'd willingly do anything you wanted, *ma chère.*'

'I might hold you to that…' With a teasing but knowing smile, Rose held her hand softly against his cheek…

# CHAPTER SIX

ROSE HAD IMMEDIATELY sensed the man beside her tense when she'd asserted that she would hold him to his comment about doing anything she wanted. She hadn't meant anything by it—it had just been a bit of teasing banter. But now, up and dressed, she felt her own tension mounting as she followed him out into the living room.

She could hardly believe what had just happened between them. All she knew was that making love with Gene had made her feel more alive and vital than she'd felt in years... However, as wonderful and exhilarating as the experience had been, she'd better quickly come back down to earth and remember why she was there.

With his straight back and squared shoulders—his flawless white shirt and taupe chinos a little crumpled after his joining her in bed—Gene looked intimidating and officious. That suggested he wasn't going to be as approachable as he recently had been. Obviously he had reached a decision about the antiques store, and perhaps it wasn't the one she'd hoped for...

Would he let her down gently or would he stress that business was business and he no longer saw the building as a viable proposition for his restaurant business? Suddenly Rose was sick with nerves. How would she tell Philip about her failure to bring back the signed purchase agreement if that was the case?

She could already visualise the pain and disappointment in his eyes, even though she knew he would quickly reassure her that everything would be okay—that he would soon find another buyer and all would be well.

Her mind teeming with thoughts, most of them unhelpful, all of a sudden Rose was struck by how bare and austere the white-painted room was. Yes, it had a magnificent view, but how much more beautiful it would look if it had some warmth and personality instilled.

'What a shame you don't like antiques or even beautiful paintings,' she declared. 'The right ones would make this room look even more stunning…it would be so much more homely and inviting.'

Gene turned round. Raising a formidable dark brow, he snapped, 'But this isn't my home. It's my retreat. I don't need pictures or antiques to pretty it up. Besides, no one else is going to see it but me.'

After the intimacy they'd just shared, Rose was more than a little deflated by his sharpness. But she persisted. 'That might be the case, but what's wrong with *you* appreciating them? Surely you would find some pleasure in making your retreat look nice on the inside as well as externally?'

'You're wrong. I wouldn't. It serves a purpose—that's all it does. I'm not interested in getting any pleasure from what the furnishings look like.'

His tone was adamant…not to mention he seemed annoyed that she'd made the suggestion.

'I'm not an aesthetic like you are, Rose. I'm practical and pragmatic.'

'Yet it's important to you to wear beautifully tailored clothing, shoes made by one of the finest Italian designers and the most appealing French cologne, isn't it?'

As soon as the words were out of her mouth Rose sensed her blood throb heatedly through her veins. So hot and heavy did it pound that she was mortified. She'd revealed to Gene that she'd noticed so much. In doing so, she'd foolishly given him another edge with which to usurp her if he chose and, despite their lovemaking, she didn't doubt that he would use it…

She saw that his deliciously carved mouth had shaped a smile. Again the image of the Big Bad Wolf flashed into her mind.

'You're right. I admit that personal presentation is important to me. And to that end I believe in wearing only the very best that money can buy.'

He paused, and a muscle flexed at the side of one flawlessly carved cheekbone. 'It goes without saying that my exacting standards are important in my personal life too. For example, I very much appreciate the curves of a lovely woman…the way she smiles…the radiance of a pair of stunning long-lashed violet eyes…'

He was talking about *her.* Rose sucked in a steadying breath as her heart beat double-time. The irresistible magnetism between them which had driven them to consummate their attraction wouldn't have been there under normal circumstances, she was sure. It had probably just occurred because they'd found themselves isolated and alone in this incredible futuristic house, with nothing but the rocks, the sea and the stormy weather to keep them company. Add to that Rose's fear of lightning, and the fact that she'd let her guard down round Gene because he seemed so concerned…

A disquieting thought assailed her. What if his being concerned was just an act and in truth he just wanted to have her in his power because it stroked his ego? After all, he prided himself on having anything he wanted, didn't he? But she still couldn't understand why he didn't seem able to resist her. It just didn't make sense. *Nothing* made sense when she was around him, she realised.

Clasping her hands in front of her soft woollen sweater, she didn't shy away from meeting his gaze. She had come here for one thing and one thing only: for him to sign the documents that would make him the new owner of Philip's antiques store. That was what she should be concentrating on.

'Well, that aside… Have you made a decision about the antiques shop?'

He gave her another enigmatic smile. Yet the charismatic gesture on that too handsome face hardly reassured her. It did, however, make her catch her breath. And the restless heat that seemed to have infiltrated her body because she now knew what it felt like to be intimate with him seemed to increase disturbingly.

His comments just now suggested that he thought her beautiful, and the exhilarating thought affected Rose perhaps more than it ought to. The allure of him was becoming more and more irresistible, and along with the impulse to do what was right and be sensible it had created a war inside her that made it hard to think straight.

Her voice not quite steady, she pressed, 'Well? You need to tell me sooner rather than later, because I have a boat to catch.'

'Do you?'

He was moving closer still, and the faint drift of his arresting French cologne made her stomach clench painfully. 'What do you mean do I? How else am I going to get off this island and return home?'

'I meant does it have to be today?'

Rose widened her eyes. 'Why? Is there some reason I *shouldn't* go today?'

Gene was suddenly standing right in front of

her, and his crystalline blue gaze was hot enough to burn her. 'Yes, there is. I'd like you to stay so that we can get to know each other a little better.'

There was a dizzying rush inside her head. 'Why on earth do you think that—?'

Before she could finish what she'd been going to say her lips were captured hungrily, and suddenly there was no oxygen left to breathe—just a heady, seductive heat and the taste of something forbidden…

With a helpless groan Rose found herself responding. The thought *how can something so wrong seem so right?* flashed through her mind. Sexually, the man delivered everything he promised. She found herself strangely weak, with a hard to resist desire to be more reckless than she'd ever been before…

Last night she'd been terrified by the violent flashes outside the window that had lit up her room like every celebratory firework display in the country combined. Yet she'd been more afraid of knocking on Gene's door to let him know because of what might happen if she did. But then in the morning…*it had happened anyway.*

His hands were on her shoulders now, and they moved seductively down her back, the scalding heat from his fingertips feeling as if they were melting the very vertebrae of her spine as they travelled. Then he caught her by the waist and impelled her closer—so close that she was intimately aware of his heat and his hardness again.

He felt so good…so…so *necessary.* The man's kisses were an erotic delight that she could easily become addicted to.

He was still kissing her when he reached for the hem of her sweater and started to tug it upwards. When he lifted it over her head and let it fall onto the floor behind her Rose's heart galloped. She was wearing a sleeveless white vest over a matching cotton bra, and when Gene's searching hand dived inside to caress her breast, his fingertips lightly pinching her burgeoning nipple, she moaned feverishly. Then he carried on kissing her—as if he too was finding it hard to be free of the taste of her.

*It felt so good to be wanted and desired.* It had been a long time.

Her last and only real boyfriend, Joe Harding, had been a twenty-four-year-old trainee broker, and at the age of eighteen she had lost her virginity to him. At first he had been kind and considerate, swearing that he loved her. But as time progressed he'd become more and more driven by the demands of the City bank where he worked and hadn't seemed to have much time for anything else—including their relationship.

He'd sought to placate her by telling her that he was working hard for *her*…that he wanted to ensure that they had a happy and successful future *together*. But Rose had soon begun to suspect that that wasn't true. One night she had smelled another woman's perfume on his shirt and, when confronted, he had admitted that he'd been having an affair…as it turned out one of many.

She had been horrified and hurt that the man

she'd so eagerly given her trust and her love had so blatantly betrayed her. She'd had a short, sharp lesson in the mercenary way some men could behave…and in the lies they told to get what they wanted, not caring who they hurt in the process. Heartbroken, Rose had told him it was over. He hadn't even looked surprised, and nor had he protested. *In fact, she'd never forgotten the look of relief in his eyes…*

After that wounding experience she'd vowed to stay single and focus on her career, and she hadn't succumbed to any soulless liaisons purely for physical release either—no matter how tempted she sometimes felt—knowing it was only because she was lonely.

Yet here she was, in the arms of a man who was the ultimate practised seducer, and she would have utterly surrendered to him for a second time if he hadn't lifted his head right then to examine her with what looked like a knowing smile. If ever a man epitomised the 'cat that had got the cream', *he* did.

Her insides plunged and a deafening alarm bell rang inside her. Rose was suddenly painfully reminded of exactly who Gene Bonnaire was. He was a mercenary businessman who didn't have a single qualm about taking what he wanted—and he was just about to add her body and her capitulation to his self-aggrandising quota of conquests if she didn't take action and stop him.

Breathing heavily, she pushed his hands away and stumbled as she stepped back to collect her discarded sweater. She was still reeling from that too knowing smile. Hurriedly pulling on the garment, she wiped the back of her hand across her throbbing lips in a gesture of disgust.

Startled and disappointed, Gene shook his head.

Rory's boat couldn't arrive soon enough, as far as Rose was concerned. The sooner she was out of there and away from this man the better. However, there was still the important matter of the shop to address.

'You didn't answer my question. Do you still

intend to buy the antiques store? If the answer is yes then you'd better get on with signing the papers so I can get ready to leave for the mainland.'

She was still breathing hard as she spoke, unsure of how she would handle Gene's reaction. The feeling brought it home to her how little she knew him. Did anyone *really* know this man who had built a sanctuary for himself on a remote Scottish island?

'Why did you break off our embrace? And don't lie to me and tell me you weren't enjoying it. Or do you get some kind of perverse pleasure from leading a man on?' he demanded.

'I didn't lead you on. I've already let myself down by going to bed with you. I freed myself just now because it suddenly hit me what I was doing. You have a reputation for unscrupulously taking the things you want without giving a damn about the consequences—and I didn't come here to end up as another one of your forgettable conquests. Even though you might call me a hypocrite because of the way I've acted around you, thankfully I've come to my senses. So let's forget what just happened and get on with our business, shall we?'

Stealing a quick glance at the time on her watch, Rose swallowed hard. Although she was adamant she would stay strong, inside she was quaking.

'I've got exactly one hour before I have to be down on the shore to wait for the boat.'

Gene stood perfectly still. As he examined her, his expression was bleak. 'Well, Rose… It seems as if I've misjudged you. I thought you were different from all those people who so avidly believe everything they read in the papers about me… about my less than flattering "reputation"…but I see that I was wrong.'

All of a sudden she felt sickeningly faint. *Was* she the one who was guilty of misjudging?

The usually arresting gleam in his eyes was gone. The burnished light was dulled.

'Did you honestly doubt that I would sign the purchase papers? There was never any chance of that. I still plan to own the property. It's just that I'd hoped I might persuade you to spend some time with me and not hurry to return.'

*Rose was in turmoil.* Should she believe the desire he'd expressed to spend more time with her was because he genuinely wanted to get to know her, or because he simply saw an opportunity to engage in another sexual liaison? It was so hard to trust Gene when all she had to go on was her bitter past experience of being let down by a man who had put his ambition and desire for money before his desire to have a loving relationship…

Gene smiled—but the blue eyes were chillingly empty now, she saw. He looked as though he expected her just to wait for him to sign the papers and then walk away…

'I can see that you plainly don't want to do that. You'd better follow me into my office.'

He strode ahead of her through the door, the heels of his black Italian loafers echoing loudly against the parquet flooring. Rose had to practically run to keep up with him.

Dropping down into the sumptuous leather seat behind the elongated glass desk that occupied another vast and mostly empty white room, Gene calmly drew the sheaf of property documents towards him. Silently scanning the opening page, he reached for the glinting gold fountain pen on his blotter.

Lifting his gaze, he looked straight at Rose. 'You may as well sit down,' he told her.

Still shaken after hearing his confession that he'd hoped she might stay a little longer, she sat down in the elegant leather chair on the opposite side of the desk. She could still feel the sensation of his hot velvet mouth against hers…still taste him…and she wanted to cry—because after she'd left this remote and isolated place she would never experience such delights again.

'There's one small proviso before I sign,' he declared.

Rose's heart stalled. 'What's that?'

'I want your agreement that you'll help offload the antiques for me. I'll pay you for doing it. I've already told you *I* haven't any use for them, but that doesn't mean I want to *give* them away. I can see that some of them are valuable, and that's reflected in the price I've paid for them. You know the market, and I sense you won't let them go for a song. So, do I have your agreement, Rose?'

How could she possibly say no when Philip needed every penny to help towards his after-care when he returned home? It shouldn't be such a dilemma, Rose thought, but because it would mean she'd still have to have contact with Gene it *was…*

She sat up a little straighter in her chair. 'You know I can't refuse. But at the same time I want you to know that I'm only doing this for Philip. If it wasn't for him I *would* refuse. I shouldn't have succumbed to making our association personal.'

Back in bed, when Rose had asserted that she would hold him to his promise to give her anything she wanted, Gene had had a painful moment of disquiet when it had come to him that she might be just like all the other women he'd had liaisons with and see him only as some kind of 'meal ticket' to fame and fortune. But her words and the inflection in her tone now suggested that she felt nothing but regret in meeting him and it cut him to the quick.

*It was another first for him.* He had never known a woman *willingly* part company with him. Usually the only sensation he experienced when a liaison ended was relief. But with her beguiling violet eyes, and the rare softness that he'd never encountered before, plus the fact that she could turn his blood to molten fire with her presence alone, Rose somehow had him spellbound. So he wouldn't make it at all easy for her to walk away from him—at least not until he'd had his fill of her…

'Good. Then I'd better sign, hadn't I? And I'll need you to witness my signature with your own.'

After the documents had been dealt with, Gene stowed them away in a drawer.

'I'll make sure the money is in your boss's account as soon as you leave,' he affirmed.

'Does that mean I can check the account when I get back to London?' Rose asked warily.

Gene expelled a sigh. 'I may be a lot of things that you don't like, but I never lie about money, Rose. I've got the property that I wanted and I'm not going to delay paying what I owe. An agreement is an agreement.'

They both got to their feet.

'It's nearly time for you to meet the boat. Why don't you go and get your bag and I'll walk you down to the quay?' he suggested.

His companion's soft satin cheeks inexplicably turned pink. Was she perhaps not as set on leaving as she had indicated? he wondered?

'That won't be necessary,' she answered stiffly, immediately pouring ice water on the thought. 'I'm quite capable of getting there by myself.'

'Damn it, woman. I'm doing it for my own satisfaction. I just want to make sure you get off the island safely. There'll be a car waiting for you on the other side, like I promised. My driver will take you to the airport, and there'll be another driver waiting for you when you land, to take you back home.'

'I'm going to go to the hospital first—to see Philip.'

'Of course you are.' A flash of what felt suspiciously like jealousy at her unerring regard for the other man ricocheted though Gene's insides. 'I'll meet you out at the front. Go and get your bag.'

A mournful wind was howling as they started to walk down the hillside and, glancing at the ocean, he saw that the surging waves had a chilling bluish tint and were far from calm. The scent of last night's storm still clung to the icy air and he shivered.

Unable to help himself, he hoped that the conditions were too rough this morning for Rory to make the crossing. But then he quickly realised that even if the boatman was able to make the journey to the island there was no guarantee that the return journey would be any smoother.

*Suddenly Gene didn't want to let Rose go.* If

anything happened to her when he could have taken steps to prevent it he'd never forgive himself.

'It looks rougher than usual out there today,' he remarked, coming to a sudden standstill on the uneven stone path to survey his windblown companion.

Her expression impatient, Rose tried in vain to push her fringe out of her eyes. 'It must be because of the storm. I'm sure it will be all right. Rory strikes me as a highly competent boatman.'

'Even the most competent sailors still have to contend with the unpredictable nature of the ocean,' he said dryly. 'Why don't we go back? I'll see if I can contact him and tell him that you'll wait until

tomorrow, when the weather will hopefully be a bit calmer.'

'*No.*'

Agitated and furious, Rose turned away and started to make her way down the hillside. Her leather tote bumped awkwardly against her side as she gamely negotiated the uneven rocky surface. She'd adamantly refused to let Gene carry it for her.

'The sooner I get off this island the better!' she shouted back over her shoulder.

Too concerned for her safety to let her head off without him, in just a few long-legged strides he had joined her. 'I hadn't realised how stubborn you are, but I'm quickly learning,' he murmured.

'If you mean that I know my own mind, and won't let anyone dictate what I should or shouldn't do, then, yes—I *am* stubborn.' With a flash of sublime violet and a bewitching satisfied smile, Rose forged ahead to the carved-out landing stage in the bay where the boat would dock.

She got there before him, her back straight in her weatherproof jacket and hanging on to her tote for dear life in the unforgiving gusting wind. She stared defiantly out to sea, as if fully expecting Rory's boat to appear on the horizon any moment now just because she *willed* it…

# CHAPTER SEVEN

THE MEMORY OF Gene calling out, 'I'll be in touch soon!' as Rory steered the boat back out of the bay haunted Rose for several nights after she'd returned to London. The exclamation could so easily have sounded like a threat—but it *hadn't*. Instead she'd sensed regret in his tone, as if he genuinely hadn't wanted her to leave.

She'd watched the disturbingly lonely figure he'd made on the shoreline until he had become a mere speck in the distance that had quickly disappeared. It had left a hollow feeling inside her that was hard to explain.

But her spirits had lifted when she'd discovered that Philip had made some definite improvement while she'd been away. And when she'd given him the news that Gene had officially bought the building and the antiques, and that the money was now safely in his bank account, the worried expression Rose had become used to seeing on a daily basis had started to fade. He'd even seemed to breathe a little more easily.

Having returned to work, her aim was to finish meticulously cataloguing the antiques and then to make contact with the dealers and auctioneers she knew who would be interested and hopefully make some sales. There was still the odd 'walk in' buyer that came into the store, and she didn't mind—she'd always loved conversing with customers. But the fact was that her job was swiftly coming to an end and she was now in effect working for Gene instead of Philip.

It was a twist of fate that she couldn't have predicted…not even in her wildest dreams.

She had just got off the phone one afternoon when the bell above the door jangled to announce a visitor. Glad of the distraction, Rose left the office to see who it was. It had been an agonisingly slow day, and she had spent most of her time trying to persuade a wealthy dealer in Paris to visit the shop and view a valuable chiffonier that she knew was right up his street. Sometimes it wasn't enough simply to view an item online. A true connoisseur had to physically see and touch the artefact.

The Parisian dealer was known for his exquisite good taste, and the fact that this piece had originated in the French capital was all to the good. Its provenance was impeccable. Rose had assured him that she would foot the bill for the trip—at the back of her mind she'd told herself that Gene couldn't possibly mind as long as she secured the deal and the chiffonier was sold. After all, wasn't making a profit his main concern?

The moment she walked out onto the shop floor and saw it was Gene himself standing there, his arms ominously folded across his broad chest, devastatingly suited in flawless tailoring as if he was going on to some important business function, her heart clamoured wildly and suddenly her ability to know what to say utterly deserted her.

Clearly not sharing her dilemma, he said smoothly, 'I thought I'd drop by and see how things were going.'

He was acting as if this was the usual way he did business—simply dropping by unannounced. Didn't he have a secretary or some smartly dressed snooty PA to do his bidding? Of course he did. Hadn't Rose spoken to the woman herself when she'd requested a meeting with him? And, yes, the woman *had* sounded snooty...

Clearing her throat, she shakily combed her fingers through her hair. Not since early this morning had she even glanced in a mirror to see how she looked. She couldn't even remember applying any make-up. Telling herself that she shouldn't care how she appeared to Gene, she knew the truth was that she cared more than was probably wise...

'By that I assume you want to know how the sales are getting on? I'm sure you're anxious to have the building emptied and renovated as soon as possible.'

A maddeningly inexplicable smile played round his lips. 'Of course I'm interested to hear how many antiques you've sold on my behalf— but that's not the sole reason for my visit, Rose. I came to see how you were.'

'No doubt you were wondering if I've recovered from my ordeal on the island. It's certainly an experience I'll never forget. That was some lightning storm, wasn't it? Well, I'm still alive and kicking—as you can see.'

'That's not what I meant. We didn't exactly part on the best of terms, did we? I'd hate to think you were still angry with me.'

'I'm not. Tensions were high because of what we'd both been through…that's all.'

'Well, I missed you after you'd left. I came back the next day because the place was too empty without you.'

Rose's heart skipped a beat. *What was he playing at, making such a provocative statement?*

'Isn't that the purpose of having a sanctuary?

So that you can be alone and hopefully enjoy some peace?'

Gene grimaced, and it wasn't the reaction she'd expected. It took her aback to see the pain that had momentarily flared in his dazzling blue eyes.

'There's never any peace when you're alone with your thoughts…at least that's been my experience.'

Such a frank and very *human* confession took Rose aback once more. The world seemed to be of the opinion that a man like Gene who had everything—could have anything he wanted at the drop of a hat—was devoid of any human feelings at all. His desire for more went beyond reason, it seemed. Wasn't that how *she* had viewed him? But it had slowly crept up on her that there was far more to him than that. And, in spite of her fears about being used by him, she realised she wanted to know *more* about him…not *less*.

'I know what you mean. Thoughts can drive us crazy sometimes, can't they? Look, I was just about to make a cup of tea before you appeared. Would you like one?'

The frown that creased his indomitable brow immediately relaxed and the smile he gave her seemed perfectly genuine. 'If you could make that coffee and not tea…that would be great.'

'Coffee it is, then. We'll take it into the office.'

Gene couldn't help recalling the last time he'd been in Philip Houghton's office. He winced when he remembered how his meeting with Rose had ended. Had he intuited even at that early stage of their acquaintance that she was going to shake up his world as it had never been shaken before? With her bewitching violet eyes, and the stubborn way she had of refusing to give in to his wants and needs, she was unlike any other woman he'd known before.

The fact that she seemed far from impressed by his wealth and status, and wasn't readily going to succumb to his charms, made her even more desirable. How would she react if he confessed that he hadn't been able to stop thinking about their impassioned lovemaking on the island? That since he'd tasted her soft cherry lips and intimately known her body she'd infiltrated his blood like a contagious fever that bordered on dangerous…at least to his state of mind?

He had even been finding it hard to concentrate on work—and that was unheard of.

Now, as she sat opposite him on the other side of the desk, Gene thought she looked a little flushed. Her short dark hair was mussed, as if she'd been frequently running her fingers through it because she was stressed…or worried… He didn't particularly want to discuss her boss, but he would have to if he wanted to learn what was troubling her.

'How is Mr Houghton?' he enquired, endeavouring to keep his tone as amiable as possible.

'Better than I hoped.'

'You mean he's rallying?'

'Yes. He's by no means recovered, but the doctors tell me he's definitely made some improvement. Knowing that he's sold the antiques store and no longer has the worry of paying for his aftercare when he comes out of hospital has definitely helped.'

'That's good. But what about *you*, Rose?'

'What do you mean?'

'I mean you look like something's bothering you. What are you worrying about if it's not your boss's state of health?'

Breathing out a sigh, she sat a little further back in her seat. 'I'm not *worried*. I'm…concerned. Concerned that it's going to take me quite some time to sell all these antiques and that in the meantime I need to find a new job.'

The opportunity that Gene had hoped would come his way had just landed straight in his lap… Pausing to reflect on his good fortune, he smiled and took a leisurely sip of his coffee.

'You don't need to look for a new job. You're working for *me* now—remember?' he reminded her.

The compellingly beautiful violet eyes widened. 'I know you're paying me to source buyers for the antiques on your behalf, but it's hardly a full-time position, is it?'

'No, it's not. That being the case, I'm sure I can find you something suitable in one of my companies.'

Rose looked at him aghast. 'Like *what*, for instance?'

'Something in the administration area, perhaps… I'm assuming your organisational skills are good?'

'But I'm not an administrator, am I? I'm an antiques dealer.'

Crossly she folded her arms over her very neat crimson sweater. The fitted cashmere garment couldn't fail to highlight her beautifully shaped breasts and tiny waist, and Gene hotly sensed his hunger to make love to her again becoming an undeniable craving he couldn't resist for very much longer…

She lifted her chin. 'In any case, I don't want you to find me a job. I'm quite capable of doing that for myself.'

His thoughts were racing, and he couldn't prevent his growing frustration from spilling over into his tone. 'Do you know how many résumés my offices receive every day? On average about a hundred. Most people would give their eye teeth for the opportunity to work for me!'

'Well, good luck to them—but I'm not one of those.' Lifting her cup to her lips, she took a brief sip of her tea and clattered the vessel against the matching porcelain saucer when she set it down again.

He didn't miss the fact that her hand was shaking. *God, the woman was stubborn!* He longed for her to relent a little. He found himself momentarily lost in the memory of touching her breasts, and of the way her tender nipples had instantly hardened and contracted against his hand...

He stood up, because he suddenly couldn't stay still, and walked round the desk to study her more closely.

'I'd like to let you go so that you can look for a

job you really want, but I'm afraid I can't. What I *can* do, however, is double the fee I'm paying you so that you won't have any worries about money until you find a new position. Does that make things easier for you?'

'It's not just about the money...'

'You don't *want* to stay and sell the antiques for me? Is that what you're saying?'

'It's just too awkward...'

'Why?'

'Because I've worked all these years for *Philip*—and you're not him!'

Her upsurge of emotion took them both by surprise. Rose was breathing hard and chewing anxiously down on her fulsome lower lip and Gene's heart was thudding fit to burst. Her meaning was clear. The thought that she regarded the aging antiques dealer over him made his blood boil. He knew he had no reason to be jealous, because she'd made it clear to him that her devotion to the man was purely out of respect and kindness, but he couldn't help feeling the way he did.

Reaching down, he furiously pulled her to her feet. 'You're sorry that I'm not some elderly English gentleman who couldn't give you even *one* night of pleasure if he tried?'

He brought his face down to hers and felt her slender frame tremble.

'That's the most ridiculous notion I've ever heard. If you met him you'd know why. He's the sweetest, kindest man I've ever met and I've already told you I'm not remotely attracted to him.'

Gene heard the heartfelt words but was too far gone to be remotely gracious. He was lost in an incandescent violet sea and in a sweet perfume so seductive that he was helpless to resist the erotic delights it promised. He crushed Rose's luscious cherry lips beneath his without an ounce of remorse and devoured them.

At some point during his greedy exploration he tasted blood on his lips and didn't know whether it was his or hers. But then, incredibly, he realised that she was kissing him back—that she'd freed her hands and was hungrily urging him closer.

At the same time she was making breathless little sounds that told him she wanted and needed him as much as he did her...

His blood pounding hotly in his veins, Gene acknowledged that the sparks they'd helplessly ignited together had suddenly caught fire. And there was only one solution to dousing the flames—and that was to unrestrainedly let them *burn*...

With a heated groan he swept aside all the paraphernalia on the desk and papers and items of stationery fell haphazardly onto the floor. His gaze briefly colliding with Rose's, he gripped her arms and, as gently as he was able, helped her to lie back on the mahogany surface.

She was already pushing his suit jacket aside and urgently opening his shirt buttons so that she could touch him. When she ran her hands over his chest and round his ribcage it was an irresistible combination of heaven and hell for Gene. Heaven because being close to her in this way was beyond his wildest dreams as far as pleasure was concerned, and hell because he was so turned on it was painful…

Capturing her mouth in a hard, hot kiss, he dragged up the hem of her skirt to find her panties. When his hands fastened round the skimpy white silk that adorned her svelte hips he eagerly pulled down the garment to mid-thigh and urgently undid his zip. He was almost beyond aching to be inside her.

When Rose clasped her velvet thighs around him he needed no further invitation. He plunged his inflamed sex deep inside her moist satin centre. They both stilled for a moment—not in shock or surprise, but in wonder at the unbelievable ecstasy of their union. Then Gene's ability to think even close to straight disappeared as he was driven to thrust even deeper, at the same time pushing aside her sweater and bra to fasten his mouth on a sweetly distended nipple, nibbling at it with the edges of his teeth.

The taste of her was like the sweetest nectar imaginable and he was already addicted to it. Since their very first combustible encounter Gene had known he wouldn't easily be able to relinquish sampling it again and again...

Releasing a sensuous moan, Rose suddenly stilled beneath him.

Raising his head to glance down at her, he saw that her beautiful eyes looked startled. He saw too that the incandescent violet orbs were glazed with moisture and that it had darkened the fringe of ebony lashes that surrounded them. He didn't pause to wonder why she should shed a tear at such a pleasurable moment because he was already a mere breath away from the climactic fulfilment of his own sensual journey.

In the next instant his desire reached its zenith and his entire body vibrated with the power of it. Releasing a guttural groan that might have emanated from the undiscovered corners of his very soul, Gene lowered his head to rest it against Rose's chest. If they had been in bed together he would have gathered her into his arms and held her for the longest time. Yet again a strong wave of protectiveness had swept over him, and he couldn't help but want to express it.

He was just about to enquire if she was all right, and tell her how beautiful she was, when the lyrical sound of the shop's doorbell made them both stiffen in alarm.

'It must be a customer...' Rose said huskily, her hands already pushing him away.

Even as she spoke Gene cursed beneath his breath, hurriedly got to his feet and tidied his disarrayed clothing.

Red-faced, Rose gave him a nervous glance as she straightened her skirt and tucked in her sweater. Then she dragged her fingers through her mussed hair and went to the door.

Turning, she said, 'If you go through that door you'll find a cloakroom where you can freshen up. I'll tell whoever it is that I'm closing early today.'

'Good idea,' he muttered.

When she'd closed the door behind her he cursed again—not because they'd been interrupted, but because in the throes of a passion that had been as fierce and elemental as the lightning storm they'd witnessed on the island he'd stupidly omitted to use protection...

The unexpected caller turned out to be the persistently cheerful postman, who had once told Rose that his name was Bill. He was making a late delivery, he explained, due to the 'horrendous traffic'.

Rose didn't usually mind a bit of a chat with him, but not today...

Not when she'd left Gene in the office, waiting for her.

The explosion of passion that had erupted between them had made her head spin. There wasn't an inch of flesh on her body that didn't throb and ache, and she was pretty sure she'd inadvertently acquired a couple of bruises. *They'd made love on the office desk, for goodness' sake!* Had she completely taken leave of her senses?

It stunned her that she'd been so reckless. But at the same time, strangely, she felt no regret.

In fact she didn't feel like the woman she'd always known herself to be at all…that was someone who always strove to do what was right and act accordingly. She felt like a woman who had somehow liberated herself from the yoke of conformity that had more or less dominated her whole life because of the way she'd been raised—and the feeling was *beyond* exhilarating…

And, although she still found it hard to trust, Gene was the one responsible for her liberation. In his arms she could believe that *anything* was possible.

Bill handed over the pile of letters he'd brought and commented, 'By the way, have you seen that top-of-the-range black Mercedes in the car park? Presumably it belongs to one of your rich customers? It's got a personal number plate…reads EB1. Got any idea who that might be?'

Excruciatingly, Rose felt herself redden. She endeavoured to make her answer sound as uninterested as possible. 'No, I don't. It probably belongs to someone who's popped into the bank.

Anyway, thanks for the post. I've got to get on now. I'm shutting up shop early today.'

'Got a hot date, have you?' Bill gave her a playful wink.

Wincing, Rose went behind him to the door and pointedly held it open.

'All right, love, I can take a hint!' He smiled. 'See you next time!'

Breathing a sigh of relief when he was gone, she locked the door and turned the sign that hung there round to read 'Closed'. Then she smoothed down her newly wrinkled smart black skirt and prepared herself to return to the office and face the man who had had no compunction in making her his lover yet again…

# CHAPTER EIGHT

WHEN SHE RETURNED to the office it was to find Eugene disappearing through the back door to locate the cloakroom. The papers and stationery he'd swept onto the floor had been returned to the desk and arranged tidily. Anyone stepping into the room would not notice anything remotely amiss. They certainly wouldn't guess that Rose and a well-known billionaire had been making out on the desk!

Walking across the room to her chair, she feverishly reflected on what had happened. She couldn't still her trembling as she sat down. Anguished, she murmured aloud, 'What have I done?'

In the aftermath of the event, shock had set in. Not just shock, but guilt and a generous portion of shame too. *What would Philip think if he knew? What would her father have said if he'd been alive?* Rose felt as if she'd let them both down. But, more importantly, she'd also let *herself* down. There was a good reason why she'd always sought to behave well. When her parents had split her father's friends had intimated that her mother, Ruth, had had a 'wild streak' that her father had never really come to terms with.

Philip had once shared with Rose that her father had told him, 'Living with that woman was like building a house on top of a repository for dynamite. Not a day went by when I didn't anticipate it might blow up in my face.'

Ruth Heathcote had caused utter devastation when she'd deserted him for the wealthy and flamboyant David Carlisle. He'd been absolutely crushed by her leaving and had gone to court to make sure that Rose was raised by him and not her… Suffering the fall-out of those painful events had made Rose determined never to behave as recklessly.

But she was well aware that when nature held sway humans were more often than not powerless to resist. That was why she'd ended up in bed with Gene at the sanctuary. Yet her self-respect was paramount, and she wouldn't jeopardise that if she could help it... *Or so she'd believed.* What she hadn't been prepared for was a man like Gene Bonnaire sweeping into her life and leaving her feeling as though she'd just survived a tornado by the skin of her teeth.

And now there was something else she'd better keep in mind. They had been intimate without even giving a thought to using protection. They'd been so mesmerised by their urgent feelings that it hadn't even crossed their minds. At least Rose knew that Gene hadn't *planned* the passionate seduction. If he had, he would most definitely have brought protection. He might flirt with danger in his business life, but she was certain a man like him wouldn't take unnecessary risks in his personal one...

Although it would be easy to give way to panic, she absolutely refused to. Thankfully, she knew all about the morning-after pill, and before she went home she would go straight to a pharmacy. An unplanned pregnancy was something that definitely *wasn't* in her plans for the future...

Gene returned. The expression on his handsome face was a little shame-faced. To counteract it, a tentative smile lifted a corner of his sculpted lips and Rose's senses were immediately assailed by the seductive scent of him. In her chair, she couldn't help but clench her thighs together. Her heart raced when she thought how desperately they had made love. In his arms she had learned what it meant to be ecstatic, freed of restriction. It had felt like *flying*...

'Who was your visitor? A potential customer?' he enquired.

As he asked the question he was walking

slowly towards her, and she had ample time to admire his hard, honed physique in the impeccable bespoke suit. If Gene didn't flirt with danger in *his* personal life, then Rose knew that was *exactly* what she'd be doing in hers if she didn't tell him that turning their association into a sexual one had been a bad mistake. As much as the thought grieved her, the two hot little encounters they'd enjoyed wouldn't be happening again.

'It was the postman making a late delivery,' she told him.

'His timing could have been better.'

Rose flushed. 'He said that the traffic was bad. That's why he got held up.'

'Never mind about that… I'm more interested in what *we're* doing. I want you to come back with me to my apartment tonight. This time I want to make sure I have you all to myself. I don't want to risk our time together being interrupted again.'

He was drawing her to her feet as he spoke and his arms were wound firmly round her waist.

Finding herself once again mesmerised by his cobalt blue eyes and fit body, so soon after the intimacy they'd shared, Rose sensed her determination to hold him at bay and deny him any further intimate contact teeter precariously.

'That might be what *you* want, Gene, but it's not what *I* want.'

'I don't believe you.'

He had the temerity to look amused, and she couldn't help but take umbrage. Flattening her hands against his shirtfront, she pushed him away…or at least she *tried* to push him away.

He wasn't having any of it and held her fast.

'Look, I might have agreed to *temporarily* do a job for you,' she reminded him, 'but that doesn't mean I've agreed to be at your beck and call day and night.'

'Did I say that's what I wanted?' He sighed, and his warm breath fanned her face. 'Neither would I want to be at *your* beck and call day and night, Rose. But if we need to spend some time

together that's a different proposition entirely…
wouldn't you say?'

Noting that he had said *need* instead of *want*
sent a traitorous warm glow pulsing through
Rose. The declaration didn't make it sound as if
he intended to use her and then cast her aside so
he could go on to the next available woman he
took a fancy to.

And yet the memory of her ex Joe's behaviour
reminded her that she shouldn't give her trust
so easily—she couldn't afford to be lulled into
a false sense of security by the dangerous hope
that Gene genuinely wanted to have a relationship with her. Didn't his much-documented brief
liaisons with various models and actresses prove
that he wasn't a man who believed in long-term
relationships?

'I just don't think it's a good idea for us to
spend any more time together…at least not in
*that* way. From now on our relationship should
be a purely professional one. I'll do what you're
paying me to do as regards selling the antiques,

but there'll be no need for us to associate out-side of work.'

'I disagree.'

'I thought you might—but that's only because you want your own way. My mind is made up, Gene.'

'And what if you find out you're pregnant?'

He came back at her like a whip and his gaze was suddenly ominously cold. Rose shivered, but he still didn't release her.

'You don't have to worry about that.'

'You mean you're on the pill?'

'No. But there's a morning-after pill I can get from the pharmacy that inhibits ovulation. I'm going to get it on the way home.'

'So I don't have any say in the matter at all?'

'I thought you'd be pleased that there's some-thing we can do. I'm sure you don't want to be tied to me because of a child we created in a to-tally crazy moment of unforeseen passion.'

For a perturbing few moments Gene didn't know what to say. Everything in him felt as

though it had been shaken up and displaced—
and, worse than that, he sensed it wasn't likely
that the various parts would be returned to their
original positions any time soon...

Then he remembered what had instigated their
'crazy moment of unforeseen passion'. He'd told
Rose that she was working for *him* now, and she
hadn't seemed at all happy. She had finished
by exclaiming 'But you're not him!' as if she
mourned the fact that he wasn't her boss, Philip
Houghton.

His arms locked even tighter round her impossibly small waist. An undeniable sense of ownership and possession seized him. 'Are you intent
on taking this morning-after pill because you
don't trust me? Do you think I wouldn't take responsibility?'

Rose sighed. 'I haven't thought about anything
much beyond protecting myself. We're not in a
serious relationship and I'm equally responsible
for what just happened. I'm just being sensible.'

'Why? Has something like this happened to

you before? You indicated once that you'd been hurt by someone.'

'I was. But he didn't make me pregnant and abandon me, if that's what you were thinking. In a way what he did was worse than that. He fooled around behind my back and then lied about it as if it was nothing.'

Even though she'd endeavoured to make her tone sound matter-of-fact, Gene still heard the pain in her voice. He felt as though he'd been punched. The thought of a man regularly cheating on Rose and then lying to her instigated that primitive impulse in him to protect and defend her honour.

'I'm sorry you had to go through that,' he said, low-voiced, 'but that's not the way *I* behave. You're well rid of the jerk. Getting back to the present situation, I know you're being practical in thinking about a morning-after pill, but what about our feelings? Don't *they* come into the equation at all?'

Gene's heart was galloping as he heard himself asking the one question he'd never asked a woman before. But since meeting Rose he was being more and more drawn to acknowledge an area of his life that he'd long ago become adept at turning away from...*his emotions.*

The matchless violet gaze in front of him reflected her alarm. 'Are you seriously telling me that you have some kind of—of *feeling* about the possibility of me having a baby?'

'I'm not completely heartless. There are some things in life that cause a person to stop and think. A possible pregnancy is one of them.'

'But I've already told you—it's not just your responsibility.'

'I hear you. But I also want you to hear *me*, Rose. I don't know how or why, but we seem to have developed some kind of connection—a connection that's a little deeper than run of the mill. It's not something I want to ignore, and neither do I want to just put it down to experience.'

'I hardly know what to say...'

'In that case there's absolutely no reason why

we can't make our relationship more personal, is there?'

'Didn't we just make it about as personal as it can be?'

Rose's comment was clearly meant to be ironic. Unfortunately Gene saw no reason for humour—ironic or otherwise...

He unceremoniously released her. Scraping his fingers through his perfectly groomed hair, he was intensely frustrated that she didn't seem to want to take their relationship more seriously. Even though they'd been intimate, it was easy to sense that she was already putting up walls between them... *He wished he could knock every one of them down.*

Having never experienced a woman spurning him before, he barely knew what to do. Already he felt bereft because she wasn't in his arms... He could flex his masculinity and *insist* she came home with him, but this was the twenty-first century and Rose was an independent woman. He sensed she wouldn't take at all well to his throwing his weight around. In fact, such an action would probably drive her away completely. He would have to mull over another strategy.

Meeting her gaze, he said, 'If you won't come back to my apartment then why don't you let me drive you home?'

'There's no need. I can get the bus—like I usually do.'

'You don't drive?'

'No…I don't.'

In that volatile moment he couldn't contain his temper that things weren't going his way, and he snapped, 'Then go and get yourself ready and I'll meet you out front in my car. Our first destination will be the pharmacy…'

Rose was exiting the pharmacy and heading towards the luxurious Mercedes that waited for her outside when a man with a camera rushed towards her. Pointing it at her, he was taking continuous snaps even as he moved.

'Are you Eugene Bonnaire's new girlfriend?

What's your name, love? You might as well tell me. I saw his car. What other reason would he have for parking it there?'

Even as she reeled with shock she saw Gene hurriedly open the door next to the driver's seat. Rose registered the furious muscle that flexed in his hard-chiselled jaw.

He yelled, 'Get in the car quickly and don't tell that idiot anything!'

Rose moved almost without thinking. She all but threw herself into the luxuriously upholstered passenger seat and Gene started the engine as she was still closing the door. The precision-engineered car moved smoothly away from the kerb.

'That's exactly what I *don't* need,' he murmured.

Placing her bag down by her feet, she glanced up. 'I wouldn't have said anything, you know. I certainly wouldn't have given him my name. Does that kind of thing happen very often?'

'A little too often for my liking…I never

thought I'd miss my anonymity, but it's funny how things change.'

Genuinely surprised that he should share such a personal reflection, Rose relaxed a little. Perhaps Gene didn't seek the limelight as much as the press made out that he did? Could that be the reason he'd looked so unhappy in that photo she'd seen of him at the awards ceremony? The idea of having your every move stalked and being photographed by paparazzi must be a living nightmare. There was nothing about his life that she remotely envied. In fact she suddenly found herself feeling genuinely sad for his lack of privacy...

'I never thought I'd say this, but I feel for you, Gene...I really do. I'm glad I said we should keep our relationship on a professional footing rather than a personal one. In light of events like *that* happening, it's probably best if you stay away. We can communicate by phone.'

Turning his head towards her, he scowled. 'I won't be dictated to by anybody—least of all the media.' He returned his furious gaze to the road. 'Just give me your address and I'll take you home.'

When they pulled up outside the neat semi-detached house in the pleasant cul-de-sac where Rose lived, Gene switched off the engine and turned to gaze out of the window at the building. Rose saw him glance at the newly mown lawn and the tidy window boxes that were full of colourful perennials. It was late autumn, and she loved the fact that they were still in bloom. But he was probably thinking how ordinary the place was, she reflected.

'Have you always lived here?' he asked.

Even as she nodded, she hated the feeling that he might be judging her in some way because of where she lived.

'It's the house I grew up in with my parents. When my father died he left it to me.'

'Not your mother?'

She shook her head. 'No. They weren't together any more.'

'You mean they were divorced?'

Expelling a jaundiced sigh, Rose replied, 'Yes. She ran off with a rich unscrupulous business-man who promised her a better life.' She couldn't hide the bitterness in her tone and sensed her cheeks flush red.

Gene's brow puckered interestedly. 'And *did* he…? Give her a better life, I mean?'

'Depends what you mean by "better". As far as I know she's happy. They live in a swanky place in Paris and she doesn't want for anything. Apparently she's got the kind of life she always dreamt of…the kind of life that my father could never have afforded to give her. But she broke his heart when she left him and he never really recovered.'

'I'm sorry to hear that. But her desertion must have been tough on you too?'

Rose felt the backs of her eyes sting. 'It was for a while. But then I got over it. I had to deal with what was in front of me. In any case, who needs a mother who'd rather have the material things in life over the people that really love her?'

She thought she saw Gene wince.

'What did he do for a living? I mean your father?' he asked.

'He was an accountant…a very good one, as a matter of fact.' She was quite aware that she sounded defensive. 'But he was never as ambitious as my mother wanted him to be. Instead of seeing what a loyal and devoted husband and father he was, she saw the fact that he put spending time with his family before rising in his career as a weakness.'

'You said that your mother and her husband live in Paris? Can you tell me where?'

Again Rose sensed her face heat. She didn't doubt that Gene would know the place. She hadn't forgotten that he was French. 'It's a suburb called Neuilly-sur-Seine.'

'If they can afford to live there he *must* be rich. It's got some of the most prime real estate in the city.'

She shrugged and unbuckled her seatbelt. 'I wouldn't know. Nor do I care.'

Before she could turn and open the car door she heard the soft snick of Gene's seatbelt being freed. Leaning towards her, he captured her hand and held it fast.

'Before you go I think we need to have a serious talk, don't you?'

Like a moth drawn to a flame, she fell headlong into the dangerous fire of his glittering blue gaze and sensed herself sizzle. At the same time the sensual musky scent of him made her insides melt. Shockingly, all she could think about was the silkily hard, hot sensation of him inside her... It stunned Rose just how much she ached to experience his intimate possession again.

She bit down hard on the lower lip that was already contused from his passionate kisses. 'What kind of a talk? If it's about the sale of the antiques I told you I'd stay in touch.'

Even to her own ears her voice sounded distinctly shaky.

'You know damn well it's not about the antiques. We need to talk about what just happened between us at the shop.'

Rose forced herself to stay strong, not to let him suspect how deeply his passionate attentions had affected her. 'We had sex on my boss's desk… that's what happened. I told you I was going to take the morning-after pill to make sure I don't get pregnant, so you don't have to worry. What else do we need to talk about?'

'I don't believe for one second that's *all* you think we did, Rose.'

Suddenly Gene was lifting her hand towards his lips with strangely purposeful intent…

'We made *fire* back there—that's what we did…a fire that burned us both right down to our core. And if you deny it I won't hesitate to call you a liar.'

Even as he made the assertion he was inserting her slender forefinger into the silkily hot cavern of his mouth and sucking it…

She gasped. 'What are you…? What are you

doing?' She snatched her hand away even as she wished that she was brave enough to keep it there.

His lips formed a lazily knowing smile. 'I was reacquainting myself with your taste, Rose. It seems that I can't get enough of it.'

'Well, you're going to have to learn to do without it—because I can't and won't continue with this stupidity!'

The feeling that she was about to burst into tears was overwhelming. Because she didn't want to make an even bigger fool of herself than she'd done already, she snatched up her bag and opened the door.

As she stepped out onto the pavement Gene's inscrutable handsome features gave not the slightest clue as to his feelings, but he remarked, 'You might call it stupidity for us to spend more time together, Rose, but I don't happen to share that view. Whatever the outcome of this situation, I personally have no regrets. Be assured that I'll be in touch.'

Rose didn't reply. Instead she slammed the car door shut and headed straight for the house. Even as she heard him pull away, and as the tears she'd tried so hard to hold back started to stream down her face, she made sure not to turn and follow his progress...

# CHAPTER NINE

GENE HADN'T BEEN lying when he'd commented to Rose that he couldn't get enough of her taste. It wasn't just her taste he was addicted to either. He couldn't get enough of *her*…especially since that wild episode in Philip's office. His blood rushed and his heart pumped harder every time he thought about it.

The realisation that she was becoming more important to him than he'd ever envisaged threatened everything. Dear God, the woman had him in such a tailspin he'd barely even given the ownership of the antiques shop building a thought. How could that be? he wondered. Wasn't possession of the listed building supposed to be the icing on the cake, crowning yet another successful year of his restaurant chain as well as the other numerous lucrative investments he'd made?

*It didn't feel like that.* It made him realise there was a big difference between *being* successful and *feeling* successful—and right then he didn't feel successful at all. He felt strangely empty… as though everything he'd set such store by in his life had suddenly become meaningless.

Rose's story about her mother's desertion of her for an 'unscrupulous rich businessman' had definitely hit a nerve. It was evident that she despised her stepfather. Without a doubt Gene could probably find at least a dozen parallels with himself and the man, and it was quite possible he even *knew* him. The business community *he* was a member of only welcomed the 'elite of the elite' into their ranks…the wealthiest and most powerful of men and women…and Rose's stepfather might even be one of Gene's competitors.

Yet it wasn't that that perturbed him. It was the knowledge that he'd behaved exactly like her mother when he'd turned his back on his loved ones, believing that the simple life his parents enjoyed wasn't enough. He'd become greedy and ambitious, and hearing Rose's story had made him aware of some of the more negative consequences his desires had wrought.

He'd purchased a beautiful Georgian house for his parents a few years ago and had sensed their deep unease at accepting it.

His father had told him, 'It's a wonderful gift, son, but in truth your mother and me would rather know that you're happy and content, and have your company from time to time, than have you buy us a house. We're quite happy with our simple little terrace. All our memories are here… it's where we raised you and your sister.'

Gene had felt crass and insensitive. He'd never even considered what *they* wanted. Yet it hurt him deeply that they'd never understood how much losing his beloved sister, Francesca, had affected *him*. Knowing that life was so precarious and ephemeral had really shaken him. And the need to protect his remaining family at all costs had driven him to become more and more successful in the world. Yet he had never been able to share his feelings with them about it.

After the disappointing reception of his well-meant gift of the house he had retreated to lick his wounds and had distanced himself from them even more. Gene had numbed his discomfort and pain by acquiring even more restaurants and playing the stock market. He had been employing the only way he knew how to protect himself from further hurt.

He had been as devastated as his parents when illness had so cruelly taken Francesca from them. From time to time her beautiful face would come into his mind, and it was like a knife in his heart that he would never see her grow into a woman, would never see her fall in love, maybe marry and have children of her own...

They'd all been like ghosts after she went... alive, but not really living. And now Gene feared he'd lost his parents' respect and regard. They might tell him that they loved him, but too often when he visited he saw pain and disappointment in their eyes because of the path he'd taken. They had no idea what drove him to pursue success and money so relentlessly and probably never would. They no doubt believed it made him happy. How could they know what a high price he paid for being so driven?

Every night when he went home from his day's work—to his apartment in London or either of the desirable residences he owned in New York and Paris when he was there—more often than not he went home alone. Eugene didn't have relationships. He had joyless liaisons that were usually conducted in some luxurious hotel that was utterly devoid of anything remotely homely or comforting. It made him secretly despise the women he entertained, because they were more interested in his money than in expressing even a passing interest in the real man behind the wealthy and polished veneer...

He might have been kidding himself that that was okay, but deep down he knew it was a *lie*.

Seeing Rose's house today, in an ordinary sub-urban cul-de-sac, with its well-tended window boxes and tidily perfect lawn, he had been almost *envious* that she clearly didn't feel the need for something grander. The mere concept of being satisfied with your lot in life was a million miles away from the world Gene inhabited. And, al-though he couldn't envisage himself in a simi-lar situation to hers, it had surprisingly instilled in him a longing for some of the comforts of a real home.

*And it wasn't just that that he longed to expe-rience.*

There was a deep yearning inside him to be with someone who really cared…someone who didn't just want him for what he could provide materially but who genuinely wanted to get to know him and likewise would let him get to know *her*…

He headed for the kitchen. Whenever he was troubled and—yes—sometimes *sickened* by the relentless desire for more that had set him apart from so much that was true, he returned to the one thing that was guaranteed to give him pleasure...*cooking*. And while he gathered together the pots, pans and ingredients that he needed to make a meal his thoughts inevitably turned to Rose and the meal he'd made for her on the island.

Already it had become one of Gene's favourite memories. But thinking of her was bittersweet, because he'd left her on her own to deal with the possibility that he might have made her pregnant. *It wasn't right*. He hated the idea that she might be feeling scared and upset. Having the presence of mind to think about taking the morning-after pill might denote that she was a practical woman, but he knew she was a sensitive one too.

Frustrated that he couldn't be with her, he reached for his mobile and dialled the number of a trusted business colleague who was the owner of an exclusive jeweller's in Bond Street. After that he contacted an equally prestigious florist. If he couldn't have the pleasure of Rose's company tonight at least he could do something to show her that he cared about the compromising situation he had put her in…

The next morning Rose was roused from a restless night with very little sleep to take unexpected delivery of the most beautiful bouquet of white roses. Even as she carefully transported them into the kitchen to put them into her favourite crystal vase the scent of the flowers filled the air like a soporific hypnotic balm. Had Philip sent them to thank her for dealing with the sale of the antiques store?

With their exotic scent and lush, velvety petals, even in her sleep-deprived state they couldn't help but make Rose think of Cleopatra, Queen of the Nile. The legend went that the queen had regularly bathed in a bath of milk scented with rose petals…

Gently laying the bouquet down on the table, she bent to inhale the scent a little more closely. It was then that she saw the card that accompanied them, and tucked in amongst the flowers she saw a narrow red velvet box. Frowning, she opened the card and studied the inscription. With her pulse racing she read it.

*To the Hidden Diamond I never expected to find.*
*Gene x.*

*Gene* had sent her the flowers? To receive such a message from him was so unexpected, so exhilarating, that Rose felt quite intoxicated by it.

Pulling out a chair from the table, she sank down into it because her legs suddenly felt as though they might not support her. Her mind was racing as she strove to find an explanation of what he might mean. Then she reached into the bouquet of buttery roses for the glamorous presentation box. She opened it.

Lying on a bed of sumptuous cream silk was the most dazzling diamond bracelet Rose had ever seen. Set in white gold, the square-cut gems were flawlessly pristine and glinted up at her like brilliant sunlight radiated through a prism. What had Gene meant by sending her such an amazing and valuable gift?

Lifting the bracelet out of the box, she tried it on. It was blissfully cool against her skin and yet her whole body felt drenched with heat, just thinking about the man who'd sent it. But it was the words he'd written on the card that had taken her aback the most. *The Hidden Diamond…* Was Gene saying that *Rose* was the hidden diamond he'd never expected to find? Was the sentiment a heartfelt one or was he merely flattering her?

She suddenly felt like crying, because more than anything she wanted to believe that Gene meant every word…

The telephone rang. Rose rushed to answer it in case it might be the hospital. As far as Philip's health was concerned he was by no means out of the woods yet.

But it wasn't anyone from the hospital.

*It was Gene.*

'Rose? It's me.'

The seductive bass voice that never failed to raise gooseflesh on her skin made her instantly tingle. She hadn't yet taken off the diamond bracelet he'd sent and the glittering gems winked back at her as if daring her to remove it…

Dry-mouthed, she answered, 'What's up?'

She wanted to sound nonchalant, as if she didn't care that he should be ringing her so early in the morning, but as soon as she heard his voice her insides were deluged with a swarm of agitated butterflies.

'Tell me how you are this morning.'

'I'm—I'm fine…'

'I still wish that you'd come home with me.'

'I did the right thing. I was very tired. It's been an emotional time.'

'That's the reason why we shouldn't make any hasty decisions.'

Rose heard him take a deep breath in and remembered the comment he'd made about considering their feelings. It had knocked her for six. It certainly hadn't followed his infamous pattern of brief, 'take it or leave it' liaisons.

'I was worried that you might be upset about what happened yesterday and regret it,' he went on.

The comment made her burn as she recalled the sheer power of the elemental forces that had driven them to make love with such wild abandon in her boss's office. In the cold light of day it was hard to believe she'd behaved so recklessly.

'I'm not upset. We did what we did and I don't regret it. But, like I said…it's not going to happen again.'

She sucked in a breath and released it slowly in a bid to calm her nerves, but even as she'd said the words she'd been wishing she could take them back…

'By the way, thank you for the beautiful roses and the gift you sent.'

Frowning, she lifted her arm once again to examine the elegant diamond bracelet that adorned her wrist. The apricot silk dressing gown she was wearing, which she'd bought from a vintage clothing sale, couldn't help but complement the jewellery. The sensuous feel of the garment next to her skin made her feel like a million dollars.

Wearing both the bracelet *and* the gown, she felt like a whole other person...someone much more stylish and beautiful than the unremarkable woman she thought of herself as.

But her pleasure quickly died when she caught herself. She didn't want to give herself illusions of grandeur or to feel different or special just because she'd been given an expensive diamond bracelet. She wasn't like her mother, whose craving for the finer things in life had made her leave her loyal, dependable husband to be with a much wealthier man just because he could indulge her material desires...

'I'll keep the roses...but I'm afraid I won't be keeping the bracelet.'

There was a significant momentary silence at the other end of the phone. It was soon filled with an exasperated, 'Why not? I know how much you admire beautiful things and I wanted to give you something beautiful—so what's the problem?'

'It's a *diamond bracelet*, Gene. That's the problem. The clarity, cut and carat of the stones is amazing, so it's by no means a simple gift. Do you think that men give women gifts like that every day? They might in your exalted world, but they most definitely don't in mine. And it—it makes it hard for me to trust your motives. My ex used to give me pretty gifts when he was seeing other women behind my back and wanted to divert me from finding out. I know we're not serious, but if that's what *you're* going to do, Gene, then I'll save you wasting your time and your money by giving you the bracelet back. At least then we know where we stand.'

By the time she came to the end of her impassioned speech Rose could just imagine Gene dismissing it with a shrug of his impressive shoulders…more than likely encased in his usual impeccable tailoring. It was hard not to break down and cry… He might have talked about having feelings, but that didn't mean he'd honestly meant it.

'It sounds to me as if what happened yesterday *did* upset you, Rose. Why don't you have lunch with me today and we can talk?'

'About what a colossal mistake we made?' Even as she made the comment the churning emotion in her gut made a liar of her.

'You really believe that? A mistake suggests we had a choice in the matter and had time to think it through. If you recall, Rose, *thinking* didn't come into it. We were drawn together by an overpowering force of nature that we couldn't resist.'

And she had the sore spots on her body to prove it...

Feeling her face flame red, she replied, 'Anyway, I can't meet you for lunch. I have far too much work to do.'

'Do I have to keep reminding you that you're working for me now? You can have the whole damn day off if you want to.'

'But I don't *want* the day off.'

He made another exasperated sound and Rose was glad he couldn't see the tears that welled in her eyes.

'Meet me for lunch and let that be an end to it,' he ground out. 'I'll give you the name of the restaurant and you can meet me there. I'll pay for a cab.'

She sniffed and wiped her eyes, then stared blankly at the shimmering diamond bracelet that had slid down her slender-boned wrist to rest elegantly against her hand. 'I can pay for my own cab.'

'I might have guessed that you'd say that. Did I tell you that I think you're the most stubborn woman I've ever met?'

It was Rose's turn to shrug. 'More than once… But it probably does you good to not have your own way all the time.'

Gene chuckled, and the sound elicited a burst of warmth inside her that made her want to count the minutes—no…the *seconds* until she could be with him again…

* * *

As Rose followed the smart, straight-backed *maître d'* to the table Gene had reserved she was sure that every single diner in the exclusive little restaurant watched her progress. As soon as she'd mentioned what seemed to be the magic words 'Eugene Bonnaire' she would have sworn that every one of the stylishly dressed customers seated at the tables had turned to see who was enquiring.

The table was in an intimately cordoned off alcove, tucked away at the back of the restaurant, and Rose's heart clanged hard as Gene stood up to greet her. He was wearing a slim-fitting charcoal suit, and the single-breasted jacket hung open to reveal a navy shirt and an azure silk tie. But it wasn't the colour of his shirt or tie that transfixed her. It was the arresting glint in his incredible blue eyes...

Every single muscle in her body stiffened and contracted at the undeniably voracious glance he gave her—because he was shamelessly undressing her with his eyes. That intense examining glance left her with nowhere to go…nowhere to run and hide…

He huskily murmured, 'Hi…' but she couldn't seem to find a single word with which to respond.

The discreet *maître d'* smiled, saying he would give them a few minutes to look at the menu. Then he politely left them alone.

Despite her see-sawing emotions Rose couldn't deny she'd been looking forward to their lunch date. That being the case, she'd decided to wear what was perhaps her most eye-catching outfit. She'd bared her shoulders in a top the colour of metallic silver, and had teamed it with a black chiffon mini-skirt with ebony tights and long leather boots.

She'd wanted Gene to see that she could look chic and classy and didn't need to dress in haute couture to prove it… Showcasing what she thought of as some of her best assets for their date—namely her tiny waist, slim arms and shapely legs—made her feel good.

In fact she was beginning to realise that she felt more womanly and attractive than she'd ever felt before when she was with him, and she wanted to let him see that—however their relationship *did* or *didn't* progress.

'You look sensational.'

His low-voiced compliment confirmed that she'd opted for the right outfit.

'I definitely heard an admiring gasp when you entered the restaurant. I'll bet everyone wants to know who you are.'

Although Gene's effusive compliments had stopped her in her tracks, confidently holding his gaze, Rose murmured, 'Thanks. You scrub up nicely yourself.'

With a gravel-voiced chuckle he moved round the table to be closer to her. Then he made an elegant bow, like a gentleman from the upper echelons of society in one of those classic novels, and politely brushed the side of her cheek with a kiss.

Immediately the cool touch of his lips rendered Rose dangerously weak. *The reaction was definitely starting to become a habit.*

'Come and sit next to me...' he breathed, and it didn't once cross her mind to refuse. 'I haven't been able to stop thinking about you,' he confessed, his piercing cobalt eyes practically consuming her with their electric glance.

Rose set her handbag down on the chair next to her and twisted her hands together. 'I don't know whether that's a good or not so good thing. We're work colleagues now, remember?'

His sculpted lips shaped an amused grin, 'So our relationship is purely a working one, is it?'

'I didn't come here to talk about what's happened between us. I want to put that behind me and concentrate on doing a good job of selling off the antiques for you.'

'You can still do that...but it doesn't mean that we can't see each other outside of work.'

'Where are you going with this, Gene? I've already told you that I'd prefer it if we kept our association a professional one. Like I said before, I'm not interested in becoming one of your short-term little liaisons. In spite of what's happened, my decision hasn't changed.'

Gene sighed. As he pushed back his hair the eye-catching gold watch he wore glinted against his wrist. The bracelet was made unusually of rose gold, as was the intricate dial, set in relief against an ebony backdrop. Surely only the most confident and assured of men would be able to wear such a watch? And not only that, but wear it with enviable panache.

Rose didn't need to see the maker's name to know that it had been made by one of the most esteemed watch designers in the world. Her stomach lurched as it was brought home to her yet again just who Gene was and what he represented…

'I don't see our liaison as being a short-term one,' he told her, his tone etched with frustration. 'In fact I want us to have a *proper* relationship.'

Reaching for the water jug on the table, Rose

poured a glass and gratefully swallowed some. She was almost lightheaded with shock. 'That's impossible. I know you don't do "proper" relationships, so why would you make an exception for me?'

His expression was serious. 'Why? Because I'm tired of denying the fact that I want something more, that's why. I'm tired of isolating myself from people. I haven't seen my family for months now, and it's near killing me.'

'Why haven't you seen them?'

'Because I'm too busy working.' Looking agonised, he shook his head. 'And because all I seem to do is hurt them when we're together.'

Rose caught his hand and held it. The heartfelt confession had utterly shaken her.

'Whatever has happened between you, there's always a way to make things better.'

'Maybe there is in your world, Rose…but not in mine.'

'Have you even talked to them about your belief that all you do is hurt them? That might not be the case at all. What if they're just waiting for you to come and talk things over?'

He glanced down at her slim hand, covering his, and his faint smile of acknowledgement twisted her heart.

'Maybe they are. I just haven't considered it.'

'Then you shouldn't waste any more time in going to see them and reconciling…that's my advice.'

'See how good you are for me? *That's* why it doesn't make sense for our relationship to be purely platonic.'

Rose sighed and carefully withdrew her hand. Again the fear arose that she was lulling herself into a false sense of security. 'Yes, it does. Just look at the facts. We're oceans apart, Gene. It doesn't matter how attracted we are to each other physically. The fact is we inhabit very different worlds. An association like ours is never going to work unless we keep things purely platonic.'

'You must be joking!' His lips twisted grimly. 'You might not want to admit I'm right, but our relationship is never, *ever* going to stay platonic. That would be like touching a lit match to some dry tinder and expecting it not to catch fire. Because that's what you do to me, Rose…you make me catch fire.'

Even as he finished speaking she knew he was going to kiss her. And what was more worrying was that she knew she wasn't going to try and stop him…

# CHAPTER TEN

As GENE'S MOUTH claimed Rose's in a hotly voracious kiss the depth and power of his desire genuinely scared him. It scared him to want and need
a woman this much because it gave her a power
over him that he wouldn't be able to repudiate
easily. It wasn't just about the intense attraction
he felt towards her either. The realisation that he
might want something deeper was territory he'd
never encountered before, and potentially it made
him dangerously vulnerable.

*But he simply couldn't leave her alone.*

It would be like depriving himself of life-giv-
ing oxygen not to see her.

As his silken tongue danced with hers he heard
her moan softly with pleasure and he gathered
her into his arms. The sensation of her shapely

and slender body pressed close into his chest inevitably made him tighten. *Why hadn't he suggested she met him at his apartment instead of at the restaurant?* At least then they could have tumbled into bed and continued what they'd started on the island and yesterday...

Intimately possessing Rose in the office might have been the most red-hot sex he'd ever experienced, but it had fanned the flames of Gene's desire even more—despite his not using protection and the potential consequences.

But he didn't want to raise the topic of the morning-after pill right now...

Lifting his head, he glanced down into his lover's prettily flushed face and smiled. '*Now* do you believe me when I say a platonic relationship hasn't got a chance in hell of working? Not between you and me, Rose.'

Even though her beautiful eyes were drowsy with need, they also reflected unease. This was confirmed when she immediately extricated herself from Gene's embrace and moved further down in her seat.

'Well, we'd better not have *any* kind of relationship, then. We shouldn't have been intimate. Sex just confuses things. It always leads to trouble of some kind.'

Her words reminded him that Rose had been badly let down by an ex-boyfriend and that it wasn't just her mother running off with her rich lover that had made her so mistrustful of men...

'I told you that that's not going to happen between us. I may have played the field a little, but I've never lied to any woman about my intentions. That's why I've come clean with you and told you frankly what I've been feeling. I'm not like your ex-boyfriend and I won't let you down like he did. Can't you trust the connection we have and just be open to seeing where it goes?'

She glanced away for a second. 'I could... But it's difficult when my ex had many of the same traits you have. I don't need to go into details— all you need to know is that he put work and ambition before everything else and basically did what he liked, because he thought it was some kind of inalienable right. Our relationship came very low down on his list of priorities, and if I dared complain he'd tell me he was only working as hard as he was for *me*. Then, finally, I found out that he'd regularly been cheating on me. I felt like such a fool. That's why I can't trust my feelings—and I can't trust men like *you*, Gene.'

'Just because he had similar traits to me and hurt you, Rose, it doesn't mean I'm going to behave in the same way. The least you can do is to give me a chance to prove myself.'

'It's a risk I can't afford to take, Gene. In any case the point is that I need to focus my attention on getting a new job, and you need to…you need to—'

He might be hard, hot and frustrated, but Gene couldn't deny he wanted to hear what she had to say. Raising an eyebrow, he murmured, 'Go on. What exactly *do* I need to do, Rose?'

'Forget it. What do I know? We lead very different lives.'

'You obviously have an opinion, so you may as well share it.'

Trapped, she heaved an annoyed sigh. 'Okay… but you're not going to like it. It's never going to work out between us, whatever our relationship. The way you live your life is totally alien to me, and I think it would do you good to check in with the *real* world from time to time.'

Gene suddenly sensed that he wasn't going to enjoy hearing what else she had to say, but still he invited, 'Go on…'

'Well…you have a reputation for being able to get anything you want, and you like the power that it gives you. I sensed that the very first time I met you. There was beauty all around you but you barely even saw it. What you saw was a desirable property that you were desperate to acquire and you would do anything to get it. But let me ask you this: Don't you have enough property already? You probably don't even register what you own because you're always looking for more. It must be hard for the people who care about you because your focus can't ever be on nurturing those relationships—not if you're always so dissatisfied with what you've got. You've told me yourself that you haven't seen your parents in months, and I can see how much that hurts you. Perhaps you ought to try and heal that relationship first, before you think about having one yourself. In truth, I genuinely feel sorry for you—because I can see that your wealth has stopped you from seeing the things in life that really matter.'

Gene had never before been stunned into silence but he was now. Rose's impassioned words hadn't just unsettled him—they'd honestly disturbed him. He felt as if he'd been put under a magnifying glass in the hot sun. He was in pain and he was *furious*...

Reining in his temper, he countered, 'What do you mean I should get in touch with the "real" world? Do you think I was born with a silver spoon in my mouth and have no notion of what it's like to have to work hard for my living? My parents were immigrants and they both came from poverty-stricken backgrounds. They came over here, worked hard at various restaurants, then started up their own restaurant with minimal money and no help from anyone but each other. When I was old enough I started to help them and they taught me how to cook. When I realised I was good at it I discovered what I wanted to do in life and was determined to be a success. I've spent my life working hard to make my dreams into a reality…that's why my family and I will never be poor again. Do you think I'm going to apologise for that? Like *hell* I am!'

Rose's smooth brow puckered. 'It's commendable that you made your dreams come true, and of course I don't expect you to apologise for what you've achieved. I'm sure your parents must be very proud of you. But all I'm asking is haven't you ever thought about appreciating some of the more valuable things in life that are actually *free*?'

Gene glared irritably. 'Like what, for instance? It's been my experience that nothing is free. Fortunately I've always understood that the name of the game is money.'

'What about the ability to nurture and enjoy good relationships and—and to experience love? Do you think you have to pay for those too?'

He scowled. 'Love is a fool's game. It's too easy to lose. I prefer things that are more tangible.'

The look on Rose's face instantly conveyed her dismay, and Gene knew he would come to regret his cynical response.

'So that means that you would never risk loving someone?'

'Let me ask *you* a question, Rose. Is your mother a pretty woman? I'll bet she is. Your rich stepfather probably saw her as another desirable possession and she saw him as a better bet to take care of her than your dad because he was wealthy. Love doesn't have anything to do with it. You probably despise the man, but there was a mutually satisfying pay-off in that they both got exactly what they wanted.'

Stung, Rose shot up and grabbed her handbag. 'I don't despise him. I hate the fact that he used his wealth and fancy lifestyle to persuade my mum away from my dad. Yes, I know she wasn't entirely innocent. But I'll never admire *anyone* who uses their wealth in such a devious way—not even caring that they helped break a man's heart.'

Clutching the neat black leather bag she'd brought with her tightly against her chest, she used it as if it was a shield.

'Anyway, you can think what you like. You barely know me…much less my family.'

Rising to his feet, Gene folded his arms. 'You're right. But how can I *get* to know you when you don't trust people enough to let them get close? Going by what you said about your ex, it's clear that you have no intention of ever trusting that I might act honourably towards you.'

Her crimson-painted lips quivered and she looked as if she was about to burst into tears. As much as he wanted to comfort her and take her in his arms, he elected not to.

This time her comments hadn't just touched a nerve—they had genuinely wounded him. It had stung to hear her suggest that his desire to keep on acquiring things must end up separating him from the people who cared about him... It stung because he knew it was *true*. It made him reflect uncomfortably on what he had done to his parents—on how his quest for 'more' and 'better' had indisputably hurt them and forged a chasm between them that was growing ever harder to bridge...

'I don't think I should stay for lunch after all,' she murmured.

'Why not...? I never had you down as a coward.'

Lifting her head, Rose stared. 'I'm not. I just think it's a case of wrong place, wrong time for us—and what's the point in us both being un-happy?'

Unable to make sense of anything much right then, Gene answered. 'I agree. There clearly isn't any point.'

'Anyway, there's one more thing before I go...'

Even as he fought to gain control of his pain and disappointment that she was leaving and, yes, the undeniable sense of loss that had engen-dered, he stayed grimly silent as Rose drew out the red velvet gift box from her handbag and laid it down on the table.

'I'm sure you meant well, but I can't accept this,' she said softly.

Then, with her pretty violet eyes glistening, she turned and walked out...

By the time Rose got to the hospital to see Philip it was already late and there was just half an hour left of visiting time. As she approached the bed and saw him intently perusing an antiques cat-alogue it hardly signified that he was looking so much better, because her heart was painfully leaden at the way she'd left Gene at the restaurant.

She'd told him some unpalatable truths and he would have had to be made out of stone not to be affected by it. She hadn't meant to be cruel. But neither had she wanted to lead him astray and let him believe she was happy to have a meaningless fling with him. Her feelings for Gene were far from meaningless.

That was why she'd returned the bracelet. It might be his habit to buy women expensive gifts in payment for sharing intimacy, but Rose knew she would never take anything from him that wasn't given freely or because it was important to him. If they had a real relationship it wouldn't be one that he had to *buy*...

'Rose...how lovely to see you!' Philip couldn't hide his delight when he saw her.

She bent down to kiss him. 'You too. I'm sorry I didn't get here earlier but I lost track of the time. I've been canvassing as many dealers as I can to get them to buy the rest of the antiques. I did quite well this afternoon, I'm happy to report, so all the time and effort was worth it.'

When she pulled out the grey utilitarian chair next to the bed and tiredly dropped down into it her smile wasn't as animated as she would have wished. But, quickly gathering herself, Rose delved into her bag for the generous carton of plump red grapes that she'd brought.

'I know you'd probably prefer some of your favourite Belgian chocolate, but I thought I'd better not lead you astray.'

'Why on earth not…? Even an old fogey like me can use a little of what they fancy from time to time, can't they?'

'Well…perhaps next time I'll smuggle some in. How are you? Any news on those other tests you had?'

The time seemed to pass in a flash, and most of the other patients' visitors had left when Rose finally plucked up the courage to share what was uppermost in her mind…*Gene.*

'Philip?' Nervously smoothing her hand across the crisp white hospital counterpane, she leant towards him. 'Can I talk to you about something? It's a personal matter.'

'Of course you can, my dear. Is it to do with the shop? Are you perhaps finding it too much of a struggle to sell off the antiques as well as dealing with everything else that needs doing before Bonnaire comes in and takes over?'

Even the mention of Gene's surname had the power to make Rose ache with longing. She couldn't help wondering if she would ever see him again after their heated exchange at the restaurant. What if he sent his secretary or some minion to oversee things at the antiques store, just so he wouldn't have to come face to face with her?

It was like a dagger in her heart to think that he might so quickly forget the staggeringly powerful passion that had driven them to make love in Philip's office and treat it as though it was nothing important. Look at the risk they'd taken.

But the declaration he'd made at the restaurant that he wouldn't risk loving someone—that love was 'a fool's game'—couldn't help but fill her with more sorrow. If Rose had privately nursed an impossible hope that somehow he *could* learn to love her, his searing admission had obliterated it.

'I'm fine organising the sale of the antiques and everything else. That's not what I wanted to talk to you about. It's much more personal than that.'

Not commenting, Philip leant back against his plumped-up pillows and waited patiently for her to continue. Meeting his infinitely kind gaze, Rose assured herself that it would be all right— that he would understand and wouldn't judge her...

'I—I've fallen for someone...' she told him, even as her privately anguished feelings threatened to overwhelm her.

'Are you telling me that you're in love, Rose?'

Nodding miserably, she sensed her lip quiver. Philip smiled. He couldn't have looked happier. 'But that's *wonderful* news. Who's the lucky man?'

'You don't need to know his name…I—I'd rather keep that private for now, if you don't mind. All I can tell you is that he's someone completely unsuitable.'

'But that hasn't stopped you from having feelings for him?' he observed gently. Her comment clearly hadn't fazed him.

His reaction genuinely surprised her. 'No, it hasn't. But he's the absolute antithesis of me,' she insisted. 'It's hit me like a ton of bricks that I should feel this way about him.'

Philip was thoughtful. 'Falling in love can happen in a myriad different ways, Rose. For some it's a slow progression as they get to know each other…with others their eyes can literally meet across a room and they know instantly that he or she is the person they want to spend the rest of their life with. For others still it can knock them flat when they're simply going about their business, convinced that everything is under control and that nothing can possibly make them deviate from the path they're set on. It sounds to me, Rose, as if you fall into that category.'

'It's true. I never even *wanted* to fall in love. I schooled myself against it…especially after Joe cheated on me. Do you remember? But now that it's happened it's threatening everything I believe in. Doing what's right, I mean—the tenets that my dad taught me and stood by. Loving this man *isn't* doing what's right. I feel so guilty and I'm ashamed that I've let everyone down.'

Philip frowned. 'Everyone? Who do you imagine you've let down, Rose?'

Twisting her fingers restlessly together, she sighed. 'I've let *you* down, Philip. You've done so much for me and you deserve better'

'My dear…'

She found her agitated hands captured in his frail ones and subdued.

'You're behaving as though you've committed some heinous crime. Since when has falling in love been a criminal offence? Your feelings are no concern of anyone else's. Yes, the people who love you only want the best for you—but how does anybody know what's best for someone else? It's surely better to risk all for love than to turn away from it because of your fear of letting people down and living a life filled with regret and "if only".'

More than a little shocked, she stared. 'You sound as if you know exactly what that's like. Have you ever loved someone you turned away from because of what other people thought?'

The distinguished man nodded slowly, and his pale blue eyes couldn't hide the sadness that his memories must have aroused. 'I didn't just turn away from the lady because of what people thought, Rose…I turned away from her because I chose to focus on my career rather than go with her into the unknown. She was an artist…a rather wonderful one. She was ten years younger than me and she wanted to travel the world and be inspired by the vistas she saw to do her painting. She had no time for what she called "the safe option"—having a career, marrying someone and living what she used to call "a conventionally stultifying life of suburban boredom". She was a free spirit.'

He coughed a little and glanced away for a moment—but not before Rose spied the glint of moisture in his eyes.

'Her name was Elizabeth and I loved her more than life itself.'

'Do you mind if I ask…is that the reason why you've never married?'

Nodding again, he released her hands. 'There was never anyone for me but *her*. I could never even contemplate it. That's why you must follow your heart, Rose. There's no need for guilt and shame. Don't be like me and live a life of regret, imagining what might have been. I'm sure if your father was still here he would tell you the same.'

'And what about Elizabeth…? Did you ever see her again?'

'Sadly not… She said she thought it best that we didn't stay in touch. I just pray that wherever she is she continues to enjoy her travels and paint her pictures. It makes me happy to think of her doing what she loves.'

Leaning towards the bed, Rose affectionately brushed the side of his weathered cheek with her lips. 'Bless you, Philip. What you've just told me means more than I can say. I feel as though a great burden has been lifted from me. I feel lighter and—and more hopeful that whatever happens it will all work out. Although I'm still scared the man concerned might not feel the same...'

'I don't think you need have any fear about that.'

'Thanks. You're good for a girl's ego—you know that?'

Glancing towards the door, she noticed there was a stern-looking nurse pointing up at the wall clock to indicate that visiting hours were over.

Turning her gaze back to her boss, she said, 'I'd better go. I'll keep in touch by phone as often as I can, and let you know how I'm getting on with selling the antiques. And if there's anything you want me to put by for you, I will. One more thing: please let me know if you get a date for when you can come home, won't you?'

'Of course I will. Now, go and see your mysterious man. Maybe one day soon you'll feel able to tell me his name? In the meantime, tell him from me that the gods of good fortune smiled on him the day he set eyes on you, Rose.'

The first thing Gene saw when he opened his eyes the next morning was the red velvet jewel box. On his return from the restaurant he'd dropped it onto his dressing table as though he despised it.

Did Rose have any idea how much she'd humiliated him with her vehement little diatribe about the way he lived? And—more to the point—the way she'd all but thrown his gift back in his face? Hadn't the message he'd written meant anything to her? He was sick to his stomach that she'd scorned him.

Because he'd been so agitated, and hadn't been able to face returning to his office, he'd gone straight to his apartment and started to work from home. Deliberately focusing on his plans for the new restaurant, he'd sought to distract himself from thoughts of Rose by contacting as many of the professionals he'd previously courted who worked in the high-end hospitality business to remind them about the new Thames-side restaurant he was planning.

As Gene had confidently expected, there was plenty of interest about coming to work for him and he'd been able to get quite a few people to commit.

After imbibing a couple of glasses of the rare Bordeaux he'd brought over from his cellar in Paris, he had talked and planned and made arrangements into the early hours. And finally, when sheer exhaustion had got the better of him, he'd kicked off his shoes, pulled off his tie and fallen into bed fully clothed.

But even as his burning eyes had drifted closed

Gene hadn't been able to banish the memory of Rose's beautiful face, her mesmerising violet gaze, and the realisation had hit him that for the very first time in his life he was madly, head over heels in love.

The knowledge should have filled him with joy—but not when the sobering thought that the object of his affections was a woman who neither wanted nor regarded him had quickly followed it...

He had been utterly despondent. And that was why this morning, when he saw the red velvet box containing the diamond bracelet, he was painfully reminded that Rose had given it back to him without a qualm. She wasn't remotely impressed by his wealth or his ability to acquire whatever he wanted. In fact she definitely saw it as a negative rather than a desirable attribute.

She was refreshingly different from any of the women who moved in his so-called 'elite' circle. She wanted nothing of him other than that he start to look around and see the things in life that were important—the things that came in abundance just by dint of being born human...the things that came without a price tag, like nature and beauty and the possibility of being close to someone special...

Nothing that Gene could buy her or give her was ever going to convince Rose that underneath all his wealth and acquisitions had once been a genuinely good man who had somehow taken a wrong turn.

His understandable drive to make money and help secure his parents' future and his own after losing his sister had become insatiable... He'd started out doing it for all the right reasons, but the desire had long since become an addiction. He knew no peace and had no decent relationships to speak of. *All he did was work*. It took far more energy than people realised to maintain a position like his, and that was why he'd had no time to build relationships.

He'd had his sanctuary built in the hope that as well as not having to contend with the day-today bombardment of the press there, the isolation might one day help him deal properly with his grief so he could start to heal the out-of-control compulsion for 'more' that plagued him.

If only he had the courage to confide in Rose and explain *why* he had become so addicted. Gene would tell her that he'd thought it would protect him from the spectre of loss that haunted him… He would tell her about his sister and how she'd died unexpectedly and cruelly when she was just three years old. She had been the family's 'bright star' and they would never forget her…

Dropping his head into his hands, he thought hard. The only solution that would restore any hope for him was if he came up with a realistic plan to win Rose back—because suddenly the idea of living without her was too unbearable to contemplate…

# CHAPTER ELEVEN

ROSE HAD RESISTED making her all-important call to Gene's office until she'd finished work, telling herself that he would no doubt be working late himself. Yet the truth that lurked beneath her delay taunted her, and all that day her insides were tied in painful knots because of it. She was terrified that he might not want to talk to her… that after she'd walked out on him at the restaurant he had mulled things over and decided he just didn't need the grief of a woman who perpetually liked to speak her mind.

When she finally picked up the phone and rang him she'd worked herself up into such a state that she felt physically sick.

'Mr Bonnaire is not in the office today,' his snooty secretary informed her, her imperious tone suggesting that a nonentity like Rose was wasting her time.

Immediately that put Rose's back up.

'Well, if he's not in the office can you tell me where I can reach him? He's not answering his mobile.'

'No. I'm afraid I can't.'

'But this is important!'

The woman expelled an irritated sigh. 'If Mr Bonnaire had wanted you to reach him he would have left instructions, Miss Heathcote. All I can tell you is that he doesn't want to be disturbed by *anyone* today.'

'But—'

'Goodbye, Miss Heathcote.'

The receiver was firmly put down to signal the end of the call and now Rose really *was* worried. The thought that she'd lost her chance to make amends with Gene was agonising. Why had she left it so late to ring him? What if he was out of the country on business somewhere and wasn't going to be back for days—or maybe even *weeks*?

Unable to sit still, she found herself restlessly making tea in the kitchen as she thought hard about what to do. She was taking her first sip of the hot beverage when the answer came to her. She knew *exactly* what she had to do...

The idea so excited her that she felt dizzy. Gripped by a steely determination and a new-found daring that she hadn't known she had in her, she emptied the mug of tea, grabbed her coat and bag and turned out the lights. Then, locking the doors of the antiques shop behind her, she hailed a cab to take her to the station...

Nearly drowned by the sea spray on the turbulent crossing, Rose smoothed back her plastered hair and turned up the collar on her raincoat with damp, icy fingers. Any conversation with Rory the boatman was impossible above the eldritch mourning of the wind and with the craft's constant leaping over the waves and its rollercoaster dive back down into them.

The young man had warned her when she'd boarded. ''Tis a rough crossing you'll face today, Rose. Sure you want to risk it?'

With her heart thudding fit to burst, she'd answered, 'If you're willing to risk it, then so am I. But I don't want you to cross if you honestly feel it's too dangerous.'

In answer to that statement Rory had grinned and said, 'I've crossed in worse seas than this and lived to tell the tale. But the message you're taking to His Lordship must be powerful important if you're willing to risk life and limb to take it to him, Rose. Did you let him know you were coming?'

*So her instincts about Gene going to the island had been right.*

She'd breathed out a relieved sigh and climbed into the boat. 'No…I didn't. Let's just say I want to surprise him.'

'Doesn't strike me as a man who likes surprises

much…but I'm sure he'll make an exception for this one. He's a good man—in spite of all the rubbish the press say about him.'

True to his word, the boatman delivered Rose safely to the island. He even insisted on waiting for her to start negotiating the climb up the hill towards the house before leaving, calling out that he would bring the boat back one more time that afternoon 'just in case'.

Although she was chilled to the bone, and her damp clothing was clinging wetly to her body as she climbed the rocky incline, Rose hardly registered the discomfort. She was too tense to worry about it. But as she approached the futuristic dwelling that loomed out of the landscape the strangest sense of coming home washed over her, and she hugged the feeling to her as if it was something infinitely precious.

Glancing down at herself, she couldn't deny she wished she looked better. But then what did that signify, as long as Gene was pleased she'd made the journey? Because if he wasn't…

'Don't even *think* it…' she muttered crossly.

Remembering where to locate the dwelling's entrance, she moved her hand over the sensor and to her profound relief the curved doors slid opened. As she stepped onto the flawless parquet floor she heard the doors swish closed behind her. Swallowing hard, she nervously smoothed her hand down her damp raincoat. How was she going to let Gene know that she was there? Should she call out? Or simply just go and find him?

Still unsure, she kicked off her shoes, firmed the strap of her bag more securely over her shoulder and set off towards the living room. Even as she walked she detected the warm and tantalising scent of the Frenchman's cologne, and the provocative trail made her feel weak with excitement and longing.

'Well, well, well. Look who the wind's blown in.'

The tall, broad-shouldered Adonis with golden lights in his otherwise dark hair was staring out at the crashing waves through the panoramic windows. He turned slowly. There wasn't even the briefest acknowledgement of surprise in his piercing blue eyes. *It was just as though he'd been expecting her.*

Rose felt the strap of her bag slide off her shoulder and didn't move to stop it from falling to the floor. 'You said—you said that to me once before,' she answered, her teeth helplessly chattering.

'Did I?' Moving towards her, Gene smiled. 'I can see I'm going to have to find a new repertoire.'

'You don't look a bit surprised. How did you know that I would come here to look for you?'

'There are some things that are hard to explain…particularly when it comes to feelings. But that will have to keep for later. More importantly, you need to get out of those wet clothes and into a hot shower right now.'

Rose wasn't going to deny it. 'Yes, I do… But what about you, Gene? What do *you* need?'

His blue eyes mirrored his surprise…his pleasure too. 'What I need, sweetheart, is to join you,' he said huskily. 'You okay with that?'

Transfixed, Rose silently conveyed her agreement.

He stepped closer and his strong, muscular arm confidently encircled her waist. Feeling as though she was in a dream, it was as though her feet didn't even touch the floor as she let him lead her into the corridor and straight to his private suite.

In the state-of-the-art bathroom with a mosaic tiled floor in dazzling azure and wall-to-wall mirrors, Gene turned on the water in the spacious shower and soon the whole room was filled with hot, perfumed steam.

Even as she tried to take in what was happening the vehement desire that surged through her body easily took precedence over what was in her mind. When he came to her and helped dispense with her raincoat she was more than happy to let him.

After laying it on a nearby chair he came back to her, and his handsome face was a study of intense concentration as piece by piece he started to remove Rose's clothing. She was still shivering—but this time it wasn't from the cold.

*'Together we make fire,'* he'd told her once, and it was true.

Placing his big hands either side of her hips, he expertly removed her skimpy underwear, and she felt every touch and stroke of his flesh as though she couldn't bear to be without it.

Then he drew her towards him and, gravel-voiced, commanded, 'Kiss me.'

Rose had no intention of denying him and hungrily complied. Their mouths opened helplessly as soon as their lips collided and they were reunited with the molten heat that seemed to be generated so effortlessly whenever they were together. Now that heat intensified and burst into full scorching flame, and as their kisses became ever more urgent, with Gene's deliciously velvet mouth all but devouring her, Rose's hands started to tear desperately at his clothes.

When he was naked, for the very first time she had a true 'up close and personal' look at his magnificent body. As well as being muscular, fit and toned, he was heavily aroused, primed to take her, and she could hardly wait until the moment when they would join together...

Feeling deliriously weak and hungry, she wrapped her arms round his neck and begged softly, 'Take me into the shower...*please*...'

Lifting her against him effortlessly, so that her slim thighs clamped tightly round his lean waist, Gene stooped down to his discarded jeans and extracted a strip of slim foil packets. When he stood again, with his indomitable brow furrowing, she noticed his smile was a little self-conscious.

'I don't want to put you in the same position I put you in last time and have you worrying about getting pregnant,' he confessed.

'Would you be shocked if I admitted that I

actually thought about *not* taking that morning-after pill?' Rose asked him softly.

'Why? Why would you do that?'

'Perhaps we'd better talk about that later...' She smiled.

Gene immediately concurred. 'All I want you to think about now is the sweet, unadulterated pleasure I'm going to give you, sweetheart.'

Bending his head, he stole another incendiary, open-mouthed kiss and Rose's body all but melted as he carried her into the hot, steamy shower.

The first time he took her hard and fast, and she gasped her need and pleasure out loud as hot rivulets of water deluged their naked bodies. They ran down her hair and face and streamed over her breasts as Gene claimed her again and again, and finally Rose couldn't hold back the elemental force that threatened to take her over the edge any longer... *In his arms she came undone.*

Rapturous with the hot tide of sensual feeling

that overwhelmed her, she felt tears of joy flood into her eyes and mingle with the water from the shower. Her lover released a deep guttural groan and grew still as he climaxed.

For a while both of them couldn't speak. Then he looked down at her and carefully eased her back onto her feet. Even in the steam that enveloped them she saw his blue eyes shine as she'd never seen them shine before…

'We've been together for half an hour at least, angel, and I haven't yet told you how beautiful you are.'

Sighing with satisfaction, he pulled her against him and covered her eyelids, nose and mouth with infinitely tender kisses that made Rose catch her breath and stare at him in wonder.

'I promise I'm going to make up for that, sweetheart—starting now, by telling you that you're one gorgeous, sexy woman. I don't know what I did to bring you to me—only that I'm *beyond* grateful that you're here.'

Rose's smile was warm and loving as she

stroked a strand of glistening wet hair back from his lightly ridged forehead. Her heart was so full it was hard to put her feelings into words.

'I couldn't have stayed away, Gene. Did you think I *could*?'

Shaking his head, he captured her hand. 'When you left me in the restaurant after saying those things about the way I conducted myself...I won't lie to you and tell you that I didn't resent it—because I *did*.' He paused to lift her hand to his lips and kissed it. 'But I knew I was angry because you were the one person who had dared to tell me the truth.'

'I didn't mean to hurt you.'

'I know you didn't. But it had to be done, Rose. I was in a hell of my own making and you came along and set me free. Maybe now I have a chance to redeem myself?'

'Let's dry each other off and go to bed, shall we? I want to hold you in my arms and tell you exactly what I feel about you, Eugene Bonnaire... businessman *extraordinaire*.'

Her smile was teasing and unashamedly seductive, and she revelled in the new sensation of feminine power that she'd discovered—no holds barred.

The second time he took her Gene deliberately slowed things down. In the lavish double bed, with its satin and silk sheets, he took his time and savoured every incredible, joyous moment of making love with Rose. She was the most giving woman in every respect, and she took just as much delight and pleasure in exploring him as he did her.

Her sweetly shaped breasts, slim hips and silkily smooth thighs perfectly complemented his hard, lean physique when he took her in his arms and caressed her. And when he gazed at the stunning revelation of her bare body lying on his silk sheets he saw that she was the perfect 'pocket Venus'.

He found it hard to understand how he had ever thought any other woman beautiful. How could he have when there had always been one vitally important missing ingredient? The heart-to-heart connection that now made him hopeful and helped him look forward to a truly *joyous* future instead of one that he'd feared would bring only more sorrow.

Rose was lying atop him and had been teasingly nipping at the soft flesh of his lower lip. As much as he was enjoying it, in one deft motion Gene had manoeuvred her to lie next to him. Turning towards her, he cupped her small jaw in his big hand and for a long moment was lost in the beauty of her radiant violet gaze.

'You said it crossed your mind not to take that morning-after pill. Will you tell me why?'

Rose didn't shy away from meeting the intensity she saw in his glance and said, 'I couldn't help wondering what a child we made would look like. And for the first time in my life I realised I wanted children. I wanted a family of my own.'

'Do you still feel like that?'

'If the right man came along I wouldn't hesitate.'

Trying not to give way to a delighted grin, Gene eased out a long slow breath. 'And has he?'

'What do *you* think?'

He answered her, leaving her in no doubt, with a lingering hot kiss.

When they both came up for air he asked, 'Out of interest, how did you know I would be here on the island?' His breath hitched as he waited to hear her reply.

Rose sighed. 'How do you think? I *sensed* that you were here…that you would be waiting for me. I didn't even stop to pack. I just jumped in a cab. My only worry was that you wouldn't forgive me.'

'Forgive you for what?'

She grimaced. 'For taking it upon myself to tell you where you'd been going wrong, that's what. It's not like I'm some kind of expert. I've made plenty of mistakes too.'

Unable to resist teasing her, Gene made himself look serious. 'Oh? What kind of mistakes?'

'Funny enough, always trying to "do the right thing." Not allowing myself to really live...to trust that if I listened to my heart it wouldn't lead me astray. My dad found it hard to trust too. He was a wonderful man, but he could be unforgiving about making mistakes. And he was so afraid I was going to turn out like my mother if he didn't make certain rules about how I should behave. The thing is, she isn't a bad person—but he probably forgot all the reasons he'd once loved her when she left him and he was worried that one day I might replicate her behaviour.'

'You mean he was afraid you might run off with some unscrupulous billionaire who, after he'd seduced you, would make you fall in love with his wealthy and essentially empty lifestyle?'

Feeling the bitter bite of regret, Gene couldn't help his sardonic tone.

Immediately concerned, Rose put her hand on his shoulder and lightly stroked it. 'It's not your rich lifestyle that I fell in love with…it's the man I always sensed was beneath the aloof and polished façade. It's *you* that I love, Gene. You and no other.'

Somehow Gene's breath felt as if it was trapped inside his chest. His heart was racing so hard he could scarcely think straight. Then he realised that he was hearing the words he'd thought never to hear. Not in *this* life anyway…

'You *love* me?'

Rose looked perturbed. 'You sound as if you might doubt it?'

'It's not that I doubt you mean it, Rose. I'm just surprised…*delighted* and surprised. The truth is I don't think I'm a very lovable person. My own parents probably have trouble even *liking* me. Don't think I'm feeling sorry for myself—I can't help but be a realist.'

'I don't believe that your parents don't like you. And I certainly don't believe they don't *love* you. A parent's love is unconditional, isn't it?'

He shrugged. 'They tell me that they care, but it was my sister they adored.'

'You had a sister?'

'Yes…'

Instead of pushing the feelings of grief away, as he usually did, Gene let them come. He remembered the fierce joy he'd felt whenever he was with Francesca, and the sense that he would protect her with his life if he could. To his everlasting regret, he hadn't been able to.

Swallowing hard, he smiled painfully. 'Her name was Francesca. She died when she was just three, after a short and painful illness.'

Rose's hand stilled against his shoulder. 'Gene, I'm so sorry. How old were *you*?'

'I was nine.'

'Your poor family… You must have all been utterly devastated.'

'We were. We still are. That's why I was determined to do everything I could to make sure my parents at least never had to worry about money. Unfortunately things didn't go exactly as

I'd planned. My desire to secure their future got rather out of hand. I became addicted to the pleasure of seeing my bank balance grow larger and larger—and to the kudos of being successful… I thought it would protect me from the spectre of loss that had haunted me since losing Francesca. But I lost sight of my reasons. As you said to me at the restaurant, Rose…I just didn't know when enough was enough. And along the way, when I saw that my relationships—especially with women—weren't fulfilling, because they were mostly meaningless, I think I lost a little bit of my soul.'

'Oh, baby…'

She kissed him tenderly and it was then that Gene sensed the truth in her touch. His heart leapt.

'I love you too, Rose. The thought of not being with you for the rest of my life is torture.'

She wrapped her arms firmly around him and kissed him again. When she glanced up she was grinning. 'The last thing I want to do is torture you, my love. I want to spend the rest of my life making you happy. And I'll tell anyone who cares to listen what a good and kind man you are. The kind of man who always makes the people who love him proud.'

'On that subject: I'd like you to be with me when I go and talk to my parents, Rose. I want to tell them how I've been feeling, why I've grown more and more distant from them. I also want to share with them the way I felt after we lost Francesca. And lastly…'

'Tell me?'

'I want to tell them that I've met the woman of my dreams.'

Rose dimpled. 'Now you're going to make me cry…'

'There's something else I'd like you to do for me.'

'What's that?'

'I'd like you to take back the bracelet I gave you. I meant what I said on the note I sent with it. You *are* the hidden diamond that I didn't expect.

If you accept my gift, and the heartfelt intention that it was given with, I'll know it means that you love me for the *real* Gene Bonnaire—not the ruthless businessman that the world sees, but the very fallible and ordinary man who doesn't mind admitting that he's made quite a few mistakes in his life. However…the one mistake I'll *never* make is to walk away from the woman who is far more precious and valuable to me than anything material I could ever acquire or achieve… The woman who I hope will one day be my wife and the mother of my children.'

Rose was crying…crying inconsolably.

All Gene could do was to hold her lovingly against him until she grew quiet, all the while telling her how much he loved and adored her.

*Then he asked her to marry him.*

When she looked up at him she answered, 'Yes! Of *course* I'll marry you!' And the happiness that shone from her beautiful violet eyes shimmered like the most exquisite diamond of all… even though they were drenched with tears…

# EPILOGUE

ROSE HAD WANTED to make her afternoon visit to her husband's Parisian office a surprise. She'd agreed beforehand to meet him at a sumptuous and classy restaurant in the city, to have a late lunch with his parents and her mother and step-father, but in the end she'd made the decision to meet him at his office first, so that they could travel to the restaurant together.

She wanted to pinch herself at the way things had changed. Not only had Gene been reunited with his family, but Rose had also started to rebuild her relationship with her mother. And, to top it all, just a few short weeks ago she and Gene had been married in the most exquisite Gothic church in Kensington. Even the presence of a flock of paparazzi hadn't spoiled the day. Unbelievably, she was now Mrs Bonnaire.

Walking down the richly carpeted corridor of what she teasingly referred to as 'the presidential suite', she felt her tummy deluged with butterflies. She couldn't help being nervous at the prospect of seeing the man she adored. Their passionate relationship had been nothing less than a dream come true. Every day when she woke up next to him Rose told Gene that he took her breath away.

Today she'd donned one of her prettiest dresses underneath a stylish designer jacket, and she was particularly hoping that he would notice.

'Mrs Bonnaire. How nice to see you. Is Mr Bonnaire expecting you?'

His new smartly attired middle-aged secretary, Martine, was genuinely pleased to see her, and had made no secret of the fact that she was pleased and delighted that her handsome boss had found the woman he declared to be 'the love of his life'.

Rose sent up a silent prayer that her husband wasn't with a colleague or a client. She was literally *aching* to see him.

'No, Martine. He's not expecting me. But if he's free can I just go in and see him?'

'But of course.'

After knocking briefly on the panelled oak door, she walked inside. Gene's office was not just stylish, it was bright and beautiful too. Rose loved the way that sunlight never seemed to fail to be pouring in from the large plate-glass windows that looked out onto the busy city whenever she visited.

Today was no different. As her avid gaze fell upon her husband she saw how the light reflected burnished lights in his immaculately cut dark hair.

He turned to welcome his visitor. 'I knew it had to be you, my love.' He smiled. 'I think I'm psychically attuned to that polite little knock of yours.'

Rose moved swiftly towards him for his embrace. 'I know I said I'd meet you at the restaurant, but—'

'Is something wrong?'

Seeing his worried frown, she hastened to assure him. 'No, there's nothing wrong. I just couldn't wait to see you. Do you mind?'

'You may as well ask me if I need to breathe.' Gene chuckled. 'Not only have you decided to surprise me with an impromptu visit, but you've worn that very pretty red dress that I love on you.'

He nuzzled the side of her neck and the heat he exuded along with the seductive scent of his cologne made Rose instantly weak.

'I'm just wondering if I should lock the door and lower the blinds. And if I have time to take it off you and make love to you before we go to the restaurant.'

'Ordinarily I'd agree it was a good idea, but we're meeting both your parents and mine for lunch—remember?' Her cheeks dimpled and she gently touched her palm to his cheek. 'And not just that—I have something I need to tell you before we leave.'

Lifting her hand away, her husband pressed his lips in a briefly tender kiss against hers. 'That sounds ominous…' he remarked teasingly.

'But only in a good way, I hope?'

'Depends what it is you're going to tell me.'

'I'm pregnant. We're going to have a baby, Gene!'

His blue eyes widened, glinting in the sunlight. 'This is true? I mean, you know this for sure, Rose?'

'I took a pregnancy test this morning and it came out positive.' Her heart was hammering as she spoke, but there was no need for anxiety. Already she could see the joy in his expression.

'*Mon Dieu*…I'm going to be a father! We are going to be parents. This is the most wonderful thing I've ever heard, my love!'

Gene caught her to him and passionately kissed her. When they came up for air he pushed a button at the side of his desk. The lock on the door firmly clicked shut and the cream-coloured blinds at the windows started to lower smoothly.

He turned back to Rose and gently divested her of her jacket, and then he expertly pulled down the zip at the side of her pretty red dress.

'I've decided we definitely have time to make love before we go to lunch...' He smiled. 'Our parents won't mind if we're late... Not when we tell them that they're going to be grandparents.'

Rose's eyes moistened as she gazed up at him. 'Have you *any* idea just how much I love you?' she breathed.

For an electrifying moment Gene looked serious. 'If it comes anywhere near to the depth and breadth of the love I have for you, Rose, then I know I must be the most blessed man on earth.'

\* \* \* \* \*

# MILLS & BOON®
## Large Print – November 2015

**The Ruthless Greek's Return**
Sharon Kendrick

**Bound by the Billionaire's Baby**
Cathy Williams

**Married for Amari's Heir**
Maisey Yates

**A Taste of Sin**
Maggie Cox

**Sicilian's Shock Proposal**
Carol Marinelli

**Vows Made in Secret**
Louise Fuller

**The Sheikh's Wedding Contract**
Andie Brock

**A Bride for the Italian Boss**
Susan Meier

**The Millionaire's True Worth**
Rebecca Winters

**The Earl's Convenient Wife**
Marion Lennox

**Vettori's Damsel in Distress**
Liz Fielding

# MILLS & BOON®
## Large Print – December 2015

**The Greek Demands His Heir**
Lynne Graham

**The Sinner's Marriage Redemption**
Annie West

**His Sicilian Cinderella**
Carol Marinelli

**Captivated by the Greek**
Julia James

**The Perfect Cazorla Wife**
Michelle Smart

**Claimed for His Duty**
Tara Pammi

**The Marakaios Baby**
Kate Hewitt

**Return of the Italian Tycoon**
Jennifer Faye

**His Unforgettable Fiancée**
Teresa Carpenter

**Hired by the Brooding Billionaire**
Kandy Shepherd

**A Will, a Wish...a Proposal**
Jessica Gilmore

# MILLS & BOON®

## Why shop at millsandboon.co.uk?

Each year, thousands of romance readers find their perfect read at millsandboon.co.uk. That's because we're passionate about bringing you the very best romantic fiction. Here are some of the advantages of shopping at www.millsandboon.co.uk:

* **Get new books first**—you'll be able to buy your favourite books one month before they hit the shops

* **Get exclusive discounts**—you'll also be able to buy our specially created monthly collections, with up to 50% off the RRP

* **Find your favourite authors**—latest news, interviews and new releases for all your favourite authors and series on our website, plus ideas for what to try next

* **Join in**—once you've bought your favourite books, don't forget to register with us to rate, review and join in the discussions

Visit **www.millsandboon.co.uk**
for all this and more today!